lonely planet

New Orleans

"All you've got to do is decide to go
and the hardest part is over.

So go!"

TONY WHEELER, COFOUNDER – LONELY PLANET

THIS EDITION WRITTEN AND RESEARCHED BY
Adam Karlin, Amy C Balfour

Contents

Plan Your Trip 4

Explore New Orleans 42

Understand New Orleans 187

Survival Guide 213

New Orleans Maps 236

Left: The Neville Brothers performing at Jazz Fest (p82)

Above: Celebrating St Patrick's Day (p20)

Right: Audubon Zoo's white tiger (p128)

Welcome to New Orleans

The things that make life worth living – wine, song and feasting – are the humid air New Orleans breathes.

Epicurean Appetite

We hope you're not reading this at home or in an airport. We hope you're *actually in* New Orleans. Because if so, you're about to eat better than any armchair traveler, plus most of the rest of the world. When it comes to food, New Orleans does not play. Well, OK, it does: it takes a playful attitude to ingredients and recipes, mixing (for example) alligator sausage and cheesecake into a dessert fit for the Gods. But it creates this mind-meltingly rich food with enterprise, innovation and a dedication to perfecting one of the USA's great indigenous cuisines, a culinary aesthetic that will leave you snoring in the happiest of food comas afterwards.

Celebration Seasons

We are not exaggerating when we write the following words: there is either a festival or a parade every week of the year in New Orleans. Sometimes, like during Mardi Gras or Jazz Fest, it feels like there's a new party for every hour of the day. At almost any celebration in this town, people engage in masking – donning a new appearance via some form of costuming, while acting out the Satyr-side of human behavior. But the celebrations and rituals of New Orleans are as much about history as hedonism. Every dance here is as much an expression of community spirit as it is of joy.

Unceasing Song

New Orleans is the hometown of jazz, but neither the city nor the genre she birthed are musical museum pieces. Jazz is the root of American popular music, the daddy of rock, brother of the blues and not too distant ancestor of hip-hop – in other words, all the styles of music that have been the defining beat of global pop for decades. And every variety of music we mentioned, plus a few you may never have heard of, is practiced and played here on every corner, in any bar every night of the week. Live music here isn't an event. It's as crucial to the city soundscape as the streetcar bells.

Candid Culture

There aren't many places in the USA that wear their history as openly on their sleeves as New Orleans. This city's very facade is an architectural study par excellence. And while Boston and Charleston can boast beautiful buildings, there's a lived-in, cozy feeling to New Orleans that's easily accessible. As a result of this visible history there's a constant, often painful dialogue with the past, stretching back hundreds of years, a history that for all its controversy has produced a street culture that can be observed and grasped in a very visceral way.

Why I Love New Orleans

By Adam Karlin, Author

In New Orleans, it's all about beauty and experiencing the divine through mortal senses. There's joy, from great food to the best concert of your life, and serenity, in the shade between live oaks, or watching fireflies on Bayou St John. Whichever way of being I choose to be for the day, New Orleans indulges me. Basically, I like traveling with soft eyes, eyes that see as a child, with wonder. This town gives me soft eyes the moment I step out the door.

For more about our authors, see p256.

Above: Steamboat *Natchez* (p53)

New Orleans'
Top 10

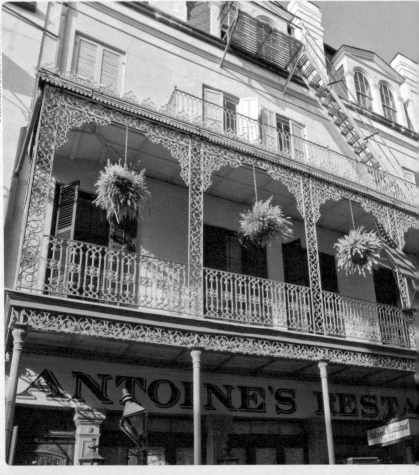

Creole Architecture (p206)

1 Looks aren't always skin deep. In this city, the architectural skin is integral to the spirit – and an undeniably distinctive sense of place. What immediately sets New Orleans apart from America is the architecture of the Creole *faubourgs* (Fo-burgs), or neighborhoods. This includes the shaded porches of the French Quarter, of course, but also filigreed Marigny homes, candy-colored Bywater cottages and the grande manses of Esplanade Avenue. Look down any of these streets and know, intuitively and intensely, you are in New Orleans.

⊙ *French Quarter; Faubourg Marigny & Bywater*

Mardi Gras (p76)

2 Let us start by saying what Mardi Gras is *not:* beads and breasts. With the exception of some rowdy crowds on Canal St, most visitors, and all locals, keep their clothes (or bodypaint) on. And oh, what clothes. You'll see the most fantastic costumes (plus some boring yellow-purple-green rugby shirts Uptown), the weirdest pageantry, West African ritual, Catholic liturgy and massive parade floats, all culminating in the single most exhausting, exhilarating day of your life. Happy Mardi Gras, baby.

EPA EUROPEAN PRESSPHOTO AGENCY B.V. / ALAMY ©

National WWII Museum *(p100)*

3 History doesn't just come alive at the National WWII Museum. It parachutes behind enemy lines, scans the horizon for invaders and slams onto Omaha Beach. Vivid photographs, first-person oral histories, compelling artifacts and an exciting 4-D movie trace America's involvement in the war, from the bombing of Pearl Harbor to the Allied victories in Germany and Japan. The New Orleans connection? The D-Day amphibious landing crafts were designed by local entrepreneur Andrew Higgins, and they were invaluable to the success of the invasion, which was a turning point in the war.

⦿ *CBD & Warehouse District*

Shopping on Magazine Street *(p138)*

4 Forget Fifth Avenue. Erase Oxford Circus. So long, Saint-Honore. Magazine St, specifically the 3-mile stretch of it that smiles along the bottom bend of New Orleans' Uptown, may be the world's best shopping street. Oh, sure, there are no big-name big boxes with thumping house music, but there is a glut of indie boutiques; tons of vintage; po'boys for the hungry; antique warehouses galore; art galleries in profusion; big shady trees; and architecture that will charm your toes off. All this, and Ms Mae's (p137).

🔒 *Uptown & Riverbend*

City Park *(p142)*

5 City Park is larger than Central Park and has alligators, so really, what are you waiting for? Oh, alright, if alligators aren't your thing there are also long lines of live oaks and weeping willows, a botanical garden that contains New Orleans in miniature, ice cream, Greek columns, a sculpture garden that surrounds the New Orleans Museum of Art, and a singing tree, festooned with wind chimes and romance – the sort of space where love and music take time to impregnate the air with giddiness. LEFT: BOTANICAL GARDENS

⦿ *Mid-City & the Tremé*

Music on Frenchmen Street
(p88)

6 You! With the Hurricane/Hand Grenade souvenir cup! Get off Bourbon St and up to Frenchmen, a locus of local live music just a few steps – and a whole world – removed from the city's tackiest tourist traps. If you can walk the few small blocks of Frenchmen – packed with joints playing rock, metal, hip-hop, folk and, of course, jazz – without hearing something you like, just keep going out of New Orleans, because this city is all about the music, and the music always plays here.

☆ *Faubourg Marigny & Bywater*

Eating a Po'boy *(p27)*

7 If by 'sandwich' we mean a portable meal that contains vegetable and meat enclosed by starch, the po'boy is perfection, the Platonic Ideal – yea, the Philosopher King – of sandwiches. But let's get to the detail: it's fresh filling (roast beef or fried seafood are the most common, but the possibilities are endless), tomatoes, lettuce, onion, mayo and pickles and a perfect loaf of not-quite-French bread. The ideal po'boy is elusive: try Mahony's (p134) on Magazine St, Domilise's Po-boys (p133) Uptown or Parkway (p149) in Mid-City.

✗ *Eating*

St Charles Avenue Streetcar (p129)

8 Some of the grandest homes in the USA line St Charles Ave, all shaded by enormous live oak trees that glitter with the tossed beads of hundreds of Mardi Gras floats. Underneath the shade joggers pace themselves along the grassy 'neutral ground' (median) while Tulane girls flirt with Loyola boys. Clanging through this bucolic corridor comes the St Charles Streetcar, a mobile bit of urban transportation history bearing tourists and commuters along a street as important to American architecture as Frank Lloyd Wright.

🏃 *Uptown & Riverbend*

Drinking Classic Cocktails *(p30)*

9 A significant case could be made that the cocktail, a blend of spirits mixed into something delicious and dangerous, was invented in New Orleans. Bitters, long considered a crucial component of any cocktail, is the homegrown creation of a French Quarter pharmacy. When someone calls a drink a 'classic cocktail,' it's because local bartenders have been making it here for centuries. The ultimate New Orleans drink is the Sazerac, enjoyed at any time of day, but always with a touch of class.

🍷 *Drinking & Nightlife*

Garden District Stroll *(p119)*

10 After the Louisiana Purchase, thousands of Americans began moving to New Orleans, until then an entirely French city. Said Yankees decided to show the Europeans they could build homes as pretty as any continental-Caribbean townhouse, and constructed enormous, plantation-ready mansions in the area now known as the Garden District. Soaking up architecture is simply magical out here; stroll under live oaks, past fine restaurants and bumping bars – and don't forget to pay a visit to the cemetery too...

◉ *Garden, Lower Garden & Central City*

What's New

All the City's a Stage

New Orleans has all the elements of a great theater town. It possesses an inherent sense of drama and has a populace that appreciates laughter, wit, absurdity and, frankly, a bit of raunch. These days, home-grown improv companies like The New Movement (p94) and indie theaters like the Shadowbox (p95) and Mudlark (p96; surreal giant puppets, anyone?) are bursting into being like live oak roots through the sidewalk.

Domenica

This downtown Italian eatery boasts delicious pizza and pasta, plus Chef Alon Shaya, who earned a James Beard nomination for Best Chef in the South at the time of research (p107).

Music on St Claude

Once considered shady by local residents, parts of St Claude Ave now host some of the most exciting live music gigs in the city (p94).

Twelve Mile Limit

A superlative neighborhood bar in a city that knows the genre, Twelve Mile Limit combines a great jukebox with well-mixed cocktails and some delicious barbecue (p151).

Satsuma

This soup, salad and sandwich cafe, which would fit in fine in Melbourne, Brooklyn or San Francisco, neatly sums up the Bywater's transition from gritty to pretty (p90).

Freret Street Corridor

Gentrification has rolled over Freret St, leaving gourmet burger bars, fancy cocktails, a wonderful comic-book store and a great hometown hot-dog stand in its wake (p132).

Green Goddess

This Goddess rules over her French Quarter domain with an exciting menu that is rooted in New Orleans techniques, while drawing on the rest of the world for influences and ingredients (p62).

Old New Orleans Rum Tour

In a gritty industrial park you'll find the Old New Orleans distillery and its varietals of delicious rum, just awaiting some slow spirit sampling (p88).

Bayou Beer Garden

Mix up sultry humidity with a town that loves its libations and you've got a sure-fire winner when it comes to outdoor beer-swilling spots (p152).

Cake Cafe

This bustling place may not take reservations, but it does dish out some of the finest breakfasts in the city, not to mention some mouth-watering baked goodness (p89).

Confederacy of Cruisers

Explore the Crescent City in style from the cushioned seat of a street-king cruiser bicycle (p88).

For more recommendations and reviews, see **lonelyplanet.com/usa/new-orleans**

Need to Know

Currency
US dollars ($)

Language
English

Visas
Required for most foreign visitors unless eligible for the Visa Waiver Program (see p223).

Money
ATMs widely available. Credit cards accepted in all accommodation and many, but not all, restaurants.

Cell Phones
Local SIM cards can be used in European and Australian phones. Other phones must be set to roaming.

Time
Central Time (GMT/UTC minus six hours)

Tourist Information
New Orleans Convention Center & Visitors Bureau (☎566-5011; www.neworleanscvb.com; 2020 St Charles Ave; ⏰8:30am-5pm Mon-Fri) Plenty of free maps and helpful information.

Your Daily Budget

Budget under $100
➡ Dorm bed $30
➡ Self-cater or cheap takeout
➡ Free music shows
➡ Rent a bicycle or use streetcars

Midrange $100–200
➡ Guesthouse or B&B room $90
➡ Neighborhood restaurant for two $50
➡ Bicycle rental or split taxi fares

Top end over $200
➡ Fine dining for two, plus wine $150
➡ Four-star hotel rooms from $200
➡ Taxis or car rental

Advance Planning

Three months before Check if any festivals are going down; book hotel rooms if you're arriving during Mardi Gras or Jazz Fest.

One month before Organize a car rental. Make bookings at high-end restaurants you don't want to miss.

One week before Read the Gambit (www.bestofneworleans.com) and check www.neworleansonline.com to see what's going on in the way of live music during your visit.

Useful Websites

➡ **Gambit** (www.bestofneworleans.com) Arts and entertainment listings.

➡ **New Orleans Online** (www.neworleansonline.com) Official tourism website.

➡ **New Orleans CVB** (www.neworleanscvb.com) Convention Center & Visitor Bureau.

➡ **WWOZ radio** (www.wwoz.org) Firm finger on the cultural pulse.

➡ **Times-Picayune** (www.nola.com) Three times a week.

➡ **Lonely Planet** (www.loneyplanet.com/usa/new-orleans) Your trusted traveler website.

WHEN TO GO

The city's most popular festivals are Mardi Gras, in late February/early March, and Jazz Fest, which runs the last weekend in April and first weekend in May.

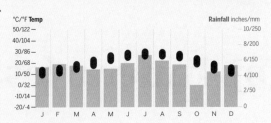

Arriving in New Orleans

Louis Armstrong International Airport (MSY) Located 10 miles west of New Orleans. A taxi to the CBD costs $33, or $14 per passenger for two more passengers. Shuttles to the CBD are $20/38 one way/round-trip per person. The E-2 bus takes you to Carrollton and Tulane Ave in Mid-City for $2.

Amtrak & Greyhound Adjacent to each other downtown. You can walk to the CBD or French Quarter, but don't do so at night, or with heavy luggage. A taxi from here to the French Quarter should be around $10; further afield you'll be pressed to spend more than $20.

For much more on **arrival**, see p214.

Getting Around

➜ **Streetcar** Service on the charming streetcars is limited. One-way fares are $1.25, and multi-trip passes are available.

➜ **Bus** Bus services are OK, but try not to time your trip around them. Fares won't run more than $2.

➜ **Walk** If you're just staying in the small French Quarter, your feet will serve fine.

➜ **Bicycle** Flat New Orleans is easy to bike across – you can cross town in 45 minutes.

➜ **Car** The easiest way to access outer neighborhoods like Mid-City. Parking is problematic in the French Quarter and CBD.

For much more on **getting around**, see p215.

Sleeping

The bedrock of the local economy is tourism, and accommodation is generally of a high standard. **Hotels** are found in the French Quarter and Central Business District (CBD). These are large, multistory affairs kitted out with amenities; hotels in the French Quarter tend to have a more boutique, historical feel, while CBD properties are more modern.

More intimate (and quirky) **guesthouses** and **B&Bs** are the norm in the Garden District, Uptown, Faubourg Marigny and the Bywater. There is one **hostel** in Mid-City.

Useful Websites

➜ **New Orleans Online** (www.neworleansonline.com) The city's official tourism website is a good starting point.

➜ **New Orleans CVB** (www.neworleanscvb.com) The Convention Center & Visitors Bureau possesses extensive hotel listings.

➜ **New Orleans Hotels** (www.neworleanshotels.com) Another good database of lodging options.

For much more on **sleeping**, see p171.

THE NEW ORLEANS COMPASS

North, south, east and west? Not in New Orleans. This city's directions are determined by bodies of water and how they flow, not a compass. Here folks say Lake, River, Up and Down. 'Lake' is Lake Pontchartrain, north of the city. 'River,' of course, is the Mississippi. 'Up' and 'down' refer to the flow of the river, which heads 'down' towards the Gulf of Mexico. So 'Down' basically means 'east,' and 'Up' basically means west. Confused? It makes more sense when you're here, honest.

Top Itineraries

Day One

French Quarter (p46)

 If you're feeling decadent, have one of a dozen varieties of poached egg at **Brennan's Restaurant**. Or do coffee and beignets at **Cafe du Monde** – it's clichéd, but it's quintessentially New Orleans. Arrive early to avoid crowds. Afterwards go on to the **Friends of the Cabildo Walking Tour**, our favorite introduction to the architectural wonders of the French Quarter.

> **Lunch** Green Goddess (p62) Unique, quirky and delicious culinary innovation.

French Quarter (p46)

Wander through **Jackson Square** and the Quarter's museums. The **Cabildo** and **Presbytère** are adjacent to each other and give a good grounding in Louisiana culture, as does the nearby **Historic New Orleans Collection**. Afterwards, take in the mighty Mississippi strolling along the **Moon Walk**, or enjoy a free afternoon concert at the **Old US Mint**.

> **Dinner** Bayona (p62) Locavore base of hometown legend Susan Spicer.

French Quarter (p46)

We're going to enjoy a night in the Quarter without stepping onto Bourbon Street (except to cross it). Forget Hurricanes and Hand Grenades and all those neon concoctions: have a real drink at **Tonique** or **French 75**. Take in a show at **Preservation Hall** or **One Eyed Jacks**, then have 3am breakfast at the **Clover Grill**.

Day Two

CBD & Warehouse District (p98)

 Spend a morning visiting the **Ogden Museum of Southern Art**. Once you've immersed yourself in aesthetics, consider pursuing some history at the **National WWII Museum**, the USA's most comprehensive museum dedicated to the conflict.

> **Lunch** Cochon Butcher (p106) Artisan meats with a Cajun twist.

Garden, Lower Garden & Central City (p113)

Stroll along Magazine St in a state of shopping nirvana. Then walk north, pop into **Lafayette Cemetery No 1**, consider having a drink at **Commander's Palace** (it helps to be well-dressed) and hop onto the **St Charles Avenue Streetcar** heading west toward **Audubon Park** and through one of the prettiest streets anywhere.

> **Dinner** Mat & Naddie's (p131) Fun fine dining in a charming riverfront cottage.

Uptown & Riverbend (p126)

Have a boozy night perusing the excellent beer menu at **Cooter Brown's** and consider having an oyster or ten on the side. Then head to the **Maple Leaf** or **Tipitina's** and rock out to whoever's playing.

Day Three

Faubourg Marigny & Bywater (p86)

 Get the day going right with oysters and grits at **Cake Café & Bakery**. Eat early so you can join the morning Creole Neighborhoods bike tour with **Confederacy of Cruisers**. This is exceptionally easy riding, and takes in all elements of the funky Marigny and Bywater, but if you don't fancy bikes, walk past **Washington Square Park** and soak up the Marigny's vibe.

> **Lunch** Lost Love (p91) This dive bar has a surprise Vietnamese kitchen.

Faubourg Marigny & Bywater (p86)

Walk along Royal or Congress Sts east ('down' in New Orleans directional-speak) and check out the colorful houses, plus **Dr Bob's Studio**. If you head north, you'll see where voodoo and yoga come together at the **Healing Center** and, if you're lucky, the new Crescent Park will have opened on Chartres St.

> **Dinner** Bacchanal (p89) Wine and cheese in a musical garden.

Faubourg Marigny & Bywater (p86)

Stay in the neighborhood to listen to live music. If you're feeling edgy, head to **St Claude Avenue** where the offerings range from punk to hip-hop to bounce to '60s mod. For more traditional Nola jazz and blues, head down **Frenchman Street**.

Day Four

Mid-City & the Tremé (p140)

 Consider renting a bicycle and riding around the Tremé – the **Café Tremé** is a good place to fuel up on coffee. You can walk around here too, but it will take longer. Driving is also an option. While in the neighborhood, don't miss the **Backstreet Cultural Museum**.

> **Lunch** Dooky Chase (p151) The queen of local soul food.

Mid-City & the Tremé (p140)

Head up **Esplanade Avenue** and gawk at all the gorgeous Creole mansions sitting pretty under the big live oaks. Take Esplanade Ave all the way to **City Park** and wander around the **New Orleans Museum of Art**, then spend some time lolling under the shade of live oaks, especially the **Singing Tree**.

> **Dinner** Café Degas (p149) Fabulously romantic French fine dining.

Mid-City & the Tremé (p140)

Have a well-mixed drink at friendly **Twelve Mile Limit**, where they serve barbecue in case you feel peckish again. Afterwards head to **Mid-City Rock & Bowl**, a mix of bowling alley and concert hall, where you can hit the lanes and the dance floor.

If You Like...

Live Music

Candlelight Lounge Wednesday night with the Tremé Brass Band is one of the most soulful shows in town. (p153)

Tipitina's Legendary live music; the Uptown has heaps more character and atmosphere. (p137)

d.b.a. Hosts local legends and international acts of acclaim throughout the week. (p93)

Mid-City Rock & Bowl Zydeco Thursday is as close as you'll come to Cajun country within New Orleans. (p152)

Spotted Cat One of the great smoky jazz bars of New Orleans. (p94)

Snug Harbor This attractive lounge is the classiest jazz establishment in town. (p94)

Hi Ho Lounge Shows range from bluegrass to punk at this eclectic venue. (p93)

Maison Attracts a younger crowd, showcasing everything from hip-hop to indie rock. (p95)

AllWays Lounge Come for frontier-pushing music, experimental stuff and damn good dance parties. (p94)

One Eyed Jack's One of the French Quarter's best bars, showcasing genres spanning rap to indie to hard metal. (p68)

Creole Cuisine

Bayona One of the first, and still best, innovators in haute Nouveau-Orleanian cuisine. (p62)

A classic Creole dish: soft-shell crab served with new potatoes and almonds

Gautreau's Consistently amazing, with a kitchen fronted by Sue Zemaneck, one of the brightest rising stars in American gastronomy. (p130)

Restaurant August Pricey, but also some of the best of New Orleans fine dining. (p107)

Brigtsen's Restaurant Incredible menu features the best of locally sourced, wonderfully prepared entrees. (p131)

Commander's Palace One of New Orleans' most legendary restaurants, a proving ground for many a young local chef. (p118)

Lilette One of the most promising kitchens in town during our research, Lilette combines great food with a cozy atmosphere. (p131)

Patois Excellent French cuisine given a New Orleans twist, housed in a wonderfully atmospheric historic home. (p130)

Galatoire's Where the New Orleans elite still gathers every Friday, a restaurant and experience of another era. (p65)

Green Spaces

City Park The largest and prettiest green space in the city of New Orleans. (p142)

Bayou St John This coffee-black waterway is one of the nicest places for a stroll in the city. (p147)

Barataria Preserve See the swamps that define southern Louisiana mere minutes from the state's largest city. (p169)

Alcee Fortier Park A tiny but wonderfully landscaped park on lovely Esplanade Avenue. (p145)

Audubon Zoo Located in lush Audubon Park, the zoo is both park area and animal encounter space. (p128)

Bars

Twelve Mile Limit A friendly neighborhood bar where the drinks are strong and the staff are smiling. (p151)

Tonique The bartender's bar, where drinks will kick your ass and you'll thank them for it. (p66)

St Joe's One of the finest neighborhood bars in the posh environs of Uptown. (p135)

The John One of the diviest of dives in bohemian Faubourg Marigny. (p92)

Cure A pioneer of both the cocktail revival and the revitalization of Freret Street. (p135)

R Bar Great neighborhood bar with a punk attitude and exceptionally strong drinks. (p92)

Sylvain Pretty French Quarter gastropub where the great food is matched by excellent drinks. (p66)

Rusty Nail An utterly unexpected dive bar in the midst of the posh Warehouse District. (p109)

French 75 Classy Quarter spot where the staff wear tuxes and the drinks are just as pretty. (p66)

Bellocq Posh downtown spot for those who dig a more modern, Manhattan-lounge vibe. (p110)

Architecture

Royal Street Quintessential French Quarter: stroll past fine Creole townhouses and wonderful iron balconies. (p52)

St Charles Avenue The live oak trees here shade some of the most beautiful plantation-style mansions in the South. (p129)

For more top New Orleans spots, see
→ Eating (p26)
→ Drinking & Nightlife (p30)
→ Entertainment (p33)
→ Shopping (p37)
→ Gay & Lesbian (p39)

Esplanade Avenue Another shady street where the villas are French-Caribbean inspired; Degas once lived here. (p145)

Faubourg Marigny & Bywater Lovely, colorful Creole cottages are scattered over this area like candy. (p86)

Museums

National WWII Museum Excellent, comprehensive museum that provides fascinating insights into the largest conflict in history. (p100)

New Orleans Museum of Art Features both contemporary work and a large archaeological section, plus gorgeous sculpture garden. (p142)

Ogden Museum of Southern Art A mesmerizing peek into the aesthetic of America's most distinctive geographic region. (p101)

Backstreet Cultural Museum Enthralling journey into the street culture of African American New Orleans. (p147)

Hogan Jazz Archive A must-see for anyone who has even a passing obsession with the history of music. (p129)

Butterfly Garden & Insectarium Bugs! Fun for kids, but also accessible to adults, especially those with an interest in the animal kingdom. (p103)

PLAN YOUR TRIP IF YOU LIKE...

Month by Month

January

Contrary to popular belief, New Orleans gets cold, and January is pretty nippy. Sports events and tourism-oriented New Year's debauchery give way to the professional partying of Carnival season by month's end.

Joan of Arc Parade

On January 6, New Orleans celebrates the birthday of the Maid of Orleans – Joan of Arc – with a family-friendly parade (www.joanofarcparade.com) that runs through the French Quarter (*bien sur*). Parade-goers dress in meticulously detailed historical costume.

Martin Luther King Jr Day

On this day, a charming midday parade, replete with brass bands, makes its way from the Bywater to the Tremé District, down St Claude Ave.

February

It's Carnival time! In the weeks preceding Mardi Gras the madness in the city builds to a fever pitch, culminating in the main event, the party to end all parties.

Carnival Season

During the three weeks before Mardi Gras, parades kick off with more frequency each day. Large krewes stage massive affairs, with elaborate floats and marching bands, that run along St Charles Ave and Canal St.

Mardi Gras Day

In February or early March, the outrageous activity reaches a crescendo as the city nearly bursts with costumed celebrants. It all ends at midnight with the beginning of Lent. (www.mardigrasneworleans.com)

March

The city has barely nursed its Mardi Gras hangover when the fun starts again. New Orleanians call this Festival Season, as small concerts and free music events kick off every weekend.

St Patrick's Day

The party picks up again the weekend of Paddy's Day (www.stpatricksdayneworleans.com) with the Jim Monaghan/Molly's at the Market parade, which rolls through the French Quarter; and the Uptown/Irish Channel parade, where the float riders toss cabbages and potatoes.

Super Sunday

St Joseph's Night, March 19, is a big masking event for black Indian gangs, who march after sunset around St Claude Ave and LaSalle St. The following Sunday (known as Super Sunday), tribes gather at AL Davis park (Washington & LaSalle St) for a huge procession of the city's Mardi Gras Indian tribes. (www.mardigrasneworleans.com/supersunday.html)

Foburg Fest

Traditionally held the weekend before Austin's SXSW music festival, Foburg Fest (www.foburgneworleans.com) turns Frenchmen St into a big indie rock event.

⚜ Tennessee Williams Literary Festival

The last weekend of March features a four-day fete (www.tennesseewilliams .net) in the playwright's honor; Williams called New Orleans his 'spiritual home.' There's a 'Stell-a-a-a!' shouting contest, walking tours, theater events, film screenings, readings and the usual food and alcohol.

✖ Louisiana Crawfish Festival

This huge crawfish feed qualifies as the epitome of southern Louisiana culture. It's fun for the family, with rides, games and Cajun music. Held in nearby Chalmette in late March/early April. (www.louisianacraw fishfestival.com)

⚜ Congo Square Rhythms Festival

This huge world-music festival (www.jazzandheritage .org/congo-square) rocks into Congo Sq in mid- to late March; expect drumming, dancing, indigenous crafts and delicious food.

April

Festival season continues – besides the events we list here, concerts and crawfish boils pick up in frequency as the weather turns a balmy shade of amazing.

⚜ Gay Easter Parade

On Easter Sunday, the GBLT population of New Orleans (and their straight friends) dress up in their hyperbolic, frilliest Sunday best, then march or ride in horse-drawn carriages past the gay bars of the French Quarter. Fabulous fun.

⚜ French Quarter Festival

One of New Orleans' finest events, the French Quarter Festival (www.fqfi.org) rocks the Vieux Carre in mid-April with stages featuring jazz, funk, Latin rhythms, Cajun, brass bands and R&B, plus food stalls operated by the city's most popular restaurants.

⚜ Jazz Fest

The Fair Grounds Race Course – and, at night, the whole town – reverberates with good sounds, plus food and crafts, over the last weekend in April and first weekend of May. See p76 for details. (www.nojazz fest.com)

May

There's another month or two before the weather starts to get soupy and, to be honest, the days are already fairly hot. So too is the ongoing music, food and parties.

☆ Chaz Fest

When local musicians felt bumped out by all the international headliners at Jazz Fest, they formed Chaz Fest (http://chaz festival.com), a wonderful celebration of New Orleans musicians and music named for local legend (and his instrument) 'Washboard Chaz.' Held first weekend in May.

⚜ Bayou Boogaloo

Mid-City gets to shine with this wonderful outdoor festival (www.thebayou boogaloo.com), held on the banks of pretty Bayou St John in mid-May. Expect the usual: food stalls, lots of bands and general good times.

✖ New Orleans Wine & Food Experience

This being a culinary town, the local food and wine fest (www.nowfe .com) is quite the affair. To join you pay a pretty penny to attend various tastings, seminars and meal 'experiences' that push the gastronomic frontiers. Late May.

July

There's a sultry romance to summer – makes you want to sit in a sweat-stained tank top or summer dress and do nothing but drink iced tea. Don't rest. The New Orleans calendar doesn't let up.

☆ Essence Music Festival

Essence magazine sponsors a star-studded lineup of R&B, hip-hop, jazz and blues performances at the Superdome around the July 4 weekend. (www.essence .com/festivals)

🏃 Running of the Bulls

Don't miss this one! In mid-July, the Big Easy Rollergirls dress up as bulls and chase crowds dressed in Pamplona-style white outfits with red scarves. The 'bulls' run through the French Quarter – trust us, this one's lots of fun. (www .nolabulls.com)

Tales of the Cocktail

Sure, New Orleans is a 24/7 festival, but this three-day event (www.talesofthe cocktail.com) sets its sights a little higher. Appreciating the art of 'mixology' is the main point, and getting lit up is only an incidental part of the fun.

August

Damn. It's hot. So very, very hot. And there may be hurricanes on the horizon. Who cares? The eating, drinking and making merry continue, and hotel rates are bottoming out.

Satchmo SummerFest

Louis Armstrong's birthday (August 4) is celebrated with four days of music and food in the French Quarter. Three stages present local talents in 'trad' jazz, contemporary jazz and brass bands. (www.fqfi.org/satchmo summerfest)

Southern Decadence

Billing itself as 'Gay Mardi Gras,' this five-day Labor Day weekend festival (www.southerndecadence.com) kicks off in the Lower Quarter. Expect music, masking, cross-dressing, dancing in the streets and a Sunday parade that's everything you'd expect from a city with a vital gay community.

White Linen Night

Get decked out in your coolest white duds and wander about the Warehouse District, as galleries throw open their doors to art appreciators and lots of free-flowing drinks on the first Saturday in August.

Top: A Mardi Gras Indian (p146)

Bottom: Celebrating St Patrick's Day (p20)

Red Dress Run

The Nola Hash House Harriers lead this charity run (www.nolareddress.tumblr.com) through the Quarter and Downtown. It's a 3- to 4-mile run with one rule: Wear a red dress. Or less. Open to men or women, so there's lots of crimson cross-dressing afoot.

Mid-Summer Mardi Gras

The Uptown Krewe of OAK (Outrageous and Kinky) holds this mini-Mardi Gras every year around the last weekend in August. Revelers parade around the Riverbend, with the party kicking off at the Maple Leaf (p137).

September

The heat doesn't let up and the threat of hurricanes gets even worse, but the music certainly doesn't take a break.

Ponderosa Stomp

Billed as the greatest celebration of American roots music in the world, the Stomp takes over Howlin' Wolf (p111) downtown in mid-September. Lots of blues, rock, folk, jazz, country and soul. (www.ponderosastomp.com)

October

Locals love dressing up, costumes, ghost stories and the supernatural, so October is a pretty big month in these parts.

Crescent City Blues & BBQ Festival

Doesn't the name alone make you want to visit? At this mid-October festival

(www.jazzheritage.org /blues-fest), there's barbecue, there's blues and there's good times in Lafayette Park on St Charles Ave.

New Orleans Film Festival

Theaters around the city screen the work of both local and internationally renowned filmmakers for one week in mid-October. (www.neworleansfilmsociety.org)

Halloween

Halloween is not taken lightly here. Most fun is to be found in the giant costume party throughout the French Quarter. It's a big holiday for gay locals and tourists, with a lot of action centering on the Lower Quarter.

Voodoo Music Experience

If you thought New Orleans was all jazz and no rock, visit during Halloween weekend. Past acts at Voodoo have included the Foo Fighters, the Flaming Lips, Queens of the Stone Age, Billy Idol and Ryan Adams (all in one year!). (www.voodoomusicfest.com)

November

The weather is cooling down and winter is arriving. Arts and entertainment events, plus some of the best sandwiches you'll ever eat, fill up the calendar.

All Saints Day

Cemeteries fill with crowds who pay their respects to ancestors. It is by no means morbid or sad, as many people have picnics and parties. It wouldn't be out of line

for families to serve gumbo beside the family crypt.

Celebration in the Oaks

This City Park celebration is New Orleans' take on Christmas in America, with 2 miles of oak trees providing the lit-up superstructure. You can view it in its entirety from your car or in a horse-drawn carriage. (www.celebrationintheoaks.com)

Fringe Fest

Dramatic boundaries are pushed throughout the city, but particularly in the Marigny and Bywater, at this festival (www.nofringe.org) of experimental theater, held around the second weekend of the month.

Po-Boy Festival

Fifty thousand sandwich lovers descend on Riverbend in November to sample po'boys from New Orleans' best restaurants. (www.poboyfest.com)

December

Christmas brings flickering torch lights, chilly winds, gray skies and a festive atmosphere to this city of festivals.

Feux de Joie

'Fires of joy' light the way along the Mississippi River levees above Orleans Parish and below Baton Rouge in December and on Christmas Eve (December 24).

New Year's Eve

Revelers – mostly drunk tourists – pack around Jackson Brewery (p74) in the French Quarter, where Baby New Year is dropped from the roof at midnight.

With Kids

New Orleans really is a fairy-tale city, with its colorful beads, weekly costume parties and daily music wafting through the air. The same flights of fancy and whimsy that give this city such appeal for poets and artists also makes it an imaginative wonderland for children, especially creative ones.

Riding Audubon Zoo's antique carousel

JUDY BELLAH / LONELY PLANET IMAGES ©

Best Animal Encounters

Exploring the Audubon Zoo

There's wildlife from around the world in this attractive zoo, but the main attraction is the excellent showcasing of local critters in the form of the Louisiana Swamp. Out in this cleverly landscaped wetland, your kids will get a chance to mug next to a genuine albino alligator, as pretty as freshly fallen snow in a bayou.

Undersea Adventures at Aquarium of the Americas

Dip a toe into the waters of marine biology at this excellent aquarium, where the aquatic habitats range from the Mississippi Delta to the Amazon River Basin. Kids and adults will marvel at rainbow clouds of tropical fish, and guess what? There's a white alligator – 'Spots' – living here too.

Bug Out in the Insectarium

You've got to love a museum dedicated to New Orleans' insects where one display focuses on cockroaches, and another is sponsored by the pest-control business. Yet this isn't a museum that focuses on insects' 'ick' factor. Rather, you'll get a sense of the beauty and diversity of the entomological world, from gem-colored beetle displays to the serenity of the Butterfly Garden.

Outdoor Adventures

Wander Through City Park

The largest green space in New Orleans is undoubtedly also its most attractive. There's plenty of big trees proving shade, lazy waterways filled with fish (and sometimes small alligators!), a model train diagram of the city built entirely of biological materials, and a wonderful carousel and sculpture garden that will be of interest to older kids. Plus Storyland – a nostalgic mini-park with more than two dozen storybook scenes reproduced on a life-sized scale.

Barataria Preserve

This green gem in the national park system crown is located just south of the city. Toddlers to teenagers will enjoy walking along the flat boardwalk, which traverses the gamut of Louisiana wetlands, from bayous to marsh prairie.

Let's Go Ride a Bike

Biking in New Orleans is pretty easy for fit kids. Younger ones can be taken on short rides through the French Quarter or the Garden District. Older kids should be able to swing bike tours like the ones offered by Confederacy of Cruisers (p88), which take in the city's older Creole neighbourhoods on big, tough, comfortable cruiser-style bicycles. Avoid biking through the traffic-congested Central Business District.

Alcee Fortier Park

By day, this little gem of a park, located on shady Esplanade Avenue, is a nice spot to stop for a lemonade in the sun and chill out on funky furniture. At night, as the weather warms up, outdoor movies are sometimes shown here, generally in the early part of the evening.

Jackson Square & the River

Jackson Square is essentially a constant carnival. At any time of day you may encounter street artists, fortune tellers, buskers putting on their shows, brass bands and similar folks all engaged in producing the sort of sensory overload New Orleans is famous for (and kids go crazy over). The square is framed by a fairy-tale cathedral and two excellent museums, and nearby are steps leading up to the Mississippi River, where long barges evoke *Huckleberry Finn* and the Mississippi of Twain mythos. Drop by Cafe du Monde if you want to treat your kids (and yourself) to some powdered sugary treats.

History & Culture for Kids

Under the City's Skin

The Louisiana Children's Museum is a good introduction to the region for toddlers, while older children and teenagers may appreciate the Ogden Museum, Cabildo and Presbytère. Little ones also often take a shine to the candy-colored houses of the city, especially those in the French Quarter, Faubourg Marigny and Uptown. The Latter Public Library on St Charles Ave has a good selection of children's literature and is located in a pretty historical mansion. The city's cemeteries, especially Lafayette Cemetery No 1 in the Garden District, are authentic slices of the past and enjoyably spooky to boot.

Festival Fun

The many street parties and outdoor festivals of New Orleans have food stalls and, of course, great music. Children will love dancing to the beat. Seek out festivals held during the day, such as Bayou Boogaloo; see Month by Month (p20) for more details.

Mardi Gras for Families

Your eyebrows may raise at that heading, but only if you're not from New Orleans. Mardi Gras and the Carnival Season are actually extremely family-friendly affairs outside of the well-known boozy debauch in the French Quarter. Along St Charles Avenue, which hosts many day parades and where lots of krewes roll, families set up grilling posts and tents where drinking revelers aren't welcome. Kids are set up on 'ladder seats' (www.momsminivan.com /extras/ladderseat.html) so they can get an adult-height view of the proceedings and catch throws from the floats. The crazy costumes add to the child-friendly feel of the whole affair. For more information, see www.neworleansonline.com/neworleans /mardigras/mgfamilies.html.

Cajun-style crawfish and red potatoes

 # Eating

In what other American city do people celebrate the harvest season of sewage-dwelling crustaceans? We're describing a crawfish boil, by the way, which exemplifies New Orleans' relationship with food: unconditional love. This city finds itself in its food; meals are both expressions of identity and bridges between the city's many divisions.

The Native Example

Settlers who arrived in Louisiana had to work with the ingredients of the bayous, woods and prairie, and developed one of America's only true native-born cuisines. As a result, some say the New Orleans palette is limited to its own specialties, that this is a town of 'a thousand restaurants and three dishes.'

That cliché is not entirely true. First, lots of restaurants are serving what we would deem 'Nouveau' New Orleans cuisine – native classics influenced by global flavors and techniques. And second, international options pop up frequently in this town, the most common being Vietnamese, Italian and Latin American food.

Still, this is a place where the homegrown recipes are the best stuff on the menu. As such, we present this guide to New Orleans/ Louisiana specialties. Note: 'Cajun' and 'Creole' are different, and both can be found here. The former refers to the rustic cuisine of the countryside; the latter to the richer, more refined meals of the city.

ROUX

Very few meals begin life in Louisiana without a roux (pronounced 'roo'): flour slowly cooked with oil or butter. Over time, the product evolves from a light-colored 'white' roux into a smokier 'dark' roux. The final product is used as a thickening and flavoring agent. While deceptively simple, local cooks insist their dishes live or die based on the foundation roux.

GUMBO

No cook is without a personal recipe for this spicy, full-bodied soup/stew, which is sort of Louisiana, food-ified. Ingredients vary from chef to chef, but gumbo is almost always served over starchy steamed rice. Coastal gumbo teems with oysters, jumbo shrimp and crabs, while prairie-bred Cajuns turn to their barnyard and smokehouses.

PO'BOY

Maybe you call it a submarine, grinder or hoagie. You are wrong. Simply put, a po'boy is an overstuffed sandwich served on local French bread (more chewy, less crispy) dripping with fillings; the most popular are roast beef, fried shrimp and/or fried oysters, and 'debris' (the bits of roast beef that fall into the gravy). When you order, your server will ask if you want it 'dressed,' meaning with mayonnaise, shredded lettuce and tomato. Say yes.

RED BEANS & RICE

A poor man's meal rich in flavor, this is a lunch custom associated with Mondays. Monday was traditionally wash day and, in the past, a pot of red beans would go on the stove along with the ham bone from Sunday dinner. By the time the washing was finished, supper was ready.

JAMBALAYA

Hearty, rice-based jambalaya (johm-buh-lie-uh) can include just about any combination of fowl, shellfish or meat, but usually includes ham, hence the name (derived from the French jambon or the Spanish jamón). The meaty ingredients are sautéed with onions, pepper and celery, and cooked with raw rice and water into a flavorful mix of textures.

MUFFULETTAS

It's only a slight exaggeration to say that New Orleans muffulettas are the size of manhole covers. Named for a round

NEED TO KNOW

Price Ranges

In our listings we have used the following price codes to indicate the cost of a main course.

$	less than $15
$$	$15 to $30
$$$	over $30

Opening Hours

➡ Generally restaurants are open from 11am to 11pm, with last seatings around 10:30pm.

➡ Breakfast usually starts around 7am.

➡ Many restaurants are closed Sunday, Monday or both days.

Reservations

➡ Where reservations are necessary, we say so in our reviews. But many restaurants have no-booking policies; Galatoire's (p65) and K-Paul's (p63) are two notable examples. This means that instead of calling ahead, you can expect to wait out on the sidewalk for a table to open.

➡ There are lots of small, family-run places in New Orleans. Call ahead to these spots if you're in a large group.

Tipping

Tipping is not optional. An adequate tip is 15%, but folks tend to be munificent here; a 20% tip is almost standard. That said, you're fine with 15%, but if the service is good, go a little higher. Some places will charge an automatic 18% gratuity for large groups (usually six or more people).

Lunch for Less

Scared off by high prices at top end restaurants? Visit during lunch, where you can usually dine on fare that's identical or close to the dinner menu for sometimes as low as half the cost.

sesame-crusted loaf, muffulettas are layered with various selections from the local Sicilian deli tradition, including Genoa salami, shaved ham, mortadella and sliced provolone cheese. The signature spread – a salty olive salad with pickled

Eating by Neighborhood

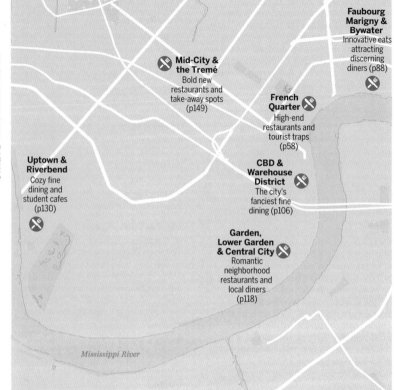

Faubourg Marigny & Bywater
Innovative eats attracting discerning diners (p88)

Mid-City & the Tremé
Bold new restaurants and take-away spots (p149)

French Quarter
High-end restaurants and tourist traps (p58)

Uptown & Riverbend
Cozy fine dining and student cafes (p130)

CBD & Warehouse District
The city's fanciest fine dining (p106)

Garden, Lower Garden & Central City
Romantic neighborhood restaurants and local diners (p118)

Mississippi River

vegetables, herbs, garlic and olive oil – is what defines the sandwich, though. It's a flavorful, greasy mess.

TASSO

This highly prized butcher-shop specialty is basically a lean chunk of ham, cured with filé (crushed sassafras leaves) and other seasonings, and then smoked until it reaches the tough consistency of beef jerky.

BOUDIN

A tasty Cajun sausage made with pork, pork liver, cooked rice and spices. A popular quick bite, especially in Cajun country.

SNOWBALLS

Shaved ice in a paper cup doused liberally with flavored syrup, snowballs are blasts of winter on a steamy midsummer afternoon.

BEIGNETS

Not so much a dessert as a round-the-clock breakfast specialty akin to the common doughnut, beignets are flat squares of dough flash-fried to a golden, puffy glory, dusted liberally with powdered (confectioner's or icing) sugar, and served scorching hot.

BREAD PUDDING

A specialty in New Orleans and Acadiana, this custardy creation is a good use for leftover bread. Local variations involve copious amounts of butter, eggs and cream, and will usually come topped with a bourbon-spiked sugar sauce.

Lonely Planet's Top Choices

Bacchanal (p89) Wine, cheese, bread and a magically lit garden.

Restaurant August (p107) Fine Creole dining in a 19th-century warehouse.

Elizabeth's (p89) Creative, fun and funky fine dining.

Cochon Butcher (p107) The pinnacle of Cajun – and carnivorous – cuisine.

Parkway Tavern (p149) Po'boy perfection served in Mid-City

Surrey's Juice Bar (p118) Best breakfast in the city.

Best for Romantic Meals

Café Degas (p149)

Adolfo's (p91)

Bacchanal (p89)

Lilette (p131)

Patois (p130)

Best for Late Night

Clover Grill (p61)

13 Monaghan (p91)

La Peniché (p90)

Trolley Stop (p120)

Buffa's (p92)

Best for Breakfast

Surrey's Juice Bar (p118)

Cake Café & Bakery (p89)

Dante's (p130)

Elizabeth's (p89)

Ruby Slipper (p149)

Best for Po'boys

Mahony's Po-Boy Shop (p134)

Domilise's (p133)

Parkway Tavern (p149)

Guy's (p133)

Rampart Food Store (p89)

Best for Classical Creole Cuisine

Bayona (p62)

Commander's Palace (p118)

Gautreau's (p130)

Galatoire's (p65)

Restaurant August (p107)

Best for 'Nouveau' New Orleans Cuisine

Green Goddess (p62)

Elizabeth's (p89)

Bayona (p62)

Herbsaint (p106)

Mat & Naddie's (p131)

Best for Vietnamese

Pho Tau Bay (p150)

Dong Phuong Oriental Bakery (p150)

Kim Son (p150)

Magasin Cafe (p133)

Lost Love (p91)

Best for Vegetarians

Green Goddess (p62)

Fatoush (p91)

13 Monaghan (p91)

Wandering Buddha (p90)

Satsuma (p90)

Best for Dessert

Sucré (p121)

Boucherie (p131)

Green Goddess (p62)

Hansen's Sno-Bliz (p135)

K-Paul's (p63)

Best for Pizza

Domenica (p107)

Slice (p118)

Crescent City Pie & Sausage Company (p149)

Nonna Mia (p150)

Mona Lisa Restaurant (p61)

Best for Burgers

Port Of Call (p59)

Yo Mama's (p65)

Elizabeth's (p89)

The Company Burger (p132)

Buffa's (p92)

Drinking & Nightlife

New Orleans doesn't rest for much. But the city isn't just an alcoholic lush. A typical New Orleans night out features just as much food and music as booze. Here they appeal to all your senses: your ear for a brass band, your taste for rich food, the feel of heat on your skin, the visual composition of a streetcar line running past historic homes, as well as your whetted thirst for another beer and shot...

Classic New Orleans Cocktails

The argument can well be made that New Orleans invented the cocktail, and while mixing spirits properly was once a lost art, today a generation of dedicated mixers are out there prepping some mean classics.

➡ **Sazerac** A potent whiskey drink that uses either rye or bourbon as its primary ingredient, with aromatic bitters (including the locally produced Peychaud's), a bit of sugar and a swish of Herbsaint.

➡ **Ramos Gin Fizz** Named for 19th-century New Orleans bartender Henry Ramos, this is a rich, frothy blend of gin, cream, egg whites, extra-fine sugar, fizzy water and a splash of orange-flower water.

➡ **Aviation** Try it on a hot day: gin, maraschino liqueur and lemon juice, plus some other trade secrets depending on which bar you're drinking in. They're very refreshing.

➡ **Pimm's Cup** A summer tipple traditionally associated with the infamous French Quarter bar, Napoleon House (p67). It's a simple mix of the British gin-based liqueur Pimm's No 1, topped with soda or ginger ale.

Beer

Nola Brewing Co (motto: *Laissez la bonne bière verser!* – Let the good beer pour!) is the only brewery based in Orleans Parish. It makes some great brews, ranging from light to dark to intensely hoppy.

That said, Abita, based in St Tammany Parish, is the most popular local brewery. All of its beers are winners, especially the seasonal varietals. Bayou Teche Brewery, based in Arnaudville, is an exciting newcomer to the local brewery scene.

Founded in 1907, Dixie Beer used to be the beer everyone associated with New Orleans, but since Katrina operations were shipped north to Wisconsin. You can still get a Dixie here, but don't think you're getting a locally produced drink.

Wine

Wine is and ever has been popular in Louisiana thanks to a strong French cultural influence, but the homegrown industry is small; this state is too humid for viticulture.

Tourist Drinks

The bars on Bourbon St feature neon, sugary beverages that will melt your face and give you an awful hangover. Still interested? OK: the Hurricane, made famous by Pat O'Brien's (p67), is a towering rum drink that gets its bright-pink hue from the healthy portion of passion fruit juice. The Hand Grenade, sold at Tropical Isle (p67), is a mix of melon liqueur, grain alcohol, rum, vodka and God knows what else. Frozen daiquiris, by New Orleans' definition, are a class of alcoholic Slurpees that come in all the brightest colors of the rainbow. You can pick them up, sometimes by the gallon from, yes, drive-through take-outs.

Nonalcoholic Drinks
COFFEE & CHICORY

Coffee here is traditionally mixed with chicory, a roasted herb root. Originally used to 'extend' scarce coffee beans during hard times, chicory continues to be added for its full-bodied flavor, which gives local coffee a slightly bitter twist. We like it served best as café au lait, which is coffee mixed with scalded (not steamed) milk poured from two cups.

ICED TEA

In hot and humid Louisiana, iced tea is more than just a drink – it's a form of air-con in a tall, sweaty glass. 'Sweet Tea' is served with enough sugar to keep an army of dentists employed. If you want a proper English cuppa, specify 'hot tea'.

Bars

In general, bars in New Orleans would often be considered 'dives' elsewhere. That's not to say bars here are grotty (although some certainly are); rather, there are many neighborhood joints in New Orleans that are unpretentious spots catering to those looking to drink, as opposed to those who want to meet and chat someone up. If you're in the latter category, head to lounges, which tend to be newer, more brightly lit and possessed of a general modern sensibility. That said, some bars, such as Mimi's in the Marigny (p92), are good spots for both a beer after work and a bit of random flirtation.

Drinking & Nightlife by Neighborhood

➡ **French Quarter** Tourist-oriented boozefests, with the occasional bar that has genuine local flavor.

➡ **Faubourg Marigny & Bywater** Amazing concentration of live music, plus friendly, arty neighborhood bars.

➡ **CBD & Warehouse District** Mix of dives and fancy lounges, often in hotels, catering to visitors.

➡ **Garden, Lower Garden & Central City** Neighborhood bars, corner dives and elegant bars attached to fine restaurants.

➡ **Uptown & Riverbend** A few good music spots and local bars, many with a student vibe.

➡ **Mid-City & the Tremé** Cheap, convivial neighborhood bars and friendly local music spots.

NEED TO KNOW

Opening Hours

Most dedicated bars open around 5pm, although some places serve drinks during lunch, and some are open 24 hours. Closing time is an ill-defined thing; officially it's around 2am or 3am, but sometimes it's whenever the last customer stumbles out the door. Cafes open early and closing times vary from lunch to late evening (around 9pm).

Prices

This is a cheap town for nighthawks. You'll rarely pay more than $5 for a beer. Sometimes domestics will go for under $3. Cocktails rarely top $6 (unless you're at a higher-end lounge), shots of hard spirits go for around $3 to $5 (more for top-shelf stuff) and everything is cheaper during happy hour. Wine can be expensive at wine bars, but is generally of very high quality. The only time prices go up to annoyingly high levels is during big events such as Mardi Gras and Jazz Fest.

Tipping

It's common to leave a dollar or more for your bartender, even if they just pop the cap off a bottle of beer. You don't have to tip for every drink, but the general rule is to leave a couple of bucks extra for every hour spent at the bar.

Bars vs Lounge vs Clubs

Many bars in New Orleans pull triple duty as live music venues and restaurants. In our reviews, we try to categorize places based on their primary 'function' – eating, drinking or music.

Lonely Planet's Top Choices

Twelve Mile Limit (p151) Casual neighborhood vibe, great spirits and drinks.

AllWays Lounge (p94) Music, scruffy attitude and funky folks.

Tonique (p66) A bartenders' bar with great cocktails.

St Joe's Bar (p135) Students and Uptown locals rub shoulders.

Mimi's in the Marigny (p92) Mixed drinks, cold beer, great music.

Cure (p135) Best spot for a fancy cocktail Uptown.

Best For Bar Food

Sylvain (p66)

Lost Love (p92)

Mimi's in the Marigny (p92)

Twelve Mile Limit (p151)

Café Negril (p95)

Best for Coffee

Fair Grinds (p152)

Rue de la Course (p136)

Who Dat Coffee Cafe (p93)

Cafe Tremé (p152)

Orange Couch (p93)

Best for Beer

Bulldog (p122)

d.b.a (p93)

Le Bon Temps Roulé (p136)

Bayou Beer Garden (p152)

Best for Wine

Delachaise (p133)

Bacchanal (p89)

Swirl (p154)

WINO (p111)

Bouligny (p136)

Best for Cocktails

Tonique (p66)

French 75 (p66)

Cure (p135)

Twelve Mile Limit (p151)

Sylvain (p66)

Best for Jukebox

St Joe's (p135)

Markey's (p92)

Pal's (p152)

Twelve Mile Limit (p151)

Lost Love (p92)

Best for Singles

Bridge Lounge (p122)

Columns Hotel (p135)

Lafitte's Blacksmith Shop (p66)

Bellocq (p110)

Bulldog (p122)

Carousel Bar (p66)

Best for Students

F&M's Patio Bar (p136)

Boot (p137)

Saint Bar & Lounge (p123)

Bulldog (p122)

Snake & Jakes (p136)

Best Historical Bars

French 75 (p66)

Napoleon House (p67)

Carousel Bar (p66)

Lafitte's Blacksmith Shop (p66)

Chart Room (p66)

Best Neighborhood Bars

Pal's (p152)

Rusty Nail (p109)

Twelve Mile Limit (p151)

Markey's (p92)

Candlelight Lounge (p153)

R Bar (p92)

Music posters stapled to the wall at live-music venue d.b.a. (p93)

☆ Entertainment

Be it live music, the visual arts, dance, film or theater, New Orleans knows how to entertain guests. We would go so far as to say the city is one great stage, and that visitors need not just watch the show, but are welcome to participate as costumed players.

Live Music

There is great live music happening every night of the week in New Orleans, which makes a strong claim to being the best live music city in the nation. Jazz is definitely not the only genre on offer: R&B, rock, country, Cajun, zydeco, funk, soul, hip-hop and genre-defying experimentation are all the norm. For more information on New Orleans' music culture, see p207.

The Arts

The city of New Orleans has been actively using the arts as a means of revitalizing neighborhoods and building cachet with 'creative class' travelers – the ones who come to a destination looking for a local aesthetic and take on beauty. The city has always been a bit of an arts colony, and creativity comes naturally to its citizens.

Many New Orleanians are aspiring and established artists, drawn by – excuse the expression – a perfect storm of conditions that

NEED TO KNOW

Price Ranges

➡ Standard cover for shows is $5 to $10; the latter price raises an eyebrow.

➡ However, during events like Jazz Fest, seeing local celebrities like Kermit Ruffins may run to $15.

Weekly Gigs

Some musicians in New Orleans are regular as clockwork, showing up at that same party time in the same party place every week. There's a great vibe at these shows, where it feels like musicians are entertaining friends. Note the following gigs are not set in stone – bands tour, after all.

➡ **Sunday** Bruce Daigrepont and the Cajun Fais Do Do at Tipitina's (p137).

➡ **Monday** King James & The Special Men at BJ's (p96); bluegrass open jam at Hi Ho Lounge (p93).

➡ **Tuesday** Rebirth Brass Band at Maple Leaf Bar (p137); Wasted Lives at AllWays Lounge (p94); Kermit Ruffins at Bullets (p153).

➡ **Wednesday** Tin Men with Washboard Chaz, and Walter 'Wolfman' Washington, both at d.b.a. (p93), Treme Brass Band at Candlelight Lounge (p153).

➡ **Thursday** Kermit Ruffins at Vaughan's (p95); Zydeco night at Mid-City Rock & Bowl (p152).

➡ **Friday** Ellis Marsalis at Snug Harbor (p94).

➡ **Saturday** John Boutté at d.b.a. (p93).

makes New Orleans an almost ideal city for the aesthetically inclined. Rents and competition, especially when compared with cities such as New York, Miami, Los Angeles and San Francisco, are relatively low, although there is a corresponding downgrade in exposure.

Plus, New Orleans has a reputation as an island for outcasts, especially in the relatively conservative American South. We're not saying all artists are eccentrics, but it's safe to say members of the arts community often march to the beat of their own drum, and there's no city of comparable size in America that bops to a more unique drum than New Orleans. Hell, this town will

probably play said drum at its own jazz funeral... Still, in a city with urgent needs for affordable housing, road repairs, increased law enforcement and improved education, arts funding has often been characterized as a low priority. In reaction, artists have taken it upon themselves to self-fund, provide mutual support and generally operate on whatever shoestring fate has currently handed them. Creative types here have a history of forming communities with extensive networks to support each other.

GALLERIES, MARKETS & ART WALKS

There's an arts event (almost) every weekend of the month in New Orleans. Galleries are concentrated on Royal St in the French Quarter, Julia St in the Warehouse District, Magazine St Uptown and St Claude Ave in the Bywater.

New Orleans Arts District (www.neworleans artsdistrict.com; ◷6-9pm) The galleries on Julia St open their doors every first Saturday; expect lots of wine and music.

St Claude Arts District (www.scadnola.com; ◷starting around 6pm) Various edgy and indie galleries open their doors in the Marigny & Bywater on the second Saturday of the month.

Freret Market (http://freretmarket.org; ◷noon-5pm) Part farmers market, part arts market, held on second Saturdays.

Bywater Arts Market (www.art-restoration .com/bam) Original, funky art; used to be held on third Saturdays, but schedule is a little more sporadic now.

Arts Council of New Orleans (www .artscouncilofneworleans.com; Palmer Park, at S. Carrollton & S. Claiborne Aves; ◷10am-4pm) Hosts a juried arts market on the last Saturday of the month.

THEATER

New Orleans has a strong theatrical bent; numerous local theater companies and a few large theatrical venues for touring productions frequently stage shows. Broadway blockbusters cross the boards at the Mahalia Jackson Theater (p148). Student plays are often performed at the **University of New Orleans** (☎280-6317; www.uno.edu; 2000 Lakeshore Dr) and Tulane University's **Lupin Theatre** (Map p250; ☎865-5106). There is also the Freda Lupin Memorial Theatre at the New Orleans Center for Creative Arts (Nocca; p95), separate from Tulane.

Entertainment by Neighborhood

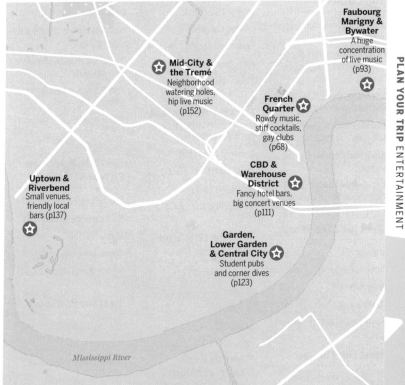

Faubourg Marigny & Bywater
A huge concentration of live music (p93)

Mid-City & the Tremé
Neighborhood watering holes, hip live music (p152)

French Quarter
Rowdy music, stiff cocktails, gay clubs (p68)

CBD & Warehouse District
Fancy hotel bars, big concert venues (p111)

Uptown & Riverbend
Small venues, friendly local bars (p137)

Garden, Lower Garden & Central City
Student pubs and corner dives (p123)

Mississippi River

In Faubourg Marigny, improv comedy can be found at the New Movement Theater (p94), while the Shadowbox Theatre (p95) and Healing Center (p96) host performances ranging from indie to classics. The Mudlark Theatre (p96) in the Bywater hosts performance art, fringe shows and, occasionally, giant puppet extravaganzas.

FILM
New Orleans has a few quality cinemas scattered about; our favorites are Prytania Theatre (p137) and Zeitgeist (p123). Indie films are sporadically screened in some bars and clubs; check www.bestofneworleans .com for the latest events. Hollywood fare is screened at the Shops at Canal Place (p112).

CLASSICAL MUSIC
The **Louisiana Philharmonic Orchestra** (☎523-6530; www.lpomusic.com) is the only musician-owned and -managed professional symphony in the USA. It performs in various churches and concert halls around town; check the website or call for details.

DANCE
The **New Orleans Ballet Association** (NOBA; ☎522-0996; www.nobadance.com; tickets $30-75) usually runs a few productions annually. The season is short, fleshed out with presentations by visiting dance companies from around the world. Performances are primarily held at the Mahalia Jackson Theater (p148) and Nocca (p95). For contemporary dance, see what's on at Nocca.

OPERA
The **New Orleans Opera** (☎529-2278; www .neworleansopera.org; tickets $30-125) rarely causes much of a stir, but remains an important part of the local culture. Productions are held at the Mahalia Jackson Theater (p148).

Lonely Planet's Top Choices

d.b.a. (p93) Consistently great live music nightly.

Hi Ho Lounge (p93) Eclectic schedule, from bluegrass to hip-hop.

Maple Leaf Bar (p137) Studenty spot for Uptown's best shows.

Mid-City Rock & Bowl (p152) Live music *and* bowling.

Snug Harbor (p94) Elegant jazz club.

Candlelight Lounge (p153) Neighborhood live music spot.

Best for Live Music

d.b.a. (p93)

Spotted Cat (p94)

Maison (p95)

Tipitina's (p137)

Hi Ho Lounge (p93)

Best for Theater

Shadowbox Theatre (p95)

Mudlark Theatre (p96)

New Movement Theater (p94)

Mahalia Jackson Theater (p148)

Best for Jazz Shows

Snug Harbor (p94)

Spotted Cat (p94)

Three Muses (p95)

Palm Court (p69)

Chickie Wah Wah (p153)

Best for Rock Music

Circle Bar (p110)

One Eyed Jacks (p68)

Checkpoint Charlie (p95)

Saturn Bar (p95)

Banks Street Bar (p153)

Best for Hip-Hop & Bounce

Blue Nile (p97)

St Roch Tavern (p93)

Maison (p95)

Dragon's Den (p96)

Best for Free Entertainment

Mardi Gras (p76)

Frenchmen Street (p88)

Bayou Boogaloo (p21)

Barkus Parade (p81)

Red Dress Run (p23)

Best Arts Events

Ogden After Hours (p101)

New Orleans Arts District arts walks (p34)

Tennessee Williams Literary Festival (p21)

Poetry slams at the Healing Center (p96)

Movie screenings at Zeitgeist (p123)

Best 'Only In New Orleans' Parties

Second Line Parades (p153)

Running of the Bulls (p21)

Mom's Ball (p76)

Chewbacchus Ball (p81)

French Quarter Festival (p21)

Best for Zydeco

Mid-City Rock & Bowl (p152)

Jazz Fest (p76)

French Quarter Festival (p21)

Bayou Boogaloo (p21)

Maple Leaf Bar (p137)

Shopping

Too many travelers assume shopping in New Orleans equals unspeakable T-shirts from the French Quarter. Wrong! New Orleans is a creative town that attracts innovative entrepreneurs and, as such, features all sorts of lovely vintage antiques, cutting-edge boutiques, functional art and amusing kitsch – and generally lacks the worst chain-store blah.

Souvenirs

There are some really great awful souvenirs out there: T-shirts, foodstuffs (you're in hot sauce heaven, here), Mardi Gras masks, stripper outfits, voodoo paraphernalia, French Quarter–style street signs and, of course, beads, beads, beads. Besides the unintentional kitsch is quite a bit of intentional tackiness – this city seems to know how to mock itself.

Arts

Music makes New Orleans go round, and this is a fantastic town for buying original CDs, vinyl and the like, plus very high-quality instruments. A large literary scene has resulted in a good number of independent bookshops, some of which have evolved into unofficial anchors of their respective communities. And visual artists will find no shortage of stores selling supplies for their work.

Antiques

Antiques are big business here, and sometimes it feels like you can't walk past parts of Royal, Chartres, lower Decatur and Magazine streets without tripping on some backyard, warehouse or studio space exhibiting beautiful examples of found furniture. Pieces tend to be relatively cheap compared to the antique action in similarly sized metropolises, and the genre goes beyond chairs and armoires to lots of old maps, watches, prints, books and similar doodads.

Fashion

This isn't a city that has a lot of time for the cold, modern school of design or fashion. Locals have opted to live in a place that drips history, and when it comes to personal style, they like to reference older eras set off with their own individualistic accents.

Probably the most-distinct face of the local shopping scene is the innumerable boutiques and vintage shops that are sprouting up all along Magazine St and in the vicinity of Riverbend. The post-Katrina arrival of artists, students and save-the-city types added a lot of funky sprinkles to an already hip fashion sundae.

Shopping by Neighborhood

➡ **French Quarter** Antique shops, souvenir stalls and art galleries.

➡ **Faubourg Marigny & Bywater** Arty, eclectic emporiums and vintage.

➡ **CBD & Warehouse District** Art galleries, clothing and shopping malls.

➡ **Garden, Lower Garden & Central City** Boutiques, antiques and vintage.

➡ **Uptown & Riverbend** More boutiques, plus student stores.

NEED TO KNOW

Opening Hours

Hours vary, but as a rule of thumb, shops are open from 9am or 10am to 7pm Monday to Friday, and 10am to 2pm Saturday and Sunday. Some stores are shut on Sunday or Monday, and sometimes both.

Buy Local

Even before Hurricane Katrina, and particularly after the storm, there was a big push in the city to promote local businesses and commerce in New Orleans. To keep abreast of the 'Buy Local' movement, visit www .buylocalbuynola.org and http://staylocal.org.

Lonely Planet's Top Choices

Dirty Coast (p138) Cleverly designed and sloganed New Orleans–themed T-shirts.

Meyer the Hatter (p112) The spiffiest headgear for your dome in town.

Fleurty Girl (p125) Cute local-themed clothing for both genders.

Maple Street Book Shop (p138) Best bookstore in town.

Crescent City Comics (p138) A great comic and graphic novel shop.

Euclid Records (p97) Awesome vinyl, old posters and knowledgeable staff.

Best for Souvenirs

Simon of New Orleans (p123)

Louisiana Music Factory (p69)

Faulkner House Books (p74)

Meyer the Hatter (p112)

Trashy Diva (p124)

Tabasco Country Store (p73)

Best Vintage Stores

Funky Monkey (p125)

Trashy Diva (p124)

Elie Monster (p70)

Bloomin' Deals (p139)

Magazine Street (p137)

Best Women's Fashion

Trashy Diva (p124)

C Collection (p139)

Pied Nu (p139)

Voluptuous Vixen (p71)

Fleurty Girl (p125)

Hemline (p71)

Best Men's Fashion

Aidan Gill for Men (p123)

Style Lab for Men (p139)

Meyer the Hatter (p112)

Dirty Coast (p138)

Best for Antiques

Bywater Bargain Center (p97)

Greg's Antiques (p71)

James H Cohen & Sons (p71)

Sword & Pen (p70)

Moss Antiques (p70)

Magazine Antique Mall (p125)

Best Music Stores

Euclid Records (p97)

Louisiana Music Exchange (p69)

James H Cohen & Sons (p71)

New Orleans Music Exchange (p125)

Peaches Records & Tapes (p70)

Best Book Stores

Maple Street Book Shop (p138)

Faulkner House Books (p74)

Crescent City Comics (p138)

Garden District Bookshop (p125)

Costumed revelers at Mardi Gras

☆ **Gay & Lesbian**

Louisiana is a culturally conservative state, but its largest city bucks that trend. New Orleans has always had a reputation for tolerance, remains one of the oldest gay-friendly cities in the Western Hemisphere and markets itself as the 'Gay Capitol of the South.' Neighborhoods such as the French Quarter and Marigny are major destinations on the GBLT travel circuit.

The Vibe

New Orleans is a pretty integrated city. Except for the lower part of Bourbon St, which we describe below, few areas or businesses feel exclusively gay. Rather, the queer vibe in the city seems to be strongest during major festivals such as the Gay Easter Parade and Southern Decadence.

History

New Orleans has always had a reputation as a city for outcasts, which for much of history has included the gay and lesbian population. Even today, in conservative states like Alabama and Mississippi, gay and lesbian youth feel the pull of the Big Easy, where acceptance of their sexuality is easy to find.

Artists such as Tennessee Williams, Truman Capote and Lyle Saxon, among many, many others, found acceptance and purpose here; Williams went so far as to dub New Orleans his 'spiritual home.' Gay Civil Rights battles were fought in New Orleans by groups like the Gertrude Stein Society. In 1997, Mayor Marc Morial extended domestic partner benefits to city employees; in the same year, Louisiana became the first state in the Deep South to pass hate crimes legislation that covered sexual orientation. One year later, New Orleans pushed new boundaries by being one of the first American cities to add gender identity to a list of groups protected from discrimination.

Sissy Culture

Queer New Orleans is a racially diverse bag, but just as there is another New Orleans living in the rough neighborhoods our guide does not cover, so too is there another, African American queer scene. 'Sissy' is local slang for gay black men – specifically gay black men who grew up in New Orleans' black neighborhoods (a middle-class, queer African American would not fit the bill). Sissy culture references the language and folkways of the black American ghetto; its most visible element to visitors is undoubtedly bounce music (see p207).

Gay & Lesbian by Neighborhood

➡ **French Quarter** The Lower Quarter, from St Philips St to Esplande Ave, is a lively gay party.

➡ **Faubourg Marigny & Bywater** Quieter gay scene largely made up of established couples.

Lonely Planet's Top Choices

Faubourg Marigny Books (p97) This bookstore is also a cornerstone of the gay community.

Country Club (p92) Clothing-optional heated pool? Sounds good.

Café Lafitte in Exile (p66) Oldest gay bar in the South.

Washington Square Park (p88) Notable for a touching HIV/AIDS memorial.

Southern Decadence (p22) One of the craziest parties in town.

Bourbon Pub & Parade (p69) It's 24-hour madness on Bourbon St.

Best Gay & Lesbian Bars

Country Club (p92)

Rawhide 2010 (p68)

Bourbon Pub & Parade (p69)

Big Daddy's Bar (p93)

Café Lafitte in Exile (p66)

Best Gay Dance Floors

Oz (p69)

Bourbon Pub & Parade (p69)

Café Lafitte in Exile (p66)

Rawhide 2010 (p68)

Best Gay Festivals

Southern Decadence (p22)

Gay Easter Parade (p21)

Mardi Gras (p76)

Halloween (p23)

Best Gay Stays

Bywater Bed & Breakfast (p178)

Green House Inn (p184)

Bourbon Orleans Hotel (p176)

Lions Inn B&B (p178)

W French Quarter (p175)

NEED TO KNOW

Gay Bars Never Close

OK, that's not entirely true, but it's safe to say that if you want a 24-hour party, the gay bars on Bourbon St (especially Bourbon Pub) are the place to be. Even the bars that aren't technically open 24 hours are often still kicking around 5am, so it's not like they attract the shrinking violet crowd.

Best Gay Online Resources

Check out these websites for information on queer travel in New Orleans.

Gay New Orleans Online (www.neworleansonline.com/neworleans/glbt) Probably the most comprehensive collection of queer listings online.

Gay New Orleans (www.gayneworleans.com) Not as polished as the above, but full of information.

Gay Cities (http://neworleans.gaycities.com) Another good online resource.

Ambush Magazine (www.ambushmag.com) Local take on queer news and issues.

Purple Roofs (www.purpleroofs.com/usa/louisiana.html) Reliable gay travel resource.

PLAN YOUR TRIP GAY & LESBIAN

Explore
New Orleans

NEW ORLEANS' TOP SIGHTS

Neighborhoods at a Glance

① French Quarter (p46)

Also known as Vieux Carré (voo car-*ray;* Old Quarter) and 'the Quarter,' the French Quarter is the original city as planned by the French in the early 18th century. Here lies the infamous Bourbon St, but of more interest (unless you happen to be in a bachelor/bachelorette party) is an elegantly aged grid of shop fronts, iron lamps and courtyard gardens. Most visitors begin exploring the city in the French Quarter; some, sadly, never leave it. That's not to say the Quarter isn't lovely, but it's definitely heavy on tourist traffic and light on locals (unless you count your bartender or waitress).

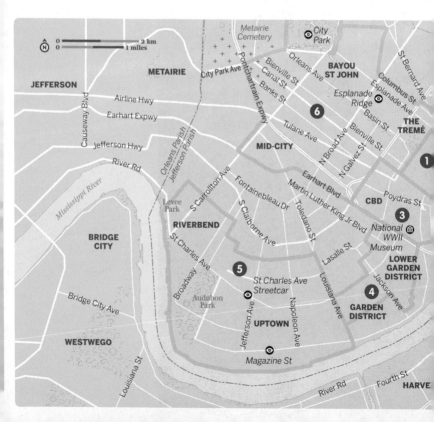

❷ Faubourg Marigny & Bywater (p86)

North of the Quarter are the Creole faubourgs (literally 'suburbs,' although neighborhood is a more accurate translation in spirit, as these areas are still very much within the city). For tourists, the Marigny and Bywater are fascinating, constituting several interesting slices of the urban landscape: an established area for gays, lesbians and successful creative class types (artists, graphic designers, etc); the edge of gentrification where exciting new bars and restaurants are opening; and areas where the rent is cheap enough to attract the young artists who will eventually gentrify the place.

❸ CBD & Warehouse District (p98)

Canal Street is the 'great divide' that splits the French Quarter from the Central Business District (CBD) and Warehouse District. Between offices and forgettable municipal buildings are some of the city's best museums, many posh restaurants, an eyesore of a casino, art galleries and excellent arts walks. That said, with all those attractions listed, this area, with its high-rise buildings and converted condos, is the least 'New Orleans' neighborhood in New Orleans.

❹ Garden, Lower Garden & Central City (p113)

Proceeding south along the Mississippi, following the curve of the river's 'U,' the streets become tree-lined and the houses considerably grander; this is the Garden and Lower Garden Districts, the beginning of New Orleans' 'American Sector' (so named because it was settled after the Louisiana Purchase). This area is home to recent graduates and young professionals, and the hip shops and bars that cater to this class are evident.

❺ Uptown & Riverbend (p126)

Uptown is the area where American settlers decided to prove to the original French inhabitants they could be as tasteful and wealthy as any old-world aristocrat. Magazine St is one of the coolest strips of restaurants and shopping outlets in town. Eventually the 'U' curves north again along the river's bend into Riverbend, popular with the university crowd.

❻ Mid-City & the Tremé (p140)

The Tremé is the oldest African American neighborhood in the country, a cluster of low-slung architecture and residential blocks, some middle class, some rotted by poverty, some gentrifying. This area runs on its west side into Mid-City, a semi-amorphous district that includes long lanes of shotgun houses, poor projects, the gorgeous green spaces of City Park, the elegant mansions of Esplanade Avenue and the slow, lovely laze of Bayou St John.

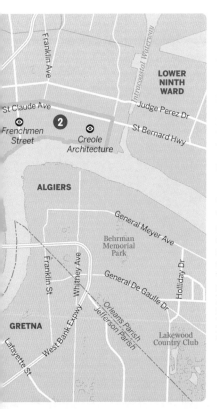

French Quarter

Neighborhood Top Five

1 Walking up and down the Mississippi River along the **Riverfront** (p56), stopping to watch crowds disembarking from ferries and listening to music and street performers along the way, before wandering into Jackson Square for, well, even more street performers.

2 Having a boozy breakfast (and possibly lunch) on Friday at **Galatoire's** (p65).

3 Catching a few drinks and the burlesque revue at **One Eyed Jacks** (p68).

4 Rubbing shoulders with local cops and journalists at **Molly's at the Market** (p66).

5 Exploring the **Cabildo** (p50) and grounding yourself in the history of Louisiana.

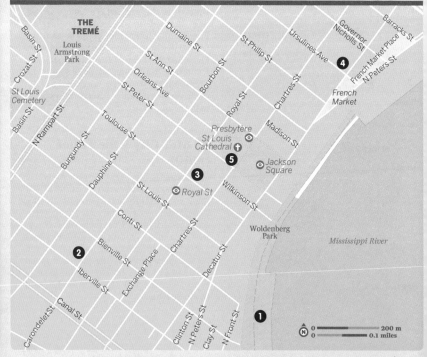

For more detail of the area, see Map p238 ➡

Explore the French Quarter

The French Quarter is pretty walkable, but if you're staying on Canal St and want to head out somewhere near Esplanade, don't discount the fact that you'll be covering around a dozen blocks (potentially more) on foot. Don't forget; it gets *hot* in New Orleans.

We would recommend exploring on your first day with the morning Friends of the Cabildo walking tour. It's an excellent introduction to both the architecture and history of the area. After the tour, take a walk along the river and consider catching a concert sponsored by the National Park Service at the US Mint. Finish the evening with dinner at either Bayona or Green Goddess, and drinks at French 75 or Tonique.

On your next day, walk up and down Royal St and consider taking a tour of the Historic New Orleans Collection. If you feel inclined, rent a bicycle from Bike Nola; you can cover lots more ground that way. Go shopping for local music at Peaches, and get yourself to Preservation Hall early enough in the evening to see the show there. As night well and truly falls, have dinner at Sylvain, and drinks at Lafitte's Blacksmith Shop.

Local Life

➡ **History** History drips though the brick walls of the French Quarter. There's a great concentration of museums, historical homes and tours that take in this city's colorful (and often criminal) past.

➡ **Music** Sure, there are good concert venues here, but you're just as likely to have a stirring auditory experience on the street, or in a national park space.

➡ **Shopping** From the kitschiest crap ever sold on God's green earth to tasteful art galleries to antique shops concealing some truly rare treasures, the Quarter is a shopper's dream.

Getting There & Away

➡ **Streetcar** The Canal and Riverfront streetcars both skirt the edges of the French Quarter.

➡ **Ferry** The 91 bus runs up Rampart St and Esplanade Ave, which are both boundary roads of the French Quarter.

➡ **Car** Parking is a hassle in the Quarter; if you're going to drive here, either be prepared to park in a garage or bring lots of quarters for meters.

Lonely Planet's Top Tip

We know: your friends told you to go to Bourbon St. We're telling you not to. Or, if you must, do so after visiting other neighborhoods. The tackiness of Bourbon is a lot more obvious after you've experienced the magic of the rest of New Orleans.

There have been frequent muggings in the part of the Quarter near Louis Armstrong Park. If you are out between Rampart St and Dauphine St past 11pm, walk with a friend.

FRENCH QUARTER

✖ Best Places to Eat

➡ Green Goddess (p62)

➡ Bayona (p62)

➡ Sylvain (p58)

➡ K-Paul's Louisiana Kitchen (p63)

➡ Port of Call (p59)

For reviews, see p58 ➡

⊙ Best Historical Sights

➡ Cabildo (p50)

➡ Presbytère (p51)

➡ Ursuline Convent (p53)

➡ Friends of the Cabildo (p54)

➡ Beauregard-Keyes House (p55)

For reviews, see p53 ➡

♉ Best Nightlife

➡ Tonique (p66)

➡ Lafitte's Blacksmith Shop (p66)

➡ Molly's at the Market (p66)

➡ Erin Rose (p66)

➡ French 75 (p66)

For reviews, see p65 ➡
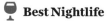

TOP SIGHTS
JACKSON SQUARE

Sprinkled with lazing loungers, surrounded by fortune tellers, sketch artists and traveling performers, and overlooked by cathedrals, offices and shops plucked from a Paris-meets-the-Caribbean fantasy, Jackson Square is one of America's great town squares. It both anchors the French Quarter and beats out the heart-rhythm of this corner of town. Whatever happens in the Quarter usually begins here. The identical, block-long Pontalba Buildings overlook the square, and the near-identical Cabildo and Presbytère structures flank St Louis Cathedral, the square's centerpiece.

The square was part of Adrien de Pauger's original city plan and began life as a military parade ground called Place d'Armes (Place of Weapons). Madame Micaëla Pontalba transformed the muddy marching grounds into a trimmed garden and renamed the square to honor Andrew Jackson, the president who saved New Orleans from the British during the War of 1812. Along the edges of that garden, you'll see street performers, artists, bands and tourists taking in the atmosphere. It's a gentle, carnival-esque scene, invariably lovely at sunset, which belies a bloody history: during the 1811 German Coast Slave Uprising, three leaders of the rebellion were hung here.

In the middle of the park stands the monument to Andrew Jackson – Clark Mills' bronze equestrian statue of the man, unveiled in 1856. The inscription 'The Union Must and Shall be Preserved' was added by General Benjamin Butler, Union military governor of New Orleans during the Civil War, ostensibly to rub it into the occupied city's face. The gesture worked. Butler was dubbed 'Beast Butler' by locals, and eventually his face was stamped on the bottom of city chamber pots (Butler deserves some credit too: during his tenure as military governor of New Orleans, he instituted health quarantines that drastically reduced yellow fever outbreaks).

DON'T MISS

➡ Street performers
➡ Artists
➡ The Andrew Jackson statue

PRACTICALITIES

➡ Map p238
➡ www.jackson-square.com
➡ Bound by Decatur, St Ann, Chartres & St Peter Sts
➡ ⊘24hr

TOP SIGHTS
ST LOUIS CATHEDRAL

One of the best examples of French architecture in the country is the triple-spire cathedral of St Louis, King of France, an innocuous bit of Gallic heritage in the heart of old New Orleans. Still used for services, the structure is packed on Christmas Eve midnight mass and is one of the most important (and beautiful) churches serving Catholics in the USA today.

Besides hosting black, white and Creole congregants, St Louis has attracted those who, in the best New Orleanian tradition, mix their influences, such as voodoo queen Marie Laveau, who worshiped here during the height of her influence in the mid-19th century. The interior stained glass and French wall inscriptions are a peek into New Orleans' Catholic heritage.

In 1722 a hurricane destroyed the first of three churches built here by the St Louis Parish. Architect Don Gilberto Guillemard dedicated the present cathedral on Christmas Eve in 1794. Pope Paul VI awarded it the rank of minor basilica in 1964. St Louis is a working cathedral; be respectful when you visit. Loud noises and obtrusive picture-taking are frowned upon.

Throughout the year, St Louis hosts events that are at the core of New Orleans' Catholic community. If you're in town during any of the following holidays, try to visit. Christmas services include 5pm vigil on December 24 and midnight mass on December 25; doors open at 11:15pm. On Palm Sunday (the Sunday before Easter), the transfixing ceremony of the Blessing of the Palms begins at 10:50am. If you can beat your hangover, come on Ash Wednesday (the day after Mardi Gras); ashes, a symbol of mourning and penitence, are distributed at 7:30am, noon and 5pm.

DON'T MISS

➡ Morning Mass
➡ Christmas services
➡ Ash Wednesday

PRACTICALITIES

➡ Map p238
➡ ☏525-9585
➡ http://stlouiscathedral.org
➡ Jackson Square
➡ admission free; donations requested
➡ ⊙9am-5pm Mon-Sat, from 1pm Sun; Mass 7:30am Mon-Sat, 5pm Sat, 9am & 11am Sun

TOP SIGHTS
CABILDO

The former seat of power in colonial Louisiana serves as the gateway for exploring the history of the state, and New Orleans in particular. It's also a magnificent building on its own merits. The Cabildo, a Spanish term for a city council, leads visitors into airy halls reminiscent of Spanish colonial design and with a mansard roof (the narrow, steep-sided roofs commonly found in Europe) added in the French style.

The exhibits, from Native American tools on the 1st floor to wanted posters for escaped slaves on the 3rd, do a good job of reaffirming the role the building and surrounding region has played in history. Highlights include an entire section dedicated to the Battle of New Orleans, anchored by an enormous oil painting by 19th-century French artist Eugene Louis Lami, a historical *Plan de la Nouvelle Orléans* from 1744 showing a four-block-deep city, and the death mask of Napoleon Bonaparte. Give yourself at least two hours to explore.

American author William Faulkner said, 'The past is never dead. It's not even past.' That quote only begins to hint at the troubled history of race relations in the South. The wing of the Cabildo dedicated to post–Civil War Reconstruction is as even-handed and thorough an attempt at explaining this difficult period as we've seen, and should be of interest to both history wonks and casual visitors alike.

The magnificent Sala Capitular (Capitol Room), a council room fronted by enormous windows and sweeping views onto Jackson Square, was the most important room in Louisiana for decades. Civic function and legal action were conducted here; this was the courtroom where *Plessy v Ferguson*, the 1896 case that legalized segregation under the 'separate but equal' doctrine, was tried. The Sala now includes a comprehensive exhibition dedicated to the Louisiana Purchase.

DON'T MISS

➡ Native American exhibition hall
➡ Reconstruction exhibits
➡ Death mask of Napoleon
➡ Sala Capitular

PRACTICALITIES

➡ Map p238
➡ ☏568-6968
➡ www.crt.state.la.us /museum
➡ Jackson Square
➡ adult/student/child $6/5/free
➡ ⏰10am-4:30pm Tue-Sun

TOP SIGHTS
PRESBYTÈRE

Visit the Cabildo to gain insights into Louisiana's past. Visit the Presbytère, a museum dedicated to contemporary Louisiana, to learn about her present and one of the most dynamic regional cultures in the USA. The structure is as elegant as the Cabildo, which makes sense as the Presbytére is that building's twin, a well-crafted reflection separated from its sibling by St Louis Cathedral.

The Presbytère was originally designed in 1791 as a place of residence (also known as a rectory, or presbytère) for Capuchin monks. That function never panned out, and the building switched from commercial to civic use for decades, finally becoming a museum in 1911. Today the museum features rotating special exhibits on local life, documenting everything from fashion to art to music, plus two noteworthy permanent exhibitions.

The wonderful permanent exhibit on Mardi Gras exhaustively explores the city's most famous holiday. Here you'll find there's more to Fat Tuesday than wonton debauchery – or at least you'll learn the meaning behind the debauchery. There's an encyclopedia's worth of material inside on the krewes, secret societies, costumes and racial histories that are the threads of the complex Mardi Gras tapestry. We particularly like the exhibit on the *'Courir'* Cajun Mardi Gras, held in rural Louisiana, and the bathrooms, which are modeled after the port-a-potties that are rare as spun gold on Mardi Gras day.

There are many spaces in New Orleans dedicated to explaining the impact of Katrina; the 'Living with Hurricanes: Katrina & Beyond' exhibit, which also tackles the issue of how this city survives (and thrives) within the hurricane zone, is the best of the lot. Multimedia displays, stark photography, several attics (literally) worth of found objects and a thoughtful layout combine into a powerful experience.

DON'T MISS

➡ Special Exhibits
➡ Mardi Gras: It's Carnival Time in Louisiana
➡ Living With Hurricanes: Katrina & Beyond

PRACTICALITIES

➡ Map p238
➡ ☎568-6968
➡ www.crt.state.la.us/museum
➡ Jackson Square
➡ adult/student/child $6/5/free
➡ ⊙10am-4:30pm Tue-Sun

TOP SIGHTS
ROYAL STREET

Royal Street, with its rows of high-end antique shops, block after block of galleries and potted ferns hanging from cast-iron balconies, is the elegant yin to Bourbon's Sodom-and-Gomorrah yang. This is where you go to engage in more acceptable vacation behavior of culinary and consumer indulgence rather than party-till-unconscious excess.

Stroll or bicycle past the patinaed, fading grace and beauty, have a chat with a local as they lounge on their porch, and get a sense of the fun with a dash of elegance that used to be the soul of the Vieux Carre.

This is one of those places where said soul still exists, but there's no getting around the fact that far more tourists in New Orleans have heard of, and spend more time on, Bourbon St than Royal St. And to be fair, Royal St is, in a sense, as artificial and manufactured as Bourbon. Blocks and blocks are dedicated to antique stores and art galleries, making Royal a sort of elegant, 19th-century, very long outdoor shopping arcade.

Few people actually *live* on the 13 blocks that constitute the French Quarter stretch of Royal, although they once did, as attested to by rows of wrought-iron balconies and closely packed Creole townhouses. You may not be able to tell from the street, but behind many of these buildings are enormous gardens and leafy courtyards, once spaces of escape from the street scene, now often utilized as dining spaces by restaurants.

The blocks of Royal St between St Ann & St Louis St are closed to car traffic during the afternoon. Musicians, performers and other buskers set up shop; you may see some teenage runaways shill for pennies, or accomplished bluesmen jam on their Fenders. Either way, the show is (almost) always entertaining.

DON'T MISS

➡ Pedestrian section
➡ Antique Stores
➡ Architecture
➡ Art Galleries
➡ Restaurants
➡ Our Sober Stroll Walking Tour (p60)

PRACTICALITIES

➡ Royal St, between Canal St & Esplanade Ave

⊙ SIGHTS

⊙ Lower Quarter

The Lower Quarter is actually the Quarter's northern end: in New Orleans, 'up' and 'down' are determined by the flow of the Mississippi rather than the cardinal compass points. This is the quieter, more residential end of the Vieux Carré, filled with museums and historical houses.

FRENCH MARKET   MARKET

Map p238 Within the shopping arcades of forgettable souvenirs, mediocre art and overrated food, it's easy to forget that for centuries this was the great bazaar and pulsing commercial heart of much of New Orleans. Today the French Market is a bit sanitized, a tourist jungle of curios, flea markets and harmless, shiny tat that all equals great family-friendly fun. Occasionally you'll spot some genuinely fascinating and/or unique arts and craftwork. Following cycles of fire and storm, the market has been built and rebuilt by the Spanish, French and Works Progress Administration (WPA).

NEW ORLEANS JAZZ
NATIONAL HISTORIC PARK   INFORMATION

Map p238 (⌨589-4841; www.nps.gov/jazz; 916 N Peters St; admission free; ⊙9am-5pm Tue-Sun) The headquarters of the Jazz National Historic Park has educational music programs

on most days of the week. Many of the park rangers are musicians and knowledgeable lecturers, and their presentations discuss musical developments, cultural changes, regional styles, myths, legends and musical techniques in relation to the broad subject of jazz. You can pick up a self-guided audio walking tour of jazz sites in the Quarter at this office – the tour can be downloaded as an MP3 file or listened to on your phone.

OLD US MINT   MUSEUM

Map p238 (⌨568-6968; http://lsm.crt.state.la.us; 400 Esplanade Ave; adult/child $6/5; ⊙10am-4:30pm Tue-Sun) The Mint, housed in a blocky Greek-revival structure, was the only building of its kind to have printed both US and Confederate currency. Today the mint is a museum showcasing rotating exhibits on local history and culture, plus the Louisiana Historical Center, an archive of manuscripts, microfiche and records related to the state. The Jazz National Historic Park hosts concerts here on weekday afternoons; check in with their office to see who is playing.

URSULINE CONVENT   HISTORIC BUILDING

Map p238 (⌨529-3040; 1112 Chartres St; adult/senior/student $5/4/3; ⊙10am-4pm Mon-Sat) One of the few surviving French-colonial buildings in New Orleans (though its design is more French Canadian), this lovely convent is worth a tour for its architectural virtues and small museum of Catholic

---

MISSISSIPPI RIVERBOATS

New Orleans' current fleet of steamboats are theme-park copies of the old glories that plied the Mississippi River in Mark Twain's day. Gone are the hoop-skirted ladies, wax-mustachioed gents, round-the-clock crap games and bawdy tinkling on off-tune pianos. Instead the steamboats offer urbane (but sterile) evening jazz cruises, and while the calliope organ survives, even this unique musical instrument loses some of its panache when applied to modern schmaltz like 'Tie a Yellow Ribbon on the Old Oak Tree.' Alas.

Still, few visitors to New Orleans can resist the opportunity to get out on the Mississippi and watch the old paddle wheel propel them upriver and back down for a spell. It's a relaxing pastime that the entire family can enjoy.

Creole Queen (Map p244; ⌨529-4567; www.creolequeen.com) A three-hour dinner-and-jazz cruise (adult/child 3-5yr/6-12yr $66/10/32, without dinner $40/free/20) features a live Dixieland jazz combo; it boards nightly at 7pm at the Canal St Wharf.

Steamboat Natchez (Map p238; ⌨586-8777, 800-233-2628; www.steamboatnatchez.com) The closest thing to an authentic steamboat running out of New Orleans today, the *Natchez* is steam-powered and has a bona fide calliope on board. The evening dinner-and-jazz cruise (adult/child 2-5yr/6-12yr $68/13.50/34, without dinner $40/free/20) takes off at 7pm nightly. The *Natchez* boards behind the Jackson Brewery.

bric-a-brac. After a five-month voyage from Rouen, France, 12 Ursuline nuns arrived in New Orleans in 1727. The Ursuline had a missionary bent, but it achieved its goals through advancing the literacy rate of women of all races and social levels; their school admitted French, Native American and African American girls.

GALLIER HOUSE MUSEUM   HISTORIC BUILDING
Map p238 (☎525-5661; www.hgghh.org; 1118 Royal St; adult/student & senior $12/10; combined with Hermann-Grima House $20/18; ⊙tours hourly 10am-2pm Mon-Fri, noon-3pm Sat) Many New Orleans buildings owe their existence, either directly or by design, to James Gallier Sr and Jr, who added Greek-revivalist,

ACTIVITIES IN THE FRENCH QUARTER

The French Quarter is packed with stuff to see; if you have a limited amount of time you may want to try some of these tours. Tours depart from the addresses listed here, and the hours we give are either tour times or times when you can stop by and find a tour.

Friends of the Cabildo (☎523-3939, 524-9118; www.friendsofthecabildo.org; 523 St Ann St; adult/student/child $15/12/free; ⊙10am & 1:30pm Tue-Sun) These excellent walking tours are led by knowledgeable (and often funny) docents who will give you a great primer on the history of the Quarter, the stories behind some of the most-famous streets and details of the area's many architectural styles.

Royal Carriage Tours (☎943-8820; www.neworleanscarriages.com; at Decatur St & Jackson Sq; 30min/1hr tour with up to 4 people $75/150; ⊙8:30am-midnight) The conductors of these mule-drawn carriage tours really know their stuff, revealing the locations of celebrity homes and sites of historic minutiae that constantly impressed us. Royal Carriages has a good animal welfare track record; they are licensed by the city and don't conduct tours if the weather is over 95°F (35°C). There are other, independent horse-tour operators you'll have to judge on a case by case basis.

Haunted History Tours (☎861-2727; www.hauntedhistorytours.com; 723 St Peter St; adult/student & senior $20/17; ⊙3pm, 6pm & 8pm Jan-May, Oct & Nov) Sure, these tours are a little cheesy, but they're fun too, and you'll learn a bit about the shady side of city history.

Tours By Judy (☎416-6666; www.toursbyjudy.com; $15) Judy Bajoie, a local scholar and historian, leads well-crafted tours of the city she loves. Contact her for departure information.

New Orleans Culinary History Tours (☎875-6570; http://noculinarytours.com; from $46; ⊙call ahead) It's hard to beat a tour that is delicious *and* intellectually stimulating, but that's what Kelly Hamilton, a history instructor at Xavier University, offers with these tours that plumb the past and local pantries.

Magic Tours (☎588-9693; www.magictoursnola.com; 441 Royal St; adult/student & senior $20/17; ⊙4pm) Led by local teachers, historians, preservationists and journalists, Magic Tours admirably gets under the skin of the city.

American Photo Safari (☎298-8876; www.americanphotosafari.com; Jackson Sq, by St Louis Cathedral; $79; ⊙call ahead) A cleverly focused tour, this: the photo safari docents don't just show you the sights, they give you lessons in how to take pictures of them as well.

American Institute of Architects (☎525-8320; www.aianeworleans.com; from $35) As you may guess, the AIA and its experts provide some of the best building and design walks in the city. Check the website or call for the schedule of tours and where they depart from.

Pedicabs – two-seater carriages powered by a leg-pumping cyclist – are a popular means of getting around the French Quarter. Pedicab 'drivers' are pretty ubiquitous. There are several companies offering their services, but the standard fare is around $1 per block.

CASKET GIRLS & WORKING GIRLS

During the early days of their work, the Ursuline nuns (see p53) quickly observed that an unusually high proportion of the colony's women were working the world's oldest profession, so they decided to call in marriageable teenage girls from France (generally recruited from orphanages or convents). The girls arrived in New Orleans, Biloxi and Mobile with their clothes packed in coffin-like trunks, and thus became known as the 'casket girls.' Educated by the nuns, the girls were brought up to make proper wives for the French men of New Orleans. Over the centuries, the casket-girl legacy became more sensational as some in New Orleans surmised the wood boxes may have contained French vampires.

Of course, prostitution never lost its luster in this steamy port. New Orleans' fabled bordellos are one of the earliest foundations upon which the city's reputation as a spot for sin and fun are built. The most famous 'sporting' houses were elegant mansions, reputedly decorated with some of the finest art and furnishings of their era and staffed with a multiracial cast of employees ranging from white to Creole to black. Around the turn of the 20th century, famously puritan city alderman (councillor) Sidney Story wrote an ordinance that moved the bordellos out of the city's posh residential neighborhoods and into that side of the French Quarter that borders the Tremé. Never ones to pass up good irony, New Orleanians dubbed their red-light district 'Storyville' in honor of Sidney.

Although there were no Lonely Planet books around at the time, visitors could explore Storyville with the help of the 'Blue Book,' a guide to the area's…attractions. Each book was imprinted with the passage: 'Order of the Garter: *Honi Soit Qui Mal Y Pense*' (Shame to Him Who Evil Thinks). Jazz was largely popularized by visitors listening to music in Storyville's storied pleasure houses. One of the most famous, the Arlington, operated at 225 North Basin Street (look for the onion-domed cupola, all that's left of the demolished bordello).

Storyville was shut down in 1917 by the federal government. At the time Mayor Martin Behrman lamented that while authorities could make prostitution illegal, 'you can't make it unpopular'.

British and American accents to the Quarter's French/Spanish/Creole architectural mélange. In 1857 Gallier Jr began work on this town house which incorporated all of the above elements. The period furniture is lovely; not so much are the intact slave quarters out back – once you see these, you'll recognize them throughout the Quarter.

BEAUREGARD-KEYES HOUSE
HISTORIC BUILDING

Map p238 (☑523-7257; www.bkhouse.org; 1113 Chartres St; tours adult/child/student/$10/4/9; ☺tours hourly 10am-3pm) This 1826 Greek-revival house is named for its two most famous former inhabitants. Confederate General Pierre Gustave Toutant Beauregard commanded the artillery battery that fired the first shots at Fort Sumter in Charleston, SC, starting the Civil War. Francis Parkinson Keyes wrote 51 novels, many of which were set in New Orleans (and one, the 1962 *Madame Castel's Lodger*, which was set in

this house). Her collection of some 200 dolls and folk costumes are on display.

1850 HOUSE MUSEUM
HISTORIC BUILDING

Map p238 (☑568-6968; 523 St Ann St; adult/child/senior & student $3/free/2; ☺9am-5pm Tue-Sun) The 1850 House is one of the apartments in the lower Pontalba Building. Madame Micaëla Pontalba, daughter of Don Andrés Almonaster y Roxas, built the long rows of red-brick apartments flanking the upper and lower portions of Jackson Square. Today, knowledgeable volunteers from the Friends of the Cabildo give tours of the apartment (every 45 minutes or so), which includes the central court and servants' quarters, with period furnishings throughout.

HISTORIC VOODOO MUSEUM
MUSEUM

Map p238 (☑680-0128; www.voodoomuseum .com; 724 Dumaine St; adult/child $7/3.50; ☺11am-5pm) Of the (many) voodoo museums in the French Quarter, this one is probably our favorite. The narrow corridors and dark rooms, stuffed with statues, dolls and paintings, are something approaching spooky, and the information placards (seemingly written by anthropology dissertation candidates with too much time on their hands) are genuinely informative, if a little dry.

VOODOO SPIRITUAL TEMPLE   MUSEUM
Map p238 (☑522-9627; www.voodoospiritual temple.org; 828 N Rampart St; donations accepted; ◎10:30am-5pm daily) Mexican crucifix? Check. Tibetan mandala? Ditto. Balinese Garuda? Why not? Miriam William's temple feels more like a mush of global religions and New Age mysticism than voodoo, but maybe that's just her interpretation of voodoo. The temple is big on the tour-group circuit and it's often entertaining to watch Miriam give her lectures on life, the universe and everything. There is, of course, an adjacent gift shop doing a brisk trade in candles, cards and gris-gris (amulets or spell bags).

LOWER BOURBON STREET   STREET
Map p238 (Bourbon St btwn St Philip St & Esplanade Ave) At St Philip St, Bourbon shifts from a Dante's *Inferno*-style circle of neon-lit hell into an altogether more agreeable stretch of historical houses, diners and bars, many of which cater to the gay community. In fact, said gay bars are the loudest residents on this, the quieter, more classically New Orleans side of Bourbon St.

◉ Upper Quarter

South of Jackson Square is where you'll find most of the booziness and souvenir stands that most tourists associate with the Old Quarter.

JACKSON SQUARE   SQUARE
See p48.

ST LOUIS CATHEDRAL   CHURCH
See p49.

CABILDO   MUSEUM
See p50.

PRESBYTÈRE   MUSEUM
See p51.

ROYAL STREET   STREET
See p52.

RIVERFRONT   PARK
Map p238 (From Bienville to St Philip St) It's supremely pleasant to stroll up to the Mississippi River as it runs by the French Quarter. The entire riverfront area has been landscaped with pedestrian paths, small public arts projects and small green spaces such as the **Woldenberg Park**. Sunset is the best time to come up here; couples walk around in love, container ships and ferries ply the water and all feels bucolic. Nearby is the **Jackson (Jax) Brewery**, a mediocre shopping mall that *does* happen to have free public restrooms.

JEAN LAFITTE NATIONAL HISTORIC PARK   INFORMATION
Map p238 (☑589-2636; www.nps.gov/jela; 419 Decatur St; admission free; ◎9am-5pm daily) This small visitor center serves as a primary visitor center for the six statewide sites of Jean Lafitte National Historic Park. Helpful rangers and a series of interactive, interpretative exhibits provide lots of insight into the history and culture of Louisiana.

NEW ORLEANS PHARMACY MUSEUM   MUSEUM
Map p238 (☑565-8027; www.pharmacymuseum .org; 514 Chartres St; adult/child $5/4; ◎10am-2pm Tue-Fri) This beautifully preserved little shop is all a-groaning with ancient display cases filled with intriguing little bottles. Established in 1816 by Louis J Dufilho, at a time when the pharmaceutical arts were – shall we say – in their infancy, the museum claims Dufilho was the nation's first licensed pharmacist, although his practices would be suspect today (gold-coated pills to the wealthy; opium, alcohol and cannabis for those with less cash).

UPPER BOURBON STREET   STREET
Map p238 (Bourbon St btwn Canal & Dumaine) Like Vegas and Cancun, the main stretch of Bourbon is where the great id of the repressed American psyche is let loose into a seething mass of karaoke, strip clubs and every bachelorette party ever. This is not New Orleans, folks: the only locals you meet are working behind the bar. But Bourbon can be fun for an evening. Everyone needs more skeletons in their closet, and you'll probably stuff a few more in after a night out here.

FROM THE MEKONG TO THE MISSISSIPPI

Following the Vietnam War, thousands of South Vietnamese fled to the US, settling in Southern California, Boston, the Washington, DC area and New Orleans. If the last choice seems odd, remember that many of these refugees were Catholic and the New Orleans Catholic community – one of the largest in the country – was helping to direct refugee resettlement. In addition, the subtropical climate, rice fields and flat wetlands must have been geographically reassuring. For a southeast Asian far from home, the Mississippi delta may have borne at least a superficial resemblance to the Mekong delta.

Most Vietnamese in Louisiana settled in New Orleans' newer suburbs: New Orleans East, Versailles, Algiers and Gretna (some also moved to rural parishes in south Louisiana). Their work ethic was legendary, their presence revitalized many formerly crumbling neighborhoods and their story is as American Dream–like as a bald eagle hatching from apple pie. The first generation of Vietnamese worked in Laundromats, nail shops, restaurants and shrimp boats; the second became doctors, lawyers and engineers. Following Hurricane Katrina, the New Orleans Vietnamese community gained the reputation as being the first back in the city, quickly rebuilding their homes and businesses.

To see where New Orleans Vietnamese work and play, you need to drive a little way out of the city proper. Although many Vietnamese refugees were Catholic, Vietnamese religion has always been pretty syncretic, and there were many Buddhists among the boat people. In New Orleans East, the **Mary Queen of Vietnam church** (☎255-9170; www.mqvncdc.org; 4626 Alcee Fortier Blvd) is a focal point for the Catholic Vietnamese community; further south, the **Chua Bo De temple** (☎733-6634; Hwy 996), about 25 minutes outside the city near English Turn golf course, is a major center for Buddhists. The latter is a typically Vietnamese Buddhist structure, filled with Chinese-style bodhisattvas (Buddhist saints), photos and offerings to dead ancestors, and lots of red and gold in the color scheme. You don't have to call ahead before visiting, but it may be polite to do so (plus, you can check if the temples are open).

Probably the most pleasant way to experience local Vietnamese culture is by eating its delicious food; to this end we've put together a list of our favorite Vietnamese restaurants in the Eating chapter (see the boxed text, p150). Most of these are in Gretna. Try not to miss the local markets either; the **Hong Kong Food Market** (☎394-7075; 925 Behrman Hwy; ☺8am-9pm) is a general Asian grocery store that serves plenty of Chinese and Filipinos, but the main customer base is Vietnamese. The closest you'll come to witnessing Saigon on a Saturday morning (lots of local Vietnamese, being southern refugees, still call it 'Saigon') is the **Vietnamese Farmers Market** (☎394-7075; 14401 Alcee Fortier Blvd; ☺6am-9am), also known as the 'squat market' thanks to the ladies in non la (conical straw hats) squatting over their fresh, wonderful-smelling produce.

MUSÉE CONTI HISTORICAL WAX MUSEUM   MUSEUM

Map p238 (☎525-2605; www.neworleanswaxmuseum.com; 917 Conti St; adult/child/senior $6.75/5.75/6.25; ☺10am-4pm) This place sells itself as one of New Orleans' 'best kept secrets,' which is like saying po'boys are undiscovered culinary gems. It's a wax museum that's kitschy and entertaining in the way wax museums should be: local historical figures include Andrew Jackson, Huey Long, Louis Armstrong and Napoleon Bonaparte (caught in the bathtub for some reason), then Frankenstein's monster (chained, for your protection) and Swamp Thing (unchained!).

HERMANN-GRIMA HOUSE   HISTORIC BUILDING

Map p238 (☎525-5661; www.hgghh.org; 820 St Louis St; tours adult/student & senior $12/10, combined with Gallier House Museum $20/18; ☺tours hourly 10am-2pm Mon-Fri, noon-3pm Sat) Samuel Hermann, a Jewish merchant who married a Catholic woman, introduced the American-style Federal design to the Quarter in 1831. Hermann sold the house in 1844 to Judge Grima, a slaveholder, after he reportedly lost $2 million during the national financial panic of 1837. Cooking demonstrations in the open-hearth kitchen are a special treat on Thursdays from October to May.

MUSICAL LEGENDS PARK PARK

Map p238 (www.neworleansmusicallegends.com; 311 Bourbon St; ☺8am-10pm Sun-Thu, until midnight Fri & Sat) This pleasant little public square is peppered with statues of some of New Orleans' great musical heroes: Louis Prima, Chris Owens, Pete Fountain, Al Hirt, Fats Domino and Ronnie Kole. Musicians play live jazz within the park from 10am until it closes.

EATING

Lower Quarter

The Lower Quarter features the best cheap eating options around, but there are a few decent high-end places here as well.

TOP CHOICE SYLVAIN CONTEMPORARY $$

Map p238 (☑265-8123; www.sylvainnola.com; 625 Chartres St; mains $12.50-25; ☺5:30-11pm Mon-Thu, until midnight Fri & Sat, until 10pm Sun, 11:30am-2:30pm Fri & Sat, 10:30am-2:30pm Sun) Sylvain is the sort of exciting new New Orleans restaurant the French Quarter sorely needs. Rather than a hokey attempt at more red beans, this rustic yet elegant gastropub draws inspiration from the dedication to ingredients and locavore love demonstrated by chefs like Thomas Keller. The duck confit served on a bed of black-eyed peas is indicative of the gastronomic experience: rich, refined and delicious.

COOP'S PLACE CAJUN $

Map p238 (☑525-9053; 1109 Decatur St; mains $8-17.50; ☺11am-3am) Coop's is an authentic Cajun dive, but more rocked out. Make no mistake: it's a grotty chaotic place, the servers have attitude and the layout is annoying (be ready for an elbow in your back at some point in the night). But it's worth it for the food: rabbit jambalaya, chicken with shrimp and *tasso* (smoked ham) in a cream sauce – there's no such thing as 'too heavy' here.

OUR NOD TO HNOC

The **Historic New Orleans Collection** (HNOC; Map p238; ☑523-4662; www.hnoc.org; 533 Royal St; admission free, tours $5; ☺9:30am-4:30pm Tue-Sat, from 10:30am Sun) sells itself to visitors as the best introduction to NOLA available. That's slightly hyperbolic, but we still love HNOC, a combination of preserved buildings, museums and research centers all rolled into one introduction to the city's history. The complex is anchored by **Merieult House** and a series of regularly rotating exhibits in the **Williams Gallery** (Map p238; admission free; ☺9:30am-4:30pm Tue-Sat). Upstairs, the meticulously researched Merieult History Tour dives into 11 galleries' worth of New Orleans' history. It's slightly overwhelming – the original Jazz Fest poster, transfer documents of the Louisiana Purchase, 1849 broadside advertising '24 Head of Slaves' (individual children for $500 or entire families for $2400) – and imminently rewarding. The building itself has served as private residence, storehouse and hotel, and is a rare survivor of the 1794 fire that gutted the Quarter.

The Williams family was always considered eccentric, and their residence, purchased in 1938 in what was then considered a dowdy neighborhood, is stuffed full of art and furniture collected in their world travels. Tours are given Tuesday to Saturday at 10am, 11am, 2pm and 3pm for $5. As entertaining as the tour is, even better is the intro video, which glosses over the source of their fortune (ie harvesting out the old-growth cypress of the Louisana wetlands).

Dedicated travelers and history heads should pop into the **Williams Research Center** (Map p238; ☑523-4662; 410 Chartres St; ☺10am-4:30pm Tue-Sat); if you have specific queries about almost anything New Orleans, the staff here can help. The archives contain more than 350,000 images and some 2 miles of manuscripts.

THE BIG MUDDY

The Mississippi River is more than the defining geographical landmark of New Orleans. It is its soul, its center and its reason for being. 'Why was New Orleans built below sea level?' folks ask. First off, only half the city is below sea level, but the reason is that this spot commands the entrance to the most important river in North America. All the trade, conquest and exploration of this continent is wrapped up in the Mississippi and her moods. It would be criminal to come here and not catch a glimpse of the Mother of Waters.

It can be difficult to appreciate just where the river is from the streets. Some of our favorite spots for river-watching include numerous benches along the levee opposite Jackson Square and the Moon Walk, a boardwalk built by and named for former mayor Moon Landrieu (not the dance).

The Mississippi is no lazy river. Through New Orleans, the river's depth averages about 200ft. Its immense volume of water and sand roils with tremendous, turbulent force, whirling and eddying and scouring at the banks of snakelike curves. It runs some 2400 miles from Minnesota to the Gulf of Mexico, and its drainage basin extends from the Rockies to the Alleghenies, covering 40% of the continental USA. The rain that falls in this vast area ultimately ends up in the Gulf, and most of it is carried there by the Mississippi. The Platte, the Missouri, the Ohio, the Cumberland and the Arkansas – mighty rivers themselves – all feed into the Mississippi, which carries their waters past New Orleans. It drains more water than the Nile, and only the Amazon and the Congo carry a greater volume of water to the sea.

It also moves up to several million tons of sediment into the Gulf every day. Thus, the river has shifted more than 1000 cubic miles of earth from north to south, depositing soil into the Gulf and spreading it to the east and west as the river changed its course. The land that is Louisiana and much of the states of Mississippi and Alabama were created by the river.

The river's name is a corruption of the old Ojibwe *Misi-ziibi* (great river). For early European settlers to the Mississippi Valley, the river initially proved too unruly to serve as a viable route inland until the advent of the steamboat in 1807. During the early part of the 19th century New Orleans' population mushroomed, largely as a result of river traffic and trade.

It is natural for deltaic rivers to flood regularly and periodically change course, and preventing the Mississippi from flooding is no simple engineering feat. The river has broken its levees on several occasions, most notoriously in 1927, when the river breached levees in 145 places. That spring, some 27,000 sq miles of farmland, from Illinois to southern Louisiana, turned into a raging sea (up to 30ft deep in places) that flowed steadily down to the Gulf. Entire towns were washed away and a million people were driven from their homes. It took several months for the flooding to recede back to within the river's banks. New Orleans, however, remained high and dry, as north of the city the floodwaters chose the Atchafalaya River's shorter path to the Gulf.

FIORELLA'S   ITALIAN, LOUISIANAN **$**

Map p238 (☎523-2155; 1136 Decatur St; mains $7-15; ⏰11am-midnight Sun-Thu, to 2am Fri & Sat) Where nearby Coop's is a Cajun Country shack hipster-ed up, Fiorella's is a Sicilian cafe (all red-checkered cloth) but run through the same punk-rock wringer. It's still bright and cozy, but this is more neighborhood spot than tourist trap, and said 'hood is the slightly grungy northern end of Decatur St. The food is quintessential Italian New Orleans: pastas, pizzas, veal cutlets and great fried chicken.

PORT OF CALL   GRILL **$$**

Map p238 (☎523-0120; 838 Esplanade Ave; mains $7-21; ⏰11am-midnight) The Port of Call burger is legendary. The meat is unadulterated and, well, meaty – when you bite into a POC burger, you *know* you are eating cow, not some preprocessed Grade E substitute. Then there's the baked potato on the side, buckling under the weight of sour cream, butter and bacon bits. It's all served in a 1960s-ish Polynesian tiki bar, dim and hot-pink lit and kitschy as hell. Be prepared to wait outside in long lines for a seat (no reservations).

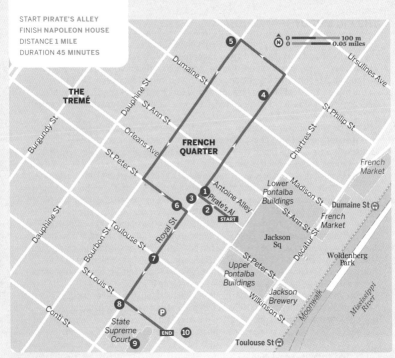

START **PIRATE'S ALLEY**
FINISH **NAPOLEON HOUSE**
DISTANCE **1 MILE**
DURATION **45 MINUTES**

Neighborhood Walk
Sober Stroll

This walk explores the French Quarter's two main drags: Bourbon St and Royal St. Goofus and Gallant, if you will. Think of this as a quick introduction to the Quarter.

Begin at Pirate's Alley, an inviting walkway that cuts through the shadow of St Louis Cathedral. To the right is gated **1** **St Anthony's Garden**, a peaceful pocket in the bustling Quarter.

Halfway up the alley, stop in at **2** **Faulkner House Books**, which opened in 1990 and quickly became a focal point for New Orleans literary circles. Much of the alley is occupied by the **3** **Labranche buildings**, built by Jean Baptiste Labranche, a Creole sugar planter, which wrap around Royal St to St Peter St. Turn right at Royal St, which takes the cake for classic New Orleans postcard images.

The **4** **Cornstalk Hotel** stands behind a frequently photographed fence. Turn left at the corner at St Philip St and head towards Bourbon. A structure on the corner,

5 **Lafitte's Blacksmith Shop** is, supposedly, where pirate Jean Lafitte ran a blacksmith shop as a front. Have a drink to brace yourself for Bourbon St.

Turn left down St Peter St and get to **6** **Pat O'Brien's**. Have a look in Pat's courtyard and then continue south to Royal St (you can also walk through Pat's and emerge on Bourbon St, then head back to Royal via Toulouse St).

Go down Royal St past the **7** **Historic New Orleans Collection** and continue on to St Louis St. On this corner, in what is now **8** **James H Cohen & Sons** antique gun shop, the cocktail was supposedly invented. The premises were occupied at the beginning of the 19th century by Peychaud's Apothecary.

Turn left and walk a block of St Louis St, back to Chartres. All the while, it's impossible not to notice the **9** **State Supreme Court Building**. Nearby is **10** **Napoleon House**, where we'll end our tour over a bowl of gumbo and a beer in the courtyard.

BENNACHIN
WEST AFRICAN $

Map p238 (☑522-1230; 1212 Royal; St; mains $8-16; ☺11am-9pm, until 11pm Fri & Sat; ☑) West African cuisine (specifically Cameroonian and Gambian) doesn't pose too many challenges to the conservative palette. It's basically meat and potatoes, with a main, like beef in peanut stew or spinach and plantains, served with some kind of starch used as a scooping accompaniment. The heavy use of okra reminds you how much this cuisine has influenced Louisiana. All in all, this is a great ethnic eatery in a city that can lack in the genre.

IRENE'S CUISINE
ITALIAN $$

Map p238 (☑529-8811; 539 St Philip St; mains $16-23; ☺5:30-10pm Mon-Sat) Irene's is a romantic gem, tucked in a corner generally missed by tourists – not that that's easy to do given the overwhelming(ly good) scent of garlic emanating from this cavern of Italian intimacy. It's Italian-French, really: you can pick from seasoned rosemary chicken, seared chops, pan-sautéed fish fillets and great pasta, but leave room for the decadent pecan-praline bread pudding. Reservations are not accepted and long waits are the norm, but they're worth it.

CAFÉ AMELIE
FRENCH $$

Map p238 (☑412-8965; 912 Royal St; mains $8-32; ☺11am-9pm Wed-Sat, 11am-3pm & 6-8pm Sun) We've waxed rhapsodic over the Quarter's beautiful backyard gardens, but Amelie's, much beloved by locals, takes the cake. This may be the most romantic dining spot in the city, an alfresco restaurant that's practically as cute as the movie of the same name, tucked behind an old carriage house and surrounded by high brick walls and shade trees. Fresh seafood and local produce are the basis of a modest, ever-changing menu.

CLOVER GRILL
GRILL $

Map p238 (☑598-1010; 900 Bourbon St; mains $3-8; ☺24hr) You don't have to be gay to eat or work here. But the vibe is definitely gay-friendly. It's a little surreal, given this place otherwise totally resembles a '50s diner, but nothing says Americana like an argument between an out-of-makeup drag queen and a drunk club kid, all likely set to blaring disco music. The food is dependable diner fare and good for a hangover, or for those who can see the hangover approaching.

MONA LISA
ITALIAN $

Map p238 (☑522-6746; 1212 Royal St; mains $9-16.50; ☺11am-10pm Thu-Mon, 5-10pm Tue & Wed) An informal, quiet local spot in the Lower Quarter, Mona Lisa is dim and dark and candlelit romantic in its quirky way. Kooky renditions of da Vinci's familiar subject hang on the walls. In hair curlers, 50lb heavier or in the form of a cow, she stares impassively at diners munching on pizzas, pastas and spinach salads.

CENTRAL GROCERY
DELI $

Map p238 (☑523-1620; 923 Decatur St; sandwiches $7-10; ☺9am-5pm Tue-Sat) There are a few New Orleans names inextricably linked to a certain dish, and Central Grocery is the word-association winner for the muffuletta. That's pronounced 'muffa-lotta,' and that about sums it up: your mouth will be muffled by a hell of a lotta sandwich, stuffed with meat, cheese and great, sharp olive salad. This is a real grocery by the way, one of the last neighborhood vestiges of the New Orleans Sicilian community, and the fresh Italian produce is a draw on its own.

TUJAGUE'S
CREOLE $$$

Map p238 (☑525-8676; www.tujaguesrestaurant .com; 823 Decatur St; 6-course dinners $32-44; ☺5-10pm daily, 11am-3pm Sat & Sun) Tujague's has been holding down its corner since 1856, making it the second-oldest eatery in New Orleans. Dinner is a traditional six-course affair where diners can select from four mains based on choice offerings from the butcher and the fishmonger. Sometimes this set meal is fantastic, but part of Tujague's staying power comes from its position on several organized group tours of New Orleans, so the kitchen can get rushed. The front-room bar is nicely atmospheric.

VERTI MARTE
DELI $

Map p238 (☑525-4767; 1201 Royal St; meals $3.50-8.50; ☺24hr) Sometimes you just wanna wander the Quarter with a good burger or seafood sandwich in hand. If that's the case, get ye to Verti, a reliable deli with a take-out stand that's got a menu as long as a hot New Orleans summer day. If you're in your hotel room at 3am and craving some ribs (with two sides!), rejoice, for Verti delivers free in the French Quarter and Faubourg Marigny.

MURIEL'S
CREOLE $$$

Map p238 (☎568-1885; www.muriels.com; 801 Chartres St; mains $17-35; ⊙5:30-10pm Mon-Fri, from 5pm Sat & Sun, 11:30am-2:30pm daily) You have a good choice of settings in Muriel's: the blood-red main dining room evokes the pomp of Storyville; in the eclectic bistro, 19th-century art hangs from exposed brick walls; the courtyard bar exemplifies tropical decadence; while the balcony seating affords an elevated view of Jackson Square. The kitchen tinkers with the Creole ethos enough to steer clear of stodginess without alienating the average patron. It's also a good spot for a steak.

ANGELI ON DECATUR
DINER $

Map p238 (☎566-0077; 1141 Decatur St; mains $6-18; ⊙11am-2am Sun-Thu, to 4am Fri & Sat; ⓙ) Great philosophers have long debated one of the most pressing of human questions: what makes a late-night place great? We humbly submit: the food tastes as good sober as when you're trashed at 3am. Enter Angeli – decked out with hipster art and patrons – the burger, pasta and pizza fare here is wonderful no matter your state of mind/inebriation/whatever.

LOUISIANA PIZZA KITCHEN
PIZZA $

Map p238 (☎522-9500; www.louisianapizza kitchen.com; 95 French Market Place; mains $8-16; ⊙noon-9pm Wed-Sun) Opposite the Old US Mint, this is a popular local franchise offering wood-fired pizza crusts that resemble toasted pita bread as opposed to chain-style cheesiness. Ever had alligator sausage or crawfish on a pizza? Here's your chance.

CROISSANT D'OR PATISSERIE
BAKERY $

Map p238 (☎524-4663; 617 Ursulines Ave; meals $3-5; ⊙6am-3pm Wed-Mon) On the quieter side of the Quarter, this spotlessly clean pastry shop is where many Quarter locals start their day. Bring a paper, order coffee and a croissant – or a tart, quiche, savory pie or sandwich topped with béchamel sauce(!) – and bliss out. They're all wonderful. Check out the tiled sign on the threshold that says 'ladies entrance' – a holdover from prefeminist days.

✗ Upper Quarter

TOP CHOICE GREEN GODDESS
FUSION $$

Map p238 (☎301-3347; www.greengoddessnola .com; 307 Exchange Place; mains $12-22; ⊙11am-3:30pm daily, 6-11pm Wed-Sun; ⓙ) Who serves South Indian lentil pancakes, Jamaican coconut curry and bacon ice cream sundaes? Or crawfish and basil-fed snails on a bed of polenta? Or Vietnamese pork belly with red beans and local greens? Green Goddess, that's who. One of the most exciting restaurants in the city, the Goddess combines a playful attitude to preparation with a world traveler's perspective on ingredient sourcing and a workman's ethic when it comes to actually cooking the stuff. Oh – and it's all freaking delicious.

TOP CHOICE BAYONA
MODERN LOUISIANAN $$$

Map p238 (☎525-4455; www.bayona.com; 430 Dauphine St; mains $28-38; ⊙11:30am-2pm & 6-10pm) Bayona is, for our money, the best splurge in the Quarter. It's rich but not overwhelming, classy but unpretentious, innovative without being precocious and all around just a very fine spot for a meal. Thank chef Susan Spicer and her army of line cooks – they all seem to have a genuine love of what they do and commitment to their craft. The menu changes regularly, but expect fresh fish, fowl and game prepared in a way that comes off as elegant and deeply cozy all at once.

DOING DU MONDE

Cafe du Monde (Map p238; ☎800-772-2927; www.cafedumonde.com; 800 Decatur St; beignets $2; ⊙24hr) is an iconic fixture in the New Orleans scene, but fair warning: it's crowded and hardly romantic (unless you arrive late at night – and to be fair, du Monde is open 24 hours). The beignets (small fried doughnuts topped with powdered sugar) are usually pretty good, while the coffee is inconsistent. The other place in town for coffee and beignets is (surprise) **Café Beignet** (p65), located at Musical Legends Park. The coffee is usually better at Cafe du Monde, while the beignets tend to be a little denser and topped with more sugar – not to everyone's liking, but they don't exactly break the bank, so why not try both?

K-PAUL'S LOUISIANA KITCHEN   CAJUN $$$

Map p238 (☎596-2530; www.chefpaul.com/kpaul; 416 Chartres St; mains $27-36; ☺5:30-10pm Mon-Sat, 11am-2pm Tue-Sat) This is the home base of chef Paul Prudhomme, who is essentially responsible for putting modern Louisiana cooking on the map. Prudhomme isn't cooking here anymore, but the kitchen's still cranking out quality: blackened twin beef tenders, a signature dish, come with an incredibly rich 'debris' gravy that's been slowly cooked over a two-day period. Despite its popularity, K-Paul's retains a no-reservations policy downstairs, but takes reservations for its upstairs tables.

BRENNAN'S RESTAURANT   CREOLE $$$

Map p238 (☎525-9713; www.brennansneworleans.com; 417 Royal St; 3-course breakfasts $38, 4-course dinners $44; ☺9am-1pm Mon-Fri, 8am-2:30pm Sat & Sun, 6-9pm daily) We give Brennan's credit for reinventing the concept of 'poached eggs on bread with hollandaise.' In its quest to create the city's most extravagant breakfast, there's a dozen variations of the above eggs on offer – with andouille (spiced, smoked pork sausage), wine sauce, trout, you name it. You'll have your not-so *petit déjeuner* in one of the restaurant's 12 elegant dining rooms or its lovely courtyard, and if you're hard enough, you'll start the day with an 'eye-opener' (if you can imagine downing a Sazerac before breakfast). Bananas Foster is also recommended, as it's a Brennan's original. The dinner menu emphasizes Creole seafood and, while not quite as decadent, is still pretty indulgent.

DICKIE BRENNAN'S   STEAKHOUSE $$$

Map p238 (☎522-2467; www.dickiebrennans steakhouse.com; 716 Iberville St; mains $23-44; ☺5:30-10pm daily, 11:30am-2:30pm Fri) New Orleans, a city of seafood and swamp ingredients, isn't known as a steak town. Yet the best steakhouse in the city is considered one of the greatest in the country. There's not a lot we can say about Dickie Brennan's; they do steak, and they do it right. For a side, try the Pontalba potatoes, done up with garlic, mushrooms and ham.

ARNAUD'S   CREOLE $$$

Map p238 (☎523-5433; www.arnauds.com; 813 Bienville St; mains $24-40; ☺6-10pm Mon-Sat, 10am-2:30pm & 6-10pm Sun) Back in 1918 'Count' Arnaud Cazenave, a French immigrant with extravagant tastes, took roughly a city block's worth of buildings and turned them into a restaurant that's been serving fine upscale Creole cuisine ever since. The menu includes shrimp Arnaud (shrimp in a rémoulade sauce), oysters Bienville (an original dish with mushrooms and a white-wine sauce), speckled trout meunière (served with a rich, gravy-like sauce) and steak stuffed with oysters. Bring it on. Show up early for a mint julep at the excellent bar. And men, bring that jacket.

BROUSSARD'S   CREOLE $$$

Map p238 (☎581-3866; www.broussards.com; 819 Conti St; mains $29-40; ☺5:30-10pm daily) You wouldn't expect a native Berliner to be one of New Orleans' foremost experts on old-line Creole cuisine, but along comes chef Gunter Preuss, who heads the talented kitchen of Broussard's. This restaurant has been around since 1920, buoyed by uncommonly good executions of Creole standbys such as veal and crawfish in a béchamel sauce and redfish stuffed with shrimp, crabmeat and oysters. No T-shirts or shorts, gentlemen.

DEANIE'S   SEAFOOD $$

Map p238 (☎581-1316; www.deanies.com; 841 Iberville St; mains $16-24; ☺11am-10pm Sun-Thu, until 11pm Fri & Sat) Deanie's is a local seafood joint that's popular with the suburban crowd from out in the parishes – which in this case is a pretty good sign, as parish folk know their fish and shellfish in these parts. The stuffed flounder and crabmeat au gratin are winners.

ANTOINE'S   CREOLE $$$

Map p238 (☎581-4422; www.antoines.com; 713 St Louis St; dinner mains $22-44; ☺11:30am-2pm & 5:30-9pm) Antoine's is the oldest of old-line New Orleans restaurants, and is in fact the oldest family restaurant in America (established 1840). Kitchen and floor jobs are held for decades and passed down to family members, and 'class' is an understated description of the atmosphere; the dining rooms all look like first-class lounges on the *Orient Express* and are named for Mardi Gras krewes. That said, the food is good but not great. Even the dishes this restaurant *invented,* such as oysters Rockefeller, aren't the best in town, but hey, you're eating history. Nowhere else will you feel as if you've stepped into a Rex Ball attended by Jay Gatsby. Jackets required; denim prohibited.

MR B'S BISTRO
MODERN LOUISIANAN **$$$**

Map p238 (523-2078; www.mrbsbistro.com; 201 Royal St; mains $26-48; 11:30am-2pm & 5:30-9pm Mon-Sat, from 10:30am Sun) Mr B's is a clubby, attractively designed restaurant that, in Brennan style, adds a bit of rocket fuel to push local Louisiana food into the future, usually in the form of Asian and Latin accents. The barbecue shrimp is the stuff of legend, and arguably the best take on the stuff in the city. If water bugs aren't your thing, may we direct you to the rabbit braised in apple cider?

NOLA
MODERN AMERICAN **$$$**

Map p238 (522-6652; www.emerils.com /restaurant/2/NOLA-Restaurant/; 534 St Louis St; mains $27-38; 6-10pm daily, 11:30am-2pm Thu-Sun) Emeril Lagasse's French Quarter outpost is pretty damn good. Of course, Emeril's not in the kitchen 'Bam!'-ing your food up, but whoever is does a great job with blackberry stout glazed ribs, buttermilk cornbread pudding and other sexed-up contemporary dishes. This is one of the few top-end New Orleans restaurants that successfully whips some California-style fusion hip into Louisiana classics, but the top draw may be the waiters, who are enthusiastic and friendly as hell.

GW FINS
SEAFOOD **$$$**

Map p238 (581-3467; www.gwfins.com; 808 Bienville St; mains $22-35; 5-10pm Sun-Thu, to 10:30pm Fri & Sat) Fins focuses, almost entirely, on fish: fresh caught and prepped so the flavor of the sea is always accented and never overwhelmed. For New Orleans this is light, almost delicate dining – you'll still find the crabmeat stuffing and *tasso* toppings, but Fins also knows how to serve a rare yellowtail with a bit of fine sticky rice. It's a refreshing breath of salty air if you're getting jambalaya-ed out.

PALACE CAFÉ
CREOLE **$$$**

Map p238 (523-1661; www.palacecafe.com; 605 Canal St; mains $18-39; 5:30-10pm daily, 11:30am-2:30pm Mon-Sat, 10:30am-2:30pm Sun) One of the best things this Brennan family outpost has going for it is its space: occupying a former music store, the building's original tile floors and interior columns have been retained and a corkscrew staircase is an idiosyncratic touch to this posh affair. The menu takes a generally non-experimental but very good approach to classic Creole standards, and a lot of effort is made to source from local suppliers.

COURT OF TWO SISTERS
CREOLE **$$**

Map p238 (522-7261; www.courtoftwosisters .com; 613 Royal St; mains $18-32; 9am-3pm & 5.30-10pm) The court regularly makes at least top five in 'best place for brunch in New Orleans' lists, a standing that's as attributable to its setting as its food. The latter is a circus of Creole omelets, Cajun pasta salads, grillades, grits, fresh fruits, carved meats and fruity cocktails; the former is a simply enchanting Creole garden filled with sugar-scented warm air and a soft jazz backdrop.

OLIVIER'S
CREOLE **$$**

Map p238 (525-7734; www.olivierscreole.com; 204 Decatur St; mains $15-26; 5-10pm daily, 11am-3pm Tue-Sat) Olivier's is run by an African American–Creole family that's been in the restaurant business for five generations, passing down and refining recipes over the decades. That heritage makes for some fine Creole dining. Go for the gumbo sampler to get an education in local cuisine before digging into specialties such as Creole rabbit, crab cakes and broiled catfish. Save room for bourbon-pecan pie.

ACME OYSTER & SEAFOOD HOUSE
SEAFOOD **$$**

Map p238 (835-6410; www.acmeoyster.com; 724 Iberville St; mains $11-21; 11am-late) They still shuck oysters to order here, which is a beautiful thing, but when Acme gets busy – which is fairly often – it serves them pre-shucked. This heresy encapsulates the dance with quality Acme engages in: trying to stay true to its roots as one of the Quarter's oldest seafood joints, but within dangerous proximity of the undiscerning crowds. Acme will even serve gumbo in a bread bowl – nice if you're from California, but pure madness to local food purists.

GUMBO SHOP
LOUISIANAN **$$**

Map p238 (525-1486; 630 St Peter St; mains $8-24; 11am-11pm) For an unabashed tourist trap, Gumbo Shop (a) does pretty good gumbo, and (b) gets a fair amount of respect from locals. The décor is actually quite lovely, all frescoed out with scenes of old New Orleans. We reckon the Shop, like most heavy-turnover food factories (for that is what this is), suffers from inconsistency in the food quality, though it's never below mediocre.

THE UNENDING LUNCH

Galatoire's (Map p238; ☑525-2021; www.galatoires.com; 209 Bourbon St; mains $17-42; ⊘11:30am-10pm Tue-Sat, noon-10pm Sun) is a special place. The interior has been frozen in time for over a century, and despite being a top-end joint, the restaurant only recently started taking credit cards. That's not to say you couldn't get meals on credit; some families are allowed to have tabs at Galatoire's, a sure sign that your name rings out in the right New Orleanian social circles. The best time to come to this revered institution of the New Orleans upper crust, is Friday morning. That's when the local ladies in big hats and gloves and men who un-ironically wear bowties buy copious bottles of champagne, gossip to high hell and have eight-hour boozy lunches that, in their way, have been going on forever. There are new stories and new scandals, but they're all told by a relatively stable cast of larger-than-life characters.

Some folks act the absolute merry fool at the Galatoire's lunch, proving the old saying: 'What's the difference between crazy and eccentric? Money.' If you can't make it on Friday – and the lines do sometimes stretch around the block – that's OK. Show up whenever and ask a tuxedo-clad waiter what's fresh. When you visit, dress the part; jackets are definitely a must for men. The food is old-line masterpieces and mainstays: pompano meunière, liver with bacon and onions, and the signature chicken *clemenceau*.

YO MAMA'S
AMERICAN $

Map p238 (☑522-1125; www.yomamasbarandgrill.com; 727 St Peter St; mains $7-14; ⊘11am-3am) 'Where we eatin' tonight?' 'Yo Mama's.' Chortle, chortle, chortle. Now that *that's* out of the way, let's lay it on the line: peanut butter and bacon burger. Yep, it looks like a cheeseburger, but that ain't melted cheddar on top – it's peanut butter, and honest, it's great. If you've got the backbone, compliment it with a heaping mound of sour cream, butter and bacon bits on the accompanying baked potato.

CAFÉ BEIGNET
CAFE $

Map p238 (☑524-5530; 331 Royal St & 311 Bourbon St; meals $6-8; ⊘7am-5pm) In a shaded patio setting with a view of Royal St, this intimate café serves omelets, Belgian waffles, quiche and beignets. There's a low-level war among foodies over who does the better beignet, here or Café du Monde, with the general consensus being this spot uses less powdered sugar as a topping. Whether this makes Café Beignet beignets better is all down to your sweet tooth and tolerance for mess making. Another location is at **Musical Legends Park** (Map p238; 311 Bourbon St; ⊘8am-10pm Sun-Thu, until midnight Fri & Sat).

ALIBI
DINER $

Map p238 (☑522-9187; 811 Iberville St; mains $5-10; ⊘24hr) Alibi is more bar than restaurant, but we're including it here because it's one of the better 24-hour joints in the Quarter (popular wisdom holds that local strippers head here after their shifts). The grub (definitely 'grub') is decidedly greasy, unhealthy and perfect after a long night of doing whatever it was you were doing on Bourbon St a few minutes ago – yes you, bleary eyes. Alibi does burgers and fried stuff, although salads are on the menu and, rumor has it, occasionally emerge from the kitchen.

JOHNNY'S PO-BOYS
PO'BOYS $

Map p238 (☑524-8129; 511 St Louis St; dishes $4-10; ⊘8am-3pm Mon-Fri, until 4:30pm Sat & Sun) We don't generally like to grab our po'boys in the touristy Quarter, but we make an exception for Johnny's. A local favorite since 1950, it's the only traditional po'boy joint around, all checkered tablecloths, hustle, bustle and good food served by good folks. Breakfast is simple and delicious.

🍷 DRINKING & NIGHTLIFE

There's a lot going on in the Old Quarter, from boozy Bourbon St to quiet Pirate's Alley. Head down to lower Decatur St for a collection of interesting dives and locals' pubs, which lead in a boozy trail all the way to the fun on Frenchman St. We haven't reviewed most of the cheese-ball Bourbon St action – these megabars are a dime a dozen.

TOP CHOICE TONIQUE
BAR

Map p238 (☎324-6045; 820 N Rampart St; ⊙5pm-late) Tonique is a bartender's bar. Seriously: on a Sunday night, when the weekend rush is over, we've seen no less than three of the city's top bartenders and their staff come in here to unwind. Why? Because this French Quarter gem mixes some of the best drinks in the city, and they have a spirits menu as long as a Tolstoy novel to draw upon. Did we mention it's dark, intimate and cozy? That doesn't mean boring, by the way – folks misbehave after a few Sazeracs.

TOP CHOICE MOLLY'S AT THE MARKET
PUB

Map p238 (1107 Decatur St; ⊙10am-6am) We've favorably mentioned bars that are popular with service-industry regulars. Now it's time to highlight a waterhole patronized by another form of lush: the journalist. Molly's is the *Times-Picayune* bar, and much more. It's also popular with cops, firefighters and Irish Americans; the home of a fat cat that stares stonily at its booze-sodden kingdom; heart of Irish activities in the Quarter (ie St Patty's Day fun); and provider of shelf space for the urn containing the ashes of its founder.

TOP CHOICE FRENCH 75
BAR

Map p238 (☎523-5433; 813 Bienville St; ⊙5pm-late) The bar at Arnaud's is led by Chris Hannah, widely considered one of the best bartenders in the city. This spot is all wood and patrician accents, but staff are friendly and down to earth while still able to mix high-quality drinks that will make you feel (a) like the star of your own Tennessee Williams play about decadent Southern aristocracy and (b) drunk.

TOP CHOICE LAFITTE'S BLACKSMITH SHOP
BAR

Map p238 (941 Bourbon St; ⊙noon-late) This gutted brick cottage also happens to be the oldest operating bar in the country and one of the most atmospheric in the Quarter. Rumors suggest this spot was once the workshop of Jean Lafitte and his brother Pierre. Whether true or not (historical records suggest 'not'), the house dates to the 18th century and endured the fires that destroyed most of the French Quarter during the Spanish era. Tourists and locals gather round the back-room piano and sing along to Fats Domino and Otis Redding tunes.

CHART ROOM
BAR

Map p238 (300 Chartres St; ⊙24hr) The Chart Room is simply a great bar. There's a historical patina on the walls, creaky furniture inside, outdoor seating for people-watching and a cast of characters plucked from an Edward Hopper painting that passed through a carnival.

ERIN ROSE
DIVE

Map p238 (811 Conti St; ⊙24hr) The Rose is only a block from Bourbon St, but feels a world away. Few tourists make it in here, but it's the go-to cheap spot for off-shift service folks, who hit up Tonique for fancy drinks and the Rose for a beer and some sports.

SYLVAIN
GASTROPUB

Map p238 (625 Chartres St; ⊙5:30-11pm Mon-Thu, until midnight Fri & Sat) Sylvain is more restaurant than bar but, lord, is the bar doing something right. The cocktail menu features the best mixed drinks you'll find this close to Jackson Square; if you like whiskey, try the Almonaster's Delight, with white whiskey, whiskey bitters and Dolin Blanc.

CAROUSEL BAR
BAR

Map p238 (214 Royal St; ⊙11am-late) At this smart-looking spot inside the historic Monteleone, the circular bar revolves and is canopied by the top hat of the 1904 World's Fair carousel with running lights, hand-painted figures and gilded mirrors. Wednesday night is Louis Prima Night. It takes 15 minutes for the bar to complete a revolution. If it's spinning too fast for you, ease up, pal. Careful on your way out.

CAFÉ LAFITTE IN EXILE
BAR

Map p238 (www.lafittes.com; 901 Bourbon St; ⊙24hr) This spot, with its huge video screens and mood lighting, doesn't exactly feel like a historical property, but it's actually the oldest dedicated gay bar in the USA. Tennessee Williams and Truman Capote both drank here, as do many men and women seeking a quieter drink (not too quiet, mind you). What's in a name? The owners used to run Lafitte's Blacksmith Shop a block away; when they lost their lease in 1953, they moved here and opened Lafitte in Exile. Hosts lots of parties; check website for details.

FAHY'S
BAR

Map p238 (540 Burgundy St; ☺1pm-late) One of the surest signs of a good bar is its popularity with chefs, who generally demand a high-quality drink after a long day in the kitchen. Fahy's is very popular with French Quarter service staff getting off their shifts, which is as high a praise as any local bar could hope for. Dogs are welcome and generally in abundance (another sign of a friendly spot), and the pool tables clack until the wee hours.

JEAN LAFITTE'S
OLD ABSINTHE HOUSE
BAR

Map p238 (240 Bourbon St; ☺10am-4am) The Old Absinthe House attracts Bourbon St boozers, but it's also one of the city's fabled historic bars. Here's the skinny: this historic spot was opened in 1807. A number of bars in New Orleans, including this one, served absinthe before it was outlawed in 1914. The mysterious beverage had a psychotropic allure – wormwood was the active ingredient – but it allegedly sent enthusiasts to the loony bin. Today, Herbsaint, a locally produced anisette, is a relatively safe stand-in for old absinthe-based drinks.

NAPOLEON HOUSE
BAR

Map p238 (500 Chartres St; ☺11am-late) Napoleon House is a particularly attractive example of what Walker Percy termed 'vital decay.' By all appearances, its stuccoed walls haven't received so much as a dab of paint since the place opened in 1797; the diffuse glow pouring through the open doors and windows in the afternoon draws out the room's gorgeous patina.

THE EMPEROR'S ABORTED ALCOHOLIC EXILE

The Napoleon House has a colorful connection to its namesake. After Waterloo and the subsequent banishment of the emperor to St Helena, a band of loyal New Orleanians reputedly plotted to snatch him and set him up in this building's 3rd-floor digs. It didn't happen, but you can easily imagine Napoleon whiling away his last days in this pleasant spot, telling fishing stories about conquering Europe.

PAT O'BRIEN'S
BAR

Map p238 (718 St Peter St; ☺10am-4am) For a tourist trap, Pat O'Brien's has genuine atmosphere and history, even if the Bourbon St boozeoisie have the run of the joint. The back courtyard, lit by flaming fountains, is genuinely lovely, but the bar could be in a barren white room and folks would still pack in for the trademark drink: the Hurricane, a lethal 29oz blend of rum, orange juice, pineapple juice and grenadine. 'Hey, this doesn't taste strong at all!' Thirty minutes later: 'Dude. I love you sho much. Whash yer name agin?'

PIRATE'S ALLEY CAFE
BAR

Map p238 (622 Pirate's Alley; ☺noon-late) The narrow pedestrian alley hidden in the shadow of St Louis Cathedral is a natural spot for a tiny little bar, and this nook fits the bill perfectly. It's owned by friendly folk and has the atmosphere of a little Montparnasse hideaway with no claim to fame. You can snag a stool at the bar and meet the regular characters who seem to drop by every few minutes, or claim a table out on the alley and soak up the atmosphere of the Old Quarter. There's lots of pirate-themed fun going on.

PRAVDA
BAR

Map p238 (1113 Decatur St; ☺5pm-late) If you couldn't guess from the name, Pravda trades on a Soviet-chic theme. But while the lighting, all dark and red and sexy, would probably make a KGB officer happy, the vintage furniture and inked-up bar staff are distinctly New Orleans. The soft atmosphere belies a fun-loving clientele sipping (or shooting) off the best vodka and absinthe menu in the city; if strong spirits are your thing, this bar is a must-try.

TROPICAL ISLE
BAR

Map p238 (721 Bourbon St; ☺24hr) Everyone has a Tropical Isle memory. Usually, it's pretty fuzzy. This is an unabashed Bourbon St tourist bar that serves 'Hand Grenades'; you can tell thanks to a subtle marketing campaign where a guy in a hand-grenade suit stands outside the bar. Drinking more than two Hand Grenades is usually the kicker to a night that involves screaming 'Sweet Home Alabama'/'Sweet Child O' Mine'/Insert Other 'Sweet' Titled Song Here, table dancing, bead tossing, bead receiving, the random mashing of tongues down strangers' throats and the eventual gathering of the limp shreds of your dignity the next day. Woo!

RAWHIDE 2010 · LEATHER BAR

Map p238 (740 Burgundy St; ⊙1pm-5am Sun-Thu, 24hr Fri & Sat) If you're not into the half-naked hard body scene on Bourbon St, come to Rawhide, the oldest operating gay bar in the Quarter. This place caters more to bears and S&M types, although anyone will appreciate the cheap, cold beer.

ABBEY · DIVE

Map p238 (1123 Decatur St; ⊙24hr) There's a lot of roughnecks, of the studded pants and face tattoo sort, congregating in this atmospheric Decatur St dive. You needn't be pierced or tattooed to fit in, but a little Joe Strummer swagger won't hurt. The jukebox reflects these sensibilities, but also includes rocking sides by the original Man in Black. And if you're seeking Lee Hazelwood's brand of trouble, the juke here has that covered, too. At least stop in for a shot if you're prowling the Lower Quarter.

DOUBLE PLAY · LOUNGE

Map p238 (439 Dauphine St; ⊙4pm-late) Even though Double Play is technically a bar, we're tempted to put it in the Entertainment section since this friendly spot is also drag central. You'll likely see a lot of queens here ripping on each other's outfits in a sometimes playful, sometimes catty manner. If not, the drinks are still delightful.

BOMBAY CLUB · LOUNGE

Map p238 (830 Conti St; ⊙5pm-late) 'Why yes Lord Snarkypants, I did indubitably have a very fine martini in the colonies.' 'Surely you jest, Sir Tweedybottom! Wherever did you find one?' Right here, guys. In complete defiance of the Bourbon St jungle, Bombay is a study in Raj-era refinement, all over-stuffed armchairs and candlelit tables. Things we love: an intimidating list of over 100 martini cocktails, the fact cigar smoking is permitted and even encouraged, and frequent live jazz.

 **ENTERTAINMENT**

ONE EYED JACKS · LIVE MUSIC

Map p238 (☎569-8361; www.oneeyedjacks.net; 615 Toulouse St; cover $5-15; ⊙9pm-4am) If you've been thinking, 'I could use a night

at a bar that feels like a 19th-century bordello managed by Johnny Rotten,' well, you're in luck. Jacks is just a great venue; there's a sense dangerous women in corsets, men with Mohawks and an army of bohemians with bottles of absinthe could come charging out of the walls at any moment. The acts, which consist of punk, post punk and the like, are consistently good.

BALCONY MUSIC CLUB · LIVE MUSIC

Map p238 (1331 Decatur St; ⊙5pm-late) Balcony is all about the acts; if there's a dud band playing you can pass it up, but on good nights it forms a very convenient step in the French Quarter–Faubourg Marigny Decatur St stumble o' fun. The 1920s flapper nights, held on a semi-regular basis, are the best; if you've ever seen the 1996 movie *Swingers,* it's like the scene in the Brown Derby. If that cultural reference soared past, imagine walking into a speakeasy during the Al Capone days.

HOUSE OF BLUES · LIVE MUSIC

Map p238 (☎310-4999; www.houseofblues.com; 225 Decatur St; tickets $7-25) House of Blues may be a chain, but they've put a lot of admirable work into making their New Orleans outpost distinctive: there's tons of folk art and rustic, voodoo-themed murals and sculptures lying about, and the effect is more powerful than kitschy. It helps that a full calendar of headliner acts, from local talent to major touring bands, makes this space a winner just about every night of the week. A few doors down, HOB's small auxiliary club, the **Parish**, is a great spot; you

---

A BIT OF BURLESQUE

There's a dearth of strip clubs in the French Quarter, but if you're in the mood for some skin, we'd recommend catching the burlesque show put on by **Fleur de Tease** (☎319-8917; http://fleurdetease.com). These talented ladies, many of whom claim professional dance backgrounds, manage to blend vintage vibe with a modern, in-your-face post-feminist sexuality that is pretty enticing for men and women. The girls perform all over town, but there's a semi-regular show at One Eyed Jacks that goes on every other Sunday.

PREPARING FOR PRESERVATION HALL

Preservation Hall (☑522-2841; www.preservationhall.com; 726 St Peter St; cover $15; ◎8-11pm), housed in a former art gallery that dates back to 1803, is one of the most storied live music venues in New Orleans. Barbara Reid and Grayson 'Ken' Mills formed the Society for the Preservation of New Orleans Jazz in 1961, at a time when Louis Armstrong's generation was already getting on in years. The resident performers, the Preservation Hall Jazz Band, are ludicrously talented, and regularly tour around the world. These white-haired grandpas and their tubas, trombones and cornets raise the roof every night.

With that all said, here are some caveats you should know before seeing a show here. First: the set is only about an hour long, and that seems short for $15. Still, you're paying to see musical history as much as music, so we're OK with that. But if we do pay $15, we want to be able to see the band. The Hall is atmospheric, but it is also small and popular. Sets play on the hour, and you need to show up early – an hour before, folks – to snag a seat. Otherwise you'll be standing and, likely as not, your view will be blocked by people in front of you. When it's warm enough to leave the window shutters open, those not fortunate enough to get in can join the crowd on the sidewalk to listen to the sets. Also note: no booze or snacks are served in the club, and the bathroom is in next-door Pat O'Brien's. We love the Hall, don't get us wrong. Just be aware of the above before you visit.

can get pretty up-close-and-personal with artists during gigs.

DUNGEON CLUB
Map p238 (☑523-5530; www.originaldungeon.com; 738 Toulouse St; cover $5; ◎midnight-late) Yes, some bouncers have filed their teeth, and yes, this is a goth and black metal club, but having descended into the basement chambers, we still ran into some yuppies. DJs keep things throbbing until dawn's early light (egads! sunlight!) and several barkeeps serve up ghoulish cocktails (with creepy names like the Witches Brew and the Dragon's Blood), which the bar promises will help you 'leave your troubles behind.' Such caring, warmhearted sentiments! Dungeon, we had you all wrong!

BOURBON PUB & PARADE CLUB
Map p238 (☑www.bourbonpub.com; 801 Bourbon St) The Bourbon is the heart of New Orleans' gay scene, or at least the nightlife and party scene. Many of the events that pepper the city's gay calendar either begin, end or are conducted here; during Southern Decadence (p22), in particular, this is the place to be. The sisterhood is welcome as well, but this is pretty much a bar for the boys.

OZ CLUB
Map p238 (www.oznewtorleans.com; 800 Bourbon St; ◎24hr) Your traditional shirtless, all-night-party, loud-music, lots-of-dancing-boys

bar, where there are bowls of condoms set out for the customers.

PALM COURT JAZZ CAFÉ LIVE MUSIC
Map p238 (☑525-0200; www.palmcourtjazzcafe.com; 1204 Decatur St; cover around $5; ◎7-11pm Wed-Sun) Fans of trad jazz who want to hang out with a mature crowd should head to this supper-club alternative to Preservation Hall. Palm Court is a roomy venue that has a consistently good lineup of local legends; you really can't go wrong if you're a jazz fan. Shows start at 8pm.

🛍 SHOPPING

[TOP CHOICE] **LOUISIANA MUSIC FACTORY** MUSIC
Map p238 (☑586-1094; www.louisianamusicfactory.com; 210 Decatur St; ◎10am-7pm Mon-Sat, noon-6pm Sun) Here's your first stop if you're looking for music. The selection of new and used CDs delves deep into New Orleans and Louisiana musical culture, with recordings from the 1900s to this week. The listening stations are a great way to familiarize yourself with local artists. There's also a nice selection of cool T-shirts that you won't find elsewhere, along with books, DVDs and posters. Live performances on Saturday afternoons rock the joint.

FRENCH QUARTER GALLERIES

Royal St and Chartres St are packed with art galleries that showcase the creativity of artists from across the Gulf South.

A Gallery for Fine Photography (Map p238; ☎568-1313; www.agallery.com; 241 Chartres St; ⊗10am-6pm Thu-Sat, noon-4pm Sun & Mon) This impressive gallery usually has prints such as William Henry Jackson's early-20th-century views of New Orleans and EJ Bellocq's rare images of Storyville prostitutes, made from the photographers' original glass plates. The gallery also regularly features Herman Leonard's shots of Duke Ellington and other jazz legends, as well as the occasional Cartier-Bresson enlargement (available at second-mortgage prices).

Harouni Gallery (Map p238; ☎299-8900; www.harouni.com; 829 Royal St; ⊗noon-5pm Thu-Sat) Artist David Harouni is a native of Iran who has lived and worked in New Orleans for several decades. He creates works of absorbing depth by painting and scraping multiple layers of medium; the finished product has a surreal eerie beauty.

Kurt E Schon Ltd Gallery (Map p238; ☎524-5462; www.kurteschonltd.com; 510 St Louis St; ⊗9am-5pm Mon-Fri, to 3pm Sat) For moneyed art collectors, and the rest of us who just like to look at great artwork, Kurt E Schon is an immense gallery and storehouse that purveys fine paintings from the 19th century. The gallery is like a small museum showcasing the works of the lesser-known contemporaries of the master impressionists; most of the works on display are pieces of remarkable beauty.

Michalopoulos Gallery (Map p238; ☎558-0505; www.michalopoulos.com; 617 Bienville St) Michalopoulos has become one of New Orleans' most popular painters in recent years, in part on the strength of his best-selling Jazz Fest posters. His shop showcases his colorful and expressive architectural studies and paintings that look like van Gogh meets the Vieux Carré. The gallery holds frequent openings on Friday night. Check out the website or call ahead for hours and to check on specific events.

Rodrigue Studio (Map p238; ☎581-4244; www.georgerodrigue.com; 721 Royal St; ⊗noon-5pm Wed-Sun) Cajun artist George Rodrigue's gallery is the place to go to see examples of his unbelievably popular 'Blue Dog' paintings. He just keeps painting and painting that darn dog. Look for topical works, in which the dog quietly comments on post-Katrina issues.

TOP CHOICE ELIE MONSTER   VINTAGE

Map p238 (☎592-3596; 538 St Philip St; ⊗1-8pm Wed-Mon) Eleanor 'Elie Monster' Lahey knows a thing or two about tasteful vintage. Sometimes she finds the right piece; sometimes she finds the right potential and and uses her sewing skills to embroider old clothes and turn them from vintage into 'Vintage' with a capital 'V', the sort of timelessly funky style that you know is good when you see it. Many of the clothes here play on a peasant or Cowboy Western theme.

MOSS ANTIQUES   ANTIQUES

Map p238 (☎522-3981; 411 Royal St; ⊗10am-5pm, closed Sun) Watch your head when you enter this gallery of low-hanging chandeliers. Oof! Too late! Moss is a Royal St institution in the local antiques trade. Only the finest quality antiques and *objets d'art* are sold here. You'll find the perfect thing for your Garden District mansion. Or perhaps you can take home the busted chandelier they made you pay for.

PEACHES RECORDS & TAPES   MUSIC

Map p238 (☎282-3322; 408 N Peters St; ⊗10am-8pm Mon-Sat, 11am-7pm Sun) Peaches has been around since 1975, doing the holy work of promoting, cataloguing and marketing the best in local New Orleans music. This enormous record store dominates its corner of Peters St, and is a must-see stop for anyone who wants to take a piece of the city's musical heritage home.

SWORD & PEN   MILITARY MEMORABILIA

Map p238 (☎523-7741; 528 Royal St; ⊗10am-5:30pm) Military memorabilia nerds, rejoice. There are armies of miniature soldiers here marching past Confederate kitsch, WWII posters, recruitment buttons from every conflict of the 20th century (apparently) and anything else that could fulfill a little kid, or grown travel writer's, most lurid toy-soldier fantasies.

VOLUPTUOUS VIXEN BOUTIQUE

Map p238 (☑529-3588; 818 Chartres St; ⊙10am-6pm Mon-Thu, until 7pm Fri & Sat, 11am-6pm Sun) This Vixen is less about vamping it up, and more about providing designer chic to women sizes US 12 and up, and lingerie for sizes 34–48 C–JJ. Which isn't to say there aren't clothes within this place that aren't good for a little vamping – but there are also casual sundresses, pretty accessories and elegant tops as well.

HEMLINE BOUTIQUE

Map p238 (☑592-0242; 609 Chartres St; ⊙10am-6pm Sun-Thu, until 6:30pm Fri & Sat) An upscale yet affordable women's retailer with branches across Louisiana, Texas and Kansas City, Hemline's original outpost is right here in the French Quarter. The first store is still one of the more charming ones, carrying labels such as Nicole Miller, Corey Lynn Calter and BCBG. See if you can find another pair of the strappy sandals you fell in love with in the large mark-down section.

JAMES H COHEN
& SONS ANTIQUES, MEMORABILIA

Map p238 (☑522-3305; www.cohenantiques.com; 437 Royal St; ⊙10am-6pm Mon-Sat) From the sidewalk windows, you might be inclined to pass this one by if you're not interested in guns. Cohen & Sons does sell antique guns including flintlocks, colts, Winchester '73s and even a French musket or two. Beyond weaponry, the place is like a museum, stuffed with relics and historical curiosities, from swords to maps and coins. Try not to break anything; the owners are armed, clearly.

ARCADIAN BOOKS
& ART PRINTS ANTIQUARIAN & USED BOOKS

Map p238 (☑523-4138; 714 Orleans Ave; ⊙10am-6pm) Arcadian is a small, crowded shop that's filled with Southern literature and history, as well as many volumes in French. Owner Russell Desmond speaks French fluently and is a wonderful, if cynical, ambassador for New Orleans.

GREG'S ANTIQUES ANTIQUES

Map p238 (☑202-8577; www.gregsantiques.net; 1209 Decatur St; ⊙noon-10pm Tue-Sun) Besides rooms full of salvaged furniture and antiques, Greg's regularly exhibits works by

New Orleans underground and outsider artists, which can also take the form of found and folk art sourced from across the city.

BECKHAM'S
BOOKSTORE ANTIQUARIAN & USED BOOKS

Map p238 (☑522-9875; 228 Decatur St; ⊙10am-5pm) Across the street from House of Blues, this large, neatly organized store has two floors of used books, and also sells used classical LPs. It's definitely worth a browse.

LIBRAIRIE BOOKS ANTIQUARIAN & USED BOOKS

Map p238 (☑525-4837; 823 Chartres St; ⊙10am-6pm) A jam-packed little shop of delights for the avid bookworm and collector. The emphasis here is squarely on very old (and sometimes dusty) volumes. You might dig up an ancient copy of Herbert Asbury's *The French Quarter,* or other tales of old New Orleans. And there are scholarly texts and ample material of more general interest as well.

CENTURIES ANTIQUE PRINTS & MAPS

Map p238 (☑568-9491; 408 Chartres St; ⊙10am-6pm) OK, it's a little on the stodgy side, with its selection of 19th-century lithographs and old maps. But flip through the inventory (all of it well organized by theme, date or locale) and you just might find yourself slowing down to look things over. Particularly interesting are the Civil War and Black History sections. You're sure to be absorbed by the ancient maps here, which are beautifully drawn with outdated demarcations and occasional glaring cartographic errors – why yes, Asia is apparently half the size of Europe.

COLLECTIBLE ANTIQUES ANTIQUES

Map p238 (☑566-0399; 1232 Decatur St; ⊙10:30am-6pm) You never know what you'll find between the piles of old furniture stacked along the walls of this large, garagelike emporium of tantalizing junk. Perhaps you collect old photographic portraits from long defunct studios. You might find everything you need for that tiki bar you're slapping together in the basement. Or maybe you're just after an art-deco martini shaker, an old dented trumpet, a Pewee Herman doll, a heavy army-surplus coat or some silverware.

LUCULLUS ANTIQUES

Map p238 (☑528-9620; 610 Chartres St; ⊙9:30am-5pm Mon-Sat) Peeking in the window, you'll see a battery of ancient copper pots that appear to have generations of dents tinkered out of their bottoms. Owner Patrick Dunne is an advocate of using, not merely collecting, culinary antiques. Follow his advice and add more ritual and elegance to your life with an antique café au lait bowl or an absinthe spoon for creating your evening cocktails. Don't just pop open your champagne and pour it; chill it in a silver bucket. You get the idea.

MS RAU ANTIQUES   ANTIQUES

Map p238 (☏523-5660; www.rauantiques.com; 630 Royal St; ☺9am-5pm Mon-Sat) With a massive 30,000-sq-ft showroom (you'd never know it passing by on Royal St), and after nearly a century of doing business, MS Rau ranks among New Orleans' most venerated dealers of antiques. It's a bit serious – these are the sort of frosty antiques that require their own insurance policies – but it's a family business and the professional salespeople are quite approachable. You'll find fine art, jewelry, music boxes, clocks, Judaica, 19th-century globes – all in impeccable condition and unbelievably expensive.

LE GARAGE   ANTIQUES, USED GOODS

Map p238 (☏522-6639; 1234 Decatur St; ☺10am-6pm) Got to admit, we liked the name better when it was simply 'The Garage.' But why quibble over a little ironic Frenchness? The place is still a garage loaded with interesting stuff to paw through. Things for sale here include odd items of clothing, hats, army surplus, curtains, yellowed pool balls, tattered Mardi Gras costumes from yesteryear, knitted Coors-beer-can caps, furniture and oodles of objects d'art to ogle or even buy. Treasures galore, we tell you. Dive in.

PHOTO WORKS   ART, PHOTOGRAPHY

Map p238 (☏593-9090; www.photoworksneworleans.com; 839 Chartres St; ☺10am-5:30pm Thu-Mon) This is a polished showroom for the accomplished photographer Louis Sahuc (*sigh*-ook), who has been shooting New Orleans for years and years. Sahuc's beautiful prints capture timeless images of the city in a manner that's far more accomplished than your average Jackson Square sketcher.

FRENCH MARKET

Truth be told, from a shopping standpoint, the French Market is a bit of a disappointment. It no longer plays a vital role in French Quarter life, and locals don't rely on it as they once did for their foodstuffs. For the most part, it now caters to tourism. Still, it's an atmospheric old market with a range of shops and vendors, and is a hive of activity most days, but especially on weekends.

The market is split into two sections – the Farmers Market and Flea Market – and neither is particularly special. In a pinch, the French Market will supply the visitor with cheap gimcracks to give away back home, but for quality shopping you'll have to look elsewhere.

Shoppers can pick up some unique southern Louisiana products at the Flea Market any day of the week. There is a motley assortment of T-shirt and sunglasses vendors, as well as African art (mass-produced), inexpensive silver jewelry, chintzy Mardi Gras masks and dolls, music tapes and CDs of dubious origin, and enough preserved alligator heads to populate a polyurethane swamp. Most prices at the Flea Market are negotiable. Officially the Flea Market is open 24 hours, but most vendors keep their own hours and are open from 9am to 5pm.

Only a vestige of former market activity remains at the Farmers Market, where large freezer trucks have replaced the small trucks of farmers. Still, you might occasionally see an old pickup truck on sagging springs heading from the market to sell a load of fresh produce on an Uptown street.

Merchants in the Farmers Market offer fresh fruit and vegetables, such as green beans, mangoes, papayas, bananas, plantains, peaches, strawberries, watermelons, apples and pecans, as well as cold drinks. In addition, there are lots of kitchen supplies, spices and condiments (including a large selection of hot sauces), garlic and chili strings, and cookbooks for the tourist trade. The Farmers Market opens up early every morning and gradually peters out in the afternoon.

TABASCO COUNTRY STORE
CONDIMENTS, GIFTS

Map p238 (🖉539-7900; 537 St Ann St; ⏱10am-6pm) Bet you thought Tabasco was either red or green and always hot, right? Guess again: there's Tabasco ketchup, mayonnaise, cookbooks, plenty of souvenirs and a fairly incredible range of hot (and not so hot) sauces. Don't you need a 500-count pack of mini-Tabasco bottles?

JAVA HOUSE IMPORTS
GIFTS

Map p238 (🖉581-1288; 913 Decatur St; ⏱10am-7pm, from 9am Fri & Sun, 9am-8pm Sat) There are, indeed, cool imports and statues from Java here, as well as Balinese and West African masks, Indian-style Buddhas, lacquerwork from Lombok and all the other items that prove what a savvy traveler you are.

SAVE NOLA
GIFTS

Map p238 (🖉558-1951; 600 Decatur St; ⏱10am-6pm) The Save NOLA store, located inside the Jackson Brewery, sells handbags, souvenirs, shirts and such; proceeds go towards the group of the same name and are invested in community rebuilding projects such as Habitat for Humanity. The sort of store where your need for retail therapy is a good deed.

BOUTIQUE DU VAMPYRE
GIFTS

Map p238 (🖉561-8267; 712 Orleans Ave; ⏱10am-7pm) Dark candles and gothic gargoyles look down on you, promising a curse of blood and terror and the undead on those who only browse but do not buy! Mwa ha ha! Or...not. All kinds of vampire- and voodoo-themed gifts stock this cool, dungeon-esque store; our favorite item was a deck of tarot cards with truly surreal, somewhat disturbing artwork.

CENTRAL GROCERY
GROCERIES

Map p238 (🖉523-1620; 923 Decatur St; ⏱9am-5pm Tue-Sat) A hyper-busy store offering many of the cooking ingredients typically found in Louisiana kitchens: Zatarain's Creole Seasoning and Crab Boil, McIlhenny Tabasco or Crystal hot sauce, chicory coffee and filé for making gumbo. While you're here, grab a jar of Central Gro Co's famous olive relish, the not-so-secret weapon of the muffuletta sandwich.

FLORA SAVAGE
FLOWERS

Map p238 (🖉581-4728; 1301 Royal St; ⏱11am-6pm Mon-Sat) In town for an anniversary? Met someone you want to impress in a hurry? Take care of your floral needs here. You'll soon be festooning your hotel room with romantic aromas and colors, and your sweetheart will be swooning with romantic feelings for you.

FLEUR DE PARIS
HAUTE COUTURE

Map p238 (🖉525-1899; www.fleurdeparis.net; 712 Royal St; ⏱10am-6pm, from noon Sun) Some stores in New Orleans exist to indulge the most eccentric and particular interests a person can possibly have. This boutique in the Labranche Building is a case in point. The woman who wants to appear ready for the 1904 St Louis World's Fair need look no further. The custom hats are bouquets of plumage, fur felt, lace and, here and there, a snatch of black netting. The evening gowns are devastating showstoppers guaranteed to make a dapper Dan in spats swoon.

MASKARADE
MASKS & GIFTS

Map p238 (🖉568-1018; www.themaskstore.com; 630 St Ann St; ⏱10am-7pm) This shop deals in high-quality masks by local and international artisans, and the selection includes everything from classic *commedia dell'arte* masks from Venice to more way-out designs for your wigged-out end-of-Mardi-Gras state of mind. If your nose is too small, many of the selections here can correct the problem. Maskarade also sells beguiling handcrafted gifts as well. How about a little demon paperweight for your office mate?

HOVÉ PARFUMEUR
PERFUME

Map p238 (🖉525-7827; www.hoveparfumeur.com; 824 Royal St; ⏱10am-5pm Mon-Sat) Grassy vetiver, bittersweet orange blossoms, spicy ginger – New Orleans' exotic flora has graciously lent its scents to Hové's house-made perfumes for more than 70 years. A brief sniffing visit will leave your head swirling with images of the Vieux Carré's magnificent past. Thus intoxicated, you can ask staff to custom-mix a fragrance for you.

LEAH'S PRALINES
PRALINES

Map p238 (🖉523-5662; www.leahspralines.com; 714 St Louis St; ⏱10am-6pm Mon-Sat, until 5pm Sun) In the heart of the French Quarter, this old candy shop specializes in that special Creole confection, the praline. Here you'll get some of the very best in town. If you've already tried pralines elsewhere and decided that you don't care for them, we suggest you try some at Leah's before making

VISITING YOKNAPATAWPHA COUNTY

Like many American authors, William Faulkner did a New Orleans stint, briefly renting an apartment in a town house on Pirate's Alley in 1925. While living in the city he described as a 'courtesan, not old and yet no longer young,' Faulkner worked for the *Times-Picayune*, contributed to literary magazine *Double Dealer* and consorted with local literati. Later in his life, the author would go on to redefine the genre of Southern and, arguably, American literature, setting many of his novels in mythical Yoknapatawpha County (kudos if you got our box headline).

The flat Faulkner rented in New Orleans is now a business and a bona-fide literary attraction: **Faulkner House Books** (Map p238; ☑524-2940; www.faulknerhousebooks .net; 624 Pirate's Alley; ⊙10am-5:30pm). Faulkner House is an essential stop for any bibliophile. It's a pleasant space, with beautifully crafted shelves packed floor to ceiling, lending it the dignified atmosphere of a private library. It's not a large store – if there are more than five or six customers at a time, it starts to feel crowded – but it offers a commendable mix of new titles and first editions. The selection of books by local and Southern authors is particularly strong, and naturally William Faulkner is a staple. The shop is something of a literary hub, and local authors (Richard Ford, Andrei Codrescu etc) regularly stop by.

up your mind completely. The creamy pralines are deadly. Try one with rum in it if you don't mind a nice extra zing. Grab a box and have it expressed to your friends back home. Throw in some of the pecan brittle or rum pecans while you're at it.

BOURBON STRIP TEASE — CLOTHING

Map p238 (☑581-6633; 205 Bourbon St; ⊙10am-8pm) If you've just asked to be excused while you 'slip into something more comfortable,' but haven't actually packed anything 'comfortable,' sneak down to this shop. It has all manner of dainty things to put on before you take 'em off, starting with lacy lingerie and progressing to edible undies and sleazy toys. *Very* comfortable stuff.

JACKSON (JAX) BREWERY — SHOPPING MALL

Map p238 (☑566-7245; www.jacksonbrewery.com; 600 Decatur St; ⊙10am-7pm; P) This site really was a brewery once but, despite its proximity to boozy Bourbon St, the company failed, and the old brick structure was converted into a shopping mall. Jax has dozens of shops and eateries, most of them singing siren songs to unwary tourists. Proceed with caution or your next credit card statement will include charges for such items as Cajun golf clothing (?!), novelty ties, old-time photographic portraits and the like. However, if you're looking for a crawfish T-shirt for your cool niece or a new pair of sunglasses, or are just in need of a bathroom break, come on by. There's an ATM on the sidewalk.

HUMIDITY SKATE SHOP — SPORTING GOODS

Map p238 (☑529-6822; http://humidityskateshop .net/; 515 Dumaine St; ⊙11am-7pm) Graffiti chic, Vans shoes, Element, Darkstar and Organika decks, grip tape, Krux trucks and Zero wheels – if any of that made sense to you, make your way up to Dumaine St. If not, you may want to avoid this store.

SOUTHERN CANDY MAKERS — SWEETS

Map p238 (☑800-344-9773; 334 Decatur St; ⊙10am-7pm) Sweet-smelling confections with a Southern accent are created in this neat little shop. A visit is guaranteed to put a big ol' Dolly Parton smile on your face. The toffee is divine and the pralines are to die for. The shop does special candies for every holiday (fat Santas for Christmas, fat bunnies for Easter, chocolate hearts for Valentines) and you can have something sent off to loved ones around the country.

MARY JANE'S EMPORIUM — TOBACCO & PIPES

Map p238 (☑525-8004; www.maryjanesemporium .com; 1229 Decatur St; ⊙10am-midnight) By 'Mary Jane,' they're not referring to shoes. This is an essential stop for smokers of legal tobacco products, including finer brands of cigarettes not sold at your basic corner store. Also, a variety of apparatus for the smoking of unsanctioned herbal products and such is sold here. All right, it's basically a head shop.

ZOMBIE'S HOUSE OF VOODOO
VOODOO & OCCULT

Map p238 (☑486-6366; 725 St Peter St; ☺10am-11:30pm) Just around the corner from Bourbon St, this voodoo shop gamely makes its pitch amid the drunken hordes. Step inside and it's plain to see this is one religious store that's not bent on snuffing out the party. There's an altar at the entry with a serious note not to disrespectfully take photos, and then there is the truly splendiferous display of plaster-of-Paris statuettes imported from the Santeria realms of Brazil. All of them are fun and charming, and many are simply beautiful. Some make great gifts to take back home – such as the smiling bust of Louis Armstrong.

VIEUX CARRÉ WINE & SPIRITS
WINE

Map p238 (☑568-9463; 422 Chartres St; ☺10am-9pm) This is a densely stocked shop run by two Italian-born brothers who can often be found socializing at a table near the front door. It has an impressive selection of wines from California, Australia, France and Italy, and a commendable choice of international beers. If you're really serious about wine and willing to pay good money for it, ask to see the back room, where the rare vintages are kept.

SANTA'S QUARTERS
CHRISTMAS DECORATIONS

Map p238 (☑581-5820; 1025 Decatur St; ☺10am-6pm) This place keeps the Christmas spirit alive year-round, with ornaments, lights and every festive trinket imaginable. Now, you have to wonder about people who might be tempted to purchase Christmas ornaments on one of August's most sultry days. And what about the zero-receipt days this shop surely endures for much of the year. So is it a front for something sinister? A vanity concern for St Nick? Is the fat man indulging a local filly on the side? Anyway, on with your shopping...

Mardi Gras & Jazz Fest

'Festival Season' in New Orleans

No two events encapsulate New Orleans like Mardi Gras and Jazz Fest. These festivals are more than celebrations: they contain within themselves every thread of the colorful, complicated New Orleans tapestry.

'Stop exaggerating, Lonely Planet,' you may say, to which we reply: 'there's no need to exaggerate'. These festivals are incredible. Imagine a bunch of grown men and women riding giant neon shoes and plaster dinosaurs through the street, or Bruce Springsteen, Al Green, Dr John, Tom Petty, Cee-lo, Feist and the Carolina Chocolate Drops playing in the same venue in one weekend, or you slip through the looking glass into MOM's Ball and see a band of zombies playing for naked folks in body paint and a cast of costumes that appear to be lifted from Jim Henson's most lurid fantasies.

During Mardi Gras and Jazz Fest, all this happens. The city's flights of fancy and indulgence are realized like at no other time. And every thing that makes New Orleans...well...New Orleans becomes a lot more... *New Orleansy*. Like, let's take food. The best food in the city all of a sudden becomes booth fare in Jazz Fest. During Mardi Gras, restaurants throw their doors open to folks dressed like goblins and faeries. Which speaks to the creativity, be it via music (Jazz Fest) or the visual arts,

crafts and theater (as exemplified by Mardi Gras floats and costumes). These festivals reveal the soul of a city that is obsessed with beauty, with both redefining the concept and appreciating it in every way possible.

Finally, these festivals speak to the history of the city. Jazz Fest is the celebration that it is because this is the most important musical city in America, and artists from around the world come here to pay tribute to that fact. Mardi Gras has an older, more mysterious history, which we go into at length later in this section. But rest assured: the time between late January, when Carnival Season begins, and late April/early May, when Jazz Fest happens, is pretty much back-to-back celebrations in New Orleans, or as folks like to call it down here, festival season. There are lulls here and there, but by the time mid-March rolls around it feels like there's a small festival to bridge these two big festivals every weekend.

What are you saying, Lonely Planet, that's there's basically a half year of festivals in New Orleans?

Hey, we're not exaggerating.

From top

1. Mardi Gras Indians in their full regalia
2. Masks are a popular Mardi Gras accessory

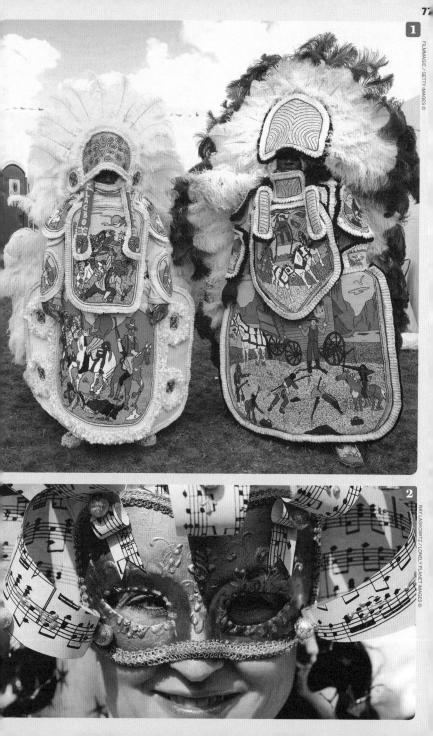

Saga of a Celebration

Pagan Rites

Carnival's pagan origins are deep. Pre-spring festivals of unabashed sexuality and appetite indulgence are not a rarity around the world. Neither is the concept of denying these appetites as a means of reasserting human forbearance in the face of animalistic cravings.

The early Catholic Church failed to appreciate these traditions, but after trying unsuccessfully to suppress them, the Church co-opted the spring rite and slotted it into the Christian calendar. In Rome it came to be known as *carnevale* (farewell to the flesh), referring to the fasting that began on Ash Wednesday (but also perhaps an oblique reference to the divinity of Christ and the Lenten fast that followed). This was a day when the commoners could literally be profane – the word comes from Pro fane, 'to come before the temple.' Nothing was sacred on this sacred day, which was celebrated in France and spread to French outposts in the New World.

The Creole Connection

Early generations of Creoles loved to dance and mask, and on Mardi Gras people would wear grotesque disguises and attend balls, concerts and theater. From the beginning Carnival crossed race lines. Creoles of color held Carnival balls to which slaves were sometimes invited. Several times, masking was altogether outlawed by authorities who distrusted the way costumes undermined the established social order. On Mardi Gras, the citizenry tended to blend into an unruly, desegregated mob. The situation hasn't entirely changed.

Following the Louisiana Purchase, Mardi Gras faded for a while, until a secretive group of wealthy Anglos who called themselves the Mistick Krewe of Comus made their first public appearance in spectacular horse-drawn floats illuminated by flambeaux (torches) in 1857. New clubs

Clockwise from top left
1. Blaine Kern's Mardi Gras World (p103) **2.** A float krewe, Mardi Gras **3.** A trombonist from Krewe du Vieux

modeled themselves on the Comus, calling themselves 'krewes' (a deliberately quirky spelling of 'crews').

Modern Mardi Gras

Rex first appeared in 1872, Momus a year later and Proteus in 1882. Mythological and sometimes satirical themes defined the parades, making these processions coherent theatrical works on wheels. These old-line krewes were (and for the most part remain) highly secretive societies comprising the city's wealthiest, most powerful men.

Many enduring black traditions emerged around the turn of the 20th century. The spectacular Mardi Gras Indians began to appear in 1885; today their elaborate feathered costumes, sewn as a tribute to Native American warriors, are recognized as pieces of folk art. The black krewe of Zulu appeared in 1909, with members initially calling themselves the Tramps and parading on foot. By 1916, when the Zulu Social Aid & Pleasure Club was incorporated, the krewe had floats, and its antics deliberately spoofed the pomposity of elite white krewes.

Ironically, today's Zulu's members include some of the city's more prominent black citizens, and their annual ball is as full of pomp and posturing as Comus'.

Today's 'superkrewes' began forming in the 1960s. Endymion debuted as a modest neighborhood parade in 1967; now its parades and floats are the largest, with nearly 2000 riders and one of its immense floats measuring 240ft in length.

OUR FAVORITE BIG PARADES

➡ **Krewe de Vieux** Old school walking parade with sharply satirical floats.

➡ **Muses** All-female krewe with creative floats.

➡ **Zulu** Traditionally African American krewe throws coconuts to crowd.

➡ **Rex** Old-line royalty of Mardi Gras.

➡ **Le krewe d'Etat** Raunchy, satirical floats.

➡ **Thoth** Family-friendly Uptown day parade.

➡ **Bacchus** Super-krewe with lots of flash.

All on a Mardi Gras Day

The parade season is a 12-day period beginning two Fridays before Fat Tuesday. Early parades are charming, neighborly processions that whet your appetite for the later parades, which increase in size and grandeur until the spectacles of the superkrewes emerge during the final weekend.

A popular preseason night procession, usually held three Saturdays before Fat Tuesday, is Krewe du Vieux. By parading before the official parade season and marching on foot, Krewe du Vieux is permitted to pass through the French Quarter. The themes of this notoriously bawdy and satirical krewe clearly aim to offend puritanical types.

Watch for Le Krewe d'Etat, whose name is a clever, satirical pun: d'Etat is ruled by a dictator rather than a king. Another favorite is Muses, an all-women's krewe that parades down St Charles Ave with thousands of members and imaginative, innovative floats; their throws include coveted hand-decorated shoes.

Mardi Gras weekend is lit up by the entrance of the superkrewes, with their monstrous floats and endless processions of celebrities, flashy as a Vegas revue. On Saturday night the megakrewe Endymion stages its spectacular parade and Extravaganza, as it calls its ball in the Superdome. On Sunday night the Bacchus superkrewe wows an enraptured crowd along St Charles Ave with its celebrity monarch and a gorgeous fleet of crowd-pleasing floats.

On Mardi Gras morning Zulu rolls along Jackson Ave, where folks set up barbecues on the sidewalk and krewe members distribute their prized hand-painted coconuts. The 'King of Carnival,' Rex, waits further Uptown; it's a much more restrained affair, with the monarch himself looking like he's been plucked from a deck of cards.

Clockwise from top left
1. The Secret Society of St Anne, Mardi Gras **2.** Krewe of Proteus float, Mardi Gras **3.** A junior member of the Wild Mohicans Mardi Gras Indian Tribe

WALKING KREWE REVIEW

Some of the best parades of Carnival Season are put on by DIY-ish, bohemian walking krewes, groups of friends who create a grassroots show that casual observers are always welcome to participate in. Just bring a costume!

➜ **Barkus** Dress your furry friends up for this all-pet parade (www.barkus.org).

➜ **Box of Wine** Crazily costumed revelers march up St Charles Ave ahead of the Bacchus (God of wine) parade, distributing free wine from boxes along the way.

➜ **Red Beans & Rice** On Lundi Gras, folks dress up in costumes made from dry beans or as Louisiana food items.

➜ **Intergalactic Krewe of Chewbacchus** Dress up as your favorite Sci-fi (but no fantasy – sorry elves!) character (http://chewbacchus.org).

➜ **Society of St Anne** Traditionally made up of artists and bohemians, St Anne marches on Mardi Gras morning from the Bywater to the Mississippi and features the best costumes of Carnival Season.

Costume Contests

Mardi Gras is a citywide costume party, and many locals take a dim view of visitors who crash the party without one. For truly fantastic outfits, score tickets to the fabled MOM's Ball (Mystic Orphans and Mutts), held the Saturday before Mardi Gras. Tickets are hard to come by, but check online, or show up to the ball itself. The costumes at MOM's need to be seen to be believed, but rest assured: you'll feel as if you've walked into a '60s acid trip.

Information

Gambit Weekly (www.bestofneworleans. com) publishes a Carnival edition during February or March, depending on the date of Mardi Gras. Mardi Gras New Orleans (www.mardigrasneworleans.com) is an excellent website.

New Orleans Jazz & Heritage Festival

Jazz Fest sums up everything that would be lost if the world were to lose New Orleans. Much more than Mardi Gras, with its secret balls and sparkly trinkets, Jazz Fest reflects the generosity of New Orleans, its unstoppable urge to share its most precious resource – its culture – with the rest of the world. Of course the Fest is first and foremost about music, but it isn't just about jazz. It's jazz *and* heritage, which means any music that jazz came from, and any music that jazz inspired. The multitude of stages and tents feature everything that pours in and out of jazz – blues, gospel, Afro-Caribbean, folk, country, zydeco, Cajun, funky brass, and on and on.

Roots of Roots Music

Jazz Fest began in 1970 and, of course, the idea of staging a big music festival in New Orleans couldn't have been more natural. George Wein had already organized the well-established Newport Jazz Festival, so he was brought to New Orleans to launch a similar tradition. Wein hired Quint Davis to help in the promotion of the project. Both men are still in charge of organizing the event each year.

The first festival, held in Louis Armstrong Park, featured a remarkable lineup of legendary artists, including Duke Ellington, Mahalia Jackson, Clifton Chenier, Fats Domino and The Meters. Mardi Gras Indians performed, and every now and then a second-line parade swept through the audience. The ingredients were already in place for a major cultural event with a genuine regional significance. Outside talent, such as Ellington, complemented the local talent and beefed up the event's exposure.

Only 350 people attended that first Jazz Fest. Most likely, the low numbers were due to poor promotion outside New Orleans. Out-of-towners arrived in much greater numbers for the '71 Fest, and with them came a far stronger local response. To accommodate another anticipated jump in attendance, the Fest was moved to the far larger Fair Grounds Race Track a year later, and Jazz Fest really hasn't looked back since. By the late 1970s the festival had grown from one weekend to two, with many legendary moments already solidifying the event's cultural importance. Mesmerizing performances by the likes of James Booker, the Neville Brothers and Professor Longhair have been recorded for all posterity. The musical lineup soon expanded to include big-time national acts, such as Lenny Kravitz, Kings of Leon and Bon Jovi, as well as international acts from South America, the Caribbean and Africa.

....

Clockwise from top left
1. The Neville Brothers, Jazz Fest 2. Jazz Fest crowds
3. A stilt walker, Jazz Fest

Experiencing Jazz Fest

Some people choose to do Jazz Fest over and over again, year after year, so obviously there's something addictive about the experience. It doesn't hurt that there are umpteen ways to approach this gargantuan feast of music, food and culture.

Setting the Stage

The first thing to decide is: one weekend of Jazz Fest or two? And if one's enough, then which one?

No one will laugh if you choose one weekend. The drawback is you may have to pick your dates before the Fest schedule is announced. The schedule isn't announced until early February at the earliest. Still, there's statistical logic to making blindfolded decisions this way, as both weekends are always equally packed with big-name show-stoppers and unheard-of talents. Sometimes you'll miss out on a personal favorite if you're not attending every day of the Fest, but in the end something along the way will make up for the loss.

For those who make their Jazz Fest plans late – that's to say, after February – there's the advantage of knowing the schedule. Free-spenders are still likely to find a pricey suite of rooms in the French Quarter at this point, but thrifty types might be frustrated. If you decide to do both weekends, you'll have four days for bopping around town, or maybe driving out to Cajun Country for Festival International de Louisiane (www.festivalinternational.com) in Lafayette. 'Festival' is the largest free francophone music festival in North America, and is held during the third weekend in April.

At the Fair Grounds

It takes a well-bred racehorse about two minutes to circumnavigate the Fair Grounds track, but the average human will require up to 10 minutes to get from

Clockwise from top left
1. Dancing up a storm to Cajun music
2. Rebirth Brass Band, Jazz Fest
3. It's not all jazz; Dave Grohl of the Foo Fighters

one stage to the next. The only way to get from stage to stage is to walk or half-jog through dense crowds and all kinds of tempting food stalls and vendors. Jazz Fest consists of a dozen performance tents:

➡ **Gospel Tent** A cherished chapel of earth-shaking live gospel music.

➡ **Jazz Tent** The lineup here leans more toward the contemporary side of things: Irvin Mayfield, Terence Blanchard, Ellis Marsalis and the like.

➡ **Jazz & Heritage Stage** Smaller stage where brass bands and the Mardi Gras Indians perform.

➡ **Economy Hall Tent** Stomp your feet to New Orleans 'trad' jazz with the likes of the Preservation Hall Jazz Band, Walter Payton and the Tremé Brass Band.

➡ **Lagniappe Stage** Varied entertainment. The stage's isolation from the rest of the Fair Grounds makes it ideal for intimate performances.

➡ **Blues Tent** Blues, R&B, funk and occasionally, some rock.

➡ **Fais Do Do Stage** Cajun and zydeco music is the emphasis at this always hopping stage.

➡ **Congo Square** This stage has become the venue for world acts from Africa and Latin America.

➡ **Acura Stage** Main stage where the biggest names appear.

➡ **Gentilly Stage** Secondary main stage.

➡ **Kids Tent** Children's music and family-friendly activities.

➡ **Food Demonstration Stage** Local live cooking lessons.

Food, Glorious Food

Jazz Fest is justifiably famous for its food stalls, many of which have cult followings. Some of the more popular Fest foods are fried soft-shell crab, Crawfish Monica (cream crawfish sauce over fusilli pasta), crawfish bread, *cochon de lait* (roast suckling pig), po'boys, spinach and artichoke casserole, Cuban sandwiches and Jamaican chicken. Of course, you'll also find jambalaya, red beans and fried catfish.

Faubourg Marigny & Bywater

Neighborhood Top Five

1 Wandering around **Frenchmen Street** (p88) starting at, say, 7pm, having dinner, listening to music, getting drunk, listening to more music, dancing a little bit, seeing who's playing on the corner of Chartres, scarfing some late-night tacos, then hey! More music!

2 Indulging in praline-coated bacon and a campfire-smoked steak with eggs for breakfast at **Elizabeth's** (p89).

3 Watching some hilarious improv comedy at the **New Movement Theater** (p94).

4 Watching music, from punk to bluegrass to hip-hop, on rapidly changing **St Claude Ave** (p94).

5 Lounging in your swimsuit, or in the buff, in the hot tub of the **Country Club** (p92).

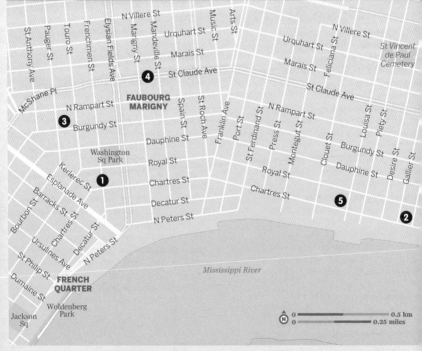

For more detail of the area, see Map p242 ➡

Explore Faubourg Marigny & Bywater

On your first day, wander around the Marigny by walking up Decatur St and onto Frenchmen St. Then head east along Royal St, taking in the architecture and sampling some of the local cafes and restaurants on the way. Your nighttime activity consists of heading back to Frenchmen St to either party, listen to music or both.

On the second day, either bike or drive out to the Bywater. Again, you'll want to just walk (or bike) around this compact neighborhood, eating, drinking and shopping wherever the spirit moves you. In the evening, head out to catch some shows along St Claude Ave, or see if there's anything interesting at one of the local theater companies.

Faubourg Marigny is bounded by Rampart St to the west, the railroad tracks at Press St to the east and Esplanade Ave to the south. The Bywater extends from Press to Poland St. St Claude Ave is the northern border of both neighborhoods, but as there are more and more places of interest opening north of St Claude, we include some of those spots as well. The southern boundary of the Bywater is easy to spot: it's the Mississippi River.

Local Life

⇒ **Music** It's everywhere! These neighborhoods have the best concentration of live music in the city, so enjoy this resource whenever you can.

⇒ **Theater** It takes plenty of forms here, from the brick-and-mortar playhouses such as the Shadowbox to the street theater of local artists putting on impromptu performances.

⇒ **Bars** Speaking of bars, there's a lot of them out this way, and each one has its own special character. Even if you're not big on drinking, rubbing shoulders with locals at spots like Markey's (p92) gets you under the skin of the city.

Getting There & Away

⇒ **Bus** Bus 5, which you can catch on Canal and Decatur Sts, runs up Decatur and onto Poydras and Dauphine into the heart of Marigny & Bywater.

⇒ **Car** Free street parking is quite plentiful in the Bywater, and only a little less common in Faubourg Marigny. There are no time restrictions, except on Esplanade Ave.

Lonely Planet's Top Tip

As you enter the Bywater on Chartres St, look towards the levee walls of the Mississippi River. By the time you read this, Crescent Park, a collection of green spaces and performance venues inspired by riverfront projects like San Francisco's Embarcadero, may already be compete. See www.reinventingthecrescent.org for more information.

Best Places to Eat
⇒ Bacchanal (p89)
⇒ Elizabeth's (p89)
⇒ Cake Café & Bakery (p89)
⇒ The Joint (p89)
⇒ Rampart Food Store (p89)

For reviews, see p88 ⇒

Best Places to Drink
⇒ Country Club (p92)
⇒ The John (p92)
⇒ Mimi's in the Marigny (p92)
⇒ R Bar (p92)
⇒ Lost Love (p92)

For reviews, see p92 ⇒

Best Places for Entertainment
⇒ Spotted Cat (p94)
⇒ Vaughan's (p95)
⇒ d.b.a. (p93)
⇒ Hi Ho Lounge (p93)
⇒ AllWays Lounge (p94)

For reviews, see p93 ⇒

FAUBOURG MARIGNY & BYWATER

◉ SIGHTS

FRENCHMEN STREET
STREET

Map p242 (From Esplanade Ave to Royal St) The 'locals Bourbon' is how Frenchmen is usually described to tourists who hate Bourbon and want to know where New Orleanians listen to music. Just toddle a little north of the Quarter here, where bars and clubs are arrayed back to back for several city blocks in what may well be the best concentration of live-music venues in the country. At night, Frenchmen becomes a carnival, as street performers and drunks occupy the street and random acts play in the grassy lot at the intersection of Frenchmen and Chartres Sts.

OLD NEW ORLEANS RUM DISTILLERY TOUR
DISTILLERY

off Map p242 (☎945-9400; www.neworleansrum.com; 2815 Frenchmen St; $10; ☉tours at noon, 2pm & 4pm Mon-Fri, 2pm & 4pm Sat) A short drive north of the Marigny is the Old New Orleans Rum distillery. Founded by local artist James Michalopoulos and his artist/musician friends, the distillery makes great spirits you'll find in most local bars. You can sample all of the delicious spirits, including a rare vintage unavailable outside the factory, on an entertaining 45-minute distillery tour; you may want to visit on a full stomach.

ST ROCH CEMETERY
CEMETERY

off Map p242 (☎945-9400; cnr St Roch Ave & N Roman St; ☉9am-4pm) One of New Orleans' more interesting cemeteries is a few blocks from Faubourg Marigny (driving is recommended). Named for St Roch, a semilegendary figure whose prayers supposedly averted the Black Death, the site became popular with New Orleans Catholics during yellow fever outbreaks. Walk through the necropolis to the 'relic room,' filled with ceramic body parts (ankles, heads, breasts), prosthetics, leg braces, crutches and false teeth; these are *ex-votos*, testaments to the healing power of St Roch. Marble floor tiles are inscribed with the words 'thanks' and '*merci*.'

MUSICIANS' VILLAGE
NEIGHBORHOOD

off Map p242 (www.nolamusiciansvillage.com; bounded by North Roman, Alvar & North Johnson Sts) North of the Bywater is this 8-acre tract of 72 houses, built primarily (but not exclusively) for musicians, a vital component of the city's cultural and economic landscape. The brightly painted homes look like skittles scattered over the cityscape. The centerpiece of the Village is the **Ellis Marsalis Center for Music** (http://ellis marsaliscenter.org; 901 Bartholomew St), where cultural events and seminars are held. A plea: this is a living neighborhood. Don't take pictures of village residents without asking permission.

WASHINGTON SQUARE PARK
PARK

Map p242 Also known as 'Marigny Green,' this park is a popular spot for locals to play with their dogs, toss Frisbees and, based on the frequent smell, smoke things that aren't cigarettes. There's a touching HIV/AIDS memorial on the northern side of the park.

PLESSY V FERGUSON PLAQUE
HISTORICAL SITE

Map p242 (cnr Press & Royal Sts) This plaque marks the site where African American Homer Plessy, in a carefully orchestrated act of civil disobedience, tried to board a whites-only train car. That action led to the 1896 Plessy vs Ferguson trial, which legalized segregation under the 'separate but equal' rationale. The plaque was unveiled by Keith Plessy and Phoebe Ferguson, descendants of the opposing parties in the original trial, now fast friends.

ACTIVITIES IN FAUBOURG MARIGNY & BYWATER

Our favorite bicycle tours in New Orleans are offered by **Confederacy of Cruisers** (☎400-5468; http://confed eracyofcruisers.com; tours from $45 per person), who set you up with cruiser bikes that come with fat tires and padded seats for Nola's flat, pot-holed roads. The main 'Creole New Orleans' tour takes in the best architecture of the Marigny, Bywater, Esplanade Ave and the Tremé. Confederacy also does a History of Drinking tour ($45, and you have to be 21 or over) and tasty culinary tour ($85).

EATING

The food cachet of the Marigny and Bywater is increasing by the month, and there's a general bohemian vibe and plethora of good cheap eats in this part of town.

THE LOWER NINTH WARD

The Lower Ninth Ward received the most media attention following Hurricane Katrina, even though neighborhoods such as Lakewood and Gentilly were similarly affected. Parts of the Lower Ninth remain pretty devastated, more wilderness than ruins. From the Bywater, drive a few minutes across the industrial canal on Claiborne or St Claude St and make your second left on Deslonde; you'll see a mix of empty lots and the architectural wonderland of LEED-Green-Building-certified homes built by Brad Pitt's **Make It Right Foundation** (http://makeitrightnola.org).

Roland Lewis, a Ninth Ward native and former streetcar worker and union rep, showcases the heritage of his home neighborhood in his actual home, which has been converted into the **House of Dance & Feathers** (957-2678; www.houseofdanceandfeathers.com; 1317 Tupleo St). This museum-turned-community-center brims with exhibits on Mardi Gras Indians, Social Aid and Pleasure Clubs, and is the gestalt of a unique American neighborhood. To get here you'll need a car; call Roland beforehand, as the museum is open by appointment only. Donate with generosity when you arrive.

Rather than just driving through the neighborhood or visiting via a tour bus, make an appointment with **Ninth Ward Rebirth Bike Tours** (909-9599; http://ninthward rebirthbiketours.com). These guys work closely with Lower Ninth Ward residents to provide a tour that is more of a dialogue between visitors and locals. Stops include local businesses and the House of Dance & Feathers.

TOP CHOICE BACCHANAL
WINE & CHEESE $$

Map p242 (948-9111; www.bacchanalwine.com; 600 Poland Ave; sandwiches $11, cheeses per piece from $5; 11am-11pm;) You may be surprised to hear one of the best eating experiences in New Orleans sits just across the water from the Lower Ninth Ward. From the outside, Bacchanal looks like a leaning Bywater shack; inside are racks of wine and sexily stinky cheese sold at just above retail. On many nights, musicians play in the garden, while cooks dispense delicious meals on paper plates from the kitchen in the back; on any given day you may try chorizo-stuffed dates or seared diver scallops that will blow your gastronomic mind.

TOP CHOICE ELIZABETH'S
AMERICAN $$$

Map p242 (944-9272; www.elizabeths-restaurant.com; 601 Gallier St; mains $11-28; 11am-2:30pm & 6-10pm Tue-Fri, 6-10pm Sat, 8am-2:30pm Sun) Elizabeth's is deceptively divey. But its food's as good as the best New Orleans chefs can offer. This is a quintessential New Orleans experience: all friendliness, smiling sass, weird artistic edges and overindulgence on the food front. Dinners can be as humble as beer-barbecued oysters or as refined as seared duck with port sherry. Brunch and breakfast are also top draws – the praline bacon is probably an utter sin to consume, but hey, consider us happily banished from the Garden.

THE JOINT
BARBECUE $

Map p242 (949-3232; www.alwayssmokin.com; 701 Mazant St; mains $7-17; 11:30am-2:30pm Mon & Tue, to 9pm Wed-Sat) The Joint's smoked pork has the olfactory effect of the Sirens' sweet song, pulling you, the proverbial traveling sailor, off course from your Ithaca into the gnashing rocks of savory meat-induced blissful death (classical Greek analogies ending *now*). Knock back some ribs or pulled pork or brisket with some sweet tea in the backyard garden and learn to love life.

RAMPART FOOD STORE
PO'BOYS $

Map p242 (1700 N Rampart St; po'boys under $10; 8am-8pm) This convenience store is so barren you'd think it was a front for something shady. It's run by Vietnamese immigrants; their English isn't great, but they know to call you 'baby' and how to make some of the best, most overstuffed po'boys in New Orleans.

CAKE CAFÉ & BAKERY
BREAKFAST $

Map p242 (943-0010; www.nolacakes.com; 2440 Chartres St; mains $10 & under; 7am-3pm) Come weekend mornings, the line is quite literally out the door here. Biscuits and gravy (topped with andouille), fried oysters and grits (seasonally available) and all the omelets are stand-outs. Lunch is great, too, as are the cakes (king cake!) whipped up in the back.

LATE NIGHT NOSH IN THE MARIGNY

This being New Orleans – city of music, 24-hour partying and good food – you would think that there would be some great late-night eating options on the city's major live music strip. This used to be the case when food trucks set up on Frenchmen, offering barbecue-food, tacos and po'boys, but sadly the city threw some bureaucratic roadblocks up, leaving us drunk revelers with hunger pangs.

Never fear: Lonely Planet is here. Here's where you can get good food late at night in the Marigny:

➡ **Café Negril** (p95) Delicious tacos ($2), tamales ($3) and burritos ($4), which you can take outside and snack on in the street. Serves until closing time, which is flexible and usually late – around 3am.

➡ **13 Monaghan** (p91) Need 24-hour vegetarian food? Bam! There's meat too, carnivores.

➡ **La Peniché** (p90) Serves 24-hour breakfast food. Enough said.

➡ **Buffa's** (p92) Bit of a walk from Frenchmen, but it's worth it for the cheeseburgers. Open 24 hours.

➡ **Gene's** (p92) If you're up on St Claude hit up this pink palace for a hot sausage po'boy, available 24 hours.

➡ **Angeli On Decatur** (p62) Pasta, pizza, burgers, salads and sandwiches, until 4am Friday and Saturday and 2am Sunday through Thursday. In the French Quarter, but just a short walk from Frenchmen St.

➡ **Wandering Buddha** (p90) In the Hi Ho Lounge; serves vegan Korean fare until midnight.

It's also worth noting that DIY caterers regularly risk the police and set up shop on Frenchmen, selling tacos, grilling steak sandwiches, burgers and hot dogs and providing all those other great, greasy things you need after a night out.

MAUREPAS FOODS   AMERICAN $$

Map p242 (☎267-0072; www.facebook.com/maurepasfoods; 3200 Burgundy St; mains $7-16; ⊗11am-midnight, closed Wed; ☌) Maurepas isn't your typical Bywater spot. It's got high ceilings, minimalist décor, polished floors and metal fixtures. And holy hell, is the food good! Try the organic chicken, market greens, grits and poached egg, all delicious. Vegetarians should snack on the soba noodles, and everyone should get drunk on the craft cocktails.

WANDERING BUDDHA   VEGETARIAN $

Map p242 (☎945-9428; www.wanderingbuddha.com; 2239 St Claude Ave; mains $10-11.75; ⊗5pm-midnight Tue-Sun; ☌) Located within the Hi Ho Lounge, the Buddha is one of the best vegetarian bets in New Orleans. The marinated tofu alone is reason to come; stay for the stir-fried rice cakes and chilled buckwheat noodles. We know vegetarians are stereotypically non-violent, but we've seen people fight for the last bits of kimchi.

SATSUMA   HEALTH FOOD $

Map p242 (☎304-5962; www.satsumacafe.com; 3218 Dauphine St; breakfast & lunch under $10, dinner mains $8-16; ⊗7:30am-5pm & 6-10pm; ☌) God, is this place *cute*. With its chalkboard menu of organic soups and sandwiches, Mediterranean-inspired salads, pasta, seafood and lamb, ginger limeade (seriously, this drink on a hot day – heaven), graphic/pop art–decorated walls and *lots* of Macbooks, it's like the cute hipster with thick eyeglass frames you've secretly had a crush on given restaurant form. The fact members of said subculture, plus young parents and local artists, are largely the clientele of this place confirms: the Bywater might become Brooklyn.

LA PENICHÉ   AMERICAN $

Map p242 (1940 Dauphine St; mains $6-14; ⊗24hr Thu-Tue) La Peniché is open 24 hours, and tends to get interesting later on when night owls, club-hoppers, drag queens and insomniacs (you know, interesting folks) file through its doors for fried seafood and delicious breakfast.

SUIS GENERIS
FUSION **$**

Map p242 (☑309-7850; www.suisgeneris.com; 3200 Burgundy St; mains $7.50-8.50; ☺10am-3pm Sat & Sun, 6pm-11pm Wed-Sun; ☑) Punky bartenders and serving staff are offset by slick molded furniture and quirky concoctions like redfish with a pistachio crust and Brazilian meat pies. Thursday is South of the Border Fantasia – that means yummy tacos, folks.

MOJITO'S
CARIBBEAN **$$**

Map p242 (☑252-4800; www.mojitosnola.com; 437 Esplanade Ave; mains $15-22; ☺4pm-1am Mon-Thu, until 2am Fri, 11am-late Sat & Sun) As you may have deduced from the name, Mojito's is the kind of place that specializes in rum and rum drinks, which just feels like a damn good idea given the huge outdoor courtyard, where live music often plays on a sultry evening. The food's a treat – jalapeno cheese grits and shrimp, and braised Cuban short ribs add that right Caribbean kick.

SCHIRO'S CAFÉ/LITTLE JULIE'S INDIA KITCHEN
DINER, INDIAN **$**

Map p242 (☑944-6666; www.schiroscafe.com; 2483 Royal St; mains $5-16; ☺9am-10pm Mon-Sat; ☑) Yes, you read it right: diner *and* Indian. One menu at Schiro's is typical New Orleanian greasy spoon, offering po'boys, blackened catfish, hushpuppies and gumbo; the other serves *saag paneer* (spinach curry with un-aged cheese), *tikka masala* and vindaloo. Oh, and the other part of the business? A launderette, naturally.

STELLA!

Tennessee Williams fans, listen up. The home at the center of *A Streetcar Named Desire* is, according to local legend, the red house on the corner of Elysian Fields Ave and Dauphine St (Map p242). Please note that it's a private home, so take your picture and move on, and save the 'Stella!' screams for the Tennessee Williams festival in late March (see p21).

If you ever wondered where the title for that iconic play comes from, yes, it does allude to the 'desire' that rips apart the lives of the main characters; but it's also a literal reference to the old Desire streetcar line that once ran up Elysian Fields Ave.

ADOLFO'S
ITALIAN **$$**

Map p242 (☑948-3800; 611 Frenchmen St; mains $8-20; ☺6-11pm Mon-Sat) If you take a date to this intimate Italian cubby squeezed on top of a jazz club (the Apple Barrel; see p95) and get nowhere afterwards, they were too hard to please. Adolfo's is as romantic as hell and the food isn't bad either, all working-class Italian-Americano fare with some requisite New Orleans zing. Cheap reds by the carafe emerge from the kitchen and raise a diner's spirits, and if they don't, go back to your little black book.

LOST LOVE
VIETNAMESE **$**

Map p242 (2529 Dauphine St; mains under $10; ☺kitchen 11am-5pm Mon-Thu, until 1am Fri & Sat, until midnight Sun) This divey neighborhood bar also has a Vietnamese kitchen in the back serving up great pho, *banh mi* (Vietnamese po'boy) and spring rolls. Just be aware the atmosphere isn't standard Vietnamese-American dive (formica, old Republic flag, karaoke); this place is more of a neighborhood bar/inked-up smoky hideaway.

FATOUSH
MEDITERRANEAN **$**

Map p242 (☑371-5074; 2372 St Claude Ave; mains under $10; ☺8am-10pm; ☑☎) Located in a vibrantly purple building next to the Healing Center (p96), Fatoush whips up Mediterranean fare with a focus on Middle Eastern staples: quality falafel, kebab and fresh salads, plus screamingly good squeezed juices.

13 MONAGHAN
DINER **$**

Map p242 (☑942-1345; www.13monaghan.com; 517 Frenchmen St; mains under $11; ☺11am-4pm; ☑) '13', as it's usually called, is a diner with a twist: much of its delicious greasy-spoon fare is actually vegetarian. A Philly cheese-steak, for example, comes with portabello mushrooms or tofu instead of beef. There's also a meat version, plus great pizza and other diner classics.

PRALINE CONNECTION
SOUL FOOD **$$**

Map p242 (☑943-3934; 542 Frenchmen St; mains $13-20; ☺11am-10:30pm Sun-Thu, to midnight Fri & Sat) If you've never had soul food before, the PC might blow you away, but connoisseurs of the genre may find this popular tour-group stop middling. The food is pretty good, in a mom's-kitchen kind of way – standbys are of the meat-loaf, fried-chicken and étouffée school of cooking – but this restaurant hovers in that frustrating space between 'meh' and 'wow.'

GENE'S
PO'BOYS **$**

Map p242 (☏943-3861; 1040 Elysian Fields Ave; po'boys $7; ☺24hr) It's hard to miss Gene's: with its pink and yellow exterior, it's one of the most vividly painted buildings on Elysian Fields Ave. The hot sausage po'boy with cheese, and the fact it is served 24/7 with a free drink, is the reason you come here.

MARDI GRAS WORLD
GROCERIES **$**

Map p242 (2706 Royal St; po'boys around $8; ☺24hr) This unexpectedly huge neighborhood grocery store/emporium of weird stuff – Mardi Gras beads (yes) and camping equipment (?) – has a good hot-food stand that's open until midnight, and high-end groceries for sale all night.

🍷 DRINKING & NIGHTLIFE

Music listings follow in the Entertainment section.

TOP CHOICE MIMI'S IN THE MARIGNY
BAR

Map p242 (Royal St; ☺5pm-late) The name of this neighborhood bar could justifiably change to 'Mimi's *is* the Marigny'; we can't imagine the neighborhood without this institution, and we don't think its army of loyal patrons would ever want to consider such a horrifying possibility. Mimi's is as attractively disheveled as Brad Pitt on a good day, all comfy furniture, pool tables, an upstairs dance hall decorated like a Creole mansion gone punk, and dim, brown lighting like a fantasy in sepia. Everyone knows your name, and very likely what your next drink will be.

TOP CHOICE COUNTRY CLUB
BAR

Map p242 (www.thecountryclubneworleans.com; 634 Louisa St; ☺bar 10am-1am, restaurant 11am-9pm) In a city of unexpected surprises, the Country Club is the ultimate island of Serendib (that's the old name for Sri Lanka, which when unexpectedly discovered became the root of the word 'Serendipity' – feel free to use in a pub quiz!). From the front, it's a well-decorated Bywater house. Walk inside and there's a restaurant serving

pizza, salads and New Orleans standbys, a sauna (!), a leafy patio with bar, heated outdoor pool and 25ft projector screen (!!), a hot tub (!!!), all clothing optional (!!!!). There's a $10 towel rental fee if you want to hang in the pool area, a popular carousing spot for the gay and lesbian community (all sexualities welcome).

TOP CHOICE R BAR
BAR

Map p242 (1431 Royal St; ☺3pm-late) 'Look man,' an R Bar customer explains, 'I seen one guy get kicked out here. After 14 years of living in this city: one guy. I mean, you could get up on that bar and [expletive] and these cats would probably let you stay. Probably.' But why try to get kicked out of the bar named for R (Royal St)? Where a beer and a shot costs a few bucks, the pool tables constantly crack, the jukebox is great and you can get a haircut on Mondays for $10.

THE JOHN
DIVE

Map p242 (2040 Burgundy St; ☺6pm-late) The clever name comes courtesy of the toilet bowl seats and tables arrayed around an otherwise pretty open interior space. The *extremely* strong drinks come courtesy of friendly bartenders, who serve them in mason jars – bonus. An excellent spot to start a Frenchmen St bar crawl.

LOST LOVE
DIVE

Map p242 (2529 Dauphine St; ☺5pm-late) Dark, smoky and sexy, the Lost Love is that vampy Marigny girl or moody artist your momma told you to stay away from, mixed with a bit of blue-collar dive sensibility. Don't listen to her. The drinks are cheap, the pours are strong, there's regular karaoke, they show HBO shows on a projector and there's an excellent Vietnamese kitchen in the back.

MARKEY'S
BAR

Map p242 (640 Louisa St; ☺2pm-2am) Markey's stands out for two reasons: its barn-red exterior, and the fact that it is a straight-up good neighborhood hangout. There's shuffleboard, cheap beer, sports on the TV and an excellent jukebox. Score.

BUFFA'S
BAR

Map p242 (www.buffasbar.com; 1001 Esplanade Ave; ☺24hr) Buffa's wears a lot of hats. First and foremost it's a neighborhood bar with a backroom stage that hosts the occasional band, quiz night, open mic and TV/movie screening. Second, it's a 24-hour spot that serves one of the best damn cheeseburgers in town. What's not to love?

WHO DAT COFFEE CAFE
CAFE $

Map p242 (2401 Burgundy St; coffees & pastries $3-5; ⊗7am-10pm; 🖋🛜) A supremely comfortable coffee shop, the Who Dat has good pastries, better sandwiches, lovely coffee and cupcakes, many baked with a bit of booze.

ORANGE COUCH
CAFE $

Map p242 (2339 Royal St; coffees & pastries $3; ⊗7am-10pm; 🛜) An icebox-cool cafe, all Ikea-esque furniture, polished stone flooring, local artwork and photography on the walls, graffitied restrooms and, yes, an orange leather couch in the midst of it all. Very Marigny, the sort of place where a tattooed attorney takes out a Mac and a tort law manual and cracks away for hours.

FLORA GALLERY & COFFEE SHOP
CAFE $

Map p242 (2600 Royal St; coffees & pastries $3-5; ⊗6:30am-midnight; 🖋🛜) Flora is almost the perfect New Orleans cafe. If you could smoke inside, as in the old days, it'd be 10 out of 10. No offense nonsmokers, but it's just the sort of place – madcap art, antique-store furniture, lush gardens and a Parisian bohemian atmosphere – that demands the accompaniment of clouds of tobacco smoke. Alas, the latter isn't there, but for the majority of you readers, that only makes Flora better.

ST ROCH TAVERN
DIVE

Map p242 (1200 St Roch Ave; ⊗5pm-late) First: if you don't like smoke, don't come here. The cigarette cloud hits you like a foggy brick when you open the door. If you *do* like white crust-punks with face tattoos and African American locals from around the way, and the weird synergy that occurs when these two cultures mix (they generally don't in New Orleans), come by. Hosts crazy, sweaty bounce parties on Saturday nights. Not a place to wear the suit and tie.

BIG DADDY'S BAR
BAR

Map p242 (2513 Royal St; ⊗4pm-2am) If it's too crowded at across-the-street Mimi's, or if you're gay and tired of the *thumpa-thumpa-bass* queer scene on Bourbon, head to this friendly 'gayborhood' bar, a quiet spot where all sexualities are welcome for friendly banter and cheap drinks.

YUKI IZAKAYA
LOUNGE

Map p242 (525 Frenchmen St; ⊗5pm-3am) If you want a clean feeling in the morning after a night on the town, order off the extensive sake menu at Yuki. As you sip your rice wine, chill out to house/lounge music and achieve hipster Zen watching subtitled Japanese art-house flicks projected onto the walls.

⭐ ENTERTAINMENT

[TOP CHOICE] HI HO LOUNGE
LIVE MUSIC

Map p242 (📞945-4446; www.hiholounge.net; 2239 St Claude Ave; ⊗5pm-late) This is one of the best bars in town on Monday nights, when a very friendly bluegrass jam session goes from 8pm to 10pm; some mandolin music and the $1 red beans and rice are the ingredients of New Orleans nirvana. Alt-country, folk, rock, punk, brass bands and Mardi Gras Indians regularly take the stage other nights of the week. When the music isn't playing, the Hi Ho is simply a great neighborhood bar.

[TOP CHOICE] D.B.A.
LIVE MUSIC

Map p242 (📞942-3731; http://dbabars.com/dbano; 618 Frenchmen St; ⊗5pm-4am; 🛜) Swank d.b.a. consistently schedules some of the best live music in town. Listening to John Boutté's sweet tenor, which sounds like birds making love on the Mississippi, is one of the best beginnings to a Saturday night in New Orleans. Then there's

---

MOD DANCE PARTY!

New Orleans is the kind of town where the young fall in love with the old school. A good example of this phenomenon is the Mod Dance Party, a celebration of pure vinyl joy, including soul, funk, R&B, Motown classics, New Orleans, Detroit, Merseybeat and anything else from the era of beehive hairdos and heavy eyeliner. There's a good mix of ages and a lot of smiling and grooving going on at this shindig, which is usually held at the Saturn Bar on weekends. Search out Mod Dance Party New Orleans on Facebook for an updated schedule.

THE ST CLAUDE SHUFFLE

St Claude isn't the city's prettiest roadway, to be sure, but the stretch of the avenue between Touro and Mandeville St has become the hot new live music strip in New Orleans. If you want a night out with all locals and good music, head up here and check out the Hi Ho Lounge or any of these great venues:

AllWays Lounge (Map p242; ☑218-5778; http://theallwayslounge.net; 2240 St Claude Ave; ⊗6pm-midnight Tue-Sun, until 2am Fri & Sat) In a city full of funky music venues, the AllWays stands out as one of the funkiest. On any given night of the week you may see experimental guitar, local theater, thrashy rock or a '60s-inspired shagadelic dance party. Also: the drinks are super cheap.

Siberia (Map p242; ☑265-8855; www.siberianola.com; 2227 St Claude Ave; ⊗4pm-late) There's always an interesting crowd of inked-up punks, sensitive hipsters and hoodie-clad hardcores (or wanna-be hardcores) in Siberia, which hosts everything from punk rock to singer-songwriter nights to heavy metal to bounce shows.

Kajun's Pub (Map p242; 2256 St Claude Ave; ⊗24hr) Kajun's is a guarantee for a good cast of characters. We suppose this bar is technically a live music venue too...if you count karaoke as live music. Whatever; the karaoke is awesome (sometimes awesomely bad) and the beer flows 24/7.

Sweet Lorraine's (Map p242; ☑945-9654; www.sweetlorrainesjazzclub.com; 1931 St Claude Ave; ⊗5pm-late Tue-Sat, 11am-3pm Sun) A neighborhood jazz club where you can hear good 'trad jazz' and contemporary grooves. Thursday night is blues night with Chucky C and Clearly Blue, while on Sunday, Lorraine's hosts a delicious jazz brunch with Danon Smith.

If you're hungry after all this, grab a spicy hot sausage po'boy at **Gene's** (Map p242; 1040 Elysian Fields; ⊗24hr); the oddly pink exterior conceals a scruffy interior and tasty sandwiches. Finally, don't wander north of St Claude on foot; that area was infamous for crime at the time of writing.

Wednesday with the Tin Men and Washboard Chaz, a man who demonstrates how a breastplate and two spoons can be the groundwork for Mozart-level musical genius. Plus, they have an amazing beer selection. Seriously d.b.a., you freaking *win*. Gigs usually start at 7pm, 10pm and 2am.

TOP CHOICE SNUG HARBOR LIVE MUSIC

Map p242 (☑949-0696; www.snugjazz.com; 626 Frenchmen St; cover $5-25; ⊗5pm-midnight) There might be bigger venues but overall Snug Harbor is the best jazz club in the city. That's partly because it usually hosts doubleheaders, giving you a good dose of variety, and partly because the talent is kept to an admirable mix of reliable legends and hot up-and-comers; in the course of one night you'll likely witness both. Plus, the acoustics and sight lines in this spot are superb. Charmaine Neville and Ellis Marsalis are regular acts.

TOP CHOICE NEW MOVEMENT THEATER THEATER

Map p242 (☑302-8264; www.newmovement theater.com; 1919 Burgundy St) We're gonna be honest: improv theater, by its nature, can be hit or miss. The best sort hits more than half the time; the New Movement, we can happily report, hits well above this average. The company has a cast of regular players from around the way and a stable schedule of classes that train new talent in the art of off-the-cuff comedy. The theater hosts regular shows on the weekends, usually around 9pm; check the website for details.

SPOTTED CAT LIVE MUSIC

Map p242 (☑943-3887; http://spottedcatmus icclub.com; 626 Frenchmen St; ⊗6pm-late) It's good the Spotted Cat is across the street from Snug Harbor. They're both great jazz clubs, but where the latter is a swish, non-smoking martini sorta spot, the former is a smoky, thumping sweatbox where drinks are served in plastic cups. They're both wonderful venues; hit up Snug when you want to get dressed up under mood lighting, and the Cat when you want to dance to Dixieland with a bunch of flushed drunks.

VAUGHAN'S
DIVE, LIVE MUSIC

Map p242 (☏947-5562; 800 Lesseps St; cover $7-15; ⏰11am-3am daily, shows 11pm Thu) On most nights of the week this is a Bywater dive, but Thursday is when Kermit Ruffins, the trumpet-playing king of New Orleans, brings the house, the neighborhood and likely a surrounding 10-mile radius *down*. This is a great show, but it gets crowded and hot, so be warned. In between sets Kermit himself dishes out red beans and jokes. He might even share some of his smokes with you.

SATURN BAR
DIVE, LIVE MUSIC

Map p242 (☏949-7532; 3067 St Claude Ave; ⏰7pm-2am) In the solar system of New Orleans bars, Saturn is planet punk. Originally it was an eclectic neighborhood bar where a crew of regulars appreciated, in an unironic way, the outsider art and leopard-skin furniture and a general, genuinely unique aesthetic. Then the navies of the skinny-jean empire began the colonization process. Today the Bywater community, punk scene and hipster enclaves are united by neon-lighting fixtures, flashy gambling machines and great live music, primarily of the rock/punk school.

CHECKPOINT CHARLIE
LIVE MUSIC

Map p242 (☏281-4847; 501 Esplanade Ave; ⏰24hr) Charlie's is so grungy it could start a band in early '90s Seattle. Acts you've likely never heard of (plus some you probably know) tromp through the stage, playing a mix of rock, metal and punk, most of it very good.

MAISON
LIVE MUSIC

Map p242 (☏371-5543; www.maisonfrenchmen.com; 508 Frenchmen St; ⏰5pm-late) With three stages, a kitchen and a decent bar, Maison is one of the more eclectic performance spaces on Frenchmen St. On any given night you may be hearing Latin rumba in one hour, indie rock in another and Nola brass to round the evening out.

THREE MUSES
LIVE MUSIC

Map p242 (☏252-4801; www.thethreemuses.com; 536 Frenchmen St; ⏰4pm-late Wed-Mon) This excellent nonsmoking restaurant hosts jazz every night it's open, and the incomparable Glen David Andrews is a regular performer. It's perfect for a night when you need to combine good food and music loud enough to enjoy, but soft enough to keep your ears from bleeding.

CAFÉ NEGRIL
LIVE MUSIC

Map p242 (☏944-4744; 606 Frenchmen St; ⏰6pm-late) When you spin the Frenchmen St musical wheel, Negril is the reggae-blues-Latin-world music stop. So if you're craving that sort of groove, and the dancing that goes with it (this is definitely one of the 'dancier' clubs on Frenchmen), roll on in.

APPLE BARREL
LIVE MUSIC

Map p242 (☏949-9399; 609 Frenchmen St; ⏰5pm-late) The Barrel is roughly the size of its namesake: you can maybe fit a dozen customers in here without going elbow to elbow. It fits in musicians, too, who tend to play some very fine jazz, blues and folk.

SHADOWBOX THEATRE
THEATER

Map p242 (☏298-8676; http://theshadowbox theatre.com; 2400 St Claude Ave) This small

THE NEW ORLEANS CENTER FOR CREATIVE ARTS

New Orleans, like few American cities of its size, lives and dies by its arts scene. This is a city unapologetically in love with (and largely built on) the work of its musicians, painters and writers, and many of the next generation of artists are educated at the **New Orleans Center for Creative Arts** (Nocca; Map p242; ☏940-2787; www.nocca.com; 2800 Chartres St). Admission to this prestigious center, one of the best arts schools in the USA, is by audition only. If accepted, students (who are concurrently enrolled in their normal schools) specialize in fields ranging from the visual arts and creative writing to dance and cooking, instructed by artists at the top of their craft. The school can't be missed; the distinctive campus, itself an expression of architectural form and fancy, is located just by the tracks that separate the Marigny from the Bywater. As it is a school, Nocca understandably isn't open to visitors 24/7, but there's a heavy theater, dance, gallery display and reading schedule; check the website for details.

theater regularly features plays written and performed by local New Orleanians, as well as established shows from outside the city, plus events like poetry slams. There's an indie flavor to what's on offer, and the cozy atmosphere you get from witnessing a community of like-minded artists perform together.

MIMI'S IN THE MARIGNY LIVE MUSIC, CLUB

Map p242 (☑872-9868; www.miminsinthe marigny.net; 2601 Royal St; ☺4pm-late) Mimi's hosts regular DJs, bands and dance parties in its upstairs room. Our favorite semi-regular party, held every other Friday, is Alligator Chomp! Chomp!, a celebration of the music of the Gulf states (Louisiana, Mississippi, Alabama and Texas), from zydeco to funk to Tex-Mex to brass.

MUDLARK THEATRE THEATER

Map p242 (1200 Port St) In old English slang, 'mudlarks' were orphans, which sets an appropriate tone for this cast of punky bohemians and their theater of fantasy. Surreal giant puppets adorn the walls (seeing them is worth the visit alone) and edgy performers take the stage – on our last visit we saw some queer-radical spoken word followed by street performers from Philadelphia. No website or phone given, but search on facebook for Mudlark Public Theatre for a performance schedule.

BJ'S LIVE MUSIC

Map p242 (4301 Burgundy; ☺5pm-late) This Bywater dive attracts a good crowd from the surrounding neighborhood for occasional live sets, especially the Monday weekly blues-rock show by King James & the Special Men, which starts around 10pm.

DRAGON'S DEN CLUB

Map p242 (☑949-1750; www.myspace.com/drag onsdennola; 435 Esplanade Ave; cover $5-10; ☺shows start around 9pm) When it comes to rock, ska, punk, drum-and-bass, dubstep and hip-hop, the Den consistently hosts some of the best acts in New Orleans.

HEALING CENTRAL

One of the surest signs of change along once-dilapidated St Claude Ave is the bright orange facade of the **Healing Center** (Map p242; 2372 St Claude Ave; http://newor leanshealingcenter.org), a sort of mall for all things New Age, full of shops whose owners would likely murder us for comparing them to a mall if they weren't all non-violence practitioners.

Sorry, we don't mean to be cute. This is a place in touch with its chakras and proud of it. You enter and look upon mandalas drawn upon the floor and rotating artwork ranging from modern sculpture to paintings of Hindu gods and goddesses. Then take your pick of macrobiotic life experiences. Call ahead for hours if they're not listed:

Crossroads Arts Bazaar (☑343-4084) A community arts fair of locally made painting, sculpture, crafts, costumes and masks.

Wild Lotus Yoga (☑899-0047) Widely considered one of the best and friendliest yoga studios in town.

New Orleans Food Co-op (☺9am-9pm) The healthiest store in town, specializing in localvore and organic groceries.

Café Istanbul (www.cafeistanbulnola.com) Multi-functional arts space that regularly hosts musicians, poets, dance recitals and movie screenings.

Maple Street Book Shop (www.maplestreetbookshop.com; ☺10am-6pm Mon, Tue & Fri, until 8pm Wed & Thu) Another outpost of the best indie bookshop in town.

Island of Salvation Botanica (☺10am-5pm Tue-Sat) Run by wonderfully genial owners who sell vodoo spells, cards, spell components and the like for serious practitioners of the faith.

There's plenty more to discover inside, including a cast of alternative-medicine practitioners who rotate in and out of the center's studio spaces. Offices for various New Orleans NGOs can be found on the 2nd floor of the center.

BLUE NILE
CLUB

Map p242 (☎948-2583; www.bluenilelive.com; 532 Frenchmen St; ☺6pm until close) Hip-hop, reggae, jazz, soul and funk are the live music staples in the downstairs section of the Nile. Things get pretty sweaty, sensual and meat-markety in the upstairs balcony room, with its dedicated dance floor, as the night goes on.

🔒 SHOPPING

TOP CHOICE FAUBOURG MARIGNY
BOOK STORE
BOOKS

Map p242 (☎947-3700; 600 Frenchmen St; ☺noon-10pm) The South's oldest gay bookstore is a ramshackle, intellectual spot, and a good place to pick up local 'zines and catch up on the New Orleans scene, gay or otherwise. Look for the subtle (enormous) rainbow flag.

TOP CHOICE EUCLID RECORDS
MUSIC

Map p242 (☎9487-4348; www.euclidnola.com; 3401 Chartres St; ☺11am-7pm Mon-Sat, noon-6pm Sun) New Orleans is the kind of town that deserves really cool record shops, and Euclid is happy to oblige. It's got all the ingredients: racks of rare vinyl, old concert posters, a knowledgeable staff that looks plucked from a Nick Hornby novel (except they're all friendly, eschewing the music-snob stereotype) and a board listing whatever live music you should see while in town.

BYWATER BARGAIN CENTER
ANTIQUES

Map p242 (☎948-0007; 3200 Dauphine St; ☺11am-6pm) Tucked away in the Bywater, this emporium is a treasure trove of, well, treasures, if you follow the old adage that one man's junk is another's...you know. There found objects, old door frames and random bits and bobs on the one hand, and handmade crafts, plaster alligators playing zydeco and lord knows what else on the other. Most impressive is a collection of Mexican folk art, including Oaxacan sculpture, bright masks and some Dia del Muerte paraphernalia.

DR BOB'S STUDIO
ART

Map p242 (☎945-2225; 3027 Chartres St; ☺call ahead) Self-taught outdoors artist Dr Bob is a fixture in the Bywater, and you're sure to recognize his signature work – the 'Be Nice or Leave' signs that appear in restaurants and bars around town. Garbage-can lids, bottle caps, trashed musical instruments and essentially anything that strikes Dr Bob's interest is turned into art. His gallery is really a fascinating junkyard of art, with a sculpture garden comprising spray-painted lawn ornaments. The man himself is a character (he is not, to put it lightly, politically correct) and not always in – call ahead.

NEW ORLEANS ART SUPPLY
ART SUPPLIES

Map p242 (☎949-1525; www.art-restoration.com /noas/index.htm; 3620 Royal St; ☺10am-5pm Mon-Fri) If you're one who likes to sketch while traveling, here's a good place to go for a fresh supply of pencils, paint and pads. The selection is very high quality. The shop is an annex of the New Orleans Conservation Guild.

GREEN PROJECT
SUSTAINABLE GOODS

Map p242 (☎945-0240; 2831 Marais St; ☺9am-5pm) You probably don't need salvaged building materials if you're visiting New Orleans, but you should still stop by this wonderful store to see what a good business can do for its community. The Green Project sells salvaged building material at extremely cut-rate costs to New Orleanians, providing cheap housing supplies that also preserve the unique architectural facade of the city. It also runs a recycling center, donates paints and art supplies to schools and artists, plants community gardens, runs garden workshops and does outreach in surrounding neighborhoods.

ELECTRIC LADYLAND
TATTOOS

Map p242 (☎947-8286; 610 Frenchmen St; ☺noon- midnight, 1-9pm Sun) New Orleans is an old port filled with bars, right? Then a tattoo is just about the coolest souvenir you can get here. This is a clean, brightly lit spot that also happens to be a bit of an informal community center with the inked crowd.

CBD & Warehouse District

Neighborhood Top Five

1 Immersing yourself in the dramatic sights and sounds of WWII at the **National WWII Museum** (p100) with oral histories, wall-sized photos, a multi-sensory 4-D movie and a 1940s-style meal.

2 Soaking up the atmosphere at the **Ogden Museum of Southern**

Art (p101), then strolling gallery-lined Julia St (p104).

3 Animal-watching at the **Aquarium of the Americas** (p103) and the **Butterfly Garden & Insectarium** (p103).

4 Living the highlife at the **Roosevelt New Orleans Hotel** (p180) with dinner at Domenica (p107) and a

nightcap at the Sazerac Bar (p109).

5 **Bar-hopping** (p109) in the Warehouse District on S Peters St and Fulton St.

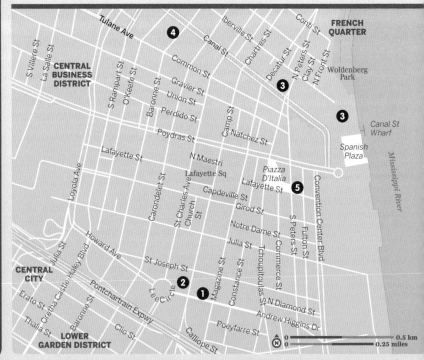

For more detail of the area, see Map p244 ➡

Explore CBD & Warehouse District

The Central Business District (CBD) stretches from the I-10 and the Superdome to the river and is bordered by Iberville St (just beyond Canal St) and the elevated I-90. Poydras St runs through the heart of the district, from the river to beyond the Superdome. The Warehouse District and Lafayette Square are two neighborhoods within the CBD.

In this chapter, the CBD is the downtown area that runs from the Superdome to St Charles Ave, with a small sliver above Poydras St that extends beyond St Charles to the river. The neighborhood features posh hotels, the Superdome, the Audubon museums and Harrah's casino, and is easily walkable.

On your first morning, eat breakfast at Mother's or Le Pavillon before visiting the Audubon Aquarium and nearby Butterfly Garden & Insectarium. Later, catch a game at the Superdome or take a river cruise on the Mississippi. End with a cocktail at one the CBD's many hotel bars. The French Quarter, just across Canal St, is within easy walking distance too.

Spend your second day in the Warehouse District, bounded by the I-90, St Charles Ave, Poydras St and the river. The WWII Museum, the Ogden Museum of Southern Art and the Civil War Museum are clustered near Lee Circle. Grab lunch at the American Sector or Cochon Butcher, then visit the Julia St galleries.

Restaurants, bars and live music are the draw in the evening. Walk along Fulton St, S Peters St or Tchoupitoulas St to find the action.

Local Life

➡ **Live Music** It's an easy walk from Howlin' Wolf (p111) to Republic (p111).

➡ **Lunch Deals** The city's nicest restaurants often serve affordable lunches. Enjoy top chefs at Herbsaint (p106), Drago's (p108) and Emeril's (p109).

➡ **Hangouts** Shoot the breeze at Cochon Butcher (p106) or catch a game and sip brews at Rusty Nail (p109).

Getting There & Away

➡ **Car** From the airport, most hotels are easily accessible off the elevated I-90. Cars coming in from the east should exit off the I-10.

➡ **Taxi/shuttle** A cab from Louis Armstrong airport to the CBD costs $33 for one or two people. Shuttles cost $20 per person one-way.

➡ **Train** The Amtrak station borders Loyola Ave near the Superdome. A new streetcar line should open by the end of 2012, running from the station to Canal St.

Lonely Planet's Top Tip

Canal St separates the French Quarter from the CBD. If you want to be near, but not in, the Bourbon St craziness, book a hotel room in the CBD. Walking just two or three extra blocks will bring quieter streets and hotels.

✖ Best Places to Eat

➡ Cochon Butcher (p106)
➡ Cochon (p107)
➡ Herbsaint (p106)
➡ Restaurant August (p107)
➡ American Sector (p108)

For reviews, see p106 ➡

☗ Best Places to Drink

➡ Rusty Nail (p109)
➡ Lucy's Retired Surfers Bar (p109)
➡ Swizzle Stick Bar (p109)
➡ Sazerac Bar (p109)
➡ Loa (p110)

For reviews, see p109 ➡

☖ Best Places to Shop

➡ New Orleans School of Glassworks & Printmaking Studio (p104)
➡ Center for Southern Craft & Design (p101)
➡ Crescent City Cooks (p112)
➡ The Flea Market at the Butterfly Garden & Insectarium (p103)
➡ Meyer the Hatter (p112)

For reviews, see p111 ➡

The National WWII Museum drops you into the action. Wall-sized photographs capture the confusion of Omaha Beach. Major Dick Winters, of Band of Brothers fame, describes his parachute drop behind enemy lines in a riveting oral history. A German Enigma machine highlights the complexities of subterfuge and code-breaking. It's exhibits like these that make this grand facility so engaging; artifacts and battle strategies are humanized through personal recollections, vivid quotes and heat-of-the-battle images.

The museum, which opened in 2000 as the National D-Day Museum, became America's National WWII Museum after a Congressional designation. How did this fascinating place land in New Orleans instead of Washington, DC? The reconstructed LCVP or 'Higgins boat,' on display in the Louisiana Pavilion, provides the link. Originally designed by local entrepreneur Andrew Jackson Higgins for commercial use on Louisiana's bayous, these flat-bottomed amphibious landing craft were instrumental in moving tens of thousands of soldiers onto Normandy's beaches during the D-Day invasion on June 6, 1944.

The Louisiana Pavilion holds four exhibit galleries: *The Home Front*, *Planning for D-Day*, *The D-Day Beaches* and *The D-Day Invasion in the Pacific*. Large artifacts, including a restored Boeing B-17 bomber, are visible from catwalks in the US Freedom Pavilion: The Boeing Center (set to open in November 2012). Here you can enjoy an immersive submarine experience inspired by the last patrol of the USS *Tang*. Across the street, the movie *Beyond all Boundaries* takes a 4-D look at America's involvement in the war – from Pearl Harbor to final victory – on a 120ft-wide screen. Get ready for rumbling seats and a dusting of snowflakes! End your explorations with a crab-meat pie and apple honey soda in John Besh's upbeat Americana diner, the America Sector.

DON'T MISS

- Louisiana Pavilion
- US Freedom Pavilion
- Beyond All Boundaries
- American Sector

PRACTICALITIES

- Map p244
- ☑528-1944
- www.nationalww2 museum.org
- 945 Magazine St (Entrance on Andrew Higgins)
- adult/child/senior $19/9/15, with movie $24/12/19
- ⊙9am-5pm; movie times vary

TOP SIGHTS
OGDEN MUSEUM OF SOUTHERN ART

The Ogden Museum sits just a few steps away from the Civil War Museum and the city's iconic statue of Robert E Lee, but this vibrant collection of Southern art is certainly not stuck in the past. It's one of the most engaging museums in New Orleans, managing to be beautiful, educational and unpretentious all at once.

The collection got its start more than 30 years ago when Roger Ogden and his father began purchasing art as gifts for Roger's mother. Ogden soon became a passionate collector and by the 1990s the New Orleans entrepreneur had assembled one of the finest collections of Southern art anywhere – one that was far too large to keep to himself. Today his namesake museum and its galleries hold pieces that range from impressionist landscapes and outsider folk-art to contemporary installation work.

The glass-and-stone Stephen Goldring Hall, with its soaring atrium, provides an inspiring welcome to the grounds. The building, which opened in 2003, is home to the museum's 20th- and 21st-century exhibitions as well as the Museum Store and its Center for Southern Craft & Design. 'Floating' stairs between floors will lead you to select pieces from regional artists as well as Southern landscapes, ceramics, glasswork and eye-catching works from self-taught artists. The Ogden's 18th-, 19th- and early-20th-century collections will be showcased in the Patrick F Taylor Library and the Clementine Hunter Education Wing, both under renovation.

The Ogden is affiliated with the Smithsonian Institute in Washington, DC, giving it access to that bottomless collection. On Thursday nights, pop in for Ogden After Hours, when you can listen to great Southern musicians and sip an Abita with a fun-loving, arts-obsessed crowd in the midst of the masterpieces.

DON'T MISS

➡ Southern Landscapes
➡ Self-Taught, Outsider and Visionary Art
➡ Center for Southern Craft & Design
➡ Museum Store
➡ Ogden After Hours

PRACTICALITIES

➡ Map p244
➡ ☑539-9600
➡ www.ogdenmuseum.org
➡ 925 Camp St
➡ ⊙10am-5pm Wed-Mon, 6-8pm Thu
➡ adult/child/senior $10/5/8

⊙ SIGHTS

⊙ CBD

Hotels and skyscrapers fill the CBD, a no-nonsense grid of bland buildings anchored by the hulking Superdome. A few historic buildings add character, particularly in the area surrounding Lafayette Sq, the heart of the former Faubourg St Mary.

LOUISIANA SUPERDOME   SPORTS ARENA
Map p244 (📞587-3663; www.superdome.com; Sugar Bowl Dr) The Superdome hovers like a giant bronze hubcap between the elevated I-10 freeway and downtown's skyscrapers. The immense indoor stadium, which seats more than 73,200, has hosted NCAA Final Four basketball games, presidential conventions, the Rolling Stones (largest indoor concert in history) and Pope John Paul II. The site of six Super Bowls, it will host its seventh in 2013. On New Year's Day the college-football Sugar Bowl is played here, and in fall this is the home turf of the New Orleans Saints. In 2011 the facility completed a six-year, $336 million renovation project that fully modernized the building and ensured occupancy by the Saints through 2025. All of this excitement occurs in a structure built on top of an ancient burial ground, which some say is the source of the Saints' seemingly cursed 40-year history.

The Superdome gained notoriety in 2005 when it was designated a 'refuge of last resort' during Hurricane Katrina. Some 25,000 to 30,000 people huddled under the dome as Katrina's winds blew off part of the roof. Power went out and food and water supplies were quickly depleted as people lived in squalor and waited nearly a week for buses to carry them out of the flooded city. Initial unconfirmed reports of rape, riot and murder within the Dome have been debunked. In all, six people died inside the Superdome (one apparent suicide, one overdose and the rest from natural causes, mainly elderly or infirm who suffered from pre-existing conditions), plus several more in the immediate vicinity.

GALLIER HALL   HISTORIC BUILDING
Map p244 (📞658-3623; www.nola.gov; 545 St Charles Ave) Architect James Gallier Sr designed this monumental Greek-revival structure, which was dedicated in 1853. It served as New Orleans' city hall until the 1950s, and far outclasses the city's current city hall (a few blocks away). Today the building is used for private functions and VIP funerals (both Confederate president Jefferson Davis and homegrown R&B legend Ernie K-Doe have lain in state here – only in New Orleans) and is a focal point for Mardi Gras parades, most of which promenade past the grandstand erected here on St Charles Ave.

NEW ORLEANS PUBLIC LIBRARY   LIBRARY
Map p244 (NOPL; 📞529-7323; www.nutrias.org; 219 Loyola Ave; ⊙10am-6pm Mon-Thu, 10am-5pm Fri & Sat; @☎) The Louisiana Room, on the 3rd floor, is a good resource of regional history. The computer room on the 2nd floor is handy for getting online for free (you'll need picture ID). Free wi-fi is also available.

ACTIVITIES IN CBD & WAREHOUSE DISTRICT

The **Canal Street Ferry** (Map p244; www.algierspoint.org; Canal St Wharf; vehicles/pedestrians $1/free; ⊙6am-12:15am) runs from the foot of Canal St to Algiers Point. It's the easiest way to get out on the Mississippi River and admire New Orleans from the traditional river approach (mmm, smells like mud, poo and petroleum). Ride on the lower deck next to the water, and you're likely to see the state bird, the brown pelican. The state-run ferry leaves Canal St on the quarter hour, and returns from Algiers on the hour and half hour. On the Algiers side, stretch your legs and learn about Louis Armstrong and other jazz greats on the Jazz Walk of Fame along the levee.

⊙ Warehouse District

The old warehouses that line most of the streets in this part of town have proved perfectly suitable for the arts district that now thrives here. The museums and galleries are joined by some of the city's finest restaurants (see p106).

NATIONAL WWII MUSEUM   MUSEUM
See p100.

OGDEN MUSEUM OF
SOUTHERN ART   MUSEUM

See p101.

BUTTERFLY GARDEN & INSECTARIUM   ZOO

Map p244 (www.auduboninstitute.org; US Custom House, 423 Canal St; adult/child/senior $16/11/13; ⊙10am-5pm Tue-Sun, plus Mon Jun-Aug; ⏢) At this lively museum, visitors do more than just stare at exotic bugs. They listen to them, touch them and, if they dare, even taste them. Opened by the Audubon Institute in 2008, the insectarium is a multi-sensory treat that's especially fun for kids. Munch on chocolate chirp cookies (topped with crickets) or mealworm dip in the **Bug Appetit room** or pet a thumb-sized Madagascar roach in the **Metamorphosis Gallery**. The eight-minute film *The Tiniest Show on Earth* spotlights the world's most amazing insects while **The Louisiana Swamp Gallery** and **Insects of New Orleans** highlight regional creepy crawlies. The latter exhibit examines yellow fever, a mosquito-borne virus that killed more than 40,000 people in the city between 1805 and 1905. A revamped **butterfly exhibit** opened in 2012, with lighting, plants and 500 to 600 butterflies co-existing inside an Asian-style garden. The insectarium's retail shop, **The Flea Market**, sells a variety of bug-related gifts, from huggable stuffed bumble bees to *Peterson's Field Guide to Insects* to a start-your-own-ant-colony kit.

The museum is located inside the carriageway of the city's historic US Custom House. Construction of the building began in 1848, but it took 33 years and nine architects to complete it. Confederate soldiers were imprisoned on the site when Union forces occupied New Orleans during the Civil War. Today, because it is a federal building, visitors' bags will be searched – so leave pocket knives and mace at your hotel.

AQUARIUM OF THE AMERICAS   AQUARIUM

Map p244 (www.auduboninstitute.org/visit/aqua; Canal St, at Mississippi River; adult/child/senior $21/14/17; ⊙10am-5pm Tue-Sun, plus Mon Jun-Aug; ⏢) Also part of the Audubon Institute, the immense Aquarium of the Americas is loosely regional, with exhibits that delve beneath the surface of the Mississippi River, Gulf of Mexico, Caribbean Sea and far-off Amazon rainforest.

One highlight is Spots, a rare white alligator who usually draws a large crowd to the **Mississippi River Gallery** where

---

ℹ️
AUDUBON EXPERIENCE
••••••••••••••••••••••••••••••••••••••

Families and travelers who *really* like animals may want to visit all three of the facilities managed by the Audubon Institute: the aquarium and insectarium (in the CBD), and the zoo (in Audubon Park in Uptown). If that's the case, buy the **Audubon Experience package** (www.auduboninstitute.org; adult/child/senior $35/19/19) and see all three, as well as an IMAX movie, at a reduced overall price.

he suns himself. The **Caribbean Reef** has a 30ft-long glass tunnel that runs under a 130,000-gallon tank, and the sea-horse gallery and penguin colony are perennially popular. At the new **Parakeet Pointe**, purchase a $1 stick of birdseed and feed the colorful birds – they'll even land on your hand!

Some 10,000 fish were lost when Hurricane Katrina wiped out the aquarium's filtration and temperature-control systems, but the aquarium reopened the following year. Unfortunately, there are no exhibits directly discussing Hurricane Katrina or the BP oil spill, two of the biggest events to affect southern Louisiana's waterways in the last decade. You will find, however, BP's aquarium sponsorship plaque near an exhibit that touts the benefits of oil rigs as artificial reefs.

At press-time, the adjacent **IMAX Theatre** (adult/child/senior $10.50/7.50/9.50) was screening several movies, including *Hurricane on the Bayou*, which examines the impact of Hurricane Katrina and the connection between hurricanes and the region's disappearing wetlands.

BLAINE KERN'S MARDI
GRAS WORLD   MUSEUM

off Map p244 (☎361-7821; www.mardigrasworld.com; 1380 Port of New Orleans Pl; adult/child/senior $20/13/16; ⊙8:30am-4:30pm) We dare say that Mardi Gras World is one of the happiest places in New Orleans by day – but at night it must turn into one of the most terrifying funhouses this side of Hell. It's all those *faces,* man, the dragons, clowns, kings and fairies, all leering and dead-eyed...sorry. Maybe it's just us.

That said, we love Mardi Gras World – the studio, as it were, of Blaine Kern (Mr

Mardi Gras), who has been making parade floats since 1947. Kern learned the trade from his father and passed it down to his sons. At press time the family was involved in a lawsuit over company management, but Kern's employees are still building the best floats in the city. You can see many of them up-close, any time of the year. There are 20,000 props in their inventory! You might also see figures built for the studio's

GALLERY HOPPING

With the most impressive concentration of serious galleries in New Orleans, Julia St, between Commerce and Baronne Sts, is the core of New Orleans' Arts District. Nearby, the excellent Ogden Museum of Southern Art and the Contemporary Arts Center are easily worked into an afternoon of gallery hopping. Drop by the Contemporary Arts Center or any gallery to pick up a comprehensive guide to the area's art dealers. Learn more about the artists and their work during the Art Walk the first Saturday of the month between 6pm and 9pm (p34; www.neworleansartsdistrict.com).

Arthur Roger Gallery (Map p244; www.arthurrogergallery.com; 432 Julia St; ⊙10am-5pm Mon-Sat) One of the district's most prominent galleries, Arthur Roger represents several dozen artists, including Simon Gunning, whose landscapes are haunting records of Louisiana's disappearing wetlands.

Bergeron Studio & Gallery (Map p244; www.bergeronstudio.com; 406 Magazine St; ⊙9am-5pm Mon-Fri, 11am-3pm Sat) This gallery has a superb collection of historic photographs by key artists who worked in New Orleans over the past century. A recent exhibition highlighted 1800s daguerreotypes.

George Schmidt Gallery (Map p244; www.georgeschmidt.com; 626 Julia St; ⊙12:30-4pm Tue-Sat) New Orleans artist George Schmidt, a member of The New Leviathan Oriental Fox-trot Orchestra, describes himself as a 'historical' painter. Indeed, his canvasses evoke the city's past, awash in a warm, romantic light. His Mardi Gras paintings are worth a look.

Heriard-Cimino Gallery (Map p244; www.heriardcimino.com; 440 Julia St; ⊙10am-5pm Tue-Sat) Established contemporary artists from across the USA are represented in this elegant space. The emphasis is on abstract and figurative paintings, but you might also encounter photography and sculpture here.

Jean Bragg Gallery of Southern Art (Map p244; www.jeanbragg.com; 600 Julia St; ⊙10am-5pm Mon-Sat) The 'Food Court' collection, with its small paintings of beignets, shrimp and other Louisiana fare, will make your stomach growl at this jam-packed gallery, which is also a good source for the Arts and Crafts-style Newcomb Pottery, which originated at New Orleans' own Newcomb College. Bragg also deals in classic landscapes by Louisiana painters and every month she features the work of a contemporary artist.

Lemieux Galleries (Map p244; www.lemieuxgalleries.com; 332 Julia St; ⊙10am-6pm Mon-Sat) Gulf Coast art is the emphasis in this nationally recognized gallery, and it's a good place to get a handle on the breadth of the regional arts scene. Works here include Shirley Rabe Masinter's realistic paintings of New Orleans – note the wonderful local signage – and Jon Langford's depictions of local musicians.

Soren Christensen Gallery (Map p244; www.sorengallery.com; 400 Julia St; ⊙10am-5:30pm Tue-Fri, 11am-5pm Sat) This impressive space showcases the work of nationally renowned painters and sculptors. The gallery is known for its nontraditional sensibility.

New Orleans School of Glassworks & Printmaking Studio (Map p244; www.newsorleansglassworks.com; 727 Magazine St; ⊙11am-5pm Mon-Sat) This school and gallery impressively fills 25,000 sq ft of an old brick warehouse. Glassworks is the sister school of the Louvre Museum of Decorative Arts, and excellent pieces are sold here. On Saturday afternoon you'll usually find artists at work, and glass blowing is always worth seeing. Artists also specialize in stained glass, fine silver alchemy, copper enameling, printmaking, paper sculpture and bookbinding.

other commercial projects, including the ubiquitous Chik-Filet cows.

Tours start with a 15-minute movie, followed by king cake and coffee, then continue into the depths of the warehouse (one of 17 storage buildings). If you're staying at a nearby hotel, you may be able to catch their free shuttle. Otherwise, parking is $10 in the lot beside the entrance.

CONTEMPORARY ARTS
CENTER   ARTS CENTER
Map p244 (CAC; www.cacno.org; 900 Camp St; admission varies; 11am-4pm Tue-Sun) The grand modernist entrance to the CAC, an airy, spacious vault with soaring ceilings and conceptual metal and wooden accents, is almost reason enough to step into this converted warehouse. Almost. The best reason for visiting is a good crop of rotating exhibitions by local artists, plus a packed events calendar that includes plays, skits, dance and concerts that draw names as big as Death Cab for Cutie.

CIVIL WAR MUSEUM   MUSEUM
Mapp244(523-4522;www.confederatemuseum .com; 929 Camp St; adult/child & senior $8/5; 10am-4pm Tue-Sat) Tattered gray uniforms, rebel swords, faded diaries and a lock of General Robert E Lee's silver hair. This collection of Civil War memorabilia pays homage to the Confederacy and the local boys who fought for the rebel cause. Once known as the Confederate Museum, this is Louisiana's oldest operating museum. It's a smallish space centered in the Confederate Memorial Hall, a chamber of dark wood and exposed cypress ceiling beams with a decidedly stately vibe. The museum used to be a center of Confederate apologia; today it's been largely politically corrected, although there's a lack of material relating to slavery, perhaps because of the paucity of material possessions slaves could have left behind. This really is a collection of *things* as opposed to a contemporary, interpretation-driven educational museum.

The permanent exhibition includes the second-largest compilation of Confederate artifacts in the world, including lots of swords, guns, buttons, flags and uniforms. The most moving exhibits are the handful of signs describing local heroes and tragic maidens, including Winnie Davis, daughter of Confederate president Jefferson Davis. After the war, vociferous Southerners demanded that she call off her engagement to

STREET PARKING IN THE CBD

Free parking is nearly impossible to find downtown, and parking meters typically run from 8am to 6pm Monday through Saturday. Sidewalk parking kiosks that accept coins and credit/debit cards are common, but you'll still find plenty of the old coin-gobbling meters. If you're out of coins, use your debit or credit card to get a receipt from one of the kiosks. You're permitted to put it on your dashboard at a metered spot. The maximum time allowed for most spots is two hours ($3). Double-check all signs for variances.

her true love – a damn Yankee. She subsequently died alone at 34.

LOUISIANA CHILDREN'S MUSEUM   MUSEUM
Map p244 (523-1357; www.lcm.org; 420 Julia St; admission $8; 9:30am-4:30pm Tue-Sat & noon-4:30pm Sun;) This educational museum is like a high-tech kindergarten where the wee ones can play in interactive bliss till nap time. Lots of corporate sponsorship equals lots of hands-on exhibits. Several exhibits offer a New Orleans spin, including the Cajun Cottage and the Little Port of New Orleans. Children under 16 must be accompanied by an adult. From early June through August, the museum is also open Mondays, and the daily closing time is 5pm.

SOUTHERN FOOD
& BEVERAGE MUSEUM   MUSEUM
Map p244 (569-0405; www.southernfood.org; Riverwalk Mall, Julia St entrance; adult/student & senior $10/5; 10am-7pm Mon-Sat, noon-6pm Sun) Foodies, mixologists and history buffs will most enjoy this compact museum, packed tight with information about food staples and dishes of the South, and New Orleans and Louisiana in particular. The display of Southern cookbooks is especially fun – there's one dedicated to potato salad and coleslaw – and there's an informative exhibit about the effects of Hurricane Katrina and the BP oil spill on local industries. The history of absinthe is explored in an adjoining room, and there's a wall dedicated to 19th-century artists and writers who found inspiration in the drink's murky depths. In the midst of it all is a 16ft Brunswick bar salvaged from Lake Pontchartrain

after Hurricane Katrina. The bar once sat inside Bruning's, the third oldest restaurant in New Orleans until it was destroyed by the hurricane (it opened in 1859).

The attached **Museum of the American Cocktail** isn't much more than a small exhibit hall, but admission is free with the food museum and, hey, how often do you get to see 19th-century ads for Sazerac or a picture gallery of 19th-century bartenders complete with handlebar moustaches?

FREE PRESERVATION
RESOURCE CENTER   HISTORIC BUILDING

Map p244 (⌀581-7032; www.prcno.org; 923 Tchoupitoulas St; ⊙9am-5pm Mon-Fri) Interested in the architecture of New Orleans? Or a self-guided walking tour? Then start here. The welcoming Preservation Resource Center, located inside the 1853 Leeds-Davis building, offers free pamphlets with walking-tour maps for virtually every part of town. Helpful staff share information about everything from cycling routes to securing low-interest loans to buy and restore your dream shotgun house. Upstairs, a library contains volumes on local history and architecture. The neighborhood brochures are also available online.

LEE CIRCLE   MONUMENT

Map p244 Called Place du Tivoli until it was renamed to honor Confederate General Robert E Lee after the Civil War, Lee Circle is a tragic example of an urban junction planned horribly wrong. The presence of a nearby elevated freeway mars what should be a pleasant roundabout. Oh well; the **Robert E Lee monument** at its center, dedicated in 1884, is attractive, and still refuses to turn its back on the North. It's within two blocks of the Civil War Museum and the National WWII Museum.

SCRAP HOUSE   MONUMENT

Map p244 (Convention Center Blvd, near John Churchill Chase St) Artist Sally Heller designed this sculpture, built entirely out of found and recycled material, and dedicated it to the victims of Hurricane Katrina. A ruined shack that resembles Dorothy's house blown off-track sits in a tree constructed from pieces of oil drums. Inside, a light shines for those seeking to return home. It's a powerful piece of work that sits in an appropriate setting – across from the Convention Center, where so many refugees were displaced in the aftermath of the Storm.

HARRAH'S CASINO   CASINO

Map p244 (⌀533-6000; www.harrahsneworleans .com; 4 Canal St; ⊙24hr) You'd think all manner of vice would be welcome in the Big Easy, but Harrah's, near the foot of Canal St, doesn't get much local love. It's a big ol' casino – 115,000 square feet for gaming – that's part of a national chain, and it pretty much feels exactly like that. Nevertheless, people do trickle in for the casino gambling, buffet dining, free parking and hotel discounts. In 2006 the casino developed a small pedestrian mall, lined with restaurants and watering holes, on nearby Fulton St. Harrah's manages the newly opened Manning's sports bar and restaurant.

✕ EATING

New Orleans' downtown isn't great for cheap eats (with a few exceptions), but as far as fine dining goes, you've hit the mother lode. Most of the city's big-name chefs – John Besh, Donald Link, Susan Spicer – have opened posh outposts downtown. That said, even the high-end restaurants here have affordable lunchtime menus if you want to sample fine food on the cheap.

TOP
CHOICE COCHON BUTCHER   SANDWICHES $

Map p244 (www.cochonbutcher.com; 930 Tchoupitoulas St; mains $8-12; ⊙10am-10pm Mon-Thu, 10am-11pm Fri & Sat, 10am-4pm Sun) This tiny sandwich and meat shop, tucked behind the slightly more formal Cochon, calls itself a 'swine bar & deli.' We call it one of our favorite eateries in the city. We also think it encapsulates the best of New Orleans. There's always a small but convivial crowd filling the handful of tables out front. Inside, savory sandwiches – pork belly, bacon melt, roasted turkey – are stuffed with abandon and accompanied by heaping servings of palate-pleasing sides. Easygoing but efficient staff, an intriguing list of cocktails, and wallet-friendly prices round out this gastronomic holiday. The North Carolina-style barbecue is succulent but messy – you'll go through some napkins on this one.

HERBSAINT   MODERN LOUISIANAN $$

Map p244 (⌀524-4114; www.herbsaint.com; 701 St Charles Ave; mains lunch $15-18, dinner $26-36; ⊙11:30am-10pm Mon-Fri, from 5:30pm Sat) Herbsaint's duck and andouille gumbo

CBD LANDMARKS

Scattered throughout the CBD are historic buildings where some of the city's biggest (and, in some cases, most notorious) wheelers and dealers operated. Keep an eye out for them when wandering through the neighborhood.

New Orleans Cotton Exchange (Map p244; 231 Carondelet St) Some would say New Orleans was built on cotton. In the mid-19th century, when one-third of all cotton produced in the USA was routed through New Orleans, the receiving docks on the levee were perpetually covered by tall stacks of cotton bales ready to be shipped out. The Cotton Exchange was founded in 1871 to regulate trade and prices. The building here, dating from the 1920s, is the third Cotton Exchange to occupy this site.

United Fruit Company (Map p244; 321 St Charles Ave) A cornucopia of tropical produce graces the entrance to this building. The United Fruit Company, infamous for controversial neocolonial practices in Central America, was based here from the 1930s until the 1970s. For many decades, the company held a virtual monopoly on the banana trade throughout much of the world. It's now part of Chiquita Brands International, based in Cincinnati, OH.

might be the best restaurant gumbo in town. The rest of the food ain't too bad either – it's very much modern bistro fare with dibs and dabs of Louisiana influence, courtesy of owner Donald Link. Kurobuta pork belly comes with a local white-bean sauce, while the shrimp and grits come with Tasso and okra. The dining room, warmly lit by windows, is especially pleasant for lunch; there's also a 1:30pm to 5:30pm limited bistro menu available. Reservations are a good idea if you're coming for dinner.

TOP CHOICE RESTAURANT

AUGUST   MODERN CREOLE $$$
Map p244 (299-9777; www.restaurantaugust.com; 301 Tchoupitoulas St; mains lunch $20-36, dinner $32-43; 5:30-10pm daily, 11am-2pm Mon-Fri) Restaurant August, which opened in 2001, is the flagship of Chef John Besh's nine-restaurant empire, and its converted 19th-century tobacco warehouse earns a nod for most aristocratic dining room in New Orleans, with flickering candles and warm, soft shades. Its delicious meals will quite likely take you to another level of gastronomic perception: speckled trout Pontchartrain with lump crabmeat, wild mushrooms and hollandaise, and a five-course, two-hour tasting menu ($95 per person, with wine pairings $139) that makes local foodies weep. There's also a $20 prix-fixe lunch with various options available.

COCHON   MODERN CAJUN $$
Map p244 (588-2123; www.cochonrestaurant.com; 930 Tchoupitoulas St; mains $15-25; 11am-

10pm Mon-Fri, 11am-11pm Fri & Sat) The phrase 'everything but the squeal' springs to mind when perusing the menu at Cochon, regularly named one of New Orleans' best restaurants. At this bustling eatery Donald Link pays homage to his Cajun culinary roots, and the menu revels in most parts of the pig, including pork cheeks stuffed with goat cheese, fried boudin and beer-braised sausage. There are plenty of other meats on offer, including some excellent rabbit livers on toast and fantastic oysters. The food could be overly rich, but ends up being just hearty and smoky enough without being totally coma-inducing.

DOMENICA   ITALIAN $$
Map p244 (648-6020; http://domenicarestaurant.com; 123 Baronne St; mains $13-30; 11am-11pm) Domenica lures in first-timers with half-price gourmet pizzas between 3pm and 6pm. These 'rustic' pies are loaded with non-traditional but savory toppings – spicy lamb meatballs, roast pork shoulder – and are big enough that solo diners should have a slice or two left over. Newbies will likely become regulars, moving on to creative pastas, smoky meats and an intriguing line-up of soft, hard and blue cheeses. With its wooden refectory tables, white lights and soaring ceiling, Domenica feels like a village trattoria gone posh. Domenica is run by partners John Besh and Alon Shaya, the latter a Jewish chef who prepares the occasional Passover dinner with an Italian touch. Beer and wines by the glass are also half-price during happy hour.

CAFÉ ADELAIDE
CREOLE $$$

Map p244 (☏595-3305; www.cafeadelaide.com; 300 Poydras St; mains lunch $14-21, dinner $22-36; ☺breakfast & lunch Mon-Fri, brunch Sat & Sun, dinner 5:30-9pm Sun-Thu, until 10pm Fri & Sat) Straw hats, seersucker suits and dainty parasols wouldn't be out of place at this jazzy restaurant, a Brennan family tribute to their endearingly eccentric aunt Adelaide. Try dining in the 'Turtle Room,' where two shelled lovers dance a reptilian pas de deux on the wall. The motto here is the namesake's own: 'Eat, drink and carry on,' a philosophy realized by haute Creole cuisine cooked, apparently, by a pleasantly insane jester. Examples? Rye whiskey pork chops with bacon-smashed potatoes, chicken that's roasted in duck fat and a Cobb salad that comes with jumbo lump crabmeat and avocado. It's all as good as it sounds, and the attached Swizzle Stick is one of downtown's better bars.

AMERICAN SECTOR
AMERICAN $$

Map p244 (www.nationalww2museum.org/american-sector; 945 Magazine St; mains $7-26; ☺11am-9pm Sun-Thu, until 11pm Fri & Sat) At first glance, John Besh's ode to the Greatest Generation looks like a 1940s doo-wop diner: white-capped waitstaff beside the tables, black-and-white photos on the wall, and chicken-fried steak and meatloaf on the menu. Then you notice the John Besh touches: jalapeno cheese grits, shrimp in a cup with spicy aioli, crabmeat pies and, finally, the kicker – a snappy central bar with an uptown cocktail list that will surely put a spring in grandma's step. Next to the movie theater at the National WWII Museum, this

is a nice spot to unwind after wandering the exhibits. The seafood gumbo is some of the best around.

ROCK-N-SAKE
SUSHI $$

Map p244 (www.rocknsake.com; 823 Fulton St; sushi $2-16, entrees $11-15; ☺5-10pm Tue-Wed & Sun, 5-11pm Thu, 11am-2:30pm & 5:30pm-midnight Fri, 5pm-midnight Sat) For serious sushi fans, Rock-n-Sake can be off-putting, especially on a weekend night. It's a little too hip, the sushi chefs might look sullen, and the music is probably too rockin' if you're in the mood for relaxing. In other words, it's a scene. But this scene shouldn't detract from the fact that Rock-n-Sake serves some of the best sushi around. To best enjoy it, pop in early. The popular New Orleans roll pays homage to the city with spicy crawfish, spicy tuna and chili-mayo sauce. And those sullen sushi chefs? They open up pretty quickly if you ask about the rolls.

DRAGO'S SEAFOOD RESTAURANT
SEAFOOD $$

Map p244 (www.dragosrestaurant.com; 2 Poydras St; lunch mains $12-20, dinner most mains $17-31; ☺11am-10pm) You used to have to truck out to Metairie to enjoy the oyster creations of Drago Cvitanovich, one of the many Croatian immigrants who brought a heady knowledge of shellfish from the Dalmatian to the Gulf Coast. Now Drago's has an outpost in the downtown Riverside Hilton. The surf-and-turf menu is alright (we like the 'Shuckee Duckee' – a duck breast topped with oysters), but the real draw is the char-broiled oysters, dripping with butter, garlic, parmesan and their own juices after kissing an open fire.

BON TON CAFÉ
CAJUN $$$

Map p244 (☏524-3386; www.thebontoncafe.com; 401 Magazine St; mains $16-38; ☺11am-2pm & 5-9pm Mon-Fri) Whoa, where did all these people come from? Bon Ton looks low-key and stuffy beneath its Magazine St awnings, but step through the door at lunchtime and you'd think half of downtown is here, all chattering and primed to enjoy their meals with gusto. This classy but sassy joint, an old-style Cajun restaurant that's been open for half a century, maintains an old-school (and pricy) menu of red fish, rice, steak and lots of butter. Don't pass on the rum-soaked bread pudding.

ℹ

LE PAVILLON BREAKFAST BUFFET

Businessmen know that one of the best breakfasts downtown is the hearty buffet ($19.99) at Le Pavillon (p180). Stroll past the man in the top hat, walk straight through the opulent lobby and glide into the Crystal Room where scrambled eggs, apple smoked bacon, biscuits and gravy, and Bananas Foster waffles stand ready to shred your diet.

EMERIL'S
MODERN CREOLE $$$

Map p244 (☑528-9393; www.emerils.com; 800 Tchoupitoulas St; lunch mains $14-21, dinner $26-45; ☺6-10pm daily, 11:30am-2pm Mon-Fri) The noise level can be deafening, but Emeril's remains one of New Orleans' finest dining establishments. The kitchen's strengths are best appreciated by ordering the daily specials. The full-on Emeril experience includes partaking of the cheese board with a selection from the restaurant's eclectic wine list. The bar is a favorite with visiting celebrities and is a fun see-and-be-scene spot with locals.

MOTHER'S
DELI $

Map p244 (www.mothersrestaurant.net; 401 Poydras St; meals $8-26; ☺7am-10pm) At lunchtime, expect to see a line out the door. Mother's is a longtime crowd-pleaser near the Warehouse District that has drawn locals, conventioneers and tourists for years. The quality isn't what it was in the storied past, but the history and come-as-you-are hospitality make up the difference. Mother's invented the 'debris' po'boy and serves the justifiably famous 'Ferdi Special,' a po'boy loaded up with ham, roast beef and debris. But in general its sandwiches don't compare with other city stalwarts. Breakfast is your best bet – it's standard meat-and-eggs stuff, but brilliantly done and served in enormous portions.

NOLA GROCERY
DELI $

Map p244 (http://nolagrocery.com; 351 Andrew Higgins Dr; mains $3-15; ☺7am-7pm) Scruffy, delicious and hidden-in-plain-sight – just how we like it. The friendly dudes behind the counter at this tiny deli make their boudin on-site and do up some mean po'boys. It's the best cheap feed for under $10 you're likely to find in the CBD. If it's too warm out, they might not be making the gumbo.

🍷🍸 DRINKING & NIGHTLIFE

Downtown may look like a nightlife wasteland, but there's some great live music peppered about the office blocks. More pertinently, New Orleans, while home to many great dives, can lack in the hip lounge stakes; the CBD works to remedy this situation.

RUSTY NAIL
BAR

Map p244 (www.therustynail.biz; 1100 Constance St; ☺4:30pm-midnight or later) The Rusty Nail is a dive bar for newbies. Yeah, it lurks in a dark spot under the I-90 overpass, but it's also flanked by residential loft complexes that look downright trendy. The twinkling white lights on the exterior are kinda cute too and, heck, they even have a Trivia Night. Inside? It's dark, small, Zeppelin's playing, a couple of guys are watching the game and maybe a couple of other guys are setting up to play music in the corner. Come on in, have a beer or a scotch (they have long list) and kick back. And oh, this dive is nonsmoking, and they don't serve food. Always open until midnight, but will stay open later especially on weekends.

SWIZZLE STICK BAR
BAR

Map p244 (www.cafeadelaide.com; 300 Poydras St; ☺11am-midnight) Swizzle dee dee! This swell bar is the tipsy companion to Café Adelaide, and its good-time vibe seems poised to spill into the lobby of the adjoining Loews Hotel. A dash of adult fun massaged with heavy levels of quirkiness, it's a good spot for an after-work drink or a pre- or post-convention tipple. On a recent cocktail menu, the names of the drinks reflected the bar's sense of fun, from the Wild Magnolia to the Mad Hatter to Oh What a Night! Depending on the crowd, the Swizzle Stick may stay open until 1am or 2am.

LUCY'S RETIRED SURFERS BAR
BAR

Map p244 (www.lucysretiredsurfers.com; 701 Tchoupitoulas St; ☺varies, generally 11am-late) There's always, always, always somebody sipping a drink at one of the sidewalk tables at Lucy's, a beach-bum kinda spot oddly plopped in the middle of downtown. It draws the 20- and 30-something crowd but it's also decent for an after-work drink. Have something colorful and cold, and we'll see you at the next bar.

SAZERAC BAR
BAR

Map p244 (☑636-1891; http://therooseveltneworleans.com; 523 Gravier St; ☺5pm-late Tue-Fri, from 9pm Sat) Walking through the Hotel Roosevelt's chandeliered lobby and into the polished glow of the Sazerac Bar, you feel as if you've stepped back into a well-heeled era of hushed wheeling and dealing and high-society drinking. Who'd blink an eye if former governor and hotel regular Huey Long strolled through the door? With its art-deco murals, plush couches and romantic glow, the Sazerac Bar is an inviting alternative to the rowdy bars jamming the French Quarter just across Canal St. So sidle up to the bar, order a sazerac (created in New Orleans) and gossip like it's 1929.

BELLOCQ   COCKTAIL BAR

Map p244 (www.thehotelmodern.com/bellocq; 936 St Charles Ave; ⏰5pm-midnight Mon-Thu, 4pm-2am Fri & Sat, 4-10pm Sun) White candles, plush Victorian chairs, intimate nooks, deep purples and blacks – Bellocq has a boudoir style suited for upscale vampires and well-heeled denizens of the night. If only that dour statue of General Lee wasn't passing judgment from his perch across the street. Named for a pre-prohibition maritime photographer who secretly snapped photos of ladies of the night, Bellocq pays homage to the golden age of drink with 'cobblers' and other 1800s cocktails. Inside the new Hotel Modern on Lee Circle, Bellocq is the latest brainchild from the owners of Freret's St's stylish Cure (p135).

CAPDEVILLE   BAR

Map p244 (www.capdeville.com; 520 Capdeville St; ⏰11am-2pm & 5-11pm Mon-Thu, 11am-1am Fri & Sat) Where is the New Orleans' tech crowd talking shop and knocking back drinks these days? The compact Capdeville, an upscale bistro with retro roots – check out that jukebox and the album covers – on the 1st floor of the Intellectual Property building just off Lafayette Sq. After a stroll past the Julia St galleries or a date in the Federal District Court, pop in for a whiskey at the elevated bar or nosh on a gouda-topped burger or a BLFT – a BLT with a fried-green tomato.

TOP 5 HOTEL BARS IN THE CBD
....

➡ Swizzle Stick, Loews Hotel

➡ Sazerac Bar, Roosevelt Hotel

➡ Bellocq, Hotel Modern

➡ Loa, International House

➡ Polo Club Lounge, Windsor Court Hotel

POLO CLUB LOUNGE   BAR

Map p244 (300 Gravier St; ⏰11:30am-midnight Mon-Thu, 11:30am-1am Fri & Sat, 11am-midnight Sun) You probably didn't come to New Orleans to fox hunt, but if you were interested, this bar in the Windsor Court Hotel would be a good place to psych yourself up. The overstuffed chairs, tweedy bookshelves, nightly jazz and soft clink of hushed merry-making is meant to evoke aristocratic old England. A cognac or brandy anyone? Those looking for trendier libations can check out the latest in mixology at the new Cocktail Bar off the 1st-floor lobby.

CIRCLE BAR   DIVE, LIVE MUSIC

Map p244 (☎588-2616; 1032 St Charles Ave; ⏰4pm-late, shows 10pm Thu-Sat) The Circle Bar was recently renovated, but if you picture a grand Victorian mansion all disheveled and punk, you've still caught the essence of the place. It's one of those joints where the bartender doesn't ask his or her customers what they want or if they want a refill; knowledge is simply and safely assumed and institutionalized. Live acts, ranging from the folk to the rock to the indie (all of varying quality), often occupy the central space, where a little fireplace and a lot of grime speak to the coziness of one of New Orleans' great dives.

LOA   LOUNGE

Map p244 (www.ihhotel.com/bar.html; 221 Camp St; ⏰5pm-late) Off the lobby of the fashionable International House (p181), Loa is a great place to grab a daytime drink. Huge windows overlook the CBD's streetscape of dedicated worker bees, and watching them while getting tipsy is a pleasure akin to munching on doughnuts among people sweating it out at the gym. In the evening, live music runs the gamut of world beats, and everyone looks good bathed in candlelight. If you practice voodoo, or you're after a full-coverage religious plan, you can leave an offering at the voodoo altar on your way out.

WHISKEY BLUE   LOUNGE

Map p244 (www.gerberbars.com; 333 Poydras St; ⏰5pm-2am Mon-Thu, until 4am Fri & Sat) Whiskey Blue feels scarily out of place in this city: a sleek, sexy bar where people get dressed up like extras in *The Matrix* and sip what very clearly isn't a bottle of Dixie. But you know what? Not all bars

IN WINO VERITAS

Topping our list of New Orleans acronyms is WINO – the **Wine Institute of New Orleans** (Map p98; ☎324-8000; www.winoschool.com; 610 Tchoupitoulas St). The 'institute' runs classes on wine tasting, food pairing and the like, aimed at both amateur enthusiasts and folks planning to be professionally employed in the wine and spirit industry. The casual classes generally run from $35 to $45 whereas professional certification classes will cost you $650.

But we're going to assume that beyond the classes, you just want to try some very good wines. Aren't you in luck? Pop by WINO and sample some 120 different types of vino, plus a fair amount of beer and pâté, cheese, chocolate and charcuterie plates. Call ahead for hours, find a designated driver and get ready to bliss out, fermented-grape style.

must be dives or neighborhood joints where brass bands get the party started. Downtown is a neighborhood, too, albeit an increasingly modern and manicured one; and Whiskey Blue, inside the W Hotel, reflects those tastes.

VIC'S KANGAROO CAFÉ   BAR

Map p244 (☎524-4329; www.satchmo.com/vics; 636 Tchoupitoulas St; ⊙5pm-3:30am Mon-Thu, 11am-4:30am Fri, 6pm-4:30am Sat & Sun) Here's a little something to make Australians either sick or prone to bust out the Anzac Day regalia: Vic's phone number is, no joke, 524-GDAY. There are all kinds of other Australia-themed paraphernalia here, and while we admittedly haven't met any diggers at the bar, there must be some around. There's a kangaroo with boxing gloves on the sign, right? Well, if there aren't any Australians here, there's certainly plenty of service staff from downtown's restaurants, who pour into Vic's when they get off their shifts and generally turn it upside down under (heh).

MANNING'S   SPORTS BAR

Map p244 (www.harrahsneworleans.com; 519 Fulton St; ⊙11am-10pm Sun-Thu, until 11pm Fri & Sat) We're not 100% sure that locals have fully embraced this glossy sports bar opened by Eli and Peyton's dad Archie in conjunction with Harrah's, but it's only been around since January 2012. Gleaming from a prime corner on the Fulton St promenade, it's a convenient place for a conventioneer looking to play hooky and catch the big game. There are 30+ flat screens and, for die-hard fans, a 13ft-by-7.5ft jumbo screen in back.

⭐ ENTERTAINMENT

The following venues are on S Peters St, within walking distance of several good restaurants, hotels and bars. To make a night of it, grab dinner before a show then see what's happening later on.

HOWLIN' WOLF   LIVE MUSIC

Map p244 (☎522-9653; www.thehowlinwolf.com; 907 S Peters St; cover free-$15; ⊙varies) One of New Orleans' best venues for live blues, alt-rock, jazz and roots music, the Howlin' Wolf always draws a lively crowd. It started out booking local progressive bands, but has become a regular stop for big-name touring acts such as the Smithereens, Hank Williams III and Allison Krauss. The club is now offering comedy acts on Tuesday and Thursday.

REPUBLIC NEW ORLEANS   LIVE MUSIC

Map p244 (☎528-8282; www.republicnola.com; 828 S Peters St; cover $5-32; ⊙varies, most shows start at 10pm) Republic showcases some pretty awesome live acts, including George Clinton and other good funk and blues talent, but it's also the kind of place where teenagers from the 'burbs come to behave very badly. There's your conundrum: your night may consist of a potentially great show, but there's a very good chance it will also include screeching girls, lots of jostling and the person next to you being sick all over the sidewalk.

🛍 SHOPPING

This part of town is chiefly concerned with business and art (see the boxed text, p104). It's not good for window shopping, but if you know what you're looking for you may find yourself zeroing in on that perfect little specialty shop.

TOP CHOICE MEYER THE HATTER   HATS

Map p244 (www.meyerthehatter.com; 120 St Charles Ave; ☺10am-5:45pm Mon-Sat) This cluttered shop, just a half block from Canal St, has a truly astounding inventory of world-class headwear. Biltmore, Dobbs, Stetson and Borsalino are just a few of the classy milliners represented. Fur felts dominate in fall and winter, and flimsy straw hats take over in spring and summer. We will say, sadly, that the selection of lids for the ladies seemed paltry and lackluster when compared to the high-kickin' men's collection.

THE SHOPS AT CANAL PLACE   MALL

Map p244 (www.theshopsatcanalplace.com; 333 Canal St; ☺10am-7pm Mon-Sat, noon-6pm Sun) No, you didn't come to New Orleans to shop at Ann Taylor, Brooks Brothers, J Crew or Saks Fifth Avenue, but if someone spills a hurricane over your last white shirt or you forgot to pack your heels, this glossy mall will be a blessing.

RIVERWALK MARKETPLACE   MALL

Map p244 (www.riverwalkmarketplace.com; 500 Port of New Orleans Place; ☺10am-7pm Mon-Sat, noon-6pm Sun) Riverwalk is half a mile long, stretching from Poydras St to Julia St along the river. There's a handful of national chains inside but most stores are off the national radar. Come here for elevated river views, the Southern Food & Beverage museum and New Orleans gift stores like **New Orleans Famous Praline Company** (www.neworleansfamouspraline.com). **Crescent City Cooks** (www.crescentcitycooks.com) sells Louisiana cookbooks and spices and offers cooking classes daily at 10am ($30).

Garden, Lower Garden & Central City

Neighborhood Top Five

1 Sipping 25¢ martinis and savoring bread pudding soufflé at ever-stylish **Commander's Palace** (p118) is one of the most enjoyable ways to live like a local. Walk off the meal with a sidewalk stroll past lush lawns and stately mansions.

2 Learning about the past at **Lafayette Cemetery No 1** (p115) where above-ground crypts hold tragic tales.

3 Popping into clothing boutiques, art galleries, music shops and day spas on **Magazine Street** (p123).

4 Wandering past paintings of local musicians and Mardi Gras at the **McKenna Museum of African American Art** (p117).

5 Celebrating like an Irishman at a neighborhood bar in the **Irish Channel** (p116).

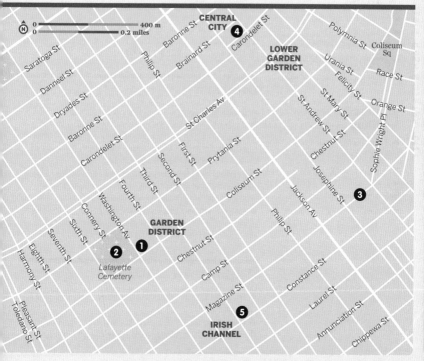

For more detail of the area, see Map p247 ➡

Lonely Planet's Top Tip

Avoid parking hassles on Magazine St by using public transportation. From the French Quarter and CBD, hop on the St Charles Ave streetcar at Canal St in the morning, then catch Bus 11 on Magazine St to return to your hotel in the afternoon.

✖ Best Places to Eat

➡ Commander's Palace (p118)

➡ Coquette (p118)

➡ Surrey's Juice Bar (p118)

➡ Slice (p118)

➡ Sucré (p121)

For reviews, see p118 ➡

🍸 Best Places to Drink

➡ Bridge Lounge (p122)

➡ Tracey's (p121)

➡ Bulldog (p122)

➡ Rendezvous (p122)

For reviews, see p122 ➡

🛍 Best Places to Shop

➡ Thomas Mann Gallery I/O (p124)

➡ Gogo Jewelry (p124)

➡ Aidan Gill for Men (p123)

➡ Fleurty Girl (p125)

➡ Funky Monkey (p125)

For reviews, see p123 ➡

Explore Garden, Lower Garden & Central City

The Garden District, Lower Garden District and Central City are three distinct neighborhoods, each offering a different experience. Two days is enough time to explore all three.

The Garden District exudes Old Southern excess with its historic mansions, lush greenery, chichi bistros and upscale boutiques. Your first morning, soak up the mixture of tropical fecund beauty and white-columned old-money elegance on a walking tour (p119) where stately homes and colorful gardens shimmer beside sidewalks bursting with Banyan roots. The Garden District is a rectangular grid bounded by St Charles Ave, Jackson Ave, Magazine St and Louisiana Ave. Magazine St and St Charles Ave are the main commercial thoroughfares; Prytania St is the most scenic (and the quickest).

Between the CBD and the Garden District, the Lower Garden District is somewhat like the Garden District but not quite as posh. Here the houses are pleasant, not palatial. There's a student vibe about, and plenty of bars and restaurants for those with university-stunted wallets and university-sized appetites for fun. The Lower Garden District is upriver (in this case, south) from the CBD. Magazine St is the main thoroughfare.

Central City, which lies between the CBD and Lower Garden District, is very much in transition. While there are large stretches of blight here, there is also a wonderful concentration of community activist organizations rebuilding what was once one of the most important African American neighborhoods in the city.

Local Life

➡ **Breakfast Joints** At Surrey's Juice Bar (p118), everything's seriously good, from the boudin to the shrimp and grits. At Slim Goodie's Diner (p121), the hip décor ain't sweet like mama's kitchen, but nobody minds at this always-crowded joint.

➡ **Pampering** Massages and lotions lure ladies to Beladonna Day Spa (p116) while men settle in for a shave at Aidan Gill (p123), a metrosexual's man-cave.

➡ **Neighborhood Bars** Saints football games are the draw at Tracey's (p121). Bringing your dog is A-OK at the canine-friendly Bridge Lounge (p122).

Getting There & Away

➡ **Bus** Bus 11 runs along Magazine St from Canal St to Audubon Park.

➡ **Streetcar** The St Charles Ave streetcar travels through the CBD, the Garden District and Uptown.

STEPHEN SAKS / LONELY PLANET IMAGES ©

TOP SIGHTS
LAFAYETTE CEMETERY NO 1

Gray crypts line up shoulder to shoulder under lush greenery in this moody place, a tiny bastion of history, tragedy and Southern gothic charm in the heart of the Garden District. It's a place filled with stories – of German and Irish immigrants, deaths by yellow fever, social societies doing right by their dead – that pulls the living into New Orleans' long, troubled past.

Established in 1833 by the former City of Lafayette, the cemetery is divided by two intersecting footpaths that form a cross. Look out for the structures built by fraternal organizations such as the Jefferson Fire Company No 22, which took care of its members and their families in large shared crypts. Some of the wealthier family tombs were built of marble, with elaborate detail rivaling the finest architecture in the district, but most tombs were constructed simply of inexpensive plastered brick. You'll notice many German and Irish names on the aboveground graves, testifying that immigrants were devastated by 19th-century yellow-fever epidemics.

The cemetery filled to capacity within decades of its opening (more than 10,000 people are buried here), and before the surrounding neighborhood reached its greatest affluence. By 1872, the prestigious Metairie Cemetery had already opened and its opulent grounds appealed to those with truly extravagant and flamboyant tastes.

In July 1995, author Anne Rice staged her own funeral here. She hired a horse-drawn hearse and a brass band to play dirges, and wore an antique wedding dress as she laid down in a coffin. The event coincided with the release of one of her novels.

The spell here is broken the moment a black-and-white-clad waiter strides past the cemetery's grated gates, hurrying to his shift at Commander's Palace next door. He's a vivid reminder that time marches on and that, yes, perhaps you are ready for lunch and a 25¢ martini. This is New Orleans after all.

DON'T MISS

➡ Social society crypts
➡ Cemetery tour (p116)

PRACTICALITIES

➡ Washington Ave at Prytania St
➡ main entrance: Washington Ave
➡ admission free
➡ ⊘7am-2:30pm Mon-Fri, until noon Sat

⊙ SIGHTS

⊙ Garden & Lower Garden Districts

Leafy, lovely and very walkable, the Garden and Lower Garden Districts are good places to soak up 19th-century architecture, bright flowers and the haunting trees that give this city its distinctive, subtropical character. Magazine St is good for window-shopping and restaurant- and bar-hopping.

LAFAYETTE CEMETERY NO 1 CEMETERY
See p115.

IRISH CHANNEL NEIGHBORHOOD
Map p247 The name Irish Channel is a bit of a misnomer; although this historic neighborhood was settled by poor Irish immigrants fleeing the potato famine in the 1840s, it has also been the home of many German and black residents living together in a truly multiculti gumbo. Still, 'Irish Channel' sounds better than 'Mixed-ethnicity/nationality Channel,' right? Paradoxically, wage-earning Irish were widely regarded as more economical than slaves, particularly for dangerous assignments, since it cost nothing to replace an Irish laborer who died on the job. This is still a working-class cluster of shotgun houses and you may not want to walk around alone at night, but in general it's pleasant for ambling. Come St Patty's day (p20), the biggest block party around takes over Constance St in front of Parasol's (p118).

HOUSE OF BROEL HISTORIC BUILDING
Map p247 (☑522-2220; www.houseofbroel.com; 2220 St Charles Ave; adult/child $10/5; ⊙tours 11am-3pm Mon-Fri) The House of Broel, built in the 1850s, is a bit of a funhouse. The entire two-story building was elevated in 1884 to allow for the construction of a new 1st floor. This was done so that the new owner could throw elaborate parties for his three daughters in a more spacious setting. Look for the black marble fireplace and original mirror framed by carved tobacco leaves. Current owner Bonnie Broel, a long-time New Orleans dress designer and fashion maven, displays some of her ballgowns as well as her astounding collection of themed, highly detailed dollhouses. The Best Little Whorehouse in Texas includes a lady of the night on a teeny tiny bed. Besides these exhibits, the house also hosts weddings and other events.

ST VINCENT'S INFANT ASYLUM HISTORIC BUILDING
Map p247 (1507 Magazine St) This large, red-brick orphanage was built in 1864 with assistance from federal troops occupying the city. It helped relieve the overcrowded orphanages filled with youngsters of all races who lost their parents to epidemics and the Civil War. The orphanage is now a hotel, but is not otherwise open to the public.

GOODRICH-STANLEY HOUSE HISTORIC BUILDING
Map p247 (1729 Coliseum St) This historic home was built in 1837 by jeweler William M Goodrich. Goodrich sold the house to the British-born merchant Henry Hope Stanley, whose adopted son, Henry Morton Stanley, went on to gain fame for finding the missing Scottish missionary, Dr David Livingston, and uttering the legendary question, 'Dr Livingstone, I presume?' He was subsequently knighted and founded the Congo Free States. The house originally stood a few blocks away, at 904 Orange St, and was moved to its current spot in 1981. Not open to the public.

ACTIVITIES IN GARDEN, LOWER GARDEN & CENTRAL CITY

After a few hard days of getting stuffed with rich Creole food and sloshed on gallons of Abita, it's time to treat yourself to a little cleansing experience at the **Belladonna Day Spa** (Map p247; ☑891-4393; www.belladonnadayspa.com; 2900 Magazine St; ⊙9am-6pm, to 8pm Wed & Thu). When you're done spoiling yourself, take home fragrant lotions and colorful cleansers for some home-grown renewal.

The non-profit **Save Our Cemeteries** (☑504-525-3377; www.saveourcemeteries.org) leads tours of Lafayette Cemetery No 1 at 10:30am Monday through Saturday for $20 per person. The entire proceeds are used for cemetery restoration, documentation and restoration. Reservations are recommended because spots are limited.

TOP HISTORIC SITES & SPORTS BARS

Melissa Smith, author of *Historic Photos of New Orleans*, archivist at Amistad Research Center, and writer of the fan site www.chicksinthehuddle.com, shares local favorites.

Top Historic Sites

➡ **Bayou St John** (p147) It's a great area to visit. Not only do you have things to do, like go to NOMA or the Botanical Gardens, but you also have a lot of great history. Before it was filled in, it was an outlet between the lake and the river. Prior to the Colonial period, the bayou was used heavily by American Indians [for] trading, and some of our oldest structures are actually in that part of town. It's where the Pitot House is, as well as Ursuline High School. I find it one of the most beautiful areas of town.

➡ **Cemeteries** So much of the vicinity's history is in its cemeteries. They actually speak to you in many ways – more so than, at times, what the written word can say. Some of the groups I've studied over time are benevolent societies. [Their crypts] tend to be in some of the mid-city cemeteries; you have wonderful names like Oddfellows Rest and the Katrina Memorial.

➡ **Cabildo** (p50) It's one of the oldest buildings in the city. It was also the seat of government. The upstairs promenade is just breathtaking when you can see the whole city, and it feels like history comes alive when you walk in there – not because it's a museum but just because of what it represents across the board. It's also just a beautiful, beautiful building.

Best Bars for Watching the Saints

➡ **Cooter Brown's** (p136) They have so many televisions [and] really, really good bar food. It's a great atmosphere, and it's one of the few bars in town that really attracts a cross-section of society. Whether it's student versus local versus tourist.

➡ **Lucy's Retired Surfers Bar** (p109) A lot of Saints players hang out there, so that tends to be a hot spot as well to watch Saints games.

GRACE KING HOUSE HISTORIC BUILDING
Map p247 (1749 Coliseum St) Behind a handsome wrought-iron fence, this papaya-hued house was named for the Louisiana historian and author who lived here from 1905 to 1932. It was built in 1847 by banker Frederick Rodewald and features Greek Ionic columns on the lower floor as well as Corinthian columns above. Not open to the public.

◉ Central City

Some areas here can get dodgy after dark. For the three sites listed here, check websites or call ahead to get information on their respectively packed events calendars.

MCKENNA MUSEUM OF AFRICAN AMERICAN ART MUSEUM
Map p247 (www.themckennamuseum.com; 2003 Carondelet St; adult/child/student & senior $5/2/3; ⊙11am-4pm Thu-Sat, by appointment Tue & Wed) Although the displayed work at this beautiful two-story institution comes from all over the African diaspora, most of it is created by local New Orleans artists. Images of Mardi Gras and the New Orleans music scene are highlights. The artwork is part of a collection amassed during some 30 years of collecting by Dr Dwight McKenna. Real standouts are the temporary exhibitions such as *Becoming Home*, a photographic depiction of life for African Americans along the Louisiana's plantation-heavy River Rd.

ASHE CULTURAL ARTS CENTER ARTS CENTER
Map p247 (☑569-9070; www.ashecac.org; 1712 Oretha Castle-Haley Blvd) An important anchor for the local African American community, Ashe (from a Yoruba word that could loosely be translated as 'Amen') regularly showcases performances, art exhibitions, photographs and lectures with an African/African American/Caribbean focus and beyond. Their 2012 calendar included *The Vagina Monologues*, a Brazilian dance class and a screening of the movie *Revenge of the Electric Car*. The on-site **Diaspora Boutique** (⊙10am-6pm), with clothing and earrings, is also worth a look.

BIG TOP GALLERY & THREE RING CIRCUS
ARTS CENTER

Map p247 (☑569-2700; www.3rcp.com; 1638 Clio St) Just bordering downtown, this arts and education center is essentially a very funky cross between an art gallery (2pm to 6pm Thursday to Saturday and by appointment), studio space and something like a circus of dreams for emerging artists. There's a small main stage that occasionally hosts some great live performances.

✖ EATING

Foodies here can pick and choose from studenty Mexican burrito shops, old-line Creole cafes and some truly excellent breakfast nooks and lunchtime diners. With a high student population, there's a decidedly young, hip and economical bent to the food on offer in the Lower Garden. There's not as much variety in the Garden District – just one of the most storied restaurants in the country.

TOP CHOICE COMMANDER'S PALACE
CREOLE $$$

Map p247 (☑899-8221; www.commanderspalace .com; 1403 Washington Ave; lunch $15-30, dinner $26-45; ☺6:30-10pm daily, 11:30am-2pm Mon-Fri, 11:30am-1pm Sat, 10:30am-1:30pm Sun) Commander's Palace is the most dapper of hosts, a seer-suckered bon vivant ready to wow you with white-linen dining rooms, decadent Creole dishes and attentive Southern hospitality. Owner Ella Brennan takes pride in her ability to promote her chefs to stardom; Paul Prudhomme and Emeril Lagasse are among her alumni. The nouveau Creole menu runs from fig and foie gras beignets to quail with apples stuffed with local blue crab. The dress code actually adds to the charm and sense of uniqueness – no shorts or T-shirts allowed and jackets are preferred at dinner. The general sense is that you are in a *very* nice place. Of course, some of that stiff upper lip is put on; the lunch special, after all, is the 25¢ martini. Reservations are required.

TOP CHOICE SURREY'S JUICE BAR
AMERICAN $

Map p247 (☑524-3828; www.surreyscafeandjuice bar.com; 1418 Magazine St; mains $6-13; ☺8am-3pm) Surrey's manages to make even a bacon and egg sandwich taste – and look – like the most delicious meal you've ever been served

for breakfast. And you know what? It probably *is* better than most breakfasts you've been served. Boudin biscuits, biscuits swimming in salty sausage gravy, eggs scrambled with salmon, and a shrimp-and-grits-and-bacon dish that should be illegal. And the juice, as you might guess, is blessedly fresh. This, friends, is how a champion (or a hungover tourist) starts their day. Cash only.

COQUETTE
MODERN FRENCH $$

Map p247 (☑265-0421; www.coquette-nola.com; 2800 Magazine St; lunch $17-20, dinner $26-36; ☺11:30am-3pm Wed-Sat, 5:30-10pm daily) A bright and beautiful addition to the crowded Magazine St eating scene, Coquette mixes up wine-bar ambience with friendly service and a bit of white linen; the combined result is a candlelit place where you don't feel bad getting a little tipsy. Don't just focus on the respectable wine menu, though – there's some great French-inspired Louisiana-sourced food served here, such as a succulent red snapper on pillowy risotto. The small plates are eclectic and highly recommended.

SLICE
PIZZA $

Map p247 (☑525-7437; www.slicepizzeria.com; 1513 St Charles Ave; pizzas $17-22; ☺11am-11pm Mon-Sat, until 10pm Sun) If you're staying in the Lower Garden District for more than a few days, Slice is one of those places you'll find yourself returning to again and again. It's notable for its nice staff, Abita Amber pints for $2 during Happy Hour (2pm to 6pm) and damn good pizza. In fact, it's our favorite pizza in New Orleans. Toppings for the thin crust pies can be as artisanal or run-of-the-mill as you like. The shrimp and andouille pizza is crammed with shrimp and sausage. The salads are good and hearty too. Order by the slice (starting at $2.50).

PARASOL'S
PO'BOYS $

Map p247 (www.parasolsbarandrestaurant.com; 2533 Constance St; po'boys $7-16; ☺11am-9pm Sun-Thu, until 10pm Fri & Sat) Parasol's isn't just in the Irish Channel; it sort of *is* the Irish Channel, serving as community center, nexus of gossip and, naturally, watering hole. Because yes, this is, first and foremost, a bar. But there is a little seating area in the back where you can order some of the best po'boys in town (see the boxed text, p121). That big ol' roast beef – a messy, juice-filled conduit of deliciousness – will

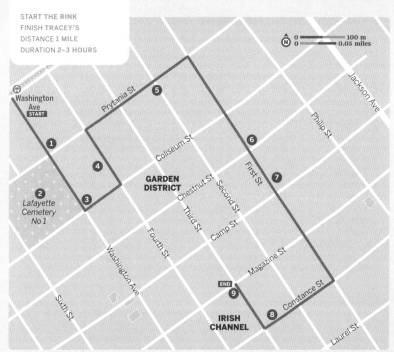

START **THE RINK**
FINISH **TRACEY'S**
DISTANCE **1 MILE**
DURATION **2–3 HOURS**

Neighborhood Walk
Green, Green New Orleans

Soak up the 'green' of New Orleans, from the historic, magnolia-shaded streets of the Garden District to the Emerald Island heritage of the Irish Channel.

From the CBD, take the St Charles Ave streetcar to Washington Ave. Walk one block south to ❶ **The Rink**, an 1880s skating rink turned 21st-century mini-mall. ❷ **Lafayette Cemetery No 1** (p115), one of the city's oldest, is across Prytania St, as is the dapper ❸ **Commander's Palace** (p118), the elegant crown jewel of the Brennan restaurant empire. Pop in for a 25¢ martini at lunchtime but remember – no shorts allowed.

Around the corner at 1448 Fourth St is ❹ **Colonel Robert Short's House**, designed by architect Henry Howard. The home of a Confederate officer, it's an exemplary double-gallery home with fine cast-iron details, including a cast-iron cornstalk fence.

Continue to the ❺ **Women's Guild of the New Orleans Opera Association** at 2504 Prytania, a Greek Revival home designed by William Freret in the late 1850s.

Turn right onto First St where you'll find ❻ **Joseph Carroll House** at No 1315, a beautiful center-hall house with double galleries laced with cast-iron. In back there's a similarly impressive carriage house.

❼ **Rosegate**, at 1239 First St, is the former home of author Anne Rice. The vampire-tale spinner lived here for many years, and regularly invited fans to tour her home. Which, by the way, is beautiful but disappointingly free of bats, organ music and Tom Cruise mooning about in a frilly jacket. No longer open to the public.

South of First St, homes quickly become shotgun shacks. This is the Irish Channel, home to working-class Irish, Germans and African Americans. Head down First St, turn right into Constance and wander along until you come to ❽ **Parasol's** (p118) on the corner of Third St and ❾ **Tracey's** (p121) on the corner of Third and Magazine Sts. These are two quintessential New Orleans neighborhood bars with dueling roast beef po'boys (see the boxed text, p121). Dig in.

FROM MYTHS TO THE MOVEMENT

Dryades St, named for legendary Greek tree spirits, is still known as such in much of town, but the official new name of this road is Oretha Castle-Haley Blvd (often shortened to OC Haley). The road is named for a local legend and Civil Rights activist who was a founding member of the Congress of Racial Equality, one of the leading organizations in the 1960s Civil Rights movement. Castle-Haley organized boycotts of segregated businesses and was one of the main leaders of local civil-disobedience and direct-action campaigns. Ironically, Castle-Haley's successful battle for integration helped hasten the decline of the street eventually named for her. When African Americans could shop anywhere they wanted, they began moving away from the traditionally black businesses clustered around Dryades, while simultaneous white flight contributed to an economic downturn across the city.

This part of town was once a major center for African American health care. The Keystone Insurance Company (now defunct) was one of the few of its kind that would fund pensions, funerals and, of course, medical treatment for black citizens. Said individuals may have been treated at Flint Goodridge Hospital (at Louisiana and Freret Sts); up until the 1950s, this was the only facility in the city where black doctors could legally practice medicine. The First African Baptist Church of New Orleans, at 2216 3rd St, was founded in 1817 and is the oldest continually operating black church in Louisiana.

In testament to this area's contribution to the Civil Rights struggle, there is a statue of Martin Luther King at the corner of Martin Luther King Blvd and S Claiborne Ave.

help to layer against the copious amounts of booze you may be tempted to drink here. There's a mad cast of characters both behind and ordering from the bar, but don't ever feel threatened; all in all this is one of the friendliest neighborhood spots in New Orleans. This place is also St Paddy's Day headquarters, when a huge block party happens on the street.

STEIN'S DELI
DELI $

Map p247 (www.steinsdeli.net; 2207 Magazine St; sandwiches $7-12; ⊙7am-7pm Tue-Fri, 9am-5pm Sat & Sun) How good is Stein's? Well, it's arguably more of a center for the city's Jewish population than any one synagogue. If lunch, for you, rests on quality sandwiches, cheese and cold cuts, this is as good as the city gets. Owner Dan Stein is a fanatic about keeping his deli stocked with great Italian and Jewish meats and cheeses, and some very fine boutique beers; the man even hosts his own beer-brewing classes. We tip our hats to you, sir.

JUAN'S FLYING BURRITO
MEXICAN $

Map p247 (www.juansflyingburrito.com; 2018 Magazine St; mains $5-13; ⊙11am-10pm Sun-Thu, until 11pm Fri & Sat) The answer to that perennial question, 'What happens when you cross a bunch of skinny jean-clad hipsters with a tortilla?' is (ta da) Juan's. The food is about as authentically Mexican as Ontario, but

that doesn't mean it's not good; the hefty burritos pack a satisfying punch against your hunger. Plus, the margaritas are tasty and it does a quesadilla with ground beef, bacon and blue cheese – yes, please.

CAFÉ RECONCILE
DINER $

Map p247 (http://reconcileneworleans.org; 1631 Oretha Castle-Haley Blvd; mains $5-9; ⊙11am-2:30pm Mon-Fri) Café Reconcile fights the good fight by recruiting and training at-risk youth to work as kitchen and floor staff. The food, which consists of daily specials, is simple and, frankly, really good. It's very much of the humble New Orleans school of home cookery: red beans and rice, fried chicken, shrimp Creole and the like. In summary: good food, good service and by eating at Reconcile you're doing a good thing for the city. Get over here already.

TROLLEY STOP
DINER $

Map p247 (1923 St Charles Ave; mains $5-15; ⊙24hr) All aboard! When we last stopped in at this 24-hour diner – where you can chow down while watching the St Charles trolley ding past – we were called about every variation of 'baby,' 'darling,' 'sweetie,' 'honeychile' and 'sugar' out there. The 1-2-3 Special – one egg, two strips of bacon, three silver dollar pancakes – will set you back $5.50. Sandwiches and burgers are also on the menu. And yeah, this sort of food isn't particularly original (although it is very good), but hey sweetie-honeychile-sugar-plum-darlin'-gooeycheeks, who's complaining when the service is this friendly?

TRACEY'S
PO'BOYS **$**

Map p247 (http://traceysnola.com; 2604 Magazine St; mains $5-12; ⊙11am-10pm Sun-Thu, until midnight Fri & Sat, bar 11am-until late) This neighborhood bar, known for its roast beef po'boys, is where you go to watch the Saints play on a lazy Sunday afternoon – the joint's got 20 TVs. Order your pub grub at the window, grab a buzzer, then settle in until you're buzzed (in both senses of the word). The crowd sitting outside can look kind of scruffy but c'mon in – it's a welcoming place, and the trendy exposed-brick wall will give urban hipsters a modicum of comfort. And as for those parasols hanging from the ceiling...see the boxed text for a clue.

JOEY K'S
DINER **$**

Map p247 (www.joeyksrestaurant.com; 3001 Magazine St; mains $9-18; ⊙11am-9pm Mon-Sat) Don't peek in the window here on a Saturday night unless you're ready to commit. You'll immediately want to step inside this cozy place that's full up with happy people, like a scene from a Norman Rockwell painting. Well, a scene by Norman's twisted brother. The snarky signs posted here and there, like the one that reads 'No sushi,' keep the vibe more New Orleans than middle America. Joey's serves good local diner comfort food and Cajun basics with a great

menu of daily specials. The cheese fries should be patented, while specialties such as fried pork chops and white beans are as satisfying a meal as you'll find for under $20 in the Lower Garden.

SUCRÉ
CHOCOLATE **$**

Map p247 (www.shopsucre.com; 3025 Magazine St; individual cookies & chocolates $2-7; ⊙8am-10pm Sun-Thu, until midnight Fri & Sat) Willy Wonka's chocolate factory has put away its top hat and purple suede coat and gone chic. Artisanal chocolates, cupcakes, chocolate bars, toffee, marshmallows and other confections preen behind glass at this glossy box of deliciousness. One chocolate macaroon will set you back $2, but as you fork over your cash you can gain comfort from the fact that Sucré, by a very wide consensus, is the best chocolate in town. It's a place you go to celebrate, a place to smile – or smack the table – while savoring dollops of single espresso beans encased in bittersweet darkness like a silk kiss.

SLIM GOODIE'S DINER
DINER **$**

Map p247 (3322 Magazine St; mains $5-16; ⊙6am-3pm; ☑) There's always a crowd waiting on the sidewalk outside this hip retro diner. This happenin' place, all overlaid with some punk-rock sensibility, was among the first restaurants to reopen after Hurricane Katrina, so it deserves a hell of a lot of credit just for that substantial accomplishment. Burgers, shakes, all-American breakfasts and other short-order standards

---

PARASOL'S V TRACEY'S: ROAST BEEF PO'BOY SMACKDOWN

So here's the backstory, but you've got to stop sipping your beer and listen close because it's confusing. It's also tangled up in rumor so everything you hear might not be true.

In any case, in 1949 there was a bar called Tracey's at the corner of 3rd St and Constance St in the Irish Channel. Parasol's (p118) took over the spot in 1952 and long reigned supreme when it came to serving up roast beef po'boys and Irish conviviality. John Carreras managed the place from the late 1990s until 2010, when Parasol's owners put it up for sale. Carerras made a bid but lost out to John and Thea Hogan, who were, unfortunately, emigrants from the miserable state of Florida. Interlopers! Grumbling ensued, and Carerras packed up his famous po'boy recipe and marched in a Second Line (a jazzy dancing parade; p153) to a brand new location that was... one block away. And what did he name his new bar? Tracey's. And to complicate the whole thing further, Thea Hogan is actually a New Orleans native, only briefly ruined by Florida. Who knew?

So Parasol's tweaked its roast beef po'boys – the bread is now swiped with garlic butter – and Tracey's churns out the originals. People took sides, and the battle of the roast beef po'boys began. Who's are better? There's no accounting for taste, so you're just going to have to chow down on both of them for yourself.

round out the menu; it's good, if not exactly awe-inspiring stuff. Vegetarians are treated well here, thanks to the presence of items such as latkes (potato pancakes) and black-bean nachos on the menu.

SAKE CAFÉ UPTOWN
JAPANESE $$

Map p247 (www.sakecafeuptown.us; 2830 Magazine St; sushi & mains $12-22; ⊘11:30am-10:30pm Sun-Thu, until 11:30pm Fri & Sat) Believe it or not, fish in this town doesn't have to come fried, swimming in a thick sauce or stuffed with bacon/crawfish/crabmeat/whatever. Sake Uptown (the original is in Metairie) serves decent sushi that's popular with the younger, yuppier types that populate the Lower Garden District and around.

BLUE PLATE CAFÉ
DINER $

Map p247 (300 Prytania St; mains $7-13; ⊘8am-2:45pm Mon-Fri, 8am-1:45pm Sat) Cheap and cheerful and colorful, too, the Blue Plate does some solid servings of breakfast and lunch stuff that's firmly of the Louisiana diner genre. The three-egg omelets are a satisfying treat. It gets packed on Saturday mornings, and justifiably so – this is one of the city's better cheap breakfast options.

🍷 DRINKING & NIGHTLIFE

Bars in this part of New Orleans tend to attract a youngish student and post-student crowd. Magazine St is, in its way, as much fun as Bourbon or Frenchmen Sts. It's wild without being ridiculous or idiotic (unlike Bourbon St) and while it lacks the live-music scene of Frenchmen, it makes up for that with a better variety of bars, many of them filled with beautiful (and not-so-beautiful) people.

BRIDGE LOUNGE
BAR

Map p247 (www.bridgeloungenola.com; 1201 Magazine St; ⊘4pm-late Mon-Thu, from 5pm Sat & Sun) Can a bar be simultaneously sexy and dog friendly? Bridge Bar answers that question with an affirmative woof. White candles provide a sultry glow and the black booths are made for smooching, but the pups on the sidewalk and the black-and-white dog photos on the wall keep things cuddly. The Bridge also hosts lots of free crawfish boil nights and is a center for the local singles scene, due in no small part to friendly bar staff who mix a mean cocktail – the mint julep is a paragon of the genre.

BULLDOG
BAR

Map p247 (www.draftfreak.com; 3236 Magazine St; ⊘2pm-late Mon & Tue, noon-late Wed-Fri, from 11am Sat & Sun) With 50 brews on tap and 100 by the bottle – from Belgium to Turkey and points in-between – the Bulldog works hard to keep beer enthusiasts happy. The best place to sink a pint or a pitcher is in the courtyard, which gets fairly packed with the young and the beautiful almost every evening when the weather is warm enough.

RENDEZVOUS
DIVE

Map p247 (www.therendezvoustavern.com; 3101 Magazine St; ⊘3pm-late Mon-Fri, noon-late Sat & Sun) Dart boards, a pool table, a long dark bar, old-looking mirrors on the wall and a few slot machines. And Billy Squier's The Stroke on the speakers. Yup, this place meets all requirements for a legitimate New Orleans dive bar. Very much a locals' hang-out, the Rendezvous attracts a mixed bag: the pool table and Golden Tee arcade game keep the collegiate crowd happy, while yuppie types stumble toward their favorite bartenders for another beer and late-night banter.

BALCONY BAR
BAR

Map p247 (☎894-8888; 3201 Magazine St; ⊘4:30pm-late) See the earlier description for the Rendezvous Bar but add a balcony and subtract the dart board. This student-centric neighborhood bar is a good place for pizza, carousing and sitting on the eponymous balcony while watching the Magazine St parade march by on balmy nights. The kitchen is open from 4pm until 2:30am or 3am.

STILL PERKIN'
CAFE $

Map p247 (http://neworleanscoffeeshop.com; 2727 Prytania St; mains $2-7; ⊘7am-6pm Mon-Fri, 8am-6pm Sat & Sun; 🛜) Perched on the corner of Prytania St and Washington Ave, this bright coffee shop is a great place to start or finish a Garden District walking tour or a visit to Lafayette Cemetery, which is located on the opposite corner. In addition to lattes and iced coffees, there's a decadent selection of scones and other treats plus a few sandwiches and wraps. It's in the 1880s Rink, as is the Garden District Bookshop.

IGOR'S LOUNGE   DIVE

Map p247 (☑522-2145; 2133 St Charles Ave; ⊙24hr) Pool tables, slot machines AND a laundromat? Hells to the yeah. And you know it's time to leave this dive if the sinuous bar starts looking like it's straight. Igor's constant rotation of characters makes it a good place to drop in if you're making your way up or down St Charles Ave. Or make this your terminus if you're staying nearby.

HALF MOON   DIVE

Map p247 (www.halfmoonnola.com; 1125 St Mary St; ⊙noon-late) On an interesting corner, just half a block from Magazine St, the Half Moon beckons with a cool neighborhood vibe. The place is good for a beer, short-order meal or an evening shooting stick. The kitchen is open 5pm to 2am. Look for the sweet neon sign.

SAINT BAR & LOUNGE   DIVE

Map p247 (www.thesaintneworleans.com; 961 St Mary St; ⊙7pm-late) The Saint? Of what? How about a great backyard beer garden enclosed in duck blinds and filled with tattooed young professionals, Tulane students, good shots, good beers, good times and a photo booth that you will inevitably end up in before the night is through. In fact, it may be a Louisiana law that visitors are not allowed to leave New Orleans without having one stupid series of pictures taken in the Saint's photo booth. It's not the cleanest bar (nickname: the Taint), but it sure is a fun one.

☆ ENTERTAINMENT

ZEITGEIST   CINEMA

Map p247 (☑352-1150; www.zeitgeistinc.net; 1618 Oretha Castle-Haley Blvd; adult/student/senior $8/7/6) This old movie house has been around since the 1920s and screens independent and art films.

🛍 SHOPPING

Magazine St is by far New Orleans' best shopping strip, and as a center for commercial activity it begins in the Lower Garden District, near its intersection with Felicity St. From here you can follow Magazine west

all the way to Audubon Park and essentially shop or window browse in antique stores and boutiques almost the entire way.

🏛 Lower Garden District

Magazine St gets cooking in the Lower Garden District. There is a heady concentration of galleries, boutiques, restaurants and other shops between St Mary St and Jackson Ave. Galleries may occasionally open or close at times that differ from those given here. You may want to call first before making a special trip.

TOP CHOICE AIDAN GILL FOR MEN   BARBER, ACCESSORIES

Map p247 (☑587-9090; www.aidangillformen.com; 2026 Magazine St; ⊙10am-6pm Mon-Fri, 9am-5pm Sat, noon-6pm Sun) Shave and a haircut...40 bits. Or $40. Apiece. But who's counting dollars at this suave and clubby barbershop, where smartly dressed mobsters of the Prohibition era would surely have felt comfortable. At Aidan Gill, it's all about looking neat and stylish, in a well-heeled, masculine sort of way. High-end shaving gear, smart cufflinks and colorful silk ties are sold in front, and the popular barber shop is in back.

ANTIQUES ON JACKSON/ SIMON OF NEW ORLEANS   ART, ANTIQUES

Map p247 (☑524-8201; 1028 Jackson Ave; ⊙10am-5pm Mon-Sat, 11am-4pm Sun) Local artist Simon Hardeveld has made a name for himself by painting groovy signs that are hung like artwork in restaurants all over New Orleans. You'll probably recognize the distinctive stars, dots and sparkles that fill the spaces between letters on colorfully painted signs such as 'Who Died & Made You Elvis?' The gallery, which moved around the corner from its old perch on Magazine St, is now part of Antiques on Jackson, which Handeveld owns with his wife Maria.

THOMAS MANN GALLERY I/O   JEWELRY
Map p247 (581-2111; www.thomasmann.com; 1810 Magazine St; 11am-5pm Mon-Sat) A giant crawfish. A robot made of wood. Jewelry. Baskets. Candle holders. If you need a funky but finely designed gift, pop in here. The 'I/O' in the name stands for 'insight-full objects.' Local craftsman Thomas Mann specializes in jewelry and sculpture, and his gallery is a smorgasbord of glass and metal.

GOGO JEWELRY   JEWELRY
Map p247 (www.ilovegogojewelry.com; 2036 Magazine St; 11am-6pm Mon-Sat) We're not sure why there's a mounted deer head on the wall, but hey, we'll just go with it because we're funky that way. But ladies, if you're looking for stylish, one-of-a-kind jewelry – rings, necklaces, cuffs – with a bit of sass, GoGo is a good place to start.

JIM RUSSELL RECORDS   MUSIC
Map p247 (www.jimrussellrecords.com; 1837 Magazine St; 11am-5pm Mon-Sat) A dense emporium of used 45s, with some very rare, collectible and expensive disks featuring all the blues, R&B and soul stars of the past. (Collecting Johnny Adams' singles? This is the place.) The used LPs have mostly given way to CDs, with an uneven selection available. Turntables make it possible to assess the quality of your purchases before you lay down some greenbacks.

TRASHY DIVA   CLOTHING
Map p247 (www.trashydiva.com; 2048 Magazine St; noon-6pm Mon-Fri, 1-5pm Sat) It isn't really as scandalous as the name suggests, except by Victorian standards. Diva's specialty is sassy 1940s- and '50s-style cinched, hourglass dresses and belle epoque undergarments – lots of corsets, lace and such. The shop also features Kabuki-inspired dresses with embroidered dragons, and retro tops, skirts and shawls reflecting styles plucked from just about every era.

🏠 Garden District

On Magazine St, where it forms the riverside extent of the Garden District, you'll find another intriguing pack of shops. Rink – opposite Lafayette Cemetery No 1, at the corner of Prytania St and Washington Ave – houses a small group of upscale shops and a book store (p125) and coffee shop (p122).

GARDENS OUTSIDE THE GARDENS

New Orleans has always been a green city, at least in terms of color and hue. The climate and the Caribbean-colonial planning philosophy of the city is behind a lush overgrowth effect that is noticeable even in poorer parts of the city. Indeed, the Lower Ninth Ward, which was wiped out by floodwaters, presently looks more like a wilderness than a ghetto. Nature works fast here, and is always sprouting through walls and foundations.

The trick of many New Orleanian plant lovers is channeling this awesome fecundity into plots that are both attractive and utilitarian. Enter **Parkway Partners** (620-2224; www.parkwaypartnersnola.org; 1137 Baronne St), one of the best NGOs operating in New Orleans at the time of writing. Besides funding urban tree-planting projects and similar programs, Parkway is planning to expand, with local contributions, its series of community gardens.

At the time of writing there were 32 such gardens scattered across the city, each one a lovely example of community partnerships and grass-roots beautification efforts. All are undoubtedly pretty, but some gardens also serve a functional role as a source of fresh veggies and produce for local tables, and all help to leech lead out of the local soil (New Orleans has unusually high levels of lead contamination in its soil). There's a full list of active community gardens at www.parkwaypartnersnola.com; our favorites include **Haley's Harvest** (Map p247; 1603 Oretha Castle-Haley Blvd) and **God's Vineyard** (Map p247; 918 Felicity St).

TOP CHOICE / FLEURTY GIRL · T-SHIRTS

Map p247 (www.fleurtygirl.net; 3117 Magazine St; ◷11am-6pm Mon-Thu, 10am-7pm Fri & Sat, noon-6pm Sun) Fleurty Girl celebrates New Orleans and the city's unofficial symbol – the fleur-de-lis – with a feminine, cheeky style. T-shirts sporting local and topical messages, often involving football, are its raison d'être. Memorable slogans include 'Breezus is my homeboy' and 'Free Payton' (after the Saints' coach Sean Payton's one-year suspension).

GARDEN DISTRICT BOOKSHOP · BOOKS

Map p247 (✆895-2266; www.gardendistrictbookshop.com; 2727 Prytania St; ◷10am-6pm Mon-Sat, until 4pm Sun) In the Rink, this indie bookstore sells travel guides, bestsellers, cookbooks, postcards and a select collection of 1st-edition works. It also stocks mostly new books about the region and hosts book signings with local authors, who have a habit of dropping in every now and then.

NEW ORLEANS MUSIC EXCHANGE · MUSICAL INSTRUMENTS

Map p247 (✆891-7670; www.neworleansmusicexchange.net; 3342 Magazine St; ◷10:30am-6pm Mon-Sat, 1-5pm Sun) Ladies, you might just get a 'Can I help you baby?' when exploring this large shop, which specializes mostly in secondhand instruments. It's the place to go for a nice used horn. There's an entire room of brass and woodwinds, all priced fairly. But to find it, you must weave through a maze of guitars and bass amps. It also sells guitars, guitar strings and all that other stuff. But really, you ought to go for the trumpet.

BIG FISHERMAN SEAFOOD · SEAFOOD

Map p247 (✆897-9907; www.bigfishermanseafood.com; 3301 Magazine St; ◷10am-6pm Sat-Thu, until 6:30pm Fri) If you're here in the spring, when it's crawfish season, you may develop a taste for the little mudbugs. But you haven't really had the full-on crawfish experience unless you've been invited to a crawfish boil in someone's backyard. If that hasn't happened, send some crawfish back home and invite your friends over. This busy little shop no longer ships them for you but they will box 'em up tight if you want to use a delivery company (which can cost $200!). The price fluctuates widely from season to season, so call ahead for prices. The store also sell sausages.

FUNKY MONKEY · VINTAGE

Map p247 (www.facebook.com/FunkyMonkeyNewOrleans; 3127 Magazine St; ◷11am-6pm Mon-Wed, 11am-7pm Thu-Sat, noon-6pm Sun) You'll find wigs in every color at Funky Monkey, which sells vintage attire for club-hopping men and women. The tiny shop, which can get jam-packed with customers, is a funhouse of frippery. In addition to wigs, look for jeans, jewelry, tops, sunglasses, hats and boots. Annoyingly it's turned into one of those vintage shops where the secondhand stuff is as expensive as new clothes from a big brand name, but the clothes are admittedly very hip-to-trip.

MAGAZINE ANTIQUE MALL · ANTIQUES, USED GOODS

Map p247 (3017 Magazine St; ◷10:30am-5:30pm Mon-Sat, noon-5:30pm Sun) If Sucré is too crowded for hanging out, grab your gelato and wander down to this antique-apalooza for some fab window shopping. A hobby horse. Scary baby dolls. Hats. Chandeliers. And a giant Darth Vader. Inside, rummagers are likely to score items of interest in the dozen or so stalls here, where independent dealers peddle an intriguing and varied range of antique bric-a-brac. Bargain hunters aren't likely to have much luck, though.

Uptown & Riverbend

Neighborhood Top Five

1 Savoring a blue-cheese smothered steak and a slice of alligator sausage cheesecake at **Jacques-Imo's Café** (p131) before catching the Rebirth Brass Band next door at the **Maple Leaf Bar** (p137).

2 Ogling alligators, foxes and swamp monsters in the Louisiana Swamp at the **Audubon Zoo** (p128).

3 Shopping for one-of-a-kind pottery, house wares and art on bustling **Magazine Street** (p138).

4 Dining and imbibing at locally owned eateries on newly hot **Freret Street** (p132).

5 Learning about art, jazz and African American history on the scenic campus of **Tulane University** (p129).

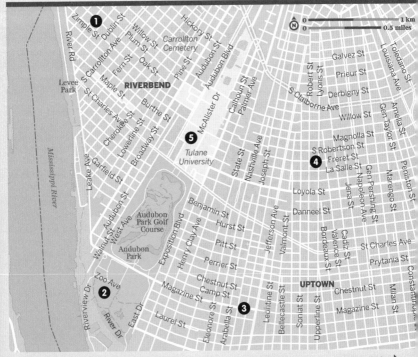

For more detail of the area, see Map p250 ➡

Explore Uptown & Riverbend

If you've only got one day, check out the Audubon Zoo in the morning. Magazine St runs past the zoo, so after your visit with the elephants and giraffes, spend the rest of the day exploring the shops and art galleries that line this busy thoroughfare. Enjoy dinner on Freret St, located above St Charles, then catch a band or grab drinks at a local dive.

If you've got another day, ride the St Charles Ave streetcar to Tulane for a bit of wandering. Continue into Riverbend to check out the shops and restaurants off S Carrollton Ave, particularly along Maple St and Oak St. For dinner, take your own po'boy challenge, sampling different versions from some of the most famous po'boy shops in the city and finding your own favorite.

Maps of New Orleans rarely agree on the area's extents, but for the purposes of this book we'll say Uptown includes everything west of Louisiana Ave, between Magnolia and the river, including the Universities and Audubon Park. St Charles Ave, Magazine St and Tchoupitoulas St are the main routes that more or less follow the contours of the river. The Riverbend is the area above the campuses and Audubon Park. Where St Charles Ave meets S Carrollton Ave is the nexus of the area.

Local Life

➡ **Exercising** Lush Audubon Park, with its 100-year-old live oaks and paved jogging trail, is beloved by runners and walkers.

➡ **Shopping** Magazine St lures the masses with indie shops, galleries and, yes, Whole Foods (p135), while boutiques and thrift stores alike draw students to Riverbend.

➡ **Dive Bars** Spending a blurry evening at grungy but loveable dives, from Ms Mae's (p136) to Snake & Jakes (p136), is part of what it means to be a New Orleanian.

Getting There & Away

➡ **Bus** Bus 11 runs along Magazine St from Canal St to Audubon Park.

➡ **Streetcar** The St Charles Ave streetcar travels through the CBD, the Garden District and Uptown.

➡ **Car** Metered parking is available on Magazine St and St Charles Ave. Free parking can be found on side streets.

Lonely Planet's Top Tip

Magazine St stretches all the way from downtown to Audubon Park, covering 4 miles in the Garden District and Uptown. To get a handle on its shops, galleries and restaurants before your trip, order the block-by-block guide printed by the **Magazine St Merchants Association** (☑342-4435; www.magazine street.com). You can also pick it up at many member stores.

Best Places to Eat

➡ Gautreau's (p130)
➡ Dante's Kitchen (p130)
➡ Patois (p130)
➡ Boucherie (p131)
➡ Dat Dog (p131)
➡ Mat & Naddies (p131)

For reviews, see p130 ➡

Best Places to Drink

➡ Cure (p135)
➡ Columns Hotel (p135)
➡ Bouligny Tavern (p136)
➡ St Joe's Bar (p135)
➡ Snake & Jake's (p136)

For reviews, see p135 ➡

Best Places to Shop

➡ Potsalot (p138)
➡ Hazelnut (p138)
➡ Cole Pratt Gallery (p138)
➡ Crescent City Comics (p138)
➡ Dirty Coast (p138)
➡ Maple Street Book Shop (p138)

For reviews, see p137 ➡

UPTOWN & RIVERBEND

TOP SIGHTS
AUDUBON ZOO

The Audubon Zoo is home to an excellent array of international animals – Asian elephants, towering giraffes, a poisonous dart frog – but it's the critters hanging out in the Louisiana Swamp that you'll likely remember most. In this wonderland of bald cypress and Spanish moss you might see a couple of gray foxes sleeping on rocking chairs near the scruffy Breaux Grocery, not too worried about the gators loitering in the sun just round the bend.

In this engaging Cajun setting you can learn how Spanish moss is used as furniture stuffing while an authentic fishing camp displays shrimp trawls, crawfish traps and an oyster dredge. Bobcats, red foxes and endangered Louisiana black bears lope (or sleep) in the swamp scrub. Human intrusions into the swamp environment are poignantly represented with a *traǎnasee* cutter, used by fish and game trappers to create access across shallow swamps. Step inside to see the famous white alligators.

Elsewhere, the **Reptile Encounter** displays representatives of the largest snakes in the world – from the king cobra that grows to more than 18ft in length to the green anaconda that reaches 38ft. Many local species of snake are also on view. Other memorable sections include the Mayan-style **Jaguar Jungle** and the **African Savanna** with its raised walkway. Poems and quotes, from Emily Dickinson to Langston Hughes, dot the walkways and add atmosphere while eco-minded plaques reinforce the precarious position of many of these animals in the wild.

The zoo is located inside Audubon Park, a lovely spot for taking a walk or simply sitting under trees and enjoying a snow cone in the summer swelter.

DON'T MISS

➡ Louisiana Swamp
➡ White Alligators
➡ Jaguar Jungle
➡ Reptile Encounter

PRACTICALITIES

➡ Map p250
➡ ☑581-4629
➡ www.audubon institute.org
➡ 6500 Magazine St
➡ adult/child/senior $16/11/13
➡ ⊙10am-4pm Tue-Fri, until 5pm Sat & Sun Sept-May; daily Jun-Aug

👁 SIGHTS

AUDUBON ZOO   ZOO
See p128.

TULANE UNIVERSITY   UNIVERSITY
Map p250 (☑865-5000; www.tulane.edu; 6823 St Charles Ave) The campus of Tulane, a premier Southern university, is an attractive tableau of live oaks, red-brick buildings and green quads spread across 110 acres above Audubon Park. This is one of the prettiest colleges in the country, and it's a pleasant place to stop and stretch your legs if you're riding the St Charles Ave streetcar across town.

Tulane has an interesting origin as a yellow-fever buster. In 1834 the Medical College of Louisiana was founded in an attempt to control repeated cholera and yellow-fever epidemics. By 1847 the University of Louisiana merged with the school, and in 1883, Paul Tulane gave the school a $1 million donation that initiated significant expansion and slapped his name on the entire institution.

Tulane boasts 13,350 students in 11 colleges and schools, including a law school whose entire student body seems to fill up Magazine St cafes during exam time, and the highly regarded medical school, now relocated downtown. Big-name alumni include former French president Jacques Chirac, Republican politician Newt Gingrich, TV presenter Jerry Springer and a very long list of Louisiana governors, judges and assorted politicos.

The **Amistad Research Center** (☑862-3222; www.amistadresearchcenter.org; Tilton Memorial Hall; ⏱8:30am-4:30pm Mon-Fri), which holds more than 15 million documents, is one of the nation's largest repositories of African American history. Despite the size of the collection, the facility is not a museum. For visitors, there is a small area on the second floor with rotating exhibits that offer insights on ethnic heritage you're not likely to get from any other source. A recent exhibit about African Americans in sports included documents and photographs related to the Negro Baseball League. The displayed works of art from the Aaron Douglas Collection are another reason to drop by.

The oral histories are the heart of the music holdings at the **Hogan Jazz Archive** (☑865-5688; http://jazz.tulane.edu; 3rd fl, Joseph Merrick Jones Hall, 6801 Freret St; ⏱9am-4:45pm Mon-Fri), a collection of New Orleans jazz artifacts which includes sheet music, photographs, journals and recordings. Most of the archive's great wealth of material is not on exhibit; the helpful staff will retrieve items for you. More casual visitors may enjoy the Storyville Room, with its emphasis on Jelly Roll Morton (who played piano in the district's bordellos during the early 20th century). Recordings include stacks of 78rpm recordings with early sides by the Original Dixieland Jazz Band in 1917.

Flanked by beautiful Tiffany stained-glass triptychs, the **Newcomb Art Gallery** (☑865-5328; www.newcombartgallery.tulane.edu Woldenberg Art Center; admission free; ⏱10am-5pm Tue-Fri, 11am-4pm Sat & Sun) is a great spot to soak up some art; just outside is a pretty green where students sunbathe, toss Frisbees and generally recede into the happiest rhythms of American higher ed.

TOURO SYNAGOGUE   SYNAGOGUE
Map p250 (☑895-4843; www.tourosynagogue .com; 4238 St Charles Ave) Despite the fact that Jews were officially banned from New Orleans under the Code Noir (Black Code), they have been calling the Crescent City home since the 18th century. Founded in 1828, Touro is the city's oldest synagogue (and the oldest in the country outside of the original 13 colonies). The synagogue

UPTOWN & RIVERBEND SIGHTS

ACTIVITIES IN UPTOWN & RIVERBEND

The clang and swoosh of the **St Charles Avenue Streetcar** (Map p250; www.norta.com; 1 ride/day pass $1.25/3; ⏱24hr) is as essential to the character of Uptown as are live oaks and stately mansions. New Orleanians are justifiably proud of their moving monument, which began life as the nation's second horse-drawn streetcar line, the New Orleans & Carrollton Railroad, in 1835. In 1893 the line was among the first systems to be electrified. Now it is one of the few streetcars in the USA to have survived the automobile era. The fleet of antique cars also survived the hurricanes of 2005, and today full service has been restored all the way to South Carrollton Ave. The line carried more than 3 million passengers in 2010.

bears a slight resemblance to a red-brick Byzantine temple, with squat buttresses and bubbly domes. The local congregation began as an amalgamation between local Spanish-descended Jews and German Jewish immigrants, a relatively rare mixed lineage in American Judaism.

LATTER MEMORIAL LIBRARY   LIBRARY

Map p250 (⌨596-2625; www.nutrias.org; 5120 St Charles Ave; ⊙9am-8pm Mon & Wed, until 6pm Tue & Thu, 10am-5pm Sat, noon-5pm Sun; @⌨) Poised elegantly above shady stands of palms on St Charles Ave, the Latter Memorial Library was once a private mansion residence, passed along from the Isaac family (owners 1907–12) – who installed Flemish-style carved woodwork, Dutch murals and French frescoed ceilings – to aviator Harry Williams and his silent-film-star wife, Marguerite Clark (1912–39), to a local horse racer named Robert S Eddy, then to Mr and Mrs Harry Latter. The couple, who converted the mansion into its current form as a library, gave the building to the city in 1948. The bottom floor and the entire exterior facade remain stately if a bit well-worn.

LEVEE PARK   PARK

Map p250 This unique public greenway runs atop the levee space that follows the curves of the Mississippi River all the way from Audubon Park to Jefferson Parish. It's a nice spot for walking, jogging or biking, but views onto the river are occasionally only so-so and there aren't enough paths connecting the levee to the street below (if you try to cross off the path, you may get ankle deep in Mississippi mud). Still, it's a good little green space.

 EATING

Uptown and Riverbend are arguably the hottest food corridors in the city. There's no shortage of options, including shotgun shack diners, po'boy-slinging bars and cute garden cottages hiding some of the best Creole fine dining in town. Freret St, which has undergone a remarkable renaissance since Hurricane Katrina (see the boxed text, p132), is the latest foodie mecca with new eateries putting a gourmet spin on old favorites such as hamburgers, pizza and hot dogs.

GAUTREAU'S   MODERN AMERICAN $$$

Map p250 (⌨899-7397; www.gautreausrest aurant.com; 1728 Soniat St; mains $22-35; ⊙6-10pm Mon-Sat) There's no sign outside Gautreau's, just the number 1728 discreetly marking a nondescript house in a residential neighborhood. But there's no secrecy once you've crossed the restaurant's threshold, just a refined but welcoming dining room where chef Sue Zemanick has won every award a rising young star can garner in American culinary circles including 'Top 10 Best New Chefs' in *Food & Wine* magazine and 'Chef of the Year' in *New Orleans* magazine. Inside, savvy diners, many of them New Orleanian food aficionados, dine on fresh, modern American fare, from sautéed snapper with a lemon burre blanc and chanterelle mushrooms to the simple-sounding but lauded roasted chicken with garlic mashed potatoes. Call several days in advance for reservations.

PATOIS   FRENCH-CREOLE $$

Map p250 (⌨895-9441; www.patoisnola.com; 6078 Laurel St; lunch $13-21, brunch $13-19, dinner $23-32; ⊙5:30-10pm Wed & Thu, until 10:30pm Fri & Sat, 11:30am-2pm Fri, 10:30am-2pm Sun) The interior of Patois feels like the cozy house of very good friends – who happen to be very good cooks. This Uptown restaurant is one of the hottest names on local foodies' lips, which isn't surprising considering the credentials of head chef, Aaron Burgau. Burgau went through the paces of New Orleans' top restaurants, including Bayona (p62) and Commander's Palace (p118), before opening Patois. The menu is French haute with New Orleans accents (or 'patois'); house-made boudin on the charcuterie plate, smoked rabbit and andouille gumbo, and new twists on surf and turf with ham-crusted scallops.

DANTE'S KITCHEN   MODERN LOUISIANAN $$

Map p250 (⌨861-3121; www.danteskitchen.com; 736 Dante St; brunch $9-14, mains $23-27; ⊙5:30-10pm Wed-Mon, 10:30am-2pm Sat & Sun) It's hard not to feel like you've stepped into the pages of a J Crew catalog during Sunday brunch at Dante's, a country cottage on the Mississippi levee. Tulane kids, grandmas and grandpas, girlfriends who brunch and a few well-behaved babies – it feels as if half of New Orleans is here or on the way. The menu melds French, American and Louisiana traditions: pork steak with kale and tasso and maple-glazed chicken with potato-bacon hash cake are good examples. The Sunday brunch is one of the best in the city. Debris and poached eggs on a caramelized onion biscuit, topped with a demi-glacé hollandaise sauce is an unbelievable way to start your day, unless, of course, you decide to opt for the bread-pudding French toast. Make reservations for dinner.

MAT & NADDIE'S
MODERN SOUTHERN $$

Map p250 (☏861-9600; www.matandnaddies .com; 937 Leonidas St; lunch $9-13, dinner $18-29; ☺11am-2pm & 5:30-9:30pm Mon-Tue & Thu-Fri, 11am-2pm Wed, 5:30-9:30pm Sat) Everything comes together at Mat & Naddie's. Set in a beautiful riverfront shotgun house with a Christmas light–bedecked patio in the back, it offers rich, innovative, even amusing food, such as sherry-marinated quail with waffles and chocolate peanut-butter gooey butter cake, and just damn friendly staff and service. It's kind of weird, it's high quality topped with quirkiness and, honestly, it's one of our favorite splurges in the city.

LILETTE
FRENCH $$

Map p250 (☏895-1636; www.liletterestaurant .com; 3637 Magazine St; lunch $12-24, dinner $24-34; ☺11:30am-2pm Tue-Sat, 5:30-9:30pm Tue-Thu, until 10:30pm Fri & Sat) Lilette is a lively little bistro with a very traditional European vibe, although tradition is not an obsession, as chef John Harris works wonders with familiar dishes, making them subtly new. Lunch is a nice way to pass a Magazine St afternoon. Dinner's nice, too; start your meal with the white-truffle parmigiana toast with wild mushrooms, then pick from a solid lineup of mains, such as grilled hanger steak, which comes with fries and marrowed bordelaise sauce. Harris opened the equally stylish Bouligny Tavern next door in 2010.

BOUCHERIE
MODERN AMERICAN $

Map p250 (☏862-5514; www.boucherie-nola.com; 8115 Jeannette St; small plates $5-12, mains $11-15; ☺11am-3pm & 5:30-9.30pm Tue-Sat) The thick, glistening cuts of bacon on the BLT can only be the work of the devil – or chef Nathanial Zimet, whose house-cured meats and succulent dishes are lauded all over town. Boucherie's signature dessert, Krispy Kreme bread pudding, is also a wonder. The heavy bread pudding becomes airy yet drool-tastically fattening when mixed with the glazed doughnuts, all topped with rum syrup. Boucherie is the permanent outpost of the Purple Truck, New Orleans' most famous mobile restaurant and the pre-cursor to the restaurant, a cute purple cottage adorned by a low-key pig. Barbecued shrimp and grits cakes are darkly sweet and savory and garlic parmesan fries are gloriously stinky. The name of the restaurant, Boucherie, is the Cajun word for a celebratory community pig-pickin'. The food here captures that downhome exuberance. As the motto says, 'It's fine dining for the people.'

DAT DOG
HOTDOGS $

Map p250 (www.datdognola.com; 5030 Freret St; mains under $7; ☺11am-10pm Mon-Sat, noon-8pm Sun) Who dat who say Dat Dog? Da whole doggone city dat's who. That's because every part of your dog, from the steamed link to the toasted sourdough bun to the flavor-packed toppings, is produced with tasty exuberance. In fact, if you can't decide which of the 13 toppings you want slathered on your link, ask for the chef's choice. They'll dress it up right. If you like your dawgs spicy, try the Louisiana hot sausage sourced from nearby Hanrahan – and grab about 10 napkins for every topping you choose. The eatery recently moved from its pint-sized original location to a new space across the street, with seating for about 45 inside and 100 outside. Cash only, but it has an ATM.

BRIGTSEN'S RESTAURANT
MODERN CAJUN $$$

Map p250 (☏861-7610; www.brigtsens.com; 723 Dante St; mains $26-38; ☺5:30-10pm Tue-Sat) Despite all the critical acclaim that has been heaped upon chef Frank Brigtsen, the restaurant that bears his name remains a decidedly unpretentious place. Set in a converted double-shotgun house, the restaurant feels homey and inviting, with service that's attentive but never oppressive. Brigsten terms his cooking 'modern Louisiana cuisine,' and those in search of haute Cajun cuisine will not be disappointed. Rabbit and duck are among his specialties. Look for the roast duck with cornbread dressing and honey-pecan gravy, or beef tournedos in a tasso wine sauce.

JACQUES-IMO'S CAFÉ
LOUISIANAN $$

Map p250 (☏861-0886; www.jacquesimoscafe .com; 8324 Oak St; mains $18-30; ☺5-10pm

Mon-Thu, 5pm-late Fri & Sat) If cornbread muffins swimming in butter aren't rich enough, how about steak smothered in blue-cheese sauce and bacon? Or the insane yet wickedly brilliant alligator sausage cheesecake? That's the whole attitude at Jack Leonardi's exceedingly popular restaurant: die, happily, with butter and heavy sauces sweating out of your pores. Jacques is just a few doors from the famous Maple Leaf Bar, and many people make an evening out of these two spots, but you don't need an excuse to dine at this dive-cum-haute-cuisine outpost. We mean that – it looks like a local's cluttered house. You can even dine in the bed of the beat-up pickup truck out front. In fairness, the kitchen does send out duds from time to time. Blame the crowds. On busy nights expect long waits to get in (reservations are not accepted). Open Sundays during Jazz Fest.

LA PETITE GROCERY   FRENCH $$
Map p250 (📞891-3377; www.lapetitegrocery.com; 4238 Magazine St; lunch $14-24, dinner $11-24; ⏰11:30am-2:30pm & 5:30-10pm Tue-Sat, 10:30am-2:30pm Sun) Now open for Sunday brunch, Petite is one of the many cozy bistros squeezed into the crowded Uptown dining scene. The dinners are good but not great for the price, and include bistro mainstays such as braised lamb shanks. We prefer the lunches, which consist of some very fine sandwiches and salads.

COWBELL   BURGERS $$
Map p250 (www.cowbell-nola.com; 8801 Oak St; mains $11-32; ⏰11:30am-3pm & 5-10pm Tue-Thu, 11:30am-3pm & 5-11pm Fri & Sat) Cowbell has a scruffy charm – local art on the walls, scuffed wooden floors, Elvis on the ceiling – that makes you want to stay awhile. And its perch by the levee is darn appealing too. But it's hard to linger at this Riverside eatery because the juicy beef burgers are just too good to leave loitering on the plate for too long. Non-beef options include grilled fish tacos and lime grill organic chicken. We hear the mac and cheese is divine. Solos will do just fine at the efficient but friendly bar, and carnivores who like their burgers medium rare will get 'em that way.

CAMELLIA GRILL   GRILL, DINER $
Map p250 (📞309-2679; 626 S Carrollton Ave; mains $3-9; ⏰8am-midnight Mon-Thu, until 2am Fri & Sat) One of our favorite New Orleans stories: apparently a woman walked into

---

DINING HOTSPOT: FRERET STREET

The revitalization of decaying Freret St into a much-lauded dining destination is one of New Orleans' biggest post-Katrina success stories. The eight-block strip, which stretches from Jefferson Ave to Napoleon Ave, had been in a state of serious decline for decades. Named for 19th-century mayor and cotton baron William Freret, the street was a prosperous business corridor in the 1920s and 1930s. The neighborhood lost families to white flight from the 1950s into the 1970s and the fatal shooting of a popular business owner in front of his store in the mid-1980s hastened the slide. Mother Nature seemed to deal the final blow in 2005 when the levee broke and several feet of water doused the neighborhood.

A few community stalwarts started the **Freret Street Farmers Market** (http://freretmarket.org; ⏰noon-5pm 2nd Sat of month) in 2007, but the revitalization really began after Neal Bodenheimer and Matthew Kohnke transformed a 100-year-old former firehouse into the craft cocktail bar Cure. City council member Stacy Head, who represents the district, helped the neighborhood win a more development-friendly zoning designation, and new eateries began trickling onto the strip. That trickle has become a storm, and by 2011 there were 11 new restaurants on Freret St with more on the way.

This new dining destination presents a bedeviling dilemma for gourmands who are only in town for a short time – how do you decide where to go? Truthfully? It's hard to go wrong. You'll find topping-slathered hot dogs and sausages at **Dat Dog** (p131), gourmet deep-dish pies at **Midway Pizza** (http://midwaypizzanola.com; 4725 Freret St), hormone-free beef at **The Company Burger** (http://thecompanyburger.com; 4600 Freret) and comfort food from the bayou and the delta at **High Hat Cafe** (http://highhatcafe.com; 4500 Freret St). And we've barely scratched the surface of the goodness. Bon Appetit!

Camellia and asked if it served low-fat dessert. The line cook's response? Dip a slice of pecan pie in melted butter and throw it on the grill. That's what you get! The other great thing about this spot, besides its great diner burger-chili-Reuben fare, is that it's the sort of place where the staff look like 50 Cent or The Ramones, and they all call each other – and you – 'baby.' All the time. Plus, they dress in tux shirts and black bow-ties, as if this place couldn't be any wonderfully weirder.

DOMILISE'S PO-BOYS   PO'BOYS $
Map p250 (5240 Annunciation St; po'boys $8-13; ⏱11am-7pm Mon-Wed, Fri & Sat) Domilise's is everything that makes New Orleans great: a dilapidated white shack by the river serving Dixie beer, staffed by folks who've worked here for decades, and prepping, if not the best po'boys in the city, at least the best seafood sandwich. Straight up; we haven't had a better oyster sandwich anywhere. Locals tell us to opt for the half-and-half (oysters and shrimp) with gravy and cheese, but honestly, we think the oyster, dressed but otherwise on its own, is the height of the po'boy maker's craft. Belly up to the bar, get another Dixie and welcome home. Cash only.

ST JAMES CHEESE CO   DELI $
Map p250 (www.stjamescheese.com; 5004 Prytania St; mains $9-15; ⏱11am-6pm Mon-Thu, until 8pm Fri & Sat, until 4pm Sun) Founded by an Englishman obsessed over all the right things (namely, meat and fermented milk products), St James is the best cheese shop in the city. We won't give all the details of what's available, but rest assured there's a veritable atlas worth of cheese in this shop. Premade sandwiches make an excellent lunch; we opt for the mozzarella with basil pesto and salami. Hosts frequent cheese tastings.

CREOLE CREAMERY   ICE CREAM $
Map p250 (www.creolecreamery.com; 4924 Prytania St; 1 scoop $2.75; ⏱noon-10pm Sun-Thu, until 11pm Fri & Sat) It's impossible to make up your mind at Creole Creamery. Every single flavor sounds uniquely delicious. Steen's molasses oatmeal cookie. Chocolate malted chop. Gingerbread cheesecake crunch. Lavender honey. Can I get a yum yum?! The good news? It's pretty clear you can't go wrong. So don't weep for the flavor you didn't try and en-

joy dancing with the one that won ya. The unique flavors rotate, but you'll always find vanilla and chocolate. You'll earn a spot in the Hall of Fame if you eat eight scoops with eight toppings.

DELACHAISE   INTERNATIONAL $$
Map p250 (☎895-0858; www.thedelachaise.com; 3442 St Charles Ave; small plates $7-18; ⏱5pm-late daily) You gotta love the cheese menu – the pictograms that explain 'stinky,' 'strong' etc are very cute. The small plates are all wonderful in their own indulgent way, especially the ridiculously over-the-top grilled cheese sandwich, apparently assembled from truffled bread and foie gras–infused cheese (that's a joke, but the thing really tastes that rich). If it's late at night, you're hungry and you need something a little more refined than a burger, head here.

IL POSTO   CAFE $
Map p250 (www.ilpostocafe-nola.com; 4607 Dryades St; mains under $11; ⏱7am-9pm Tue-Fri, 8am-9pm Sat, 8am-3pm Sun) At some point during an extended New Orleans trip, you're going to burn out on eggs benedict, house-made boudin and bread pudding. Stylish Il Posto will be there for you when that moment arrives. Order scones, croissants and bagels in the morning or stop by at lunch for a tuna salad panini or a beet and walnut salad with a glass of wine. And when it comes to the homemade Oreos, don't be indecisive. Just buy one. These babies sell quick.

MAGASIN CAFE   VIETNAMESE $
Map p250 (www.magasincafe.com; 4201 Magazine St; mains $4-11; ⏱11am-3:45pm, 6-9pm Tue-Sat) A spare and shiny cube perched on the corner of Magazine St and Milan St, Magasin won't be embraced by grouchy Vietnamese-food snobs who think pho is only good if it's served in a grubby hovel in a sketchy neighborhood far, far away. But everyone else? Come join the party. The food is fresh and light but deceptively filling. One serving of spring rolls might just fill you up. The *banh mi* sandwiches are a great deal at $4.50. One of the best parts of the experience? The service, which is simultaneously thoughtful, efficient and attentive.

GUY'S   PO'BOYS $
Map p250 (5259 Magazine St; po'boys under $10; ⏱11am-4pm Mon-Sat) It's very simple: Guy's

is basically a one-man operation that does some of the best po'boys in town. The owner is also the cashier, head shopper, chef and prep staff. Ergo your sandwich is made fresh and to order, with a level of attention you don't get anywhere else in the city. Even when the line is out the door – and it often is – each po'boy is painstakingly crafted. So yes, that loaf will take a while, but *damn* is it worth it.

REFUEL
CAFE $

Map p250 (www.refuelcafe.com; 8124 Hampson St; mains $7-12; ⊘7am-2pm Tue-Fri, 8:30am-2pm Sat & Sun) Refuel packs 'em tight on Sunday mornings but somehow still manages to look cute and breezy. This hip cafe adds a bit of much-needed chic to the local coffee culture scene, but it's hardly pretentious; service here is some of the friendliest in town. The staff serves fresh food such as California omelets with avocado, but New Orleans mainstays like grits keep the kitchen rooted in the South. Order at the counter.

KYOTO
JAPANESE $$

Map p250 (4920 Prytania St; mains $8-24; ⊘11am-2:30pm & 5-10pm Mon-Thu, 11am-2:30pm & 5-10:30pm Fri, noon-3pm & 5-10:30pm Sat) Sporting a blonde-wood interior, friendly hipster staff and chefs who truly care about creating some fine raw fish dishes, Kyoto is our favorite sushi bet in the city. The menu offers all the tuna/eel/yellowtail favorites plus some local specialties such as crawfish rolls. It's popular with students, young families and the smattering of Japanese expats we spoke with in the city, which may be the highest praise of all.

PASCAL'S MANALE
ITALIAN, LOUISIANAN $$

Map p250 (☏895-4877; 1838 Napoleon Ave; mains $18-37; ⊘11:30am-2pm Mon-Fri, 5-10pm Mon-Sat) There's a whiff of Mario Puzo in the air as you make your way past the oyster counter and clubby bar to the white tablecloths in the dining room where pasta dishes, juicy steaks and Italian standards reign supreme. Established in 1913, this old-school joint is an Uptown tradition, and the walls, bedecked with black-and-white photos of staff, patrons and the odd celebrity, pay tribute to days of yore. It claims to have invented the local take on barbecue shrimp that requires no grill (it's sautéed in a garlicky sauce).

TEE-EVA'S OLD-FASHIONED PIES & PRALINES
SOUL FOOD, CREOLE $

Map p250 (www.tee-evapralines.com; 5201 Magazine St; praline cookie $2, pint of gumbo/jambalaya $5; ⊘11am-7pm Mon-Sat, 1-7pm Sun) It's impossible to nibble a praline from Tee-Eva's over the course of a day. Trust us, after one bite, you're a goner for the whole darn thing – right then. As you're heading toward Audubon Park from the Garden District, look for a red-and-yellow sign on your right (the shop has moved from its brightly muraled former location on the 4400 block). Tee-Eva once sang backup to the late, great local legend Ernie K-Doe; now she whips out snowballs and pralines, some fine hot lunches and some very fine Louisiana sweet and savory pies.

CASAMENTO'S
SEAFOOD $

Map p250 (www.casamentosrestaurant.com; 4330 Magazine St; mains $4-13; ⊘11am-2pm & 5:30-9pm Tue-Sat early Sep–mid-May) This is as good as oysters get in NOLA. That's why you come here: to walk through the 1949 soda-shop-esque sparkling interior, across the tiled floors to a marble-top counter, trade a joke with the person shucking shells and get some raw boys with a beer. If the shucker respects the way you down your 'erster,' they might even give you a fist bump on your way out the door. If you can't take 'em raw, the thick gumbo with Creole tomatoes and oyster loaf (a sandwich of breaded and fried oysters) are suitably incredible. They keep it old school here in terms of friendly service, seasonal opening times (it's closed June to August) and trading only in cash.

MAHONY'S PO-BOY SHOP
PO'BOYS $

Map p250 (www.mahonyspoboys.com; 3454 Magazine St; po'boys $7-15; ⊘11am-10pm Mon-Sat) A convenient po'boy place with a fun atmosphere, Mahony's is a welcome if sometimes expensive choice. Digs are a converted Magazine St house with a tiny front porch. Inside, LSU pictures adorn the walls, and you might hear 'Come on Eileen' tripping from the speakers. The Peacemaker with fried oysters, bacon and cheddar is a crowd pleaser as is the grilled shrimp and fried green tomatoes, although we found the latter, at $14.95 market price, lacking in oomph.

TAQUERIA CORONA
MEXICAN **$**

Map p250 (www.taqueriacorona.com; 5932 Magazine St; mains $3-19; ⏰11:30am-2pm daily, 5-9pm Sun-Thu, 5-9:30pm Fri & Sat) Tacos start at $3 at Taqueria Corona, a friendly neighborhood/student spot that's got the requisite basket of chips on the table and Mexican bric-a-brac hanging from the ceiling. But don't let the clichéd interior put you off. Taqueria Corona serves some of the best Mexican food in the city. And gets jam-packed with families, young Uptown professionals and Tulane kids chowing down on some excellent burritos (we like the bean), tacos (go for the fish or chorizo) and flautas (mmm, the shrimp). It's a great choice for a quality budget feed.

HANSEN'S SNO-BLIZ
SNOWBALLS **$**

Map p250 (☎891-9788; www.snobliz.com; 4801 Tchoupitoulas St; snowballs $1.50-3.50; ⏰1-7pm Tue-Sun April-Aug) The humble snowball (shaved ice with flavored syrup) is New Orleans' favorite dessert (see p28). City-wide consensus is that Hansen's, which has been in business since 1939, does the best ball in town. Founder Ernest Hansen, who passed away after Hurricane Katrina, actually patented the shaved-ice machine. Now his granddaughter, Ashley, runs the family business, doling out shaved ice under everything from root-beer syrup to cream of nectar. Call or check the website before your visit to make sure it's open for the season.

WHOLE FOODS
MARKET **$**

Map p250 (www.wholefoodsmarket.com/arabella station; 5600 Magazine St; ⏰8am-9pm) What's that monstrosity across from St Joe's? I hate it! Wait, it's Whole Foods? I love it! Yep, the gleaming organic market on Magazine St triggers mixed feelings. It sells organic foods and fills a niche for the neighborhood, but its opening in 2002 signaled a change in the character of Magazine St, which is largely composed of indie stores and mom and pops. For travelers, come here to meet your self-catering needs.

🍷 DRINKING & NIGHTLIFE

There's not much difference between this drinking scene and the fun going on in the Lower Garden District; Magazine St maintains a generally young, hip, neighborhoody vibe throughout. Bars in Riverbend attract more of a student crowd, although the Maple Leaf keeps this mixed thanks to its music lineups.

TOP CHOICE CURE
BAR

Map p250 (www.curenola.com; 4905 Freret St; ⏰5pm-midnight Sun-Thu, to 2am Fri & Sat) This stylish purveyor of cocktails and spirits flickers like an ultra-modern apothecary shop, a place where mysterious elixirs are expertly mixed to soothe whatever ails you. Set in a smooth and polished space of modern banquettes, anatomic art and a Zen-garden outdoor area, Cure is where you come for a well-mixed drink, period. The bar operates on the premise that a good cocktail is the height of the bartender's craft, and takes its mixology *very* seriously. Try the appropriately dubbed Howitzer (bourbon, bitters, lemon juice and magic), which will pretty much blow your sobriety to smithereens. In the evening you need to follow House Rules: no baseball caps and after 8pm Thursday to Saturday, no shorts for guys.

COLUMNS HOTEL
BAR

Map p250 (www.thecolumns.com; 3811 St Charles Ave; ⏰3pm-midnight Mon-Thu, 11am-2am Fri & Sat, 11am-midnight Sun) With its ante-bellum trappings – a raised front porch, white Doric columns, a flanking live oak – the Columns Hotel harks back to a simpler era. Oh yes, we're going to party like it's 1859. But truthfully, it's not as aristocratic as all that; it's more a place where college students and just-graduates act the part of the Southern upper crust. This hotel bar is a great place to come and sit back with a cool glass of gin while fanning yourself and watching the St Charles Streetcar crank past. And ladies, there's still some chivalry left – a staff member is on call to walk patrons from bar-to-car.

TOP CHOICE ST JOE'S BAR
BAR

Map p250 (5535 Magazine St; ⏰5pm-late Mon-Thu, 3pm-late Fri, 4pm-late Sat, 5pm-late Sun) The mojitos at Joe's have been voted the best in town by New Orleanians several times, and the jukebox is well stocked with jazz, rock and blues. Patrons are in their 20s and 30s, friendly and chatty, as are the staff. The main draw is the layout – while narrow in the front, it leads past a series of faux-Catholic shrines into a spacious backyard that feels like a cross between an Indonesian island

and a Thai temple. It's a good spot for one of those aforementioned mojitos.

LE BON TEMPS ROULÉ
BAR, LIVE MUSIC

Map p250 (4801 Magazine St; ⊙11am-3am) A neighborhood bar – a very good one at that – with a mostly college and postcollege crowd drawn in by two pool tables and a commendable beer selection. Late at night, high-caliber blues, zydeco or jazz rocks the joint's little back room. It's the sort of bar where a lesbian punches a guy for trying to steal her girlfriend's Abita, and then all three laugh about the incident afterwards.

BOULIGNY TAVERN
COCKTAIL BAR, WINE BAR

Map p250 (☑891-8500; http://boulignytavern .com; 3641 Magazine St; ⊙4pm-midnight Mon-Thu, until 2am Fri & Sat) With its Mad Men décor, sexy lighting, inventive cocktails and extensive wine list, Bouligny is a fashionable addition to the Magazine St bar scene. Clientele come here for an after-work unwind or to prep their palate before a meal at chef John Harris' companion restaurant Lilette next door. The small plates are divine, particularly the bruschetta and the gouda beignets. You don't like gin? The wonderful Nocin Sour with aviation gin, green walnut liqueur and lemon juice will convert you. This low-key hideaway is in a house fronted by a live oak, and it's easy to miss. Look for the alluringly lit alley-way patio.

45 TCHOUP
DIVE

Map p250 (4529 Tchoupitoulas St; ⊙2pm-4am Sun-Thu, until 5am Fri & Sat) As far as dive bars go, 45 Tchoup is just as convivial as others in Uptown, but with a slightly older, less raucous crowd. But only slightly. Basically, patrons look downright glad to be at the party. Maybe it's because 45 Tchoup literally rose from the ruins of Katrina – it was constructed from salvaged materials.

COOTER BROWN'S TAVERN & OYSTER BAR
BAR

Map p250 (www.cooterbrowns.com; 509 S Carrollton Ave; mains $4-13; ⊙11am-late; 🛜) Cooter's scores points with longtime locals because it served as a community gathering place in the aftermath of Katrina. It also takes its beer seriously, serving more than 40 draft brews and hundreds of international bottled beers. College kids, local characters and Uptown swells drop in for a few brews and freshly shucked oysters, or

to shoot pool or watch sports on TV. Pause to appreciate the tavern's 'Beersoleum & Hall of Foam' – a gallery of 100 plaster bas-relief statuettes of everybody from Liberace to Chairman Mao, each holding a bottle of beer. This curious, still-growing exhibit is the work of the uniquely talented Scott Conary.

SNAKE & JAKES
DIVE

Map p250 (☑861-2802; www.snakeandjakes .com; 7612 Oak St; ⊙from 7pm) Looking like a bayou bait shack that's been tarted up for Christmas a day late, Snake & Jakes is a New Orleans institution. Some say the place even messes with the space-time continuum – enter at 3am and a mere five minutes later you're stumbling outside and the sun's coming up. If this happens to you, pat yourself on the back: you, my friend, are now a fully fledged honorary New Orleanian. If you end up here any time before 3am, it's probably too early. When you're out with your buddies and someone says, 'Let's go to Snakes,' that's a sure sign the night is either going to get much better or immeasurably worse.

F&M'S PATIO BAR
BAR

Map p250 (www.fandmpatiobar.com; 4841 Tchoupitoulas St; ⊙7pm-4am Sun-Thu, until 5:30am Fri & Sat) If you're old enough to be paying off your student loans or you have a real driver's license, you may want to give F&M a pass on weekends, when every college student in Louisiana tests the structural integrity of the bar's leopard-print pool tables by dancing on them. For the rest of the week this is a really nice place, with good pool going (on the aforementioned tables), a nice grill slinging some killer cheese fries, and a semi-outdoor area that's well-suited for a cold beer under the hot sun.

RUE DE LA COURSE
CAFE

Map p250 (1140 S Carrollton Ave; ⊙6:30am-11pm Mon-Fri, 7am-11pm Sat & Sun; 🛜) The setting alone – a cavernous former bank building on the corner of Carrollton Ave and Oak St – is reason enough to step inside for a look-see. But once over the threshold, with a glimpse at the pastries and list of hot and cold javas, and you'll surely be tempted to settle in and soak up the atmosphere. Cash only.

MS MAE'S
DIVE

Map p250 (☎895-9401; 4336 Magazine St; ☺24hr) This dimly lit dive is one of the toughest bars in the city. It's also a 24-hour den of all that is sinful and fun. Despite its gritty reputation, we hear that Ms Mae always kept the women's bathroom immaculately clean when she was running the place. Ms Mae sold the bar in 2010, and had just passed away at press time, but this legendary place across the street from the police precinct keeps tippling along. Every thread of the human tapestry gets woven into this great, grotty hole. There's even a website dedicated to the stupid behavior folks inevitably engage in here (http://msmaeswallofshame.blogspot.com).

MONKEY HILL BAR
BAR

Map p250 (www.monkeyhillbar.com; 6100 Magazine St; ☺3pm-late Mon-Sat, 6pm-late Sun) Toward the quiet end of Magazine St, Monkey Hill looks and feels like a neighborhood bar, which it basically is. But it's one of the best happy-hour spots (3pm to 8pm weeknights) in this part of town and hosts some good live music on a monthly basis. If you're near Audubon Park late in the afternoon, there's no reason not to stop in.

BOOT
BAR

Map p250 (www.thebootneworleans.com; 1039 Broadway St; ☺11am-late) Considering the Boot is almost located within Tulane's campus, it's not surprising this college bar practically doubles as student housing for that university. If you're within the vicinity of 21 years old, this place is a lot of fun; otherwise, you might think you've accidentally stumbled into Athens, what with all the Greek System types (ie frat boys and sorority girls) about.

★ ENTERTAINMENT

Many bars in Uptown and Riverbend offer live music but the following venues do it particularly well and are worth a special trip.

TOP CHOICE MAPLE LEAF BAR
LIVE MUSIC

Map p250 (☎866-9359; www.mapleleafbar.com; 8316 Oak St; usually $10, Mon free; ☺3pm-late) The premier nighttime destination in the Riverbend area, the legendary Maple Leaf's dimly lit, pressed-tin caverns are the kind of environs you'd expect from a New Or-leans juke joint. Scenes from the film *Angel Heart* (1987), in which the late, great blues man Brownie McGhee starred, were shot here. You can regularly catch performances by local stars such as Walter 'Wolfman' Washington, zydeco squeezebox virtuoso Rockin' Dopsie Jr and the funky Rebirth Brass Band (cover is $15), who currently play Tuesday nights starting at 10pm. Work up a sweat on the small dance floor directly in front of the stage or relax at the bar in the next room. There's also a nice back patio on which to cool your heels.

TOP CHOICE TIPITINA'S
LIVE MUSIC

Map p250 (☎895-8477; www.tipitinas.com; 501 Napoleon Ave; cover free-$25; ☺5pm-late Fri & Sat) 'Tips,' as locals call it, is one of New Orleans' great musical meccas. The legendary nightclub, which takes its name from Professor Longhair's 1953 hit single, is the site of some of the city's most memorable shows, particularly when big names such as Dr John come home to roost. Outstanding music from the local talent pool still packs 'em in year-round, and this is one of the few non–French Quarter bars regularly drawing tourists. The joint really jumps in the weeks prior to Mardi Gras and during Jazz Fest.

PRYTANIA THEATRE
MOVIE THEATER

Map p250 (☎891-2787; www.theprytania.com; 5339 Prytania St; tickets adult/child/senior $10/8/7, matinee $5.75) This old movie house has been around since the 1920s and screens independent and art films as well as classics. Our favorite theater in the city.

🛍 SHOPPING

Magazine St is the city's best shopping strip. You can take a good multimile window-shopping hike stretching from Audubon Park to Louisiana Ave. The area around Maple St up in Riverbend is another hopping carnival of consumption.

Fashionable shops and restaurants front a small square on Dublin St near S Carrollton Ave, where it meets St Charles Ave. To get here, take the St Charles Ave streetcar (or bus 12) to the Riverbend near Camellia Grill.

On the river side of S Carrollton, Oak St is an older neighborhood commercial zone intersecting with the streetcar line. It's

MAGAZINE STREET

For the true-blue shopper, New Orleans doesn't get much better than Magazine St. For some 6 miles the street courses through the Warehouse District and along the riverside edge of the Garden District and Uptown, lined nearly the entire way with small shops that sell antiques, art, contemporary fashions, vintage clothing and other odds and ends. The street hits its peak in the Lower Garden District (near Jackson Ave), the Garden District (between 1st and 7th Sts) and Uptown (from Antonine St to Napoleon Ave).

reasonably compact for strolling and offers a few interesting businesses, along with restaurants and the stellar Maple Leaf Bar.

TOP CHOICE DIRTY COAST   CLOTHING

Map p250 (www.dirtycoast.com; 5631 Magazine St; ⊘11am-6pm Mon-Sat, until 4pm Sun) You're not a cool new New Orleanian if you haven't picked up one of the clever T-shirts or bumper stickers (Make Wetlands, Not War), all related to local issues, inside jokes and neighborhood happenings, in this ridiculously cool store.

POTSALOT   ARTS & CRAFTS

Map p250 (www.potsalot.com; 3818 Magazine St; 10am-5pm Mon-Sat) Owners Alex and Cindy Williams, who have made and sold pottery from their Magazine St shop since 1993, call their exquisite creations functional art. Their unique, personally tested pieces are made for use in the kitchen, bathroom and den and include everything from bowls and platters to lamps and vases and, yes, lotsa pots. Their eye-catching sinks – with scallops, dimples and rolled lips – are particularly cool. Don't want to carry pottery for the remainder of your trip? Potsalot ships its wares tax-free within the US.

HAZELNUT   HOMEWARES

Map p250 (www.hazelnutneworleans.com; 5515 Magazine St; ⊘10am-6pm Mon-Sat, until 5pm in summer) Actor Bryan Batt of *Mad Men* fame – he played art director Salvatore Romano – co-owns Hazelnut, an elegant but eclectic gift and homewares shop. In addition to classically cool New Orleans-print toile, the shop also sells gilded glassware, post-modern ceramic and other interior-décor must-haves for the modern fairy-tale palace.

TOP CHOICE CRESCENT CITY COMICS   COMIC BOOKS

Map p250 (www.crescentcitycomics.com; 4916 Freret St; ⊘11am-7pm Mon-Sat, noon-6pm Sun) Helpful, on-the-ball staff members are what make Crescent City Comics shine. The store is compact, but tightly stocked, with sections dedicated to everything from local comics to underground to graphic reads. Neil Gaiman and a McSweeney's volume or two are in the book stacks. Check it out.

TOP CHOICE MAPLE STREET BOOK SHOP   BOOKS

Map p250 (www.maplestreetbookshop.com; 7529 Maple St; ⊘9am-7pm Mon-Sat, 11am-5pm Sun) The shop, founded in 1964 by sisters Mary Kellogg and Rhoda Norman, is one of the most politically progressive, well-stocked bookshops in the city. It sits in a shotgun house right next to its sister property **Maple Street Used Book Shop** (7523 Maple St; ⊘9am-6pm Mon-Sat, 11am-5pm Sun), which sells used and rare books.

COLE PRATT GALLERY   ART

Map p250 (www.coleprattgallery.com; 3800 Magazine St; ⊘10am-5pm Tue-Sat) This fine-art gallery showcases the work of 45 contemporary Gulf Coast and Southern artists. Paintings here might include Susan Downing-White's gulf coast landscapes or David Armentor's haunting black-and-white photos of sugar farms and mills.

BERTA'S & MINA'S ANTIQUITIES   ART

Map p250 (4138 Magazine St; ⊘10am-6pm Mon-Sat, noon-3pm Sun) This painting-cluttered gallery specializes in regional folk art, especially the works of the late Nilo Lanzas, whose daughter operates the shop. Lanzas began painting at 63 and produced an impressive body of work, most of it of an outsider art/religious bent. Museums and serious collectors have snatched up many of Lanzas' paintings already, but there are dozens of nice pieces, all very eye-catching and worthy of homes. Lanzas' work is, in fact, very easy to like. His daughter, Mina, also paints and her works show alongside her father's and a few other artists from the city and its surrounds. The gallery is one of the oldest on Magazine St.

C COLLECTION
FASHION

Map p250 (www.ccollectionnola.com; 8141 Maple St; ⊙10am-6pm Mon-Sat) Size zeros unite! This boutique, preening fashionably inside a converted house, does its best to keep the female population of Tulane University (and women of Riverbend region in general) looking smart with its range of tiny skirts, cute dresses, chunky belts, skinny pants and hip-hugging shorts.

STYLE LAB FOR MEN
MEN'S CLOTHING

Map p250 (www.stylelabformen.com; 3640 Magazine St; ⊙11am-6pm Mon-Fri, 10:30am-5pm Sat, noon-4pm Sun) No less an authority than *GQ* magazine has declared this shop as the place where the well-dressed New Orleanian male gets outfitted, in Ben Sherman, Diesel, Trovata and similar labels.

BLOOMIN' DEALS
THRIFT STORE

Map p250 (www.jlno.org; 4645 Freret St; ⊙10am-4:30pm Tue-Sat, 12:30-4:30pm Sun) OK, so this Junior League–run thrift store isn't exactly Bloomingdales, but some of the donations may have originated there. The women's collection is extensive – lots of jeans – and you might just pick up a unique ball gown from Mardi Gras season that was only worn once. Lots of used books for sale too ($1).

PIED NU
FASHION, HOMEWARES

Map p250 (www.piednuneworleans.com; 5521 Magazine St; ⊙10am-5pm Mon-Sat) If you need a hand-poured candle that lasts 60 hours, try one of the sweet-smelling Diptyques on sale here. As you soak up that vanilla-scented goodness, browse elephant-printed cotton T-shirt dresses, cinched poet-dresses and low-joe sneakers. Set it all off with tiny leaf earrings – you'll make yourself almost as endearing as this precious shop.

Mid-City & the Tremé

Neighborhood Top Five

1 Spending a lazy half day at **City Park** (p142), enjoying all that this great green space has to offer, from museums to toy trains to just blissing out under a live oak tree and watching the world spin by.

2 Indulging in a night of good barbecue and better cocktails at **Twelve Mile Limit** (p151).

3 Heading to **Bayou St John** (p147) at dusk for some sunset and moon shadow.

4 Seeing the Tremé Brass Band jam at the **Candlelight Lounge** (p153).

5 Eating a po'boy at **Parkway Tavern** (p149) and never going back to normal sandwiches.

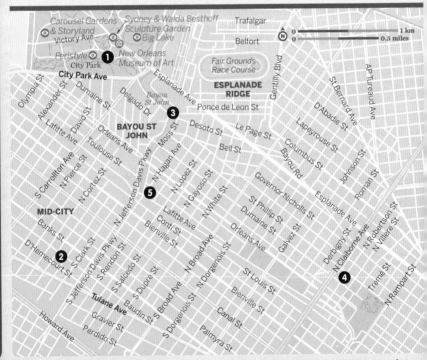

For more detail of the area, see Map p253 ➡

Explore Mid-City & the Tremé

You may want to bike here, either on your own or with the folks at Confederacy of Cruisers (p88). If you bike independently, just roll up attractive Esplanade Ave and take it all the way up to City Park, stopping at St Louis Cemetery No 3 along the way. Walk around the park and the New Orleans Museum of Art, and afterwards, stop in for dinner at Café Degas. In the evening, have a drink at Pal's or Twelve Mile Limit.

On the second day, walk around the Tremé, making sure to stop by the Backstreet Cultural Museum and St Louis Cemetery No 1. Have lunch at Dookie Chase, then drive up to Bayou St John, enjoy the serenity and consider dinner at Parkway Bakery.

Starting from the southwest, near Banks St, Mid-City is a mix of commercial lots and residential blocks. Northeast is Bayou St John, ringed with historic houses, and the great green stretches of City Park. In the southeast Esplanade Ave runs to the French Quarter. The Tremé is less amorphous, being bound by Rampart St, Louis Armstrong Park, Claiborne Ave (or Broad St, definitions vary) and St Bernard Ave.

Local Life

➡ **Food** These neighborhoods are far more residential than tourist-oriented, which is why it's all the more satisfying to know there's great, relatively undiscovered food to be found here.

➡ **Green Spaces** City Park is the obvious contender for top green space in this neighborhood (if not New Orleans), but there's also Bayou St John, Esplanade Ave and plenty of tree-lined streets.

➡ **Nightlife** As with the food scene, there's a ton of unexpected nightlife gems in this corner of town, from convivial bars to great music venues.

Getting There & Away

➡ **Streetcar** The City Park spur of Canal St hits Carrollton St, then heads up that road all the way to City Park.

➡ **Bus** The 91 bus runs up Esplanade Ave, turns into Mid-City and drops by City Park. The 27 traverses Louisiana Ave, and also hits the park. The 94 bus crosses Broad, running through both Mid-City and the Tremé.

➡ **Car** Free street parking is plentiful throughout both neighborhoods.

Lonely Planet's Top Tip

Of all the neighborhoods we cover, Mid-City & the Tremé are best explored by car. Sights are spread out in small clusters of activity across the cityscape. Walking around parts of the Tremé at night, especially near St Louis Cemetery No 1 and the Iberville projects, is not recommended.

⊙ **Best Cultural Sights**

➡ Backstreet Cultural Museum (p147)

➡ New Orleans Museum of Art (p142)

➡ St Louis Cemetery No 1 (p144)

➡ Besthoff Sculpture Garden (p142)

➡ New Orleans African American Museum (p147)

For reviews, see p145 ➡

🏹 **Best Outdoor Activities**

➡ City Park (p142)
➡ Bayou St John (p147)
➡ New Orleans Botanical Gardens (p143)
➡ Kayakitiyat Tour (p145)
➡ Esplanade Avenue (p145)

For reviews, see p145 ➡

🍸 **Best Nightlife**

➡ Twelve Mile Limit (p151)
➡ Mid-City Rock & Bowl (p152)
➡ Candlelight Lounge (p153)
➡ Pal's (p152)
➡ Chickie Wah Wah (p153)

For reviews, see p151 ➡

MID-CITY & THE TREMÉ

TOP SIGHTS
CITY PARK

Three miles long, 1 mile wide, stroked by weeping willows and Spanish moss, and dotted with museums, gardens, waterways, bridges, birds and the occasional alligator, City Park is the nation's sixth-largest urban park (bigger than Central Park in NYC) and New Orleans' prettiest green lung. It's a perfect expression of a local 'park,' in the sense that it is an only slightly tamed expression of the Louisiana wetlands – Bayou Metairie runs through the grounds – and forest that are the natural backdrop of the city. Although dubbed 'City Park,' more than 80% of the park's operating budget is self-generated.

Looking like a vague cross between Lenin's tomb and a Greek temple, the **New Orleans Museum of Art** (☑658-4100; www.noma.org; 1 Collins Diboll Circle; adult/child/senior & student $10/6/8; ☉10am-5pm Tue-Sun, until 9pm Fri) is one of the finest museums in the city and one of the best art museums in the entire South. There's strong representation from regional and American artists, but the work of masters who have passed through the city, such as Edgar Degas, is also prominent. Temporary exhibitions have consistently been daring but accessible to the average art lover, but our favorite section is the top floor, chockablock with a fantastic collection of African, Asian, Oceanic, pre-Columbian and Native American art.

Just outside the New Orleans Museum of Art, the **Sydney & Walda Besthoff Sculpture Garden** (☑488-2631; www.noma.org; 1 Collins Diboll Circle; ☉Fri-Sun) opened in 2003 with some 45 pieces from the world-renowned Besthoff collection. The growing collection includes mostly contemporary works by such artists as Antoine Bourdelle, Henry Moore and Louis Bourgeois.

DON'T MISS

- ➡ Peristyle
- ➡ Carousel Gardens/ Storyville
- ➡ Botanical Gardens
- ➡ Singing Tree
- ➡ New Orleans Museum of Art

PRACTICALITIES

- ➡ Map p253
- ➡ ☑482-4888
- ➡ www.neworleans citypark.com
- ➡ Esplanade Ave & City Park Ave
- ➡ admission free
- ➡ ☉24hr

The grounds of the **Botanical Gardens** (☑483-9386; www.neworleanscitypark.com; adult/child $6/3; ☺10am-4:30pm Tue-Sun) were almost lost to Katrina's floodwaters, but today the site has made almost a complete turnaround. Local and international flora is exhibited, and there are stirring examples of WPA workmanship and art deco design in the form of pavilions/function halls such as the Pavilion of Two Sisters and Lath House. In the northwest corner is the Train Garden, which replicates the city in 1:22 scale miniature size, cut through with 1300ft of rail.

It looks like a temple to a Greek goddess overlooks Bayou Metairie, but in fact that classical pavilion topped by Ionic columns is the **Peristyle**, built in 1907. Four concrete lions stand watch, while weddings, dances, recitals and curious tourists meander through.

We reckon anyone who doesn't like charmingly dated **Carousel Gardens** (City Park; single ride $3; ☺11am-6pm Sat & Sun) must have a heart of stone. This lovingly restored antique carousel is housed in a 1906 structure with a stained-glass cupola. In the 1980s, residents raised $1.2 million to restore the broken animals, fix the squeaky merry-go-round and replace the Wurlitzer organ. The results are spectacular in a tweedy, tinkly kind of way. You can board the tiny City Park Railroad here as well, plus a little ferris wheel, bumper cars and a tilt-a-whirl.

There are no rides at **Storyland** (admission $3; ☺10am-5pm), located next to Carousel Gardens, but the fairytale statuary provides plenty of fuel for young imaginations. Children can play with – and climb upon – the Jabberwocky from *Alice in Wonderland*, or enter the mouth of the whale from *Pinocchio*. If these characters seem strangely similar to Mardi Gras floats, it's because they were created by master float-builder Blaine Kern. During the Christmas season it's lit up like a Christmas tree; it's a good thing it rarely snows here, because the entire experience would be so magical your head might explode with fairy dust.

At **Big Lake** there are **paddleboats** (☑483-9375; off Friederichs Ave; per hr $15; ☺10am-5pm Thu-Sun) available on a first-come, first-served basis if you want to potter around this body of water, which anchors the far southeast corner of the park.

A TOUCH OF HISTORY

City Park occupies the site of the former Allard Plantation; much of the infrastructure and improvements, including pathways, bridges and the art-deco style Tad Gormley Stadium were built by the Works Progress Administration (WPA) during the Great Depression. The arboreal life is magnificent, and includes strands of mature live oaks – thousands of them, some as old as 600 years – along with bald cypresses, Southern magnolias and other species. During Hurricane Katrina nearby canals flooded and inundated more than 90% of the park in up to 8ft of saltwater. Though the ground has recovered, many priceless trees were lost. One tree that wasn't was the **Singing Oak** (or Singing Tree), festooned with chimes, some up to 14ft in length. Standing under the tree during the slightest breeze is pretty magical.

The Popp Fountain is just wonderful, and another impressive example from the WPA. Promenades planted with perennials and 26 Corinthian columns surround the centerpiece of water erupting from a bronze base of cavorting dolphins.

MID-CITY & THE TREMÉ CITY PARK

TOP SIGHTS
ST LOUIS CEMETERY NO 1

New Orleans is something of a city of cemeteries. Influenced by the massive mausoleum building cultures of the Spanish and French, large above-ground necropolises were once all the rage here. The most famous example of the genre is St Louis Cemetery No 1, opened in 1789 and today stuffed with tombs, graves and tourists.

The supposed crypt of voodoo queen Marie Laveau, where people leave offerings and candles, is the big drawcard. Debates over *which* Marie Laveau – mother or daughter, if either – was actually buried here will never be resolved, but what is known is that living members of the Glapion family consider the 'X' marks visitors scratch to be vandalism. There is no spiritual significance to these chicken scratches, and visitors are strongly discouraged from desecrating this or any other tomb – doing so is also technically illegal.

In the adjacent family tomb rests Ernest 'Dutch' Morial, New Orleans' first black mayor. Civil-rights figure Homer Plessy also rests in the cemetery, as do real-estate speculator Bernard de Marigny, architect Henry Latrobe and others.

The Italian Mutual Benevolent Society Tomb is responsible for the tallest monument in the cemetery. Like other immigrant groups in New Orleans, the Italians formed a benevolent association to pool funds and assist in covering burial costs. That fund pool got Olympic sized – the benevolent society tomb is big enough to hold the remains of thousands. In 1969, to the obvious shock of the families who own tombs here, a demented rape scene in the movie *Easy Rider* was filmed here. Take note of the headless statue *Charity* on the Italian Society tomb – urban myth maintains actor Dennis Hopper, who starred in the film, was responsible for tearing the head off.

DON'T MISS

➡ Marie Laveau Tomb
➡ Italian Mutual Benevolent Society Tomb

PRACTICALITIES

➡ Map p253
➡ http://cml.upenn.edu/nola/(unofficial)
➡ 1300 St Louis St
➡ admission free
➡ ⊙8am-3pm

👁 SIGHTS

👁 Mid-City

CITY PARK PARK
See p142.

ESPLANADE AVENUE STREET
Map p253 (Btwn Rampart St & City Park) Esplanade is one of the most beautiful streets in New Orleans, yet barely recognized by tourists as such. Because of the abundance of historical homes, Esplanade, which follows the 'high ground' of Esplanade Ridge, is known as the Creole St Charles Ave. Both streets are shaded by rows and rows of leafy live oaks, but whereas St Charles is full of large, plantation-style American villas, Esplanade is framed by columned, French-Creole style mansions.

PITOT HOUSE HISTORIC BUILDING
Map p253 (📞482-0312; www.pitothouse.org; 1440 Moss St; adult/child & senior $7/5; ⊙10am-3pm Wed-Sat) Pitot House is an excellent example of classical French New Orleans architecture, and the only Creole Colonial house situated on Bayou St John that is open to the public. Features include a shaded verandah that served the purpose of a living area when the weather got too hot and outdoor staircases (to conserve interior space). The house is named for resident James Pitot, who served as first mayor of incorporated New Orleans and lived here from 1810 to 1819.

ST LOUIS CEMETERY NO 3 CEMETERY
Map p253 (📞482-5065; 3421 Esplanade Ave; ⊙until dark) This relatively tiny cemetery was established in 1854 at the site of the old Bayou Cemetery and is worth strolling through for a few minutes (longer if you're a cemetery enthusiast). Of particular note is the striking monument James Gallier Jr designed for his mother and father, who were lost at sea. The cemetery's wrought-iron entrance gate is a beauty.

FAIR GROUNDS RACE COURSE RACE TRACK
Map p253 (📞944-5515; www.fairgroundsracecourse.com; 1751 Gentilly Blvd) Laid out in 1852, this is the third-oldest race track in the nation (during the Civil War, you could catch bear fights here). Today, besides horse races, the Fair Grounds is the site of the annual Louisiana Derby (in March) and Jazz Fest (p82). Buried in the infield are derby winners from a past era. The racing season runs from November to March on Wednesday through Sunday, with a 1:30pm post time.

ALCEE FORTIER PARK PARK
Map p253 (3100 Esplanade Ave) This pretty park, strung up with lights and lanterns and decked out with funky furniture, sits across the road from one of the most attractive stretches of Esplanade, an area replete with restaurants, shops and general breezy ambience. Movies are sometimes screened here on evenings, especially for kids.

NEW ORLEANS KRISHNA TEMPLE TEMPLE
Map p253 (📞486-3583; www.iskcon-nola.org; 2936 Esplanade Ave) The International Society of Krishna Consciousness – you probably know them better as Hare Krishnas – worships in a gorgeous house on Esplanade where they hold *pujas* (prayer ceremonies) and lectures; the interior of the temple is as colorfully close to India as you'll get in the Big Easy. The house traditionally hosts a delicious public vegetarian buffet on Sunday night, but neighbors have complained about folks parking in front of driveways and the like; call ahead before visiting.

ACTIVITIES IN MID-CITY & THE TREMÉ

It's nice to see the Bayou from the shore, but how about on the water? Get in touch with **Kayakitiyat** (📞985-778-5034; http://kayakitiyat.com; tours from $40 per person), which leads tours on the Bayou seven days a week. The best is the Pontchartrain Paddle ($60), a four-hour tour that traverses the length of the Bayou. Another favorite is the two-hour Lazy Twilight tour ($40), which takes in St John at the best time of day. Don't feel like paddling yourself? Look into getting poled around with that special someone on a gondola in City Park with **Nola Gondola** (📞985-778-5034; www.nolagondola.com; per couple $90; ⊙1-10pm Wed-Sun). Your 50-minute ride comes with crackers, cheese, chocolate and croony Italian music.

METAIRIE CEMETERY   CEMETERY
off Map p253 (☎486-6331; 5100 Pontchartrain
Blvd; ☺until dark) Established in 1872 on a
former race track (the grounds, you'll notice, still follow the oval layout), this is the
most American of New Orleans' cities of
the dead. Highlights include the Brunswig
mausoleum, a pyramid guarded by a sphinx
statue; the Moriarty monument, reputedly
the 'tallest privately owned monument'
in the country; and the Estelle Theleman
Hyams monument, with a stained-glass
fixture casting a somber blue light over a
slumped, despondent angel. Seeing everything on the 150-acre grounds is most easily
accomplished by car.

**OUR LADY OF THE
ROSARY RECTORY**   HISTORICAL BUILDINGS
Map p253 (☎488-2659; 1342 Moss St) Built
around 1834 as the home of Evariste Blanc,
Our Lady of the Rosary Rectory exhibits a
combination of styles characteristic of the
region. The high-hipped roof and wraparound gallery seem reminiscent of West
Indies houses but were actually the pre-
ferred styles of the French Canadians who
originally settled Bayou St John. However,
it's the house's neoclassical details that
make it obvious that this building is from
a later period. Call the church to discuss
visiting possibilities.

SANCTUARY   HISTORIC BUILDING
Map p253 (924 Moss St) This historic house
was built by Evariste Blanc from 1816 to
1822 on land originally granted in 1720-1 to
French Canadians. The once-swampy property was later transferred to Don Andrés
Almonaster y Roxas, the real-estate speculator who commissioned St Louis Cathedral
on Jackson Sq in the French Quarter.

MEET THE BOYS ON THE BATTLEFRONT

The most significant African American tradition of Carnival began in 1885 when
a Mardi Gras Indian gang, calling itself the Creole Wild West, paraded the city's
backstreets on Mardi Gras. Their elaborately beaded and feathered suits and head-
dresses made a huge impression, and many more black Indian gangs soon followed –
the Wild Tchoupitoulas, Yellow Pocahontas and Golden Eagles, among many others.
The new tradition, some say, signified respect for Native Americans who constantly
fought US expansion in the New World. A canon of black Indian songs was passed
down from generation to generation, with lyrics often fusing English, Creole French,
Choctaw and African words until their meaning was obscure.

From the beginning, 'masking Indian' was a serious proposition. Tribes became
organized fighting units headed by a big chief, with spy boys, flag boys and wild men
carrying out carefully defined roles. Tremendous pride was evident in the costly and
expertly sewn suits, and when two gangs crossed paths, an intense confrontation
would ensue as members of each tribe sized each other up. Often violence would
break out. As is the case with many of Mardi Gras' strongest traditions, this was no
mere amusement.

Big chiefs became pillars of communities, and some became legends – among
them Big Chief Jolly of the Wild Tchoupitoulas and Tootie Montana of the Yellow
Pocahontas. Chief Jolly, an uncle of the Neville Brothers, made his mark by recording
black Indian classics backed by the Meters. Bo Dollis and the Wild Magnolias are one
of the most dynamic Indian groups, and they appear at clubs in New Orleans and at
Jazz Fest.

Over the years, black Indian suits gained recognition as extravagant works of folk
art, and they are exhibited as such at the Backstreet Cultural Museum (p147), at the
Presbytère (p51) and at Jazz Fest (p76). Layers of meaningful mosaics are designed
and created in patterns of neatly stitched sequins. Multilayered feathered head-
dresses – particularly those of the big chiefs – are more elaborate and flamboyant
than the headgear worn by Las Vegas show performers. The making of a new suit can
take the better part of a year.

Visitors not in town for Mardi Gras are likely to have other opportunities to see the
Indians at Jazz Fest, or occasionally performing in clubs such as Tipitina's (p137).
They also parade annually on St Joseph's Night (roughly midway through the Lenten
season) and on Indian Sunday (p20; also known as Super Sunday).

NEW ORLEANS: BORN ON THE BAYOU

You wouldn't guess it today, considering it's not much more than a pleasant if occasionally smelly creek popular with canoers and kayakers, but Bayou St John is the reason this city exists. It was originally used by Native Americans as a water highway to the relatively high ground of Esplanade Ridge, but then French explorers realized the waterway was the shortest route between the Mississippi River – and by extent the Gulf of Mexico – and Lake Pontchartrain. It was essentially for this reason New Orleans was built in its commanding position at the mouth of the Mississippi. Eventually a canal built by Governor Carondelet extended the bayou to the edge of the French Quarter, and the bayou acted as the city's chief commercial harbor. Life in the area thrived; beautiful houses lined the bayou (many remain here today), and Voodoo Queen Marie Laveau and followers supposedly conducted rituals on the waterfront.

The era of steamboats made direct navigation up and down the Mississippi easier, and the bayou began to be eclipsed. Navigation ended with the filling of the canal in 1927, but the bayou remained an important geographic point of reference. Since 2005 it has also become a bone of contention between local residents and the Army Corps of Engineers. The Corps insists St John is a potential source of floodwater and have proposed sealing it off from Pontchartrain. Some residents say opening sector gates on the bayou's pump houses could facilitate the natural flow of water, which would freshen up the bayou (which can grow darkly stagnant), improve water quality and reintroduce important flora and fauna to the bayou bank.

The issue is still being fought. In the meantime, come out here to stroll along the bayou (stagnant or not, it is scenic and supremely serene, especially at sunset), enjoy a po'boy from the Parkway (p149), catch one of the many concerts played on the median that runs through the bayou and gape at the gorgeous residences. You're only allowed to enter one: Pitot House (p145), a restored mansion with a lovely set of gardens in the back.

◉ The Tremé

ST LOUIS CEMETERY NO 1   CEMETERY
See p144.

TOP CHOICE BACKSTREET CULTURAL MUSEUM   MUSEUM
Map p253 (287-5224; www.backstreetmuseum.org; 1116 St Claude Ave; donations accepted; 10am-5pm Tue-Sat) New Orleans may have the most distinctive local culture in the USA, and this is the place to see how one facet of its culture – its African American side – is expressed in daily life. The museum isn't terribly big – it's the former Blandin's Funeral Home – but if you have any interest in Mardi Gras Indian suits, second lines and the activities of Social Aid & Pleasure Clubs (the local black community version of civic associations), you need to stop by. Guided tours are usually great, but sometimes feel rushed, so be sure to ask lots of questions.

NEW ORLEANS AFRICAN AMERICAN MUSEUM   MUSEUM
Map p253 (566-1136; www.noaam.org; 1418 Governor Nicholls St; adult/child/senior & student $7/3/5; 11am-4pm Wed-Sat) This small museum has an eclectic mix of exhibits mainly dating from slavery and Reconstruction. It's an interesting spot just by dint of its location: the Meilleur-Goldthwaite House, also known as the Tremé Villa. This pretty house was the site of the city's first brick yard and is an exemplar of the Creole architectural style. In the back are restored shotgun houses and slave quarters that house supplemental exhibitions and office space.

MORTUARY CHAPEL   CHURCH
Map p253 (11 N Rampart St; donations accepted; 7am-6pm) A fear of yellow-fever contagion led the city to forbid funerals for fever victims at St Louis Cathedral. Built in 1826 near St Louis Cemetery No 1, the Mortuary Chapel offered services for victims, its bell tolling constantly during epidemics. In 1931 it was renamed Our Lady of Guadeloupe. Inside the chapel is a statue of St Jude, patron saint of impossible cases, and

VOODOO QUEEN

Voodoo became wildly popular in New Orleans after it was introduced by black émigrés from St Domingue (now Haiti) at the beginning of the 19th century, but very little is known with certainty about the legendary 19th-century Voodoo Queen Marie Laveau, who gained fame and fortune by shrewdly exploiting voodoo's mystique. Though details of her life are shrouded in myth and misconception, what has been passed down from generation to generation makes for a fascinating story.

She was born in 1794, a French-speaking Catholic of mixed black and white ancestry. Invariably described as beautiful and charismatic, at age 25 she married a man named Paris. He died a few years later, and Marie became known as the Widow Paris. She had 15 children with another man, Glapion, who is believed to have migrated from St Domingue, and may have been Laveau's first connection to voodoo.

In the 1830s she established herself as the city's preeminent voodoo queen, and her influence crossed racial lines. Mostly she reeled in stray husbands and helped people avenge wrongs done to them. According to legend, she earned her house on St Anne St as payment for ensuring a young man's acquittal in a rape or murder trial.

Marie apparently had some tricks up her sleeve. She is said to have worked as a hairdresser in the homes of upper-class white women, and it was not uncommon for these women to share local society gossip while having their hair done. In this way, Laveau gained a familiarity with the vagaries of the elite, and she astutely perceived the value of such information. At the peak of her reign as voodoo queen, she employed an entire network of spies, most household servants in upper-class homes.

Reports on Laveau's activities suggest there was more to her practice than non-practitioners were permitted to witness – which makes these reports suspect. Part of the Laveau legend involves rituals she presided over in the countryside around New Orleans. According to sensational accounts, Laveau's followers danced naked around bonfires, drinking blood and slithering on the ground like snakes before engaging in all-out orgies.

A brothel by Lake Pontchartrain called Maison Blanche was reputedly operated by Marie Laveau, but it is uncertain if this was the same Marie Laveau – there were two people known as Marie Laveau, the second being the daughter of the original Marie Laveau. The elder Laveau died in 1881 and is believed to be buried in St Louis Cemetery No 1. The younger lived into the early 20th century.

St Expedite, who may never have existed (legend says his name comes from a box of saint statues stamped with the order 'Expedite').

ST AUGUSTINE'S CHURCH CHURCH
Map p253 (☏525-5934; www.staugustinecath olicchurch-neworleans.org; 1210 Governor Nicholls St) Open since 1841, 'St Aug's' is the second-oldest African American Catholic church in the country, a place where Creoles, émigrés from St Domingue and free persons of color could worship shoulder to shoulder, even as separate pews were designated for slaves. The future of the church remains in question, so try to visit; more tourists increase the chance of preserving this historic landmark. Call ahead to see if it's possible to arrange a visit, and when there don't miss the Tomb of the Unknown Slave, fashioned to resemble a grim cross assembled from chain links.

LOUIS ARMSTRONG PARK PARK
Map p253 The entrance to this massive park has got to be one of the greatest gateways in the USA, a picturesque arch that ought rightfully be the final set piece in some period drama about Jazz Age New Orleans. The original Congo Sq is here, as well as a **Louis Armstrong statue** and a **bust of Sidney Bechet**. The **Mahalia Jackson Theater** (☏287-035; www.mahaliajacksontheater.com) has been done up with a $22 million renovation and now hosts opera and Broadway productions.

EATING

Mid-City

TOP CHOICE PARKWAY TAVERN
PO'BOYS $

Map p253 (☑482-3047; www.parkwaypoorboys.com; 538 Hagan Ave; po'boys under $10; ☺11am-10pm Wed-Mon) Let's face it: no one is going to settle the 'best po'boy in New Orleans' argument anytime soon. But tell a local you think the top sandwich comes from Parkway and you will get, at the least, a nod of respect. The roast beef in particular – a craft some would say is dying among the great po'boy makers – is messy as hell and twice as good; take one down to nearby Bayou St John, and munch that sandwich in the shade. Louisiana bliss.

CAFÉ DEGAS
FRENCH $$

Map p253 (☑945-5635; www.cafedegas.com; 3127 Esplanade Ave; mains $18-23; ☺11am-3pm & 6-10pm Wed-Sat, 10:30am-3pm & 6-9:30pm Sun) A pecan tree thrusts through the floor and ceiling of the enclosed deck that serves as Café Degas' congenial dining room. This is a rustic, romantic little spot that warms the heart with first-rate, reasonably priced French fare. Meals that sound familiar on the menu – steak *frites au poivre,* parmesan-crusted veal medallions, seared duck breast with mushroom spaetzle – are arranged with extraordinary beauty on the plate. Brunch is gorgeous; the crab crepe with hollandaise is decadent.

CRESCENT CITY PIE & SAUSAGE COMPANY
FUSION $$

Map p253 (☑482-2426; www.crescentpieandsausage.com; 4400 Banks St; mains $9-18; ☺11am-10pm Mon-Thu, until 11pm Fri & Sat, 9am-1pm Sun) We know, British and Australian travelers, that you are unimpressed with the quality of savory pies in the USA. Well, get ready to lose the smugness and gain some weight, because the meat pies here – and the handmade sausages, charcuterie and pizzas – are pretty damn amazing. Plus, during spring they host crawfish boils on the outdoor deck. On Sunday this spot becomes a cheapie brunch place called **Huevos** (mains under $10).

LOLA'S
SPANISH $$

Map p253 (☑488-6946; www.lolasneworleans.com; 3312 Esplanade Ave; mains $7-18; ☺5:30-9:30pm Sun-Thu, to 10:30pm Fri & Sat) Enjoy some wine and conversation with the clouds of Mid-City locals who swear by Lola's paellas and *fideuas* (an angel-hair pasta variation on the former). Once you get inside, it's all elbows and crowds and buzz of conversation and, incidentally, very good grub. This isn't haute Barcelona cuisine; it's the Spanish peasant fare Hemingway wrote chapters about, all rabbit and meats and hams and fresh seafood and olive oil and lots and lots of delicious garlic – vampires need not apply. Bring cash.

RUBY SLIPPER
BREAKFAST $

Map p253 (☑309-5531; www.therubyslippercafe.net; 139 S Cortez St; mains $10-17; ☺7am-3pm

---

CLOSING THE CONGO SQUARE CIRCLE

Near the main entrance to Louis Armstrong Park is one of the most important spots, arguably, in the development of modern music: Congo Square (Map p253). Once known as Place de Negres, this area used to be just outside the city's walls (Rampart St, as the name suggests, was the town limit). Under the French colonial law, slaves were allowed to gather here on Sunday. The period of rest became one of both celebration and preservation of West African rituals, which largely revolve around song and dance. Sunday became a day of letting off steam and channeling latent discontent, and it must have been, at the time, the largest celebration of traditional African culture in continental North America – slaves were forbidden from practicing traditional culture in the American colonies.

The practice was shut down when US settlers took over New Orleans, but it was alive long enough to imprint its musical stamp on the city's cultural substrate. By the late 19th century, brass bands were blending African rhythms with classical music. These bands played on a weekly basis in Congo Sq, and their sound eventually evolved, especially near the bordellos of nearby Storyville, into jazz – itself a foundation for the variations of pop music (R&B, rock 'n' roll, even hip-hop) the USA would give the world in the 20th century.

CHÚC NGON MIÊNG (BON APPETIT)!

There are all kinds of great Vietnamese restaurants in New Orleans, but a lot of them are across the river in either Gretna (6 miles south of the Tremé) or New Orleans East (about 12 miles east of City Park). While the atmosphere at all of these places is pretty locally 'Vietnamese,' there's usually a fair crowd of white, black and Latino diners as well, so don't expect to feel like an interloper. Prices are at the top end of the 'budget' category – unless you're really hungry, it's hard to spend more than $20 a head at any of these spots. Call ahead for hours, as these can be subject to some shifting.

Pho Tau Bay (☑368-9846; 113 Westbank Expressway, Gretna; ⊘9am-8:30pm daily, closed Sun & Thu) Fantastic executions of Vietnamese mains and the best pho we've tried in metropolitan New Orleans.

Dong Phuong Oriental Bakery (☑254-0296; www.dpbahnmi.com; 14207 Chef Menteur Hwy, New Orleans East; ⊘8am-6pm Wed-Sun, 8am-4pm Mon) For the best *banh mi* (Vietnamese sandwiches of sliced pork, cucumber, cilantro and other lovelies, locally called a 'Vietnamese po'boy') around and some very fine durian cake.

Kim Son (☑366-2489; www.kimsonnola.com; 349 Whitney Ave, Gretna; ⊘11am-2:45pm & 5-8:45pm Mon-Sat) A solid spot for any Vietnamese you please; the rice-paper rolls and marinated beef are off the freaking charts. The best argument for moving to Gretna we've experienced.

9 Roses (Hoa Hong 9; ☑366-7665; 1100 Stephens St, Gretna; ⊘10:30am-9:30pm Sun-Tue & Thu, 10:30am-10pm Fri & Sat) One of the oldest Vietnamese restaurants in the area, famous for its seafood soups and enormous menu.

Tan Dinh (☑361-8008; 2005 Belle Chasse Hwy, Gretna; ⊘9:30am-9pm Mon & Wed-Fri, 9am-9pm Sat, until 8pm Sun) Where else can you find jellyfish salad around here? Contends with Pho Tau Bay for some of that high-quality pho.

Tue-Sun, from 8am Sat & Sun; ☑) The Slipper serves up some of the best breakfasts in town, plus some lovely lunches as well. The fare is basic American breakfast food with a bit of a Mexican accent; the hollandaise has a kick and the migas (scrambled eggs mixed with fried tortilla strips) are divine.

MANDINA'S   ITALIAN $$
Map p253 (☑482-9179; www.mandinasrestaurant.com; 3800 Canal St; mains $10-17; ⊘11am-9:30pm Mon-Thu, to 10pm Fri & Sat, noon-9pm Sun) In the Italian-American New Orleans community, funerals were followed by a visit to this institution for the turtle soup. The menu may be conservative, but when you've been around for more than 100 years you stick to what you know. In this case that's Sicilian-Louisiana food: trout almandine, red beans and veal cutlets, and bell peppers stuffed with macaroni and meat. The dining room is as historic as any building in the city and just as crucial to its culture.

LIUZZA'S BY THE TRACK   DINER $
Map p253 (☑218-7888; 1518 N Lopez St; mains $6-14; ⊘11am-7pm Mon-Sat) This quintessential Mid-City neighborhood joint does some of the best gumbo in town, a barbecue shrimp po'boy to die for and legendary deep-fried garlic oysters. All that said, the real reason to come is the atmosphere: we've seen a former city judge and a stripper dining out together in this spot, which is as 'Only in New Orleans' an experience as you can get. Liuzza's is nearly impossible to squeeze into during Jazz Fest, naturally.

TWELVE MILE LIMIT   BARBECUE
Map p253 (☑488-8114; 500 S Telemachus St; mains under $10; ⊘food 5-10pm) Besides being an excellent bar, Twelve Mile Limit's kitchen cranks out great barbecue; the smell from outside is almost as overpowering as the rich flavor of that sweet, spicy smoked meat.

NONNA MIA CAFÉ & PIZZERIA   ITALIAN $$
Map p253 (☑948-1717; www.nonnamia.net; 3125 Esplanade Ave; pizza $12-20; ⊘11am-10pm

Sun-Thu, until 11pm Fri & Sat; ✎) Getting tired of heavy, rich Creole cuisine? How about a fresh slice of pizza and some ice tea in Nonna Mia's outdoor courtyard. The caramelized onions, goat cheese and artichoke hearts are delicious proof that pizza apparently doesn't need pepperoni to be perfect.

ANGELO BROCATO   ICE CREAM $

Map p253 (✆486-1465; www.angelobrocatoice cream.com; 214 N Carrollton Ave; desserts $2-5; ◷11am-5pm Tue-Sat) When an ice-cream parlor passes the 100-year mark, you gotta just step back and say, 'Alright. Clearly, they're doing something right.' Opened in 1905 by Signor Brocato himself, a Sicilian immigrant who scraped together his savings from working on a sugar plantation, this is the oldest ice-cream shop in New Orleans. We'd come for the beautiful copper espresso machine alone, but then there's the marble-top counter, silky gelatos, perfect cannoli, crispy biscotti and an irreplaceable sense of history. *Molto bene.*

YANG'S   PO'BOYS $

Map p253 (✆482-6080; 4840 Bienville St; po'boys under $10; ◷10:30am-7pm Mon-Sat) Other po'boy shops get more recognition but Yang's, run by a friendly Chinese family, is the epitome of the quiet corner sandwich shop beloved by generations of New Orleanians. Nothing fancy, just good food and friendly service. Cash preferred.

✗ The Tremé

DOOKY CHASE   SOUL FOOD, CREOLE $

Map p253 (✆821-0535; 2301 Orleans Ave; mains $6-15; ◷11am-3pm Tue-Fri; ✎) Ray Charles wrote 'Early in the Morning' about Dooky's, civil rights leaders used the spot as an informal headquarters in the 1960s, and Barack Obama ate here after his inauguration. Leah Chase's labor of love is a backbone of the Tremé, and her buffets are the stuff of legend. The vegetarian meal gumbo z'herbes, served on Thursday during Lent, is the great New Orleans dish done green with mustards, beet tops, spinach, kale, collards and Leah knows what else; committed carnivores should give it a try.

WILLIE MAE'S SCOTCH HOUSE   SOUL FOOD $

Map p253 (✆822-9503; 2401 St Ann St; mains $6-13; ◷11am-5pm Mon-Fri) Willie Mae's

has been dubbed some of the best fried chicken in the world by the James Beard foundation, the Food Network and other media. It thus sees a steady flow of tourist traffic from folks who want that authentic 'fried chicken from the 'hood' experience, so they drive into the Tremé, have their bird, and drive out. This sight is off-putting to some, but if you can digest it with no qualms, well, the chicken is pretty damn good.

LIL' DIZZY'S   SOUL FOOD $

Map p253 (✆569-8997; 1500 Esplanade Ave; mains $6-10; ◷7am-2:30pm Mon-Fri, to 2pm Sat) One of the city's great lunch spots, Dizzy's does mean soul food specials in a historic shack owned by the Baquet family, who have forever been part of the culinary backbone of New Orleans. The fried chicken is excellent, the hot sausages may be better and the bread pudding is divine.

CAJUN SEAFOOD   SEAFOOD $

Map p253 (✆948-6000; 1479 N Claiborne Ave; take-out under $10; ◷10:30am-9pm) The name says it all: this is a grocery store/take-out that's one of the best budget options in town for raw seafood and cooked hot plates, such as fried chicken, boudin, fish plates and the like. Their boiled shrimp are always freakishly huge, as are their shrimp po'boys.

🍺 DRINKING & NIGHTLIFE

There are some pretty good bars out this way, but they tend to be neighborhood places you may not want to drive all the way out here for. With a few exceptions... In general the scene here is lively, local and happy to share a beer and a story with a stranger. Plus, there's a bowling alley, concert hall and a bar that serves free food... just sayin'.

TOP CHOICE TWELVE MILE LIMIT   BAR

Map p253 (500 S Telemachus St; ◷5pm-midnight Mon-Thu, until 2am Fri & Sat, until 11pm Sun) Twelve Mile is simply a great bar. It's staffed by people who have the skill, both behind the bar and in the kitchen, to work in four-star spots, but who chose to set up shop in a neighborhood, for a neighborhood. The mixed drinks really are excellent, the match

THE POPULARITY OF POPEYES

Ask a New Orleanian where the best fried chicken in town is and they'll probably tell you to try Willie Mae's (p151) or Fiorella's (p59). Now ask them where *they* eat fried chicken, and they'll very likely reply, 'Popeyes.' Seriously.

Though fried chicken is not as popular here as in the rest of the South, folks still take their fried bird seriously, which is why we find it all the more amusing so many locals swear by a chain restaurant that markets a caricature of the city outside of its limits.

But hey – we trust any New Orleanian's take on food. The **Popeyes** (www.popeyes .com; numerous locations around town) here are pretty good (folks say the food tastes better than in other states and, to be honest, it just might). We'll never tell you to pass up a local business in favor of Popeyes, but if there's nothing else around…well, just sayin'.

of any mixologist's cocktail in Manhattan, and the vibe is so accepting you want to come here in your pajamas. Plus: they host free (!) buffet dinners on Monday nights, which is just perfect, really.

PAL'S   BAR

Map p253 (949 N Rendon St; ☺3pm-late) Hey – another great neighborhood bar in Mid-City. Who'd have guessed? Pal's is a little more convivial for the older generation, although it's definitely an all-ages crowd. The men's bathroom, wallpapered with vintage pinups, is like a walk through *Playboy's* history, while the backroom air hockey is always enjoyable.

FAIR GRINDS   CAFE

Map p253 (3133 Ponce de Leon St; pastries $2-4; ☺6:30am-10pm; ☏) Fair Grinds is simultaneously airy and comfy and hip and unpretentious, and the coffee's good to boot. It showcases local art and generally acts as the beating heart of Mid-City's bohemian scene; plus, it supports any number of community development associations and hosts regular folk music nights.

CAFE TREMÉ   CAFE

Map p253 (1501 St Philip St; pastries $2-4; ☺7am-7pm Mon-Fri, 9am-5pm Sat & Sun; ☏) Locally owned and operated, Cafe Tremé is a worthwhile attempt at bringing an arsty cafe that is a locus for the creative community into the Tremé. It also happens to serve damn fine coffee. This new place has already got the feel of a neighborhood cafe, which we're pretty excited about.

MID-CITY YACHT CLUB   BAR

Map p253 (440 S St Patrick St; ☺5pm-late) The Yacht Club is such a part of the neighbor-

hood that one of the owners took his boat out to save flooded Katrina victims after the storm (hence the name of the bar, which isn't anywhere near a lake or ocean). And it's so much a part of the neighborhood that the neighborhood is literally a part of it: the bar is actually made from local wood salvaged from storm debris.

FINN MCCOOL'S   BAR

Map p253 (☎486-9080; www.finnmccools.com; 3701 Banks St; ☺until late) Want a surreal New Orleans experience? Show up at Finn's at 6am when premier league soccer or big international rugby games are playing. You'll see this neighborhood bar packed with an odd mix of European sports enthusiasts, British expats and local Hispanics. Don't get us wrong, Finn's is an excellent spot for a beer any time of day (especially during St Paddy's Day), but we particularly love this spot for watching soccer. Check the website or call for game days and hours.

BAYOU BEER GARDEN   BAR

Map p253 (326 N Jefferson Davis Pkwy; ☺11am-2am) The Bayou has been sorely needed in New Orleans: a beer bar with an enormous outdoor deck that serves pub grub. Simple, right? Shows lots of sports, and thus attracts an interesting mix of jocks and punky locals on game days.

☆ ENTERTAINMENT

☆ TOP CHOICE MID-CITY ROCK & BOWL   LIVE MUSIC

off Map p253 (☎861-1700; www.rockandbowl.com; 3000 S Carrollton Ave; ☺5pm-late) A night at the Rock & Bowl is a quintessential New Orleans experience. The venue is a strange, wonderful combination of bowling alley, deli and huge live-music and dance venue, where patrons get down to New Orleans roots music while trying to avoid that 7-10 split. The best time and place in the city to experience zydeco is the weekly Thursday night dance party held here.

TOP CHOICE CANDLELIGHT LOUNGE   LIVE MUSIC

Map p253 (925 N Robertson St; ⏲2pm-late daily, closed Tue) Deep in the Tremé, the Candlelight looks like a bunker on the outside and...a slightly nicer bunker on the inside. Most nights it's neighborhood bar, but on Wednesday around 10pm (and occasionally other nights) it hosts the Tremé Brass Band ($10 cover), one of the most enjoyable live sets in the city. This is as wonderful as local music gets in this town.

CHICKIE WAH WAH   LIVE MUSIC

Map p253 (☎304-4714; www.chickiewahwah.com; 2828 Canal St; ⏲shows start around 8pm) Despite the fact it lies on one of the most unremarkable stretches of Canal St as you please, Chickie Wah Wah is a great jazz club. Local legends such as the Sweet Olive String Band or Meschya Lake, and plenty of international talent, all make their way across the small stage.

BANKS STREET BAR   LIVE MUSIC

Map p253 (☎486-0258; www.banksstreetbar.com; 4401 Banks St; ⏲11am-2am) While 'Banks Street' is a quintessential neighborhood dive, it's also renowned as a good place to catch local music seven nights a week. The bar is famous for hosting good rock shows, but they also do great reggae on Tuesday and host jazz, funk, brass and the rest. It gets *loud* in here, so don't plan on discussing representation and repression in the latter works of Terrence Malick between sets.

BULLETS   LIVE MUSIC

Map p253 (2441 AP Tureaud Ave; ⏲5pm-late) Don't be put off by the name; Bullets is just a sports bar. It's also the home base of trumpeter Kermit Ruffins, who hosts a concert here for his family and friends almost every Tuesday starting (very roughly) around 6pm.

MID-CITY & THE TREMÉ ENTERTAINMENT

SECOND LINE!

Second Lines aren't the alternate queue at the bank window, if you're wondering. No, here a Second Line specifically refers to parades put on by the city's African American Social Aid & Pleasure (S&P) Clubs. The S&P members deck themselves out in flash suits, hats and shoes and carry decorated umbrellas and fans. This snazzy crowd, plus a hired band, marches through the city pumping music and 'steppin'' – engaging in a kind of syncopated marching dance that looks like a soldier in formation overcome by an uncontrollable need to get fun-*kay*. This is the First Line, and marching behind it is the Second Line: the crowds that gather to celebrate the music. Hundreds, sometimes thousands of people – the majority African American – dance in the Second Line, stopping for drinks and food all along the parade route. Many folks bring along coolers full of beer and soda plus rolling grills too.

So what are these S&P clubs? There are theories they have their roots in West African secret societies, cultural institutions that are a big part of the societies slaves were plucked from. If you have been to West Africa and witnessed any kind of secret society activity, it's hard not to detect some similarities to the Second Line. Still, while this theory has an appealing veneer of anthropological allure, the roots of Second Lines may be more based on economics. In the 19th and 20th centuries S&P clubs functioned as insurance agencies for African Americans, as well as brokers who would help arrange the traditional (and expensive) New Orleans jazz funeral procession. The act of the parade, which the S&P helped fund, may have been eventually appended to these brokerage responsibilities.

While that role has faded, the S&P clubs remain important civic institutions. There are a few dozen in the city, and traditionally Second Lines roll every weekend, except for summers, usually in the Tremé or Central City. They're not the easiest thing to find, but keep abreast of 90.7, WWOZ (www.wwoz.org) and be on the lookout for parades and music if you're driving around on a Sunday.

SHOPPING

TOP CHOICE F&F BOTANICA   SANTERIA, VOODOO

Map p253 (☎289-2304; 801 N Broad Ave; ◎10am-6:30pm Tue-Sat) Forget all the fake voodoo shops in the French Quarter; this is a genuine Puerto Rican botanica that sells candles, gris-gris (spell bags) and spell components for use in voodoo and Santeria (the latter is a Puerto Rican religion related to voodoo). No tourist-oriented Hollywood-style dolls here; real worshippers drop in to deal with real issues, which, according to the spell lists, seem to mainly related to heartache, immigration issues and the law.

SWIRL   WINE

Map p253 (☎304-0635; www.swirlinthecity .com; 3133 Ponce de Leon St; ◎11am-8pm Mon-Fri, until 7pm Sun) This excellent wine shop has a great selection of vino and stinky cheese, and hosts awesome tasting nights on Friday evenings, usually starting around 5ish.

MASSEY'S   OUTDOOR EQUIPMENT

Map p253 (☎648-0292; 509 N Carrollton Ave; ◎10am-7pm Mon-Sat, noon-6pm Sun) Massey's is a large, well-stocked chain carrying an excellent selection of camping, hiking and general outdoors gear.

MAPLE STREET BOOKS   BOOKS

Map p253 (☎309-9815; 3141 Ponce de Leon St; ◎10am-6pm Mon-Sat, 11am-5pm Sun) This is the Mid-City/Bayou St John branch of the best independent book chain in the city.

Day Trips from New Orleans

River Road p156

Graceful antebellum mansions with elaborate gardens, majestic live oaks and clustered slave shanties offer a glimpse into a foreign but not too distant past.

St Francisville p159

Antiques, birds and ghost stories, plus a few more plantations, make a fine trip. And that's without mentioning the museum at the 18,000-acre penitentiary in Angola.

Lafayette & Breaux Bridge p161

Join the party – or the *fais do do* – in Lafayette and Breaux Bridge where Cajun dance halls and crawfish boils keep things lively. And the food? It's serious business around here.

Cajun Prairie p165

Suit up for dancing and a lot of great music in the prairielands, where a young wave of fiddlers and accordion players keep Cajun and zydeco music relevant – and fun.

Down the Bayou p168

Swamps, alligators and oil. And a whole lot of Cajun culture. Soak it all in – and enjoy fresh seafood – on a road trip that's best done slow.

River Road

Explore

Historic house tours usually take about an hour. You won't be able to visit all the ones listed here in one day, so you'll need to be selective. Note that River Road is actually two roads lining the west and the east banks of the Mississippi River. Looking at a map, the east bank is the area above the river and the west bank is the area below the river. 'Downriver' means heading southeast, as the river flows toward New Orleans. 'Upriver' means northwest, against the river's flow toward Baton Rouge. River Road has various route names along the way, yet few of the towns you pass through will display any signage to indicate the change in route numbers. Sound confusing? It's not – just follow the sinuous levees.

The Best

➡ **Sight** Laura Plantation
➡ **Place to Eat** Wayne Jacob's Smokehouse
➡ **Place to Drink** Latil's Landing

Top Tip

Bridges are not that numerous on this part of the Mississippi River. Several plantations are on the west bank, so plot your itinerary carefully and allow extra time for travel.

Getting There & Away

Direction Northwest

Travel Time From three hours to all day depending on stops

Car Take I-10 west to I-310, exit at Destrehan and follow River Road (alternately called Hwy 44) northwest from there. Don't despair if you're still on the road at 6pm and have 8pm dinner reservations in New Orleans. Even the distant upriver plantations are only a little over a one-hour drive from the city if you hop back on I-10.

Need to Know

➡ **Area Code** 985, 225
➡ **Location** 25 to 100 miles northwest of New Orleans

➡ **Tourist Office** (☏225-675-6550; 6967 Hwy 22, cnr Hwys 22 & 70, Sorrento; ⊙9am-4:30pm) Near I-10, off exit 182, the Ascension Parish visitor center has tons of information on River Road and beyond.

◉ SIGHTS

Plantations dot the Mississippi riverbanks, often tucked among oil refineries and light industrial sites. And though corridors of centuries-old live oaks present a dramatic photo opportunity, views of the river are usually blocked by the elevated levees. Plantation tours offer a fascinating look at the lives of antebellum plantation owners and, perhaps more so than in the past, provide insights into the hard lives of the slaves as well.

The plantations here are listed in geographic order, following the Mississippi upriver toward Baton Rouge.

DESTREHAN PLANTATION PLANTATION

(☏985-764-9315; www.destrehanplantation.org; 13034 River Rd/Hwy 48, Destrehan; adult/child $18/7; ⊙9am-4pm) Destrehan, the oldest plantation home remaining in the lower Mississippi Valley, is an impressive starting point for a River Road tour. Only 12 miles from New Orleans International Airport, the plantation was originally established for indigo production. Antoine Robert Robin DeLongy commissioned the original French colonial–style mansion in 1787, using *bousillage* (mud- and straw-filled) walls supported by cypress timbers. The house features a distinctive African-style hipped roof, no doubt the inspiration of the plantation's builder, who was of partial African descent. When DeLongy's daughter, Celeste, married Jean Noel Destrehan, they added the present Greek-revival facade. Destrehan was part of a tribunal, held on the property, that tried and convicted slaves involved in a revolt just upriver in 1811.

Costumed docents lead tours through the graceful home where the pirate Jean Lafitte was once a guest. Possible demonstrations include making *bousillage*, cooking in a hearth and African American herbal remedies. A highlight is seeing the historical-documents room that contains original Louisiana Purchase–era artifacts.

SAN FRANCISCO PLANTATION   PLANTATION

(☑985-535-2341; www.sanfranciscoplantation.org; Hwy 44, Garyville; adult/student $15/10; ☺9:30am-4:40pm Apr-Oct, 9am-4pm Nov-Mar) The candy-colored 'steamboat Gothic-style' San Francisco Plantation, 21 miles upriver from Destrehan, was purchased in 1830 by Edmond B Marmillion from Elisee Rillieux, a free person of color. With $100,000 and 100 slaves, Marmillion's son, Valsin, built a grand sugar plantation. Today only the architectural confection of the 1856 house and metal-domed cisterns remain. The plantation's name is a corruption of a French saying 'Sans Frusquin,' meaning 'without a penny in my pocket.' It was Valsin's joking response when asked about the mansion's expensive construction. Overall, this tour offers a bit less information than the others, but it's safe to say, based on old portraits, that Valsin and wife Louise were the most dashing couple on the river in the 1850s.

TOP CHOICE LAURA PLANTATION   PLANTATION

(☑225-265-7690; www.lauraplantation.com; 2247 Hwy 18, Vacherie; adult/student $18/5; ☺10am-4pm) West of Garyville (before Lutcher), cross over the river bridge for the blue-and-yellow Laura Plantation at Vacherie on the west bank. The West Indies–influenced plantation house was built in 1805 by Guillaume Duparc and named for his granddaughter, Laura Locoul. Four generations of women ran the plantation, and the tour – the best one on the river – describes their fascinating role in the operation's success. More than 5000 pages of plantation documents, including Laura's diary, provided first-hand details about the plantation life of women, children and slaves. More than 12 buildings – slave cabins, barns, sugar-processing stations and the like – still stand, making this one of the more complete plantations around.

OAK ALLEY PLANTATION   PLANTATION

(☑225-265-2151; www.oakalleyplantation.com; 3645 Hwy 18, Vacherie; adult/child 6-12yr/child 13-18yr $18/4.50/7.50; ☺9:30am-5pm Mar-Oct, 9:30am-4:30pm Mon-Fri, until 5pm Sat Nov-Feb) A quarter-mile corridor of majestic live oaks makes for a dramatic approach to the house. The trees – 14 on each side – were probably planted in the 1700s. More symmetry awaits at the Greek-revival plantation house where 28 columns, each 8ft

in diameter, frame the scene. Anne Rice fans will recognize this as Louis' home from the 1993 movie *Interview with a Vampire*. This property is more commercialized than most (costumed staff sells mint juleps), but you can spend the night in cottages on the peaceful grounds ($130 to $175).

RIVER ROAD AFRICAN AMERICAN MUSEUM   MUSEUM

(☑225-474-5553; http://africanamericanmuseum.org; 406 Charles St; tours per person $5; ☺by appointment) Some of the plantation tours can be light on information about slaves and the role they played in the success of the region's sugar plantations. Kathe Hambrick, a local African American woman, recognized that weakness after visiting a plantation, and she started this museum in response. Located in the town of Donaldsonville, 24 miles upriver from Laura Plantation, the collection details the history of the rural blacks of Louisiana. The emphasis is not only on slavery, but also on the achievements of black doctors, artists and others throughout history. Exhibits in the front room include a list of names of those who worked on area plantations, an 1850 bill of sale for a 14-year-old boy named Boston ($600), runaway slave notices, and shackles and slave collars. Other displays discuss the food of Africa and the diaspora, black Louisiana inventors and the rural roots of jazz. Call or visit the website to set up a tour.

While in town, don't miss **Rossie's Custom Framing** (www.alvinbatiste.com; 510 Railroad Ave; ☺10am-5pm Tue-Fri, 10am-3pm Sat) where the works of acclaimed folk artist Alvin Batiste are sold. His colorful interpretations of life in his hometown will take your breath away.

NOTTOWAY PLANTATION   PLANTATION

(☑225-545-2730; www.nottoway.com; 31025 Louisiana Hwy 1, White Castle; adult/child $20/6; ☺9am-4pm) Thirteen miles northwest of Donaldsonville, past the town of White Castle, Nottoway Plantation is known for its sheer size. The 64 rooms cover a whopping 53,000 sq ft that includes 22 columns and 200 windows. Renowned New Orleans architect Henry Howard designed the three-story Italianate-Greek-revival mansion for Virginian sugar planter John Hampton Randolph. Constructed from 1849 to 1859, it took four years to cut and dry the cypress framing timbers alone.

The circular all-white ballroom, with impressively detailed plasterwork, is perhaps the finest room in the house. Tours, which begin on the hour, are rich in the personal family history of the first owners. Stay overnight in one of the rooms within the mansion and you may get a more personal introduction to a Randolph family member: some guests have reported seeing a red-haired apparition that fits the description of the original owner's youngest daughter, Julia Marceline.

HOUMAS HOUSE — PLANTATION

(☎225-473-9380; www.houmashouse.com; 40136 Hwy 942, Darrow; admission $20; ⊙9am-5pm Mon & Tue, 9am-8pm Wed-Sun) If Judy Whitney Davis is your tour guide, you're going to learn a ton while also having a blast. Artifacts here are sometimes 'interactive,' and Whitney Davis might just play the Steinway piano or shoot a billiard ball on the 1800s Brunswick table. The original house, built in the 1790s, now forms the back end of the main Greek-revival manse, built in 1840. In its heyday, this plantation controlled 150,000 acres of sugarcane, covering modern-day towns up to 8 miles away. Most of the furnishings are not original to the house, but the current owner (and resident), Kevin Kelly, has collected some fine period antiques to fill in. Bright, towering murals of sugarcane fields flank the entranceway and set a fun mood for exploring. A fine experience is dining by candlelight in the 1790s rooms, now Latil's Landing restaurant.

CAJUN VILLAGE — VILLAGE

(☎225-675-5572; cnr Hwys 22 & 70, Sorrento; ⊙varies by store) The rustic antique, craft and coffee shops of Cajun Village are all old Creole shacks that have been moved here from around the region. Down the road you might notice the 1963 **Sunshine Bridge**, unexceptional except for the fact that it was named by Governor Jimmie Davis who rode to electoral success singing campaign songs he wrote. Ever heard 'You Are My Sunshine?'

✕ EATING & DRINKING

The eating and drinking listings are arranged geographically, heading upriver from New Orleans.

WAYNE JACOB'S SMOKEHOUSE & RESTAURANT — CAJUN $$

(☎985-652-9990; www.wjsmokehouse.com; 769 W 5th St, LaPlace; lunch $7-16, dinner $9-26; ⊙11am-2pm Mon-Fri, 5:30-8:30pm Thu & Fri, 10:30am-2am Sun) This is the place to stop on your way upriver from Destrehan Plantation. LaPlace is known for producing fantastic andouille sausages, and Wayne Jacob's smokes up some of the best. Po'boys, red beans and rice, and Cajun comfort food fill out the menu and portions are generous. There's also a long list of daily specials. But whatever you choose, make sure to include an order of the smoky chicken and andouille gumbo. It's some of the best we had in southern Louisiana. An amazing array of sausages are for sale in back.

CABIN RESTAURANT — CAJUN, CREOLE $$

(☎225-473-3007; www.thecabinrestaurant.com, cnr Hwys 44 & 22, Burnside; mains $7-20; ⊙11am-3pm Mon, 11am-9pm Tue-Thu, 11am-10pm Fri & Sat, 11am-6pm Sun) Two miles from River Road, this well-worn joint occupies a collection of slave dwellings and other dependencies rescued from the demolished Monroe, Welham and Helvetia Plantations. The interior walls are papered with old newspapers in the same manner that slaves once insulated their rough-sawn cabin walls. Besides po'boys you can get dishes like red beans and rice with sausage. The restaurant is geared to serving tourist crowds, but the gumbo is pretty good.

CAJUN VILLAGE COFFEE HOUSE — CAFE $

(☎225-675-8068; cnr Hwys 22 & 70, Sorrento; mains under $12; ⊙6am-6pm) Don't wear anything black to this rustic coffee shop if you think you might order one of the fantastic beignets. These tasty babies come smothered in powdered sugar. Full Louisiana breakfasts and plate lunches are also served, but the beignets filled with sweet and savory toppings are the real highlight.

GRAPEVINE CAFE — CAFE $$

(☎225-473-8463; www.grapevinecafeandgallery.com; 211 Railroad Ave, Donaldsonville; lunch $8-27, dinner $14-27; ⊙11am-2pm & 5-9pm Tue-Fri, 11am-9pm Sat, 11am-2pm Sun) When the white-chocolate bread pudding tastes like a cloud, you have good reason to start with dessert first. But you shouldn't miss chef Cynthia Schneider's other dishes, such as crawfish étouffée served in a pastry shell, or on top of polenta-like cornbread. Brunch is especially good.

LATIL'S LANDING

CREOLE $$$

(☎225-473-9380; www.houmashouse.com/restaurant.htm; Houmas House, 40136 Hwy 942, Darrow; mains $30-42; ⊙6-10pm Wed-Sat, 11am-3pm Sun) This exquisite little eatery occupies rooms of the original 1700s home where dishes such as bisque of curried pumpkin and crawfish, and Creole lobster risotto are served on Limoges reproductions of the plantation's original china. You dine like a sugar baron could have only dreamed thanks to modern transport and fusion cooking. Chef Jeremy Langlois' seven-course tasting menu can be paired with selections from the plantation's historic cellars.

St Francisville

Explore

Tranquil St Francisville retains nearly 150 of its original 18th- and 19th-century houses and buildings. That includes the lodging place of the town's most famous (temporary) resident, John James Audubon, who lived a few months at Oakley Plantation. He returned frequently to sketch avian species in the surrounding woodlands for *The Birds of America*.

This area was not part of the 1803 Louisiana Purchase – it stayed with Spanish-controlled Florida territory until 1810. Cotton plantations sprang up from the 1800s into the early 1900s, followed by the town.

In the morning, pick up a walking-tour brochure at the visitor center and stroll past historic homes nearby. There should be enough time to then visit two of the town's plantations. For variety, tour one plantation, then drive 25 miles to the penitentiary museum at Angola.

The Best

➡ **Sight** Louisiana State Penitentiary Museum

➡ **Plantation** Rosedown

➡ **Place to Eat** Magnolia Cafe

Top Tip

Pretty day? Pack a lunch for Rosedown Plantation. There are a few picnic tables near the visitor center.

Getting There & Away

Direction Northwest

Travel time Two hours

Car Follow I-10 west from New Orleans to Baton Rouge. Take US 110 and Hwy 61 north from there.

Need to Know

➡ **Area Code** 225

➡ **Location** 113 miles northwest of New Orleans

➡ **Tourist Office** (☎225-635-4224; www.stfrancisville.us; 11757 Ferdinand St; ⊙9am-5pm Mon-Sat, from 9:30am Sun) Information, gift shop and historical displays.

◉ SIGHTS

OAKLEY PLANTATION & AUDUBON STATE HISTORIC SITE

HISTORIC SITE

(☎225-635-3739; www.crt.state.la.us/parks/iaudubon.aspx; 11788 Hwy 965; admission $4; ⊙9am-5pm, last tour at 4pm) Outside of town is Oakley Plantation & Audubon State Historic Site, where John James Audubon spent his tenure, arriving in 1821 to tutor the owner's daughter. Though his assignment lasted only 3½ months (and his room was pretty darn spartan), he and his assistant finished 32 paintings of birds found in the plantation's surrounding forest. Several original Audubon prints hang from the walls. Restored furnishings in the small West Indies-influenced house (1806) are in the style of the Federal Period (1790–1830). The 100-acre grounds include a lovely herb and vegetable garden, two 1840s slave cabins, a kitchen with brick hearths still in working order and a barn. The half-mile wooded Cardinal Trail is great for birdwatching.

ROSEDOWN PLANTATION HISTORIC SITE

PLANTATION

(☎225-635-3332; www.crt.state.la.us/parks/irosedown.aspx; 12501 Hwy 10; adult/student

LA STATE PENITENTIARY MUSEUM AT ANGOLA

At the end of LA 66, about 25 miles northwest of St Martinsville, sits an 18,000-acre plot of farmland surrounded on three sides by the Mississippi River. The place goes by several names. Angola. The Farm. The Louisiana State Penitentiary. There are more than 5100 prisoners incarcerated here. In 2010, 86% of them were violent offenders, and 74% were serving a life sentence. Outside the front gate is the small but fascinating **Louisiana State Penitentiary Museum** (225-655-2592; www.angolamuseum.org; Angola; admission free; 8am-4:30pm Mon-Fri, 9am-4pm Sat, plus Sun in Oct). This museum displays artifacts from the prison, which had its origins on the site in the 1880s. Visitors can walk inside a tiny prison cell, look at a lethal array of prison-made weapons, and ogle a denim shirt worn by George Clooney while filming scenes from the movie *Out of Sight* (1998). Scenes from *Dead Man Walking* (1995) and *Monsters Ball* (2001) were also filmed here. The most disturbing display is Gruesome Gertie, the electric chair used at Angola between 1941 and 1991; 86 men and one woman were executed in the chair.

Angola has a long and bloody past but in recent years extensive efforts have been made to educate and rehabilitate the inmates. Prison Enterprises oversees crop production on the grounds, and prisoners grow and cultivate much of their own food. Jellies produced here are for sale in the museum's gift shop along with T-shirts reading 'Angola: A Gated Community.' The penitentiary is also known for its annual **rodeo** (www.angolarodeo.com), marketed as 'The Wildest Show in the South.' Every Sunday during the month of October inmates rope and ride in various events that are open to the public.

Angola is also the backdrop for Animal Planet's reality show *Louisiana Lockdown*, which premiered in 2012 and spotlights prisoner involvement with animal programs.

$10/4; 9am-5pm, last tour at 4pm) Get your cameras out for the corridor of live oaks fronting this lovely plantation home. Commissioned by Daniel and Martha Turnbull, the 1835 cypress-and-cedar house still contains many original mid-19th-century furnishings. Note the frighteningly narrow and well-worn circular stairwell used by slaves – they had to carry water and wood upstairs while maintaining their balance. Outside, the formal gardens have been meticulously restored based on Margaret's garden diaries. Be warned: Rosedown is a major stop on the tour-bus circuit.

MYRTLES PLANTATION & B&B   PLANTATION
(225-635-6277; www.myrtlesplantation.com; 7747 Hwy 61; adult/child $8/4, Mystery Tour $10; tours 9am-5pm daily, mystery tours 6pm, 7pm & 8pm Fri & Sat) Owners and docents alike perpetuate the idea that Myrtles is one of the 'most haunted houses in America.' And whether it's all bunk or not, this place is certifiably creepy, especially if you visit on a dark, rainy day. Tours do not seem to be quite as architecturally and historically informative as other plantation tours in the region, but they still paint a vivid picture of life during the plantation era.

Mystery tours, offered Friday and Saturday evenings, are geared toward ghost stories while daytime tours focus on details about the house and its furnishings (although ghost stories will likely be shared upon request). Brave visitors can opt to spend the night in one of the B&B rooms in the main house (c 1796). It's possibly your best chance for spotting a specter among the Carrera marble mantels and gold-leaf furnishings.

 **EATING & DRINKING**

Though there are a few places to eat in St Francisville, restaurants are not the highlight of the town.

MAGNOLIA CAFE   CAFE $$
(225-635-6528; www.themagnoliacafe.net; 5689 Commerce St; lunch $8-13, dinner $8-24; 11am-4pm Sun-Wed, to 9pm Thu & Sat, to 10pm Fri) A purple- and yellow-painted pig greets guests outside the entrance of this colorful old house where you can order fresh salads and sandwiches; try the spicy shrimp po'boy. Daily specials include Louisiana dishes and there's live music some Friday evenings.

CARRIAGE HOUSE RESTAURANT
SEAFOOD, CAJUN $$

(☎225-635-6278; www.themyrtlesrestaurant
.com; Myrtles Plantation, 7747 Hwy 61; mains
lunch $8-14, dinner $18-28; ⊙11am-2pm & 5-9pm
Wed-Sat & Mon, 11am-2pm Sun) Standard Loui-
siana fare – Cajun dishes, seafood platters,
comfort food – is offered in a plantation
setting. Eat in the courtyard or in the Myr-
tles' former carriage house, which dresses
up for dinner with white tablecloths and
starched napkins.

BIRDMAN COFFEE & BOOKS
CAFE $

(☎225-635-5446; 5695 Commerce St; ⊙7am-
2pm Thu-Tue; 🛜) Don't plan on lingering over
homemade cookies and wi-fi first thing;
this coffee shop is busy, busy in the morn-
ing. Return in the afternoon and peruse the
few used books at a more leisurely pace.

Lafayette & Breaux Bridge

Explore

In the Cajun heartland in and around La-
fayette the down-to-earth culture really
lives, with dance halls and crawfish boils
in every town. Here the roux are darker
and more earthy, and much of the seafood
is fried. Think of the Cajuns as the country
cousins of their uptown New Orleans
neighbors.

If you're planning to visit several towns,
including those in the Cajun prairie, then
Lafayette – known as the Hub City – makes
a good home base. Visit the Acadian Cul-
tural Center and a living history site in
Lafayette in the morning, then head to
Breaux Bridge for crawfish, a swamp tour
and a dance hall band. If you spend the
night, drive south to the Tabasco factory
and Shadows-on-the-Teche in New Ibe-
ria on your way back to New Orleans via
Hwy 90 the next morning. I-10 borders
the north side of Lafayette; Hwy 90 runs
north–south bisecting it.

The Best

➡ **Sight** Vermilionville

➡ **Place to Eat** French Press

➡ **Place to Drink** Blue Moon Saloon

Top Tip

Find weekly live band listings for the re-
gion in the **Times of Acadiana** (www.times
ofacadiana.com) newspaper and online at
www.arnb.org/louisiana.php.

Getting There & Away

Direction Northwest

Travel Time 2½ hours

Car Follow I-10 west all the way from
New Orleans to Lafayette.

SLEEPING IN ST FRANCISVILLE

St Francisville has a whole host of historic lodgings. If those listed here are occupied,
check out www.stfrancisville.us.

3-V Tourist Court (☎225-635-5540; www.themagnoliacafe.net/magnolia3vtouristcourts.
html; 5687 Commerce Street; r $75-125; 🛜) These 1920s motor court cabins are spare
but homey with kitchenettes, refrigerators and microwaves; the small bathrooms are
clean and well lit. Walk across the gravel drive and you're at Magnolia Cafe; the rest of
the old town is just beyond.

Butler Greenwood Plantation (☎225-635-6312; www.butlergreenwood.com; 8345 Hwy
61; 1/2 bedroom cottages incl breakfast $135/245; 🅿🛜) Stay in a 1796 plantation kitch-
en, in an enclosed hexagonal gazebo with stained-glass windows or in a three-story
windmill. All eight of the one- and two-bedroom cottages on the grounds of Butler
Greenwood are unique. Each has a full kitchen and most have Jacuzzi tubs in addition
to homey antiques and floral accents. The plantation, which has never been sold out
of the original family, is also open for **public tours** (per person $5; ⊙9am-5pm).

Need to Know

➡ **Area Code** 337

➡ **Location** 135 miles northwest of New Orleans

➡ **Tourist Office** (☏337-232-3737; www.lafayettetravel.com; 1400 NW Evangeline Thruway; ◷8:30am-5pm Mon-Fri, from 9am Sat & Sun) Pick up one of the seasonal Bon Temps guides, which has up-to-date information about the whole Cajun heartland.

◉ SIGHTS & ACTIVITIES

◉ Lafayette

Lafayette, the largest city in the region, is the self-proclaimed capital of French Louisiana. By far the largest city in the region, sprawling Lafayette is lacking in some of the quiet charm the neighboring towns and rural Cajun communities possess. It is, however, a good place to learn about Cajun history, and has recently earned praise as a top food and dining destination in the south.

THE CAJUN EXILE

Cajun culture began because of *Le Grand Dérangement*, the British expulsion of the rural French settlers from L'Acadie (now Nova Scotia) in 1755. A homeless population of Acadians searched for decades for a place to settle until seven boatloads of exiles arrived in New Orleans in 1785. The settlers spread out into the Louisiana countryside and mixed with early German peasant farmers, Isleños (Canary Islanders) and Americans. By the early 19th century some 3000 to 4000 Acadians, or Cajuns as they became known, lived in southern Louisiana. Some occupied the swamplands, where they eked out a living based on fishing and trapping, while others farmed rice.

ACADIAN CULTURAL CENTER MUSEUM

(☏337-232-0789; www.nps.gov/jela/new-acadian-cultural-center.htm; 501 Fisher Rd; admission free; ◷8am-5pm) Part of the multisite Jean Lafitte National Park, the Acadian Cultural Center is a good place to learn about Cajun history and traditions. Interpretive exhibits trace *Le Grand Dérangement* (see the boxed text, p162) and spotlight the food and music. The word zydeco, a form of Cajun music, comes from a song about hard times, 'Les Haricots Sant pas Sales,' which translates to 'The Snap Beans Aren't Salty.' Say it fast, you'll hear it. In the spring and fall, rangers lead narrated boat rides (adult/child/senior $12/8/10) describing the life of trappers and traders.

VERMILIONVILLE LIVING HISTORY

(☏337-233-4077; www.bayouvermilion.org; 300 Fisher Rd; adult/child/senior $10/6/8; ◷10am-4pm Tue-Sun) At Vermilionville, next door to the Acadian Cultural Center, costumed guides attempt to bring history to life by taking you through a 19th-century Cajun village. Among the dozen or so buildings on view are homes dating from 1795 to 1860. Bands perform in the barn, there are cooking demonstrations, and in spring and fall you can take boat tours on the bayou. There's also a restaurant La Cuisine de Maman (aka Mama's Kitchen) that serves Cajun and Creole dishes. It's all a bit corny, but entertaining. And the organisation behind the village is committed to preserving the cultural and natural resources of Bayou Vermilionville.

◉ Breaux Bridge

The sign on the namesake drawbridge in downtown Breaux Bridge welcomes you to the 'Crawfish Capital,' a title bestowed on the town by the state legislature in 1959. Since then, the town of 7500 has hosted an annual **Crawfish Festival** (☏337-332-6655; www.bbcrawfest.com) in the first complete weekend in May.

Swampy Lake Martin is 5 miles south of Breaux Bridge and several operators run two-hour water tours through the cypress and moss-filled waters. Alligators abound. If you can, try to ride with the owner of the company rather than an assistant; you may have a more informative trip.

WORTH A DETOUR

NEW IBERIA

Settled by the Spanish in 1779, New Iberia prospered on the sugarcane of surrounding plantations. Today the town's best-known native son is mystery writer James Lee Burke, whose page-turning detective Dave Robicheaux novels take place in and around New Iberia.

A top attraction is **Shadows on the Teche** (☏337-369-6446; www.shadowsontheteche.org; 317 E Main St; adult/student $10/8; ☺9am-4:30pm Mon-Sat), a grand Greek-revival plantation house on the banks of the bayou. The home stayed in the Weeks family from construction in 1831 until it was willed to the National Society for Historic Preservation in 1958. More than 17,000 papers describing the most minute details of the house's history were left in the attic, making this one of the most well-documented historic plantations in Louisiana. Tours begin 15 minutes after the hour.

Also of interest is the **Konriko Company Store & Conrad Rice Mill** (☏337-367-6163; www.conradricemill.com/tour.asp; 307 Ann St; adult/child $4/2.25; ☺9am-5pm), which celebrated its 100th birthday in 2012. It's the oldest operating rice mill in the US. Tours start at 10am, 11am, 1pm, 2pm and 3pm.

Outside town is the region's best known destination, the **McIlhenny Tabasco Factory** (☏337-365-8173; www.tabasco.com; admission free; ☺tours 9am-4pm), which sits on Avery Island. Driving here feels a bit like entering Oz. After paying the man in the tiny booth (admission $1) and waiting for the gate to lift, you drive onto the island. Which isn't really an island. It's a salt dome that extends 8 miles below the surface. The salt mined here goes into the Tabasco sauces, as do locally grown peppers. The mixture ferments in oak barrels before it's mixed with vinegar, strained and bottled. You'll get a few tiny bottles, in several flavors, after the short tour. At the gift shop, try free samples of Tabasco-spiced chili as well as jalapeno ice cream – it's surprisingly good. The store sells just about any Tabasco-imprinted item you can imagine.

In 1890 Tabasco founder EA McIlhenny started a bird sanctuary on the island. At **Jungle Gardens** (☏337-369-6243; www.junglegarden.org; adult/child $8/5; ☺9am-5pm) you can drive or walk through 250 acres of moss-covered live oaks and subtropical jungle flora. There's an amazing array of water birds (especially snowy egrets, which nest here in astounding numbers) as well as turtles and alligators.

James Lee Burke's fictional detective Dave Robicheaux likes to drop by **Victor's Cafeteria** (☏337-369-9924; www.victorscafeteria.com; 109 W Main St; breakfast $4-7; lunch plates under $10; ☺6am-1:45pm Mon-Fri, to 10am Sat, 6am-2pm Sun), and so do his fans. Get in line at the counter to order favorites such as gumbo and fried shrimp, and home-style Cajun standards in this laid-back little landmark. Note the limited hours and enter on the right.

Just down the street from Shadows-on-the-Teche, **Clementine Dining & Spirits** (☏337-560-1007; www.clementinedowntown.com; 113 E Main St; lunch $8-14, dinner $16-26; ☺11am-2pm Tue-Fri, 5-9pm Mon-Thu, until 10pm Fri, 6-10pm Sat) serves seafood, chicken and steak dishes as well as Louisiana favorites such as shrimp po'boys and oysters Rockefeller.

CAJUN COUNTRY SWAMP TOURS
SWAMP TOUR

(☏337-319-0010; www.cajuncountryswamptours.com; adult/child $20/10; ☺daily by appointment) Butch Guchereau, born and raised in the Bayou Teche area, offers two-hour eco-minded tours on quiet crawfish skiffs.

CHAMPAGNE'S SWAMP TOURS
SWAMP TOUR

(☏337-230-4068; www.champagnesswamptours.com; adult/child $20/10; ☺daily by appointment) Guides speak both French and English (if need be) on the two-hour tours. If you want to see an alligator, these guides will do their darndest to find one for you. Trips are also on a crawfish skiff.

 **EATING & DRINKING**

You'll not want for good food: Lafayette has one of the highest concentrations of restaurants per capita in the nation. In

2011 the city was named one of the Top 10 Food Cities in the South by *Southern Living* magazine and won 'Best for Food' in Rand McNally/*USA Today*'s national 'Best of the Road' competition.

Entertainment almost always goes with eating in Lafayette, which is good for families especially; restaurant-dance halls are nonsmoking and all ages are welcome.

TOP CHOICE FRENCH PRESS   CAJUN $$

(☑337-233-9449; www.thefrenchpresslafayette .com; 214 E Vermilion, Lafayette; breakfast & lunch $6-15, dinner $28-39; ☺7am-2pm Tue-Fri, 9am-2pm Sat & Sun, 5:30-9pm Fri & Sat) This place triggers plate envy. Every dish looks savory and delicious as it's carried past. Should I have ordered the Cajun Benedict? I hear it's the best thing on the menu. Maybe I should have ordered the Acadian breakfast sandwich. Or maybe the...Sweet Baby Breesus! Here it is. Three buttermilk biscuits with bacon, fried boudin balls and Steen's Cane Syrup. And a cauldron of cheese grits. I'll be juuuust fine (the dish appears to be named for Drew Brees AND the son of God). Inside a former print shop – those are typeface drawers on the wall – this new-on-the-scene restaurant also serves gourmet sandwiches and a short menu of seafood and savory meats for dinner. People like to linger and chat on weekends, so if you don't want to wait, come at 9am or 1pm.

OLD TYME GROCERY   PO'BOYS $

(☑337-235-8165; www.oldetymegrocery.com; 218 W St Mary St, Lafayette; po'boys $6-9; ☺8am-10pm Mon-Fri, 9am-7pm Sat) The shrimp po'boy here is one of the best we've eaten in the entire state of Louisiana. Step inside this busy but helpful grocery, order your po'boy at the counter, grab a bag of Spicy Cajun Zapp's chips, wander the store and then....order up! Settle in at the cozy dining room off the side or go back to your hotel room and chow down. We're hungry now with the memory.

CAFE DES AMIS   CAJUN $$

(☑337-332-5273; cafedesamis.com; 140 E Bridge St, Breaux Bridge; breakfasts $5-10, mains $14-24; ☺11am-3pm Tue, 11am-9pm Wed & Thu, 7:30am-9pm Fri & Sat, 8:30am-2pm Sun) Well-known local restaurateur Dickie Breaux does things right at this long-time local fave in a 1920s downtown storefront. The beignets are crisp and light, and spicy barbecued shrimp never tasted so good. Friday mornings you can sit under the pressed-tin ceiling and hear French spoken by all the ol' boys who gather here. Saturday morning, the place is full to capacity for the zydeco breakfast featuring live bands.

TACO SISTERS   MEXICAN $

(☑337-234-8226; www.tacosisters.com; 407 Johnston St, at Vermilion, Lafayette; mains $3-10; ☺11am-6pm Mon-Fri, 11am-2pm Sat) Opened by Molly and Katy Richard, the namesake sisters, this mango-colored taco shack serves juicy tacos and burritos with a Cajun kick. Everything's homemade and fresh, from the fish that's smoked in-house to the marinated chicken to the homemade salad dressing. Order at the first window, pay at the second and if you drop a tip in the jar they'll ring a bell. Delicious.

PREJEAN'S CAJUN DINING   CAJUN $$

(☑337-896-3247; www.prejeans.com; 3480 I-49 N, Lafayette; dinner mains $11-33; ☺7am-9pm Sun-Thu, until 10pm Fri & Sat) Live music accompanies dinner and weekend brunches (old-timer Gurvais Matte is a regular), but food takes center stage. Have crawfish omelets for breakfast, fried oyster salad for lunch, and crawfish and alligator sausage cheesecake (yummier than it sounds) followed by blackened catfish étouffée for dinner. Don't forget to say hi to Big Al, the 14ft stuffed alligator, on your way in. The restaurant is on the east-side frontage road running parallel to I-49.

☆ ENTERTAINMENT

If you get the chance to stay overnight in the area, there are some great live music options.

TOP CHOICE BLUE MOON SALOON   LIVE MUSIC

(☑337-766-2538; www.bluemoonpresents.com; 215 E Convent St, Lafayette; ☺8:45pm Fri & Sat, 6pm Sun) Dang, we love this place. And if The Lost Bayou Ramblers are hollerin' and fiddlin' it up on a Saturday night, well, you'll find us sipping a beer, hanging on the fringe of the dance floor and maybe, just maybe, howling at the blue moon. But momma doesn't think that's ladylike. Anyway, at this place the employees are happy, the patrons are happy, the musicians are

SLEEPING IN LAFAYETTE & BREAUX BRIDGE

Chain motels and hotels crowd Hwy 90, south of the intersection with I-10.

Bayou Cabins (☑337-332-6158; www.bayoucabins.com; 100 W Mills Ave, Breaux Bridge; cabins $60-125; 🔊) Welcome to the bayou! Each of the 12 cabins (one of them is a duplex) on the Bayou Teche is unique. Cabin 1 has 1949 newspapers as wallpaper (aka insulation) and cabin 6 has a 50s theme complete with Elvis. After check-in, guests are welcomed by hosts Rocky and Lisa Sonnier with Cajun hospitality and a homemade platter of boudin, cracklin's and headcheese. A full, hot breakfast is served at 9am. At night, Christmas lights twinkle from the cabin fronts, a festive backdrop if you bring home a few pounds of spicy crawfish to devour on the front porch of your cabin.

Blue Moon Guest House (☑337-234-2422; www.bluemoonpresents.com; 215 E Convent St, Lafayette; dm $18, r $70-90; 🔊) Not for the faint-of-heart, but perfect for the fun lovin', this tidy old home includes admission to Lafayette's popular down-home music venue, which is basically on a covered patio in the back of the house. The friendly owners, full kitchen and camaraderie among guests create a casual hangout environment. Prices skyrocket during festival time. The guesthouse is located on a side street in downtown Lafayette; dorms are coed.

Juliet (☑337-261-2225; www.ascendcollection.com/hotel-lafayette-louisiana-LA250; 800 Jefferson St, Lafayette; r $149-197, ste $249-279; @🔊🛏) Twenty upscale neutral rooms – with custom-made linens – occupy the former Le Parisienne department store in downtown Lafayette. Look for the lion's-head fountain gracing the curvaceous pool.

---

happy, the dancers are happy. So c'mon cher, let's *fais do do*.

ATCHAFALAYA CLUB
LIVE MUSIC

(☑337-228-7110; http://patsfishermanswharf .com; Henderson; ☺8:45pm Fri & Sat, 6pm Sun) Shuffling its feet beside Pat's Fisherman's Wharf in Henderson, the Atchafalaya Club hosts a great variety of Cajun bands. The Foret Tradition regularly belts out mean swamp music, and you might see the talented Lost Pine Boys, now familiar from HBO's *Treme*. Henderson is 8 miles east of Breaux Bridge.

BLUE DOG CAFE
LIVE MUSIC

(☑337-237-0005; www.bluedogcafe.com; 1211 W Pinhook Rd, Lafayette; brunch $23; ☺11am-2pm & 5-9pm Mon-Thu, 11am-2pm & 5-10pm Fri, 5-10pm Sat, 10:30am-2pm Sun) Make reservations if you hope to enjoy the live jazz and Cajun music brunch; any given Sunday, the line stretches out the door by 10:30am. Bayou bisque with seafood, crawfish étouffée over rice, pork grillades (thin, browned strips with gravy) and cornbread dressing. Louisiana native artist (and co-owner) George Rodrigue displays many pieces of his artwork here, including incarnations of his Blue Dog. There's live music Thursday through Saturday evenings.

LA POUSSIERE
LIVE MUSIC

(☑337-332-1721; www.lapoussiere.com; 1301 Grandpoint Hwy, Breaux Bridge; ☺7-11pm Sat, 3-7pm Sun) La Poussiere is one of the Cajun clubs around here. It doesn't serve food, just drink and dance. Live bands play Saturday and Sunday – cover charge depends on who's playing.

RANDOL'S
LIVE MUSIC

(☑337-981-7080; www.randols.com; 2320 Kaliste Saloom Rd, Lafayette; ☺5-10pm Sun-Thu, to 11pm Fri & Sat) Dishes like crab cake au gratin are quite tasty, but the nightly live Cajun tunes are the why-go. Regulars are always here scooting around the floor; sit on the bench around the dance floor (separated from the tables by some awkward plexiglass) and you *will* be asked out onto the floor.

Cajun Prairie

Explore

North of I-10 in central Louisiana the bayous and swamps give way to grasslands and prairies. The main attraction in the region's sleepy towns – Opelousas, Eunice and Mamou – is music. The best time to visit all three communities is Saturday, with a live show at Fred's Lounge in Mamou followed by the Cajun jam at the Savoy Music Center in Eunice. Spend the afternoon in area museums, then dance to zydeco in Opelousas.

Opelousas is 24 miles north of Lafayette via Hwy 49. Eunice is 20 miles west of Opelousas via Hwy 190 and Mamou is 11 miles north of Eunice. You can loop back to Lafayette taking LA 13 south to the I-10 or swinging north to Ville Platte, home of a top-notch music store, and return via Opelousas.

The Best

➡ **Sight** Pig Stand, Ville Platte

➡ **Place to Eat** Prairie Acadian Cultural Center, Eunice

Top Tip

There are four museums in Eunice, but all of them are closed on Monday. To learn more about Cajun culture and hear live music, aim for a Saturday visit.

Getting There & Away

Direction Northwest

Travel Time 3 hours

Car Head west out of New Orleans on I-10; at Lafayette, turn north on I-49.

Need to Know

➡ **Area Code** 337

➡ **Location** 155 miles northwest of New Orleans

➡ **Tourist Office** (☑337-457-2565; www.eunice chamber.com; 200 S CC Dusan St; ☺9am-3pm Mon-Fri) The Eunice Chamber of Commerce operates a visitor center downtown.

 SIGHTS

CAJUN MUSIC HALL OF FAME   MUSEUM
(☑337-457-6540; 220 S CC Duson St, Eunice; admission free; ☺9am-5pm Tue-Sat) Showcasing Cajun instruments and other musical memorabilia, this hall of fame in Eunice is worth a peek. But zydeco fans will be out of luck – Cajun is the sole focus here.

PRAIRIE ACADIAN CULTURAL CENTER   CULTURAL CENTER
(☑337-457-8499; www.nps.gov/jela; 250 W Park Ave, cnr Third St & Park Ave, Eunice; admission free; ☺8am-5pm Tue-Fri, until 6pm Sat) At 3pm there's a local Cajun music demonstration at this cultural center, which also has interpretive exhibits about the history and traditions of the prairie Acadians.

FLOYD'S RECORD SHOP   LANDMARK
(☑337-363-2138; www.floydsrecordshop.com; 434 E Main St, Ville Platte; ☺8:30am-4:30pm Tue-Sat) A good way to round out your musical tour of the prairie is to stop by Floyd's Record Shop in Ville Platte, 14 miles northeast of Mamou. In 1957 Floyd Solieau left his DJ job to start both the record shop and Flat Tire Music. Through the years, under various label names, Floyd has waxed records for dozens of French-language Cajun and swamp pop legends. The shop, still in the family, is a cultural icon and an excellent resource for all things Cajun – CDs, instruments, books and souvenirs.

✖ EATING & DRINKING

While you're on the prairie, keep your eye out for 'Slap ya Mama' seasonings. The company's hot sauces and pepper rubs, produced in Ville Platte, make spicy gifts.

PIG STAND   DINER **$**
(☑337-363-2883; 318 E Main St, Ville Platte; mains under $15; ☺7am-8pm Tue-Thu, until 9pm Fri & Sat, until 2pm Sun) It doesn't get much more Southern than a place named the Pig Stand. This one-time hole-in-the-wall has received a spiffy makeover, but thankfully they haven't changed the amazing pulled-pork sandwiches. You'll want to take some of the mustard-based barbecue sauce home.

MAMA'S FRIED CHICKEN   FAST FOOD **$**
(☑337-948-9203; 508 E Landry St, Opelousas; mains under $10; ☺10am-10pm Sun-Thu, until 11pm Fri & Sat) On a scale of 1 to 5: Ambience 0, Friendliness 3, Crispy Deliciousness 5!!!!. Yep, the orange booths and plastic tables at this fast-food style local restaurant are a bit sad, but the juicy fried chicken more than makes up for the lack of aesthetic appeal. The sides are great too and some of the choices have a local spin. Think red beans and rice, and fried okra.

⭐ ENTERTAINMENT

Eunice

SAVOY MUSIC CENTER
LIVE MUSIC

(☎337-457-9563; www.savoymusiccenter.com; Hwy 190; ⊙9am-5pm Tue-Fri, 9am-noon Sat) On Saturday mornings, this accordion factory and shop hosts a Cajun-music jam session at 9am that lasts about three hours. Musician Marc Savoy and his guitarist wife, Ann, often join in as well as son Wilson, a member of four-time Grammy nominee the Pine Leaf Boys. Look for the huge Savoy Music Company sign west of the Cajun Campground – and a long line of parked cars on Saturday morning – 3 miles east of town. It's closed for lunch on weekdays from noon to 1:30pm.

LIBERTY THEATER
LIVE MUSIC

(☎337-457-7389; www.eunice-la.com; cnr S Second St & Park Ave; adult/child $5/3; ⊙ticket office 4-6pm Sat, shows 6-7:30pm Sat) It's kind of like the Cajun version of the *Grand Ole Opry* in Nashville. But at the Liberty Theatre, built in 1924, locals dance in front of the stage where a variety of bands play for the Saturday-night radio broadcast, *Rendez-vous des Cajuns,* the live musical variety show broadcast on local radio stations every Saturday from 6pm.

Mamou

On Saturday mornings you can listen to a local Cajun radio broadcast on KVPI 1050AM starting at 9:05am. The show broadcasts from Fred's Lounge in Mamou, 10 miles north of Eunice on Hwy 190. The town's main drag, Sixth St, is a ragtag collection of slow businesses and boarded storefronts, but this little backwater attracts regulars from around the state for Fred's Saturday morning show. Live, traditional Cajun bands play upbeat two-steps and accordion-filled waltzes for a jovial crowd getting awfully merry during breakfast hours. The small brick saloon ain't much to look at, but it sure has hosted all the greats. In the 1950s the Courir de Mardi Gras started up again, and radio broadcasts begun here in 1967 helped fuel the Cajun revival.

⬡TOP CHOICE FRED'S LOUNGE
LIVE MUSIC

(☎337-468-5411; 420 6th St, Mamou; 10 oz Budweiser $3; ⊙8:15am-2pm Sat) In a world filled with finger-wagging busy bodies, it's a salvation of sorts to have a place like Fred's. On a Saturday morning here people are drinking by 9:10am, dancing by 9:15am and smoking cigarettes like it's 1965. Alfred 'Fred' Tate purchased this bar in 1946 and turned it into *the* Cajun gathering place. Today the lounge is only open during the Saturday morning concerts, but Fred's still packs them in. Doors open at 8:15am, but locals don't arrive until the broadcast starts, just after 9am. The white-haired gents and the ladies in their long prairie skirts and ballet-like dance slippers are the most fun to watch. Long-time manager and bartender Tante Sue – known for swigging shots of cinnamon schnapps from a hip flask – retired in 2011 after 40 years of service. Today the party rolls on beneath a big banner printed in her honor. *Laissez les bons temps rouler* (Let the good times roll).

Opelousas

Opelousas is the epicenter of Louisiana zydeco culture. You haven't heard the soul- and funk-mixed Acadian music till you've experienced it at Richard's Club (built in 1947) just west of town. Long a top venue in the state, Richard's has had several incarnations, most recently as Miller's Zydeco Hall of Fame, which opened in mid-2012. If you're overnighting in the area, there are a few good options for live music.

MILLER'S ZYDECO HALL OF FAME
LIVE MUSIC

(11154 Hwy 190, Lawtell; ⊙7pm-late Fri & Sat) When Richard's began, it was part of a circuit of clubs that welcomed African American musicians – such as Fats Domino – to play during pre-1960s segregation. Back then, owner Richard Eddie gave a start to many a 'French la-la' band, as he called the emerging zydeco sound. Today, new owners Dustin and Nicole Miller carry on the tradition. Tight crowds and oven-hot conditions just add to the attraction at this legendary club. The exact performance schedule can be hard to determine. Check their Facebook page or just head west on Hwy 190 toward Eunice and if you see a dance hall with a crowd, there you are.

On the right Saturday night, this wood-frame building will be packed with Louisiana Creoles dancing to bands such as Lil Nate and the Zydeco Big Timers. Mind the 'No parkin' on the dance floor' sign.

SLIM'S Y-KI-KI LIVE MUSIC
(☑337-942-6242; 182 N Main, Opelousas; ☺7pm-late Fri & Sat) Slim's is the other hotbed of zydeco activity in town, a down-and-dirty nightclub with low ceilings, a smoky atmosphere and some seriously hot Afro-Creole zydeco rhythms. Listen for big names like Chris Ardoin and NuStep.

Down the Bayou

Explore

The maze of bayous and swamps arching southwest of New Orleans, 'down the bayou' as locals say, is where the first Cajuns settled. Their traditional lifestyle is still in evidence in small part, though now it's mostly older folks who speak French and fish the waterways. The best way to experience what remains of the culture is to take a swamp tour and afterwards pull up a big plate of fresh-caught crawfish.

In the morning, drive straight to Morgan city for the 10am tour at the Rig Museum. On your return to New Orleans, either stop in Houmas for a swamp tour or drive to Thibodaux, where you can learn about Cajun culture in the wetlands region and pull off the road for a look at well-preserved slave cabins, stark reminders of the South's unsavory past. If you only have a half day for the bayou region, head south to the Barataria Preserve, where wooden walkways meander through the swamp.

The Best

➡ **Sight** Rig Museum, Morgan City
➡ **Place to Eat** Rita Mae's, Morgan City

Top Tip

Wear walking shoes to the Rig Museum. You'll climb at least 26 steep steps and do a fair bit of walking around the rig, inside and out.

Getting There & Away

Direction Southwest to Morgan City

Travel time 1½ hours

Car To get to Houma, take I-10 west to I-310, cross the Mississippi River and follow Hwy 90 west 22 miles. Take LA 182 south at exit 210 into town. Thibodaux is 20 miles northwest of Houma on Hwy 24. To Morgan City, follow Hwy 90 west for 60 miles.

Need to Know

➡ **Area Code** 985
➡ **Location** 60 miles southwest to Morgan City
➡ **Tourist Office** Houma (☑985-868-2732; cnr Hwy 90 & St Charles St; ☺8am-4pm) West of the town limits, this large office has loads of info and helpful staff. Thibodaux ☑985-446-1187; 318 E Bayou Rd; ☺8:30am-4:30pm Mon-Fri) Stop here for details about local events.

⊙ SIGHTS

RIG MUSEUM MUSEUM
(☑985-384-3744; www.rigmuseum.com; 111 1st St, Morgan City; adult/child/senior $5/3.50/4; ☺tours 10am & 2pm Mon-Sat) If you want to get a first-hand look at what it really means when American politicians say 'Drill Baby Drill,' take the 90-minute guided tour at the International Petroleum Museum and Exposition (aka The Rig Museum). This informative tour winds up, down and around Big Charlie, the first ever offshore drilling rig. It was completed in 1954, eight years after it was first proposed by creator AJ Laborde of Marksville, LA. The tour stops inside dorms, the kitchen and the rec area, and then winds outside to the actual drill site. Questions are encouraged, and you will learn a lot about life on a floating rig and how it all works. In fact, Big Charlie is still used as a training facility. Be forewarned: the tour may not always be 100% politically correct (environmentalists and feminists beware), but it is 100% interesting.

BARATARIA PRESERVE

Wanna take a walk on the wild side? Below New Orleans, the Mississippi River flows 90 miles to the bird's-foot-shaped delta, where river pilots board ships entering from the Gulf. The 20,000-acre **Barataria Preserve** (☑504-689-3690; www.nps.gov /jela/barataria-preserve.htm; 6588 Barataria Blvd, Crown Point; admission free; ⊙visitor center 9am-5pm), a unit of southern Louisiana's Jean Lafitte National Historic Park, offers hiking trips into the swamp. It's a good introduction to the wetlands environment. Though this is not a pristine wilderness (as canals and other structures offer evidence of human activity), wild animals and plants are still abundant. Even a brief walk on the boardwalks that wend their way through the swamp will yield sightings of gators and egrets. If you have several hours and want to see a variety of landscapes, walk or drive about 1 mile from the visitor center to the trailhead for the Bayou Coquille Trail and the Marsh Overlook Trail. Bring your phone to hear the free audio tour. Ranger-led wetlands walks are offered Friday to Monday at 10am. Stop by the visitor center to see where the walk will start. Gates to trailhead parking lots are open 7am to 5pm. If arriving before or after those times, park outside the gates. For information about canoeing, call or stop by the visitor center. Some waterways may be impassable due to heavy vegetation growth.

To reach the preserve, take Business Hwy 90 across the Greater New Orleans Bridge to the Westbank Expressway and turn south on Barataria Blvd (Hwy 45) to Hwy 3134, which leads to the national park entrance.

THIBODAUX · TOWN

Positioned at the confluence of Bayous Lafourche and Terrebonne, **Thibodaux** (*ti*-buh-dough; population 14,400) became the parish seat at a time when water travel was preeminent. The copper-domed **courthouse** (cnr Second & Green Sts) was built in 1855 and remains a testament to Thibodaux's glory days, now long, long past. It's history that holds the interest for visitors here. Among the cane fields, **Laurel Valley Village** (☑985-446-7456; 595 Hwy 308; admission by donation; ⊙10am-4pm), about 2 miles east of town on Hwy 308, is one of the best-preserved assemblages of sugar plantation slave structures in the state. Overall, some 60 structures (c 1755 and later) survive here, including the old general store and a school house. Exhibits at the **Wetlands Cajun Cultural Center** (☑985-448-1375; www.nps.gov/jela; 314 St Mary St; admission free; ⊙9am-7pm Mon-Tue, until 6pm Wed-Thu, until 5pm Fri-Sat) cover virtually every aspect of Cajun life in the wetlands, from music to the environmental impacts of trapping and oil exploration. Visitors learn about 'the time of shame,' from 1916 to 1968, when the Louisiana Board of Education discouraged the use of Cajun French. Cajun musicians jam at the center from 5:30pm to 7pm on Monday evenings.

HOUMA · TOWN

Numerous bodies of water (Bayou Black, Little Bayou Black, the Intracoastal Waterway and Bayou Terrebonne) wend their way through the city center of Houma, a town of 30,000 people. The city itself offers little of interest to travelers, save functioning as a place for the swamp-tour-bound to stop and eat. (Reservations are advised for all tours.)

The only company operating on a fixed schedule, **Munson's Swamp Tours** (☑985-851-3569; www.munsonswamptours.com; 979 Bull Run Rd, Houma; adult/under 12yr $20/10; ⊙tours 10am & 1:30pm, plus 4pm in summer) covers a privately owned area in the Chacahoula Swamp. Cruise the pristine waters beneath moss-draped oaks while your guides point out the area's birds and beasts.

Looking for something more lively? Black Guidry entertains passengers with an accordion while piloting them through a scenic slice of Bayou Black on **Cajun Man's Swamp Cruise** (☑985-868-4625; www.cajunman.com; Hwy 182, off Hwy 90, Houma; adult/child $25/15). The launch is 10 miles west of downtown. Eight miles west of town, **Annie Miller's Son's Swamp Tours** (☑985-868-4758; www.annie-miller.com; 3718 Southdown Mandalay Rd, Houma; adult/child $15/10) is run by the son of a local storytelling legend. He,

DISAPPEARING LANDSCAPE

Louisiana's coastal waterways are eroding, due in part to subsidence and hurricanes, and in part to flood management systems that prevent annual deposits of silt. The Army Corp of Engineers is at work on the problem, but an estimated 10 sq miles a year will be lost over the next 50 years according to the Coastal Wetlands Planning, Protection and Restoration Act. The region is hurting in these ecologically and economically tough times.

like his mom before him, has been feeding chicken drumsticks to the alligators for so long that the swamp critters rise from the muck to take a bite when they hear the motor. Captain Wendy Billiot's eco-oriented **Wetland Tours** (☑985-851-7578; www.wetland tours.com; Janet Lynn Lane, Theriot; per person $50) cruise across a swampland lake near the coast (four-person minimum). She also offers angling charters, specializing in teaching women and children (and men!) to fish. Call or email (captainwendy@wetland tours.com) for reservations and half- and full-day charter prices.

✖ EATING & DRINKING

RITA MAE'S KITCHEN   AMERICAN, CAJUN **$$**
(☑985-384-3550; www.morgancitymainstreet
.com/ritamaeskitchen.htm; 711 Federal Ave, Morgan City; ☺8am-10pm Mon-Sat, until 5pm Sun) Rita Mae's comes recommended up, down

and around the bayou. In a small house near the Hwy 90 overpass, this little cottage of deliciousness serves up comfort food like grandma used to make, but maybe just a little bit better. Heck, there's even a TV playing in the den (a tradition here it seems). Come for omelets in the morning or fill up on juicy burgers, po'boys, fried chicken, fried catfish and red beans and rice later in the day. If they're busy, just seat yourself, and they'll get to ya.

FREMIN'S   ITALIAN **$$**
(☑985-449-0333; www.fremins.net; 402 W 3rd St, Thibodaux; lunch $ $9-14, dinner $9-28; ☺11am-2pm Tue-Fri, 5-9pm Tue-Thu, 5-10pm Fri & Sat) Located in a building dating from 1878 in downtown Thibodaux, Gilded-Age Fremin's serves traditional Italian pastas as well as seafood and steaks. A few dishes, like the crawfish tortellini carbonara, have a hint of Cajun flair. At lunch, look for po'boys, burgers and sandwiches plus a few steaks.

LEJEUNE'S   BAKERY **$**
(☑337-276-5690; www.lejeunesbakery.com; 1510 Main St/Hwy 182, Jeanerette; mains less than $5) For a quick but satisfying snack between Morgan City and New Iberia, swing off Hwy 90 at Jeanerette and drive though the small downtown to Lejeune's. If the red light is on that means they still have French bread available for sale. Just walk on in and ask for a loaf – it's more factory than store – and grab some yummy ginger cakes if they've got them. That's about all they sell, but they do 'em right. The LeJeune family has been operating the bakery since 1884 and using the same recipes!

Sleeping

Where you stay in New Orleans depends largely on why you've come. You can shell out some extra cash and play the whole time in the French Quarter. Or experience the softer (but still fun) side of the city via one of its many quirky B&Bs. There's a lot of accommodation on offer; the one weakness is a lack of backpacker hostels.

Hotels

New Orleans hotels come in all the standard shapes and sizes. Most commonly you'll find either large purpose-built properties or cozier lodgings in older buildings. Figuring out which is which by an establishment's name alone is impossible (an 'inn' here might have five rooms or 500), so read reviews carefully.

B&Bs

For charm, you can't beat the Crescent City's hundreds of B&Bs – housed in everything from colorful Creole cottages to stately town houses and megamansions. Three obvious selling points are intimate surroundings, interesting architecture and, in many cases, a peaceful courtyard in which to escape the maddening crowds. The complimentary morning meal at B&Bs (and many hotels) is almost always a continental breakfast.

Longer-Term Rentals

Even if you're just staying for a week or less, renting an apartment is an option in the French Quarter, Faubourg Marigny and the Garden districts. Live in the lap of luxury at corporate digs or keep costs down by buying groceries and using a kitchen at more basic options. Independent owners list places for rent at **Vacation Rentals by Owner** (www.vrbo.com) and **Vacation Rentals Online** (www.vacationrentalsonline.com). Contrary to the name, **New Orleans Bed & Breakfast** (☑524-9918; www.neworleansbandb.com) manages unhosted properties around town.

Room Rates & Seasons

In general, lodgings in New Orleans charge by the room, rather than by person. The city is peculiar in that it's busy during the shoulder seasons of spring and fall (February through May and September through November) and slow during the summer months (due to some seriously oppressive heat June through August). Most hectic and high-priced of all are Mardi Gras (February or March), Jazz Fest (late April to early May) and other holidays and festivals (see p20). Prices listed here are for the high spring and fall seasons. Those arriving for Jazz Fest should book at one of the mansions-turned-B&B in Mid-City.

Air-Con

All accommodations listed have air-conditioning. You'd melt in the summer without it.

Parking

Note that if you're staying in the Quarter or the CBD, parking can seriously add to your bottom line (an extra $17 to $40 per night). Stashing your car while staying in other neighborhoods is usually free. If having your car accessible in a dedicated, on-site lot is important to you, look for the ℗ icon in our reviews.

NEED TO KNOW

Price Ranges
In our listings we've used the following codes to indicate the price of an en suite double room in high season.

$	less than $100
$$	$100 to $200
$$$	over $200

Reservations
➜ Conventions can fill the city any time and you'll almost always get a better rate by booking ahead.

➜ For Mardi Gras or Jazz Fest, reserve rooms six months to a year in advance.

➜ Some hotels turn over a portion of last-day bookings, at reduced rates, to the **New Orleans Welcome Center** (Map p238; ☑566-5031; 529 St Ann St; ⊘9am-5pm).

Online Resources
New Orleans Online
(www.neworleansonline.com/book)

Louisiana Bed & Breakfast Association
(www.louisianabandb.com)

New Orleans Hotels
(www.bestneworleanshotels.com)

Gay Stays
Although we list our favorite gay stays in the Gay & Lesbian overview (p40), note that all properties we list are GLBT-
New Orleans is a
hore
39.

Lonely Planet's Top Choices

Audubon Cottages (p174) Gorgeous, deceptively spacious private cottages in the heart of the French Quarter.

House on Bayou Road (p185) Old New Orleans elegance perched on bucolic Bayou St John.

Soniat House (p174) Quintessential French Quarter historic hotel.

Roosevelt New Orleans (p180) Opulent digs and central downtown location.

Columns Hotel (p184) Sip a mint julep in this Southern mansion.

Auld Sweet Olive Bed & Breakfast (p177) Hip yet cozy B&B in the heart of bohemian action.

Best For Pets

Loews New Orleans Hotel (p180)

Hotel Monteleone (p174)

Westin New Orleans at Canal Place (p177)

La Quinta Inn & Suites Downtown (p181)

Bienville House Hotel (p175)

Best For Hotel Bars

Hotel Monteleone (p174)

International House (p181)

Columns Hotel (p184)

Dauphine Orleans (p175)

Best For Families

Prytania Park Hotel (p183)

Hampton Inn St Charles Ave (p183)

Embassy Suites Hotel (p182)

Dauphine Orleans (p175)

Olivier House (p174)

Best Historic Hotels

Hotel Monteleone (p174)

Gentry Quarters (p176)

Soniat House (p174)

Hotel Royal (p175)

Degas House (p185)

Best Contemporary Cool

Loft 523 (p181)

International House (p181)

Hotel Royal (p175)

La Quinta Inn & Suites Downtown (p181)

Loews New Orleans Hotel (p180)

Best Bed & Breakfasts

Bywater Bed & Breakfast (p178)

Ashton's Bed & Breakfast (p185)

Bohemian Armadillo Guest House (p178)

Crescent City Guesthouse (p179)

B&W Courtyards (p179)

Where to Stay

Neighborhood	For	Against
French Quarter	Centrally located, so no need for a car, especially if you're staying in the Quarter. High competition means high standards of accommodation.	Touristy and loud, sometimes bordering on obnoxious. If you drove, it is difficult to find parking and maneuver in the narrow streets.
Faubourg Marigny & Bywater	Cozy, independently owned guesthouses and B&Bs. Some have an authentic bohemian vibe going; all are gay-friendly. Low-key, but close to some great live music.	Small properties means inconsistent access to major modern amenities like 24-hour room service. Less privacy than larger hotels.
CBD & Warehouse District	Best area for modern amenities. Many hotels here have excellent attached bars and restaurants. Many family-friendly spots.	The least quintessentially 'New Orleans' part of New Orleans. Many hotels are boring, convention-style places. Parking can be expensive. Potentially far from French Quarter *and* Uptown.
Garden, Lower Garden & Central City	Charming B&Bs set in wonderful historic homes, plus a few larger hotels on St Charles Ave. Walking distance to Magazine St shopping.	Not for folks who need funkier edges to their accommodation. Having a car really helps if you stay out here.
Uptown & Riverbend	Posh hotels and smaller (but just as opulent) guesthouses for those needing beauty and quiet. Within striking (sometimes walking) distance of the most exciting restaurants in the city.	Far from French Quarter and Marigny, so having a car out here is recommended.
Mid-City & the Tremé	Smaller guesthouses with character in beautiful historic neighborhoods far from the French Quarter's bustle.	You need a car out here. Stuff to do is scattered around rather than centralized. No larger hotels and their reams of amenities.

SLEEPING

🛏 French Quarter

If you are looking for the historic flavor of the Old Quarter, a general rule of thumb is the further away you stay from the CBD, the better. Bourbon St, of course, is party central. The Lower Quarter is more residential, with guesthouses and smaller hotels, and staying down there is just as convenient. Large hotels cluster around Iberville and Canal Sts.

TOP CHOICE AUDUBON COTTAGES   HOTEL $$$

Map p238 (☎586-1516; www.auduboncottages .com; 509 Dauphine St; cottages $300-800; P ⊠ 🛜) The appeal of staying in the French Quarter is the fantasy of living in a colonial (or 19th century) period house. Usually, that's a house you happen to share with about 100 other guests. Not so at the Audubon Cottages, where you get to sleep in one of seven immaculately restored historical buildings, ranging from two-bedroom suites with private courtyards and walk-in showers to former slave quarters once used as a studio by John James Audubon. You'll have your own saltwater pool, attentive staff and the satisfaction of having privacy and quiet within the Quarter while being within walking distance of all the action.

TOP CHOICE SONIAT HOUSE   BOUTIQUE HOTEL $$$

Map p238 (☎522-0570, 800-544-8808; www .soniathouse.com; 1133 Chartres St; r from $240, ste from $425; ⊜🛜) The three town houses that make up this hospitable hotel in the Lower Quarter epitomize Creole elegance at its unassuming best. The place is run with congenial efficiency. You enter via a cool loggia into a courtyard filled with ferns, palmettos and a trickling fountain. Some rooms open up onto the courtyard, while winding stairways lead to the elegant upstairs quarters. Singular attention has been paid to the art and antiques throughout. This is a genuinely romantic spot (children under 12 are not permitted).

HOTEL MONTELEONE   HOTEL $$$

Map p238 (☎523-3341, 800-535-9595; www.hotel monteleone.com; 214 Royal St; r from $250; P @) Perhaps the city's most venerable old hotel, the Monteleone is also the French Quarter's largest. (Not long after the Monteleone was built, preservationists put a stop to building on this scale below Iberville St.) Since its inception in 1866, the hotel has been the local lodging of choice for writers, including luminaries like William Faulkner, Truman Capote and Rebecca Wells. The Carousel Bar – a New Orleans classic – has appeared in numerous films and TV shows. Rooms throughout exude an old-world appeal with French toile and chandeliers. Some guests liked it so much, they never left (see the boxed text, p176).

LAFITTE GUEST HOUSE   BOUTIQUE HOTEL $$

Map p238 (☎581-2678; www.lafitteguesthouse .com; 1003 Bourbon St; r incl breakfast $140-230; 🛜) This elegant three-story 1849 Creole town house is at the quieter end of Bourbon St. Its 14 guest rooms are lavishly furnished in period style, though antique wash-basins and fireplaces seem an odd contrast to the flat-screen TVs. Many rooms have private balconies. Lafitte's Blacksmith Shop, one of the street's more welcoming (and some say haunted) drinking taverns, is on the opposite corner.

OLIVIER HOUSE   HOTEL $$

Map p238 (☎525-8456; www.olivierhouse.com; 828 Toulouse St; r from $135, 2-bedroom ste from $375; 🛜⊠) The main house was built in 1838 by Marie Anne Bienvenu Olivier, a wealthy planter's widow, and is an uncommon beauty with Greek-revival touches. Two elegant town houses expand the hotel's capacity. Rooms range from the small and relatively economical to the elaborate, with balconies and kitchens. Each has its own style, but most have furnishings evoking the early 19th century. Out back the main courtyard is lush with mature trees, thick vines and numerous flowers. A second courtyard has a small pool. The house is within a few minutes' walk of damn near everything.

THE SAINT   HOTEL $$$

Map p238 (☎522-5400; www.thesainthotelnew orleans.com; 931 Canal St; r from $200; 🛜) It's not an easy thing, designing a hotel in this town. You've got to balance the needs of those who want a bit of historic preservation versus those who don't want a place to feel too stodgy. The Saint pulls off this balance nicely, with clean duo-chromatic color schemes (white walls, dark wood floors) offset with little azure accents – quite contemporary, yet alleviated by a historic property's elegance throughout.

DAUPHINE ORLEANS
HOTEL **$$**

Map p238 (⌨586-1800, 800-521-7111; www .dauphineorleans.com; 415 Dauphine St; r incl breakfast from $259; P🛜♨) Judging from the outside of the block-long terra-cotta hotel, you'd never guess that through a courtyard there are 14 bright-yellow Creole cottage–style exterior-access rooms (once part of a carriage house). Request one of those – or one of the nine rooms with exposed cypress beams and brick across the street in the merchant Herman Howard's former home. The other rooms all have less character, but similar appointments, including earthy color schemes and high thread-count sheets. May Bailey's, once an infamous brothel, is now the bar.

HOTEL ROYAL
BOUTIQUE HOTEL **$$**

Map p238 (⌨524-3900, 888-776-3901; www .frenchquarterhotelgroup.com/hotel-royal.html; 1006 Royal St; r from $140) Lacy ironwork balconies, gas lanterns and decorative topiaries – everything an 1833 New Orleans home should be. Inside, renowned architect and designer Lee Ledbetter infused each of the 45 individually decorated guest quarters with subtle, soft-contemporary touches. A modern dark-wood four-poster bed and chocolate linens contrast nicely with the rough, white-plaster walls and plantation shutters in the king suite. Other rooms have wooden floors and exposed brick, and some have balcony access. Fragrant chicory coffee and pastries await on arrival in season (ie not summer). Rates rocket on weekends.

HOTEL PROVINCIAL
HOTEL **$$**

Map p238 (⌨581-4995, 800-535-7922; www.hotel provincial.com; 1024 Chartres St; r incl breakfast from $140; P🛜♨) Behind its stately stucco facade, this hotel fills much of the block with a series of finely restored buildings and a large parking area. The best rooms have high ceilings and open onto the interior courtyards (one with a pool). Others can be cramped and dark. Décor ranges from commercial standard to ornately historic. Check out a few rooms before booking. The back courtyard is a revelation, as is its lovely pool.

W FRENCH QUARTER
HOTEL **$$$**

Map p238 (⌨581-1200; www.whotels.com; 316 Chartres St; r from $260; P@♨) Like all W hotels, this one wears its style on its trendy, businesslike sleeve. Whether it blends with the French Quarter is questionable, but this is the flashier, less residential side of the district so maybe it does. (The Bourbon St racket is two blocks away.) Rooms vary, but all have that contemporary sleekness. The best are airy spaces opening onto an inner patio. Ponder the pool's azure waters or just enjoy a breeze while checking your email or watching a large-screen TV.

BIENVILLE HOUSE HOTEL
BOUTIQUE HOTEL **$$**

Map p238 (⌨800-535-9603, 529-2345; www .bienvillehouse.com; 320 Dectaur St; r from $150, ste from $250; P🠒♨🛜) The Bienville's the definition of a well-executed historic French Quarter hotel. The wrought iron balconies that ring the tiled lobby give way to a lovely courtyard with swimming pool; interior period design matches the promise of the Federal-meets-French-Creole exterior. Rooms are pretty, and a good size for the Quarter, which tends to offer rooms on the small side. The standard amenities you'd expect for any business traveler are available, and the hotel is both gay- and family-friendly.

HOTEL VILLA CONVENTO
HOTEL **$$**

Map p238 (⌨522-1793, 800-887-2817; www.villa convento.com; 616 Ursulines Ave; r from $150; P🛜) Classic New Orleans in every sense, the Villa Convento occupies an 1833 town house in the residential part of the Lower Quarter, complete with a three-story red-brick facade and wrought-iron balconies. Out back in the annex (probably the former servants' quarters) there are more rooms. All rooms have traditional décor, from comfy quilts to lacy canopies. It's all very low-key here in this local-family-owned and cheerfully operated hotel. There's free off-site parking, and no children under 10. Prices for budget doubles fall to as little as $89 when demand dwindles.

LE RICHELIEU
HOTEL **$$**

Map p238 (⌨529-2492, 800-535-9653; www.le richelieuhotel.com; 1234 Chartres St; r from $135; P🛜♨) Le Richelieu's red-brick walls once housed a macaroni factory, but extensive reconstruction in the early 1960s converted it into a conservative hotel. Rooms are decorated with standard synthetic floral spreads, but the price includes parking (a big plus), and there is a pool. Having an on-site bar and a restaurant are other perks here on the quiet side of the Quarter. Prices drop precipitously (down to $89) when things are slow.

BOURBON ORLEANS HOTEL HOTEL $$

Map p238 (☏523-2222, 800-521-5338; www .bourbonorleans.com; 717 Orleans Ave; r from $134; P☕☎🛜🏊) A polished-marble classic. The gray exteriors and white trim are almost as stately as the grand foyer. Combining several buildings, mostly dating from the early 1830s, the exterior hasn't made any unsightly bows to modernity. Most streetside rooms have access to the classic wrought-iron balconies. (Bourbon St, needless to say, can get noisy.) Traditional rooms feature especially comfortable beds and ergonomic desks. Note, however, that standard rooms set a new standard for smallness.

CHATEAU HOTEL HOTEL $$

Map p238 (☏524-9636; www.chateauhotel.com; 1001 Chartres St; r $120-170; 🛜🏊) Nothing is cookie-cutter here; rooms range in size and have varying floral motifs. Many feature wrought-iron beds, which echo the street-side balcony details. Though they're on the smallish side, we'd opt for the premium courtyard rooms, which are cool and peaceful and open up to a pool. The hotel is on a residential end of the Quarter, a block away from the neighborhoody, locals-oriented end of Decatur St. There's an on-site restaurant, and parking across the street.

GENTRY QUARTERS B&B $$

Map p238 (☏525-4433; www.gentryhouse.com; 1031 St Ann St; r incl breakfast from $135; ☕🛜) This charming old Creole house contains five homey rooms with kitchenettes. (Hot croissants are delivered to your door, and juice, milk and cereals are stocked in your room.) Modest but comfortable furnishings give the rooms a lived-in feel, while linens and towels are fresh and clean. Most rooms open onto a lush garden patio, where you might be visited by two friendly dachshunds. On the northern edge of the Quarter, away from the hubbub, the Gentry has loyal fans. Some guests stay a spell every year, so book ahead. Some rooms are large enough for families and there's a two-night minimum.

HAUNTED HOTELS

An eerily cold 14th-floor hallway leads to a vision of children playing; the cafe doors open and shut on their own; despite the bar being locked, guests see a patron who isn't there... Andrea Thornton, Director of Sales & Marketing at the Hotel Monteleone (p174), had heard dozens of first-hand accounts of supernatural sightings when she decided investigation was in order. In 2003 the hotel invited the International Society of Paranormal Research (ISPR) to come spend several days, during which they identified 12 disparate spirits on the property, one a former employee named 'Red'. And, indeed, hotel records showed that an engineer who went by the nickname Red worked at the hotel in the 1950s.

Hearing or seeing children is the most common of the mischievous-but-benign activities people experience in the historic hotel. Numerous guests have reported seeing a little boy in a striped suit (about age three) in room 1462. Speculation is that it's Maurice, son of Josephine and Jacques Begere, looking for his parents. While Maurice was in the hotel being watched by a nanny, his father was thrown from a coach and died instantly; his mother passed a year later.

In a town with such a strife-torn history – slavery, war, fever, flood – hauntings (if they exist) are hardly a surprise. And the Monteleone is far from the only hotel in the Quarter to report sightings. Among others, ghostbusters might want to check out the following:

Bourbon Orleans Hotel (p176) Once an orphanage and an African American convent; children have been seen and heard playing on the 6th floor.

Dauphine Orleans (p175) Bottles appear rearranged at May Bailey's bar, site of a once-infamous brothel, and moans and sounds of beds moving at night have been reported.

Hotel Provincial (p175) Building 5 was constructed on the site of a Civil War hospital; guests report sometimes gruesome visions of wounded soldiers and bloody sheets.

Lafitte Guest House (p174) 'Marie', a little girl who died of yellow fever, is said to appear in the mirror in room 21, where her mother stayed.

Le Pavillon (p180) Apparitions materialize bedside in this 1907 hotel, where the ISPR identified at least four resident spirits.

HOTEL ST MARIE
HOTEL $$

Map p238 (☎561-8951, 800-366-2743; www.hotel stmarie.com; 827 Toulouse St; r incl breakfast from $130; ☎☀⚡) The St Marie was built to look historic from the outside, but is up-to-date on the inside. Its best feature is the large and inviting courtyard, with a swimming pool and umbrella-covered tables amid lush plantings. The neocolonial guest rooms are somewhat lacking in authentic character, but are spacious and more than serviceable. Just around the corner, Bourbon St is at its most extreme.

HISTORIC FRENCH MARKET INN
HOTEL $$

Map p238 (☎561-5621, 888-538-5651; www.french marketinn.com; 501 Decatur St; r from $120; ℗☎) You hardly have to stumble out of bed to get a souvenir T-shirt or daiquiri to-go on this busy block of Decatur St, not far from the Café du Monde's aromatic chicory coffee. A good budget choice, this fairly basic hotel has 95 functional rooms with crisp linens. Most are relatively small and get little daylight; think of it as a boon if you're only just getting home at daybreak. Hidden deep within the complex is a pleasant courtyard. Some dogs are allowed.

WESTIN NEW ORLEANS AT CANAL PLACE
HOTEL $$

Map p238 (☎566-7006; www.westin.com; 100 Iberville St; r from $140; ℗☀☎⚡) With 29 stories, the Westin has some of the city's best views of the Mississippi River. (Watching the parade of freighters, tankers and barges in the wee hours beats TV.) Rooms are large and modern, with good desks and signature 'heavenly beds,' as well as small sitting areas. Some are bland, others quite elegant; have a look around. There's a rooftop pool that, needless to say, has more good views.

NINE-O-FIVE ROYAL HOTEL
HOTEL $$

Map p238 (☎523-0219; www.905royalhotel.com; 905 Royal St; r from $125; ☎) On a particularly scenic block, the Nine-O-Five eschews much of the usual NOLA shtick and opts instead for the timeless comfort you'd expect to find if this house belonged to a dignified old aunt. Front rooms with balconies are the choice for those who want to survey the always entertaining Royal St scene, but for seclusion, get a room off the cute courtyard out back. All 13 rooms have private entrances and small kitchen areas.

URSULINE GUEST HOUSE
HOTEL $

Map p238 (☎525-8509; http://ursulineguest house.com; 708 Ursulines Ave; r $100-140; ☎) Unadorned rooms in these Spanish-era buildings in the laid-back Lower Quarter have a friendly flophouse appeal. Those in front are just a short step up from the sidewalk, perhaps too close to the neighborhood's stream of yammering late-night pedestrians. Those out back are much quieter. There is a very small bunk room ('sleeps two slender adults,' heh) that goes for $59.

ST PETER HOUSE HOTEL
HOTEL $

Map p238 (☎523-5198, 800-535-7815; www.st peterhouse.com; 1005 St Peter St; r from $79) Some of the rooms in this small hotel are minuscule, but so are the prices. Each room has surprising individuality, with a carved bed or exposed brick, but not a whole lot else. Pastries are provided in the morning and you can hang out on the balconies or in the small courtyard. The St Peter is a little beyond where most of the tourists hang out, which has advantages (quiet) and disadvantages (you might want to take a cab home instead of facing the lonely walk north after a late night).

🛌 Faubourg Marigny & Bywater

Across Esplanade Ave from the Quarter, the grid-defying street pattern in the Marigny and Bywater is speckled with colorful cottages, many of which have been converted into homey, reasonable B&Bs. Savvy night owls feel the pull of the lively Frenchmen St scene. It's possible to walk to the Quarter from either neighborhood, but if you're heading back to the Bywater at night, you'll probably want to cab it.

TOP CHOICE AULD SWEET OLIVE BED & BREAKFAST
B&B $$

Map p242 (☎947-4332, 877-470-5323; www.sweet olive.com; 2460 N Rampart St; r incl breakfast from $99; ☀☎) Mardi Gras lovers take note: the Krewe de Vieux parade goes right by this grand B&B. Even if you don't come during the pre-Lenten season, you can see parade regalia like the co-owner's King Endymion costume on display. The house itself is similarly theatrical, once owned by set designer and mural artist Stephen Auld. The large double parlor (filled with games, books, videos,

SLEEPING FAUBOURG MARIGNY & BYWATER

TV, CD player, etc) resembles a banana-tree jungle; the soaking-tub room is painted to look like a night sky beneath branches. Individual rooms also have decorative touches – faux wood, or magnolia blooms – on a more refined scale.

TOP CHOICE **BYWATER BED & BREAKFAST** B&B $

Map p242 (✆944-8438; www.bywaterbnb.com; 1026 Clouet St; r without bathroom $75; ☎) This is what happens when you fall through the rabbit hole and Wonderland is a B&B. This spot is popular with lesbians (it's owned by a lesbian couple), but welcomes everyone. It's about as homey and laid-back as it gets. Don't expect someone waiting on you hand and foot. Do expect staying in what is essentially a folk art gallery with a bit of historical heritage and a hallucinogenic vibe – kind of like the Bywater itself! Guest rooms are simple and comfortable with more cheery paint and art. The owners enjoy steering guests in the right direction, whether you're looking for a great po'boy, live music or gay bars. Two-night minimum usually required.

MELROSE MANSION B&B $$

Map p242 (✆944-2255, 800-650-3323; www.melrosemansion.com; 937 Esplanade Ave; r from $120, ste from $185, all incl breakfast; P☎❄) An exquisite 1884 Victorian mansion, Melrose stands out even among its stately neighbors. This is a retreat for the well-heeled and honeymooners. Rooms are luxurious, airy spaces, with high ceilings and large French windows. Fastidiously polished antique furnishings reflect impeccable taste, with four-poster beds, cast-iron lamps and comfortable reading chairs in every room. In high season, fresh-baked breakfast pastries are accompanied by quiche, and nightly cocktails are mixed in the parlor. Full concierge service is available round the clock. Guests are pampered to death here, but it's an exquisite way to go.

LIONS INN B&B B&B $

Map p242 (✆945-2339; www.lionsinn.com; 2517 Chartres St; d $90-120, s without bathroom from $50, all incl breakfast; ☎❄❄) On a quiet Marigny block, the Lions Inn is a bright, friendly place suitable for gays and straights. Nine simply furnished guest rooms have splashes of vibrant color and no fussy antiques. The choice space is the Sun Room, which can accommodate four and has a bank of windows overlooking the back courtyard. Jump into the swimming pool and Jacuzzi or use one of the free bicycles to peddle the five blocks to the edge of the Quarter.

BURGUNDY BED & BREAKFAST B&B $$

Map p242 (✆261-9477; www.theburgundy.com; 2513 Burgundy St; r incl breakfast from $100; ☎☎) Cottage charm pervades this 1890s double-shotgun home decorated in a shabby chic style. The Chihuahua, Gizzy, welcomes you to the cheery front room. Through the six-panel door lies a guest kitchen with fridge, coffeemaker and microwave, next to a cozy dining room. No space is wasted in the four green quarters, two of which have both a queen and a single bed. The courtyard outside is more roomy, and off to the side is a (clothing-optional) spa. Gay-owned-and-operated.

DAUPHINE HOUSE B&B $$

Map p242 (✆940-0943; www.dauphinehouse.com; 1830 Dauphine St; r $104; ☎☎) The Dauphine only has two rooms, but it's actually a pretty big house, a classic Creole Esplanade-Ridge-style mansion that happens to be located in Faubourg Marigny. Those two rooms we mentioned are pretty plush; they'd put us in mind of a very luxurious house of fun sin and good times. Which is pretty much what New Orleans is, right? The owners are a valuable New Orleans travel resource, and the best of the Quarter and the Marigny is within walking distance.

COLLINWOOD HOUSE B&B $$

Map p242 (✆301-4353; www.collinwoodhouse.com; 2408 Dauphine St; r $120-225; ☎☎) This elegant, off-violet colored Creole mansion conceals old school rooms that wouldn't be out of place in a BBC period drama about lords, manors, upstairs-downstairs style romances, tweed and stiff gin (copyright prevents us from being more descriptive). We love the Shogun Room, partly modeled after an Imperial Japanese sweet; and the Continental Room, which looks perfect for an illicit (yet classy!) bonk with an aristocrat.

BOHEMIAN ARMADILLO B&B $$

Map p242 (✆598-6544; www.bohemianarmadillo.com; 735 Touro St; r incl breakfast $100-200; ☎☎) You can probably figure by the name that the Bohemian Armadillo is a pretty funky spot. And yes, the owners are classic Marigny folks – creative and enthusiastic about sharing the best of New Orleans. That said, the three quirky guest rooms are actually quite understated. The Voodoo Room, for example, with its rustic wooden walls and plush bed, fits somewhere between a *Better Homes* magazine and a folk art gallery.

CRESCENT CITY GUESTHOUSE
B&B $

Map p242 (☎944-8722; www.crescentcitygh .com; 612 Marigny St; r from $90; P🗢) This laid-back B&B is a great choice for those who want a little bit of peace and quiet but don't feel like surrendering the option of walking into the French Quarter, or onto Frenchmen St. The rooms are simple but cozy, and the owner is a very friendly treasure trove of New Orleans knowledge. The back garden is a great spot to chill with a book, or chat with the staff and other guests.

B&W COURTYARDS
B&B $$

Map p242 (☎324-3396, 800-585-5731; www. bandwcourtyards.com; 2425 Chartres St; r from $120, all incl breakfast; 🗢) One of the better B&Bs in the Marigny, the B&W is tastefully bohemian, but it's also got the right amount of historical accents. There are six highly individualised rooms; our favorite is the Peach Blossom, which has a 'Far East comes to New Orleans' vibe that's quite attractive, like a classy Chinese martial arts movie set built into a Marigny home. Service is friendly and unobtrusive, and it's within walking distance of both the French Quarter and the best Marigny bars.

LAMOTHE HOUSE
B&B $$

Map p242 (☎800-367-5858; www.lamothehouse. com; 621 Esplanade Ave; r incl breakfast from $120; P🗢) Lovely, oak-shaded Esplanade Ave is a prime jumping-off point for prowling the nightlife of Frenchmen St and the Lower Quarter. Guest rooms are furnished with antiques you may feel guilty about bumping into, and thick curtains keep the sun out when you're sleeping off a big night. If you're determined to revive early, take a dip in the pool after the continental breakfast. The cheapest rooms are slender and open onto a long courtyard. More elaborately accoutred suites somehow suggest EJ Bellocq's beautiful Storyville photographs without being lurid or seedy.

NONI'S IN NOLA
GUESTHOUSE $$

Map p242 (☎852-3418; www.noninola.com; 726 Frenchment St; r $135-220; 🗢🗢) Noni's is

located smack on Frenchmen St. You could quite literally stumble home from the clubs into your bedroom. And yet (and we mean this in a positive way) it is one of the most elegant B&Bs in the area, classy and refined but hardly stodgy. Rooms come with poster beds, some with headboards; other bits of furniture run from early-20th-century style to plush rugs and stuffed bookcases. A lovely courtyard rounds out the experience nicely.

FRENCHMEN HOTEL
HOTEL $

Map p242 (☎800-831-1781; www.frenchmenho tel.com; 417 Frenchmen St; r incl breakfast from $120; P🗢🗢) The three thoroughly refurbished 1850s houses that comprise this smart hotel are clustered around a courtyard with a swimming pool and Jacuzzi. High ceilings, balconies and some rustic exposed brick are remnant from the buildings' more elegant past. Mix-and-match furnishings have limited antique appeal. The real selling point is the hotel's proximity to everything that Frenchmen St has to offer. Concierge service is an upscale touch for a bargain hotel.

🛏 CBD & Warehouse District

The hotels in the CBD tend to be modern behemoths and posh high-rises catering to those with business-expense accounts. Even the Warehouse District, despite its artistic leanings, mostly accommodates the convention set. Prices do plummet, however, when occupancy is low. There are far more big-name chain hotels in these neighborhoods than we could possibly mention, so if you have a loyalty-point fave, look it up online.

HOTEL PARKING BLUES

Overnight parking can run as high as $40 per night in the Central Business District, an amount that can do serious damage to your budget. If convenience isn't that important to you, compare prices at one of the many public parking lots and garages on Poydras St or its offshoots. It's still expensive but you're likely to save from $10 to $20 per night and probably won't have to walk more than a few blocks.

SLEEPING CBD & WAREHOUSE DISTRICT

AIRPORT ACCOMMODATIONS

Lots of flights out of New Orleans depart at the crack of dawn. Not an easy schedule if you've been tempted to make a full night of it in the French Quarter during your last hours in the Big Easy. Nervous, conscientious types might opt for staying as near the tarmac as possible. Many airport chains have free shuttles that take just a few minutes to reach the terminals. These include the following:

Best Western (☎800-528-1238; www.bestwestern.com)

Doubletree (☎800-222-8733; www.doubletree.com)

Hilton (☎800-872-5914; www.hilton.com)

Sheraton (☎800-325-3535; www.sheraton.com)

TOP CHOICE ROOSEVELT NEW ORLEANS
HOTEL $$$

Map p244 (☎648-1200; www.therooseveltnew orleans.com; 123 Baronne St; r from $299; P@☎≋≋) The majestic, block-long lobby harks back to the early 20th century, a Golden Age of opulent hotels and grand retreats. Known originally as the Grunewald, the hotel was the city's elite establishment when it opened in 1893. In the 1930s, its swanky bar was frequented by governor Huey Long. After a meticulous $145 million renovation, the Roosevelt reopened its doors in June 2009 as part of the Waldorf-Astoria Collection. Swish rooms have classical details, but the full spa, John Besh restaurant and storied Sazerac Bar are at least half the reason to stay. Parking costs $40 per night. Wi-fi is $15 per day, but it's free in the lobby.

TOP CHOICE LE PAVILLON
HOTEL $$

Map p244 (☎581-3111; www.lepavillon.com; 833 Poydras St; r $179-259, ste from $535; P@≋≋) Oh Le Pavillon, you charmed the beads off us during Mardi Gras. Ahem, we jest, but Le Pavillon does have an old-school joie de vivre that's easy to embrace. Fluted columns support the porte cochere off the alabaster facade, and the doorman wears white gloves and a top hat (and somehow doesn't look ridiculous). Both private and public spaces are redolent with historic portraits, magnificent chandeliers, marble floors and heavy drapery. At the same time, there's a sense of fun about it all, best exemplified by the nightly serving of peanut-butter-and jelly sandwiches in the lobby at 10pm. Rates are unexpectedly low for a hotel of this quality, and during slow periods Le Pavillon offers some astounding deals. The breakfast buffet is famously good (see the boxed text, p108). Parking is $39 per night.

WINDSOR COURT HOTEL
HOTEL $$$

Map p244 (☎523-6000; www.windsorcourthotel .com; 300 Gravier St; r $260-500; P☎≋≋) Fresh from a $22 million renovation in 2011, the Windsor is ready to preen. The sparkling lobby, with its portraits of noblemen and their Brittany spaniels, could double as the drawing room at Downton Abbey. Revamped guest rooms, now painted 'robin's egg' blue, come with Italian marble bathrooms, toile with aristocratic prints, butler's pantries and frette linens. A 4500ft spa was set to open in the spring of 2012. Once you've unpacked, unwind in the clubby confines of the Polo Club Lounge (p110) or return to the lobby for a craft cocktail at the Cocktail Lounge. If the dowager countess did live here, you'd surely find her holding court nearby. Parking is $36 per night.

LOEWS NEW ORLEANS HOTEL
HOTEL $$

Map p244 (☎595-3300; www.loewshotels.com; 300 Poydras St; r $189-309; P@☎≋≋) This hotel has a snazzy, upbeat vibe that's downright inviting. The breeziness starts in the lobby where eye-catching photos of New Orleans set the tone for fun. Housed in a converted office building once occupied by a steamship company, Loews offers a boatload of amenities with a relaxed, unfussy style. The 285 rooms are larger than average, and all are located on the 11th floor and above, many with superb views. Rooms are understated yet elegantly modernist. There's an indoor lap pool and health center, plus a noted spa. Check the website for a list of packages. The WWII packages include tickets to the WWII Museum and its 4D movie. In Swizzle Stick bar, off the lobby, live jazz is performed many nights. Loews is a very pet-friendly property and charges a one-time $125 pet fee during your stay. Parking is $34 per night.

DRURY INN & SUITES
HOTEL $$

Map p244 (☎529-7800; www.druryhotels.com; 820 Poydras St; r incl breakfast r $129-170, ste

$139-195; **P@**⍟**☎**⍟) They had us at 'Three free alcoholic drinks.' And the light dinner. And the lobby piano – where guests are allowed to tickle the ivories. This Drury Inn embraces New Orleans' fun-loving spirit full-on and that's why we love it. The free drinks are served nightly between 5:30pm and 7pm along with light fare like hot dogs and baked potatoes. Hot breakfasts are complimentary too. The red-and-gold decorated rooms come with 37in flat screens, pillow-top mattresses and a microwave and refrigerator. There's also a guest laundry. Parking is $25 per night. Pets up to 75lb are allowed.

COUNTRY INN & SUITES HOTEL $$
Map p244 (☎324-5400; www.countryinns.com; 315 Magazine St; r incl breakfast $175-185, ste $205; **P@**⍟) The exterior of this 155-room hotel looks a bit uninspiring in the harsh glare of the afternoon sun, but step inside and this ugly duckling morphs into a boutiquey swan. The hotel, which opened in 2004, encompasses seven historic downtown buildings dating from the 1800s. Period touches – exposed beams, red brick, an ivy-covered courtyard – add character to this incarnation of the national chain. Because of its unusual structure, each room is slightly different in form and appearance, but all come with microwaves and refrigerators. Guests can enjoy a hot buffet breakfast in the morning and cookies in the afternoon. There's a helpful front desk and parking is $25 per night.

LOFT 523 BOUTIQUE HOTEL $$
Map p244 (☎200-6523; www.loft523.com; 523 Gravier St; r from $179-209; **@**⍟**☎**) The perfect motto for Loft 523? 'So hip it hurts.' And we mean that literally because if you fall off the bed, you're hitting a concrete floor. And if you've ever wondered what it would be like to sleep inside a piece of modern art, now's your chance. Top design magazines have recognized the industrial-minimalist style of the 18 rooms where whirligig-shaped fans circle over low-lying Mondo beds and polished concrete floors. Enjoy your free-standing half-egg tub by ordering a milk-bath in-room spa service and listening to a mixed jazz CD in surround sound (or maybe just switching on the plasma screen). And since International House is a sister property, you share their fitness center. Parking costs $32 per night, and there's a $200 flat fee for pets. And we almost forgot – the front door is so hip it's

invisible, but if you look close you'll find it between the Omni and Lucky Dogs.

INTERNATIONAL HOUSE BOUTIQUE HOTEL $$
Map p244 (☎553-9550; www.ihhotel.com; 221 Camp St; r $149-279, penthouses $979-1009; **@**⍟) The vibe is a bit too-cool-for-school, but hey, if you're a rule-breaking hipster badboy, we think you'll dig this boutique crashpad. Lavish rooms offer an array of amenities such as local wildflower arrangements, CD players with jazz CDs, ceiling fans (in addition to the air-con) and two-headed showers. Should the budget allow, go for the penthouse rooms and their sweeping terraces. One of New Orleans' most fashionable hang-outs is the Loa bar, amid soaring columns and plush tufted ottomans. There's even an iMac for those who want to check their email. Parking costs $32 per night.

HAMPTON INN NEW
ORLEANS DOWNTOWN HOTEL $$
Map p244 (☎529-5077; www.neworleanshamptoninns.com; 226 Carondelet St; r incl breakfast $149-169; **P@**⍟) Rooms are spacious, and the workout room gets a thumbs up at the Hampton Inn, which is located on the upper floors of the Carondelet Building (considered the Crescent City's first skyscraper). Per Hampton protocol, there's a complimentary breakfast buffet where you'll likely end up waffling over your choice of waffles, pancakes and more. On Wednesday nights enjoy a Manager's Reception with complimentary beer, wine and hors d'oeuvres. The location is just two blocks from the Quarter and around the corner from a streetcar. Floors are accessed with the room key. Parking is $30 per night.

LA QUINTA INN &
SUITES DOWNTOWN HOTEL $
Map p244 (☎598-9977; www.lq.com; 301 Camp St; r incl breakfast $129-149, ste from $159; **P@**⍟**☎**⍟) Oh, La Quinta. Just like every other La Quinta. Except when it's not. This one, which opened in 2009, is a new-and-shiny high-rise and it's not necessarily what you'd expect from the motel chain. Rooms are downright modern with flat-screen TVs, oversize graphic art and green throws on triple-sheeted beds. An outdoor pool, laundry facilities and continental breakfast all add to the value here, and it's just a few blocks from the Quarter. Parking is $25 per night.

HYATT REGENCY NEW ORLEANS HOTEL **$$**

Map p244 (561-1234; http://neworleans.hyatt
.com; 601 Loyola Ave; r from $209-249, ste $309-
459; P @) The streamlined lobby at the
new Hyatt, which opened in 2011, feels like
the entrance to a busy airport. But that's
not surprising considering that this colos-
sus has more than 1190 rooms. Sports fans
heading to the Superdome couldn't ask for a
better location – the hulking arena is right
next door. In the rooms, a bright fleur-de-lis
throw pillow accents white linens, and the
furniture has a hip, modern appeal. Rooms
are spread across two high-rises, and con-
necting spaces hum with energy. Those
with a fear of heights may not want to stay
on an upper floor in the main building; the
hallways overlook a central atrium from
vertigo-inducing heights. John Besh's new-
est venture, the seafood-loving **Bourgne**
(www.bourgnerestaurant.com), had just opened
at the time of writing but was already win-
ning raves. A new streetcar line on Loyola
Ave in front of the hotel should be up and
running by the end of 2012. Parking is $38
per night, and the wi-fi fee is $10 per day.

LAFAYETTE HOTEL HOTEL **$$**

Map p244 (524-4441; www.lafayettehotelnew
orleans.com; 600 St Charles Ave; r $169-199, ste
$199-229; P) This small, luxurious 1916
hotel is steps from Lafayette Sq. The surrounding blocks have a classic feel that's
generally lacking in most of the modern
CBD. (Lafayette Sq was the center of the
American St Mary neighborhood, developed after the Louisiana Purchase.) Its
44 rooms are furnished with dark woods,
antiques and king-size beds. The walls are
painted in rich, classic colors, and the bathrooms are roomy and finished in marble.
The Julia Row arts district is a short walk
from here, as are numerous cutting-edge
restaurants. Parking is $28 per night; wi-
fi is $5 per night. There is a one-time non-
refundable $50 fee for pets.

EMBASSY SUITES HOTEL HOTEL **$$**

Map p244 (525-1993; www.embassyneworleans
.com; 315 Julia St; r incl breakfast $149-199; P @
) The architecture astonishes with vast
size and a cacophony of angles, but the ec-
centric design grows on you. The soaring
atrium is indeed impressive. Every room
is a large, family-friendly suite, and no two
are exactly the same. Most have balconies;
higher floors have views of the city and
the river. Adjoining historic loft-building

rooms, in what was once a cotton ware-
house, have tall ceilings and exposed brick
walls. Complimentary cocktails are served
between 5:30pm and 7:30pm. Parking is
$30; wi-fi is $13 per night but free in the
business center.

HARRAH'S NEW ORLEANS HOTEL **$$$**

Map p244 (533-6000; www.harrahsneworleans
.com; 228 Poydras St; r from $299; P @)
Truth be told, it can be hard to snag a room
at Harrah's unless you're a regular player
with the chain. The property has 26 floors,
450 rooms, an 115,000-sq-ft casino, eight
restaurants, four blocks of retail space, and
white-gloved staff to wait on guests. Silky
purples and golds in the lobby make it seem
like Mardi Gras all year round; rooms are
similarly luxe. Parking is $30 per night; wi-
fi is $12 per day.

Garden, Lower
Garden & Central City

Stately Greek-revival town houses front
leafy lanes in the lower district, and as
you move northwest, the houses only get
more elaborate. Both historic Garden District neighborhoods are largely residential today, but you're in luck: there are a
few hotels, B&Bs – and one hostel – from
which to choose. B&B's may have a two-
night minimum stay requirement on event
weekends.

TERRELL HOUSE B&B **$$**

Map p247 (237-2076; www.terrellhouse.com;
1441 Magazine St; r incl breakfast $150-200;)
The Southern hospitality is what impresses
most at the Terrell House. Linda O'Brien is
a warm and welcoming host who's on top
of the details. And the details are many
inside this stately 1858 Georgian-revival
house with cast-iron galleries, a spacious
courtyard and exquisite touches. Original
art adds to the freshness of the simple but
tasteful carriage-house rooms. Think high-
thread-count linens, colorful spreads and
clean-lined wooden or iron beds. Suites in
the main house are more antique in na-
ture, with period furnishings, silk drap-
eries and Oriental rugs; some even have
marble fireplaces. Common rooms are gal-
leries filled with art, antiques and potted
plants. Other amenities include in-room
minifridges stocked with soda and bottled

water. Breakfasts sound divine. No children under 12.

SULLY MANSION B&B
B&B $$

Map p247 (☏891-0457; www.sullymansion.com; 2631 Prytania St; r incl breakfast $119-230; ☎) Sully Mansion stirs up just the right mix of historic Southern charm, modern style and New Orleans fun. The charm begins with the lush gardens, cast-iron fence and inviting front porch. Upon arrival Gracie, the house canine, seems just as happy to see you as hosts Guy and Nancy. The modern style leaps from the bright local artwork dotting the walls (also for sale). And the sense of fun? That comes from the many chairs and nooks that encourage socializing, and from the sweet and savory breakfasts that include apple and pear crumbles, smoked salmon crepes and French toast with molasses. The eight guest rooms are elegant, many with a fireplace and antique four-poster bed. Bathrooms are spacious and modern – there's a glass brick shower with the Royal Room and the long granite counter can double as a bar. Cheers!

GARDEN DISTRICT B&B
B&B $

Map p247 (☏895-4302; www.gardendistrict bedandbreakfast.com; 2418 Magazine St; ste incl breakfast from $90; @) The Garden District B&B is a great budget option. The private four-suite town house is like your own character-filled efficiency apartment. Each spacious room (most sleep three) has a separate entrance, kitchenette and table seating in addition to brick walls, tall ceilings and homey antiques such as a 1950s (nonworking) stove. The Patio Suite includes a wonderful little private courtyard. Fresh-made breads, muffins and fruits wrapped to go are set on the parlor table every morning and rooms are stocked with coffee, juice, yogurt and cereals. The innkeeper provides loads of local restaurant info, and respects guests' privacy. Close to the Irish Channel and within walking distance of good Magazine St shopping blocks.

PRYTANIA PARK HOTEL
HOTEL $

Map p247 (☏524-0427; www.prytaniaparkhotel .com; 1525 Prytania St; r incl breakfast from $79; P@☎♿) Prytania Park is one of the best deals going. Basic rooms can run as low as $69 to $99 on weekends, depending on what's going on in town. Wi-fi is complimentary as is parking, which is available in a guarded lot behind the property. The

CAMP BOW WOW

Pets aren't allowed at most B&Bs, which can be a problem for travelers who like to bring Fido on the road. For pet-loving vacationers, local B&B owners recommend **Camp Bow Wow** (www.campbowwow.com; 2731 Tchoupitoulas St), which provides a daytime and overnight 'camp' for dogs. But not every dog is allowed to stay here – owners and pets must complete a short interview before your canine will be allowed to board. The Camp Bow Wow folks just want to make sure your dog plays well with others and is current on shots. Once boarded, your dog will enjoy exercise, play areas and campfire treats. It's $40 per night for one dog, with a reduced price per dog if you board more than one. Anxious owners can watch their dogs on the doggie web cam. Woof woof!

hotel is one block from the St Charles Ave streetcar and within walking distance of the WWII Museum. More particular travelers may be annoyed by some of the older fixtures and quirky features (well-worn exterior hallways with unattractive views, for example), but everyone else should be just fine. Kids will get a kick out of the loft rooms that come with a spiral staircase. This place is always worth checking for last-minute reservations.

HAMPTON INN ST CHARLES AVENUE
HOTEL $$

Map p247 (☏899-9990; www.hamptoninn.hilton .com; 3626 St Charles Ave; r incl breakfast $169-189; P@☎♨♿) This Hampton Inn feels rather quiet and subdued considering its location on busy St Charles Ave across from the streetcar. But this low-key vibe may be appreciated by solo travelers whose first concern is personal security. Floors are accessible only by keycards, and there's a dedicated parking lot for guests directly behind the hotel. Nondescript mid-sized rooms come with flat screens, gold-flecked green carpets and lots of counter space in the bathroom. Weekends at this Hampton Inn book up fast, so make reservations well before your arrival date.

GREEN HOUSE INN B&B **$$**

Map p247 (☏525-1333; www.thegreenhouseinn
.com; 1212 Magazine St; r incl breakfast $139-169;
P@☎☒) Green it is – a tropical rubber-tree
green, in fact. The house's striking color
certainly stands out on the still-gentrifying
end of Magazine St closest to downtown.
A squawking macaw keeps watch over the
landscaped 24-hour pool garden (clothing-
optional); surrounded by palms and ex-
otic blooms, the color makes more sense.
Though named for flowers, the nine guest
rooms are more masculine and clean-lined
than this suggests, with hardwood floors,
exposed brick and some nautical themed
décor. The inn is a proud member of the
International Gay & Lesbian Travel Asso-
ciation. Booking ahead is preferred, and
walk-ups are not accepted. There's a $25
one-time fee for pets.

MARQUETTE HOUSE HOSTEL HOSTEL **$**

Map p247 (☏523-3014; www.hostels.com; 2249
Carondelet St; dm $16-20, s/d 35/$60; @☎)
The common areas could use some serious
TLC and the 2200 block is far from charm-
ing, but the Marquette will do if you're on
a serious budget. Dorms sleep eight to 14,
and some have en suite bathrooms. Private
rooms sleep one to six and have bathrooms.
Internet access is available in the lobby
only, the kitchenette has no stove (there's
a barbecue) and there's no on-site laundry
(but there's one in a nearby bar). The hostel
is around the block from St Charles Ave.

🛏 Uptown & Riverbend

For the most part, Uptown and Riverbend
step it up in the style department; grittier
neighborhoods are further off the beaten
path. Streetcars clank by the historic man-
sions, manicured gardens and parks that
line leafy St Charles Ave. There's a handful
of lovely places to stay in this part of town.

CHIMES B&B **$$**

Map p250 (☏899-2621; www.chimesneworleans
.com; 1146 Constantinople St; r incl breakfast
$140-170; @☎) A team from Reuters set-
tled in here after Hurricane Katrina for
an extended stay, and it's easy to see why.
The five pleasant little rooms each have an
outstanding individual touch or two – such
as a floating staircase made from 4in-thick
cypress slabs, or a sunken stone tub. All
rooms are arranged around a lovely patio

and gardens, creating a courtyard community of sorts. Other touches? The common
fridge is stocked with sodas and Abitas,
and you can buy passes for the St Charles
Ave Streetcar here before boarding. Breakfast consists of fresh-baked goods and local
Community Coffee. It's located in a quiet
residential neighborhood, but is quite close
to Magazine St. The eight namesake chimes
hang on the front porch of the main house,
offering distant music among the birdsong.
There's a two- or three-night minimum stay
required on weekends, depending on the
season.

COLUMNS HOTEL BOUTIQUE HOTEL **$$**

Map p250 (☏899-9308, 800-445-9308; www.the
columns.com; 3811 St Charles Ave; r incl breakfast
from $160; ☎) This white-porched Southern
manse, built in 1883, is a snapshot from
the past. Fortunately, the past doesn't
take itself too seriously at the Columns,
where the porches are ready-made for
people-watching and conviviality. Guests
enter through the columned front veranda
and continue past two wood-paneled par-
lors that double as a bar-cafe. A magnificent
mahogany staircase climbs past a stained-
glass window to the 20 rooms on the 2nd
and 3rd floors, ranging from smallish dou-
bles to the two-room Pretty Baby Suite
(named for the Louis Malle film shot here
in the 1970s). Elaborate marble fireplaces,
richly carved armoires and claw-foot tubs
are among the highlights. To absorb the
late-night revelry, take a front room on the
2nd floor. A lavish hot breakfast is included.

PARK VIEW GUEST HOUSE B&B **$$$**

Map p250 (☏861-7564; www.parkviewguesthouse
.com; 7004 St Charles Ave; r incl breakfast $169-
209; @☎) Next to Audubon Park, this ornate wooden masterpiece was built in 1884
to impress people attending the World Cotton Exchange Exposition. The 21 rooms and
guest lounge can feel a bit heavy with solid
wood antiques, but from the wraparound
veranda you can enjoy up-close views of
stately oaks sprinkled with Spanish beards
in the park and on St Charles Ave. Tulane
and Loyola Universities are just blocks
away – many of the hotel's frequent guests
are visiting parents. Extended-stay rates
are available. Although there's no business
center, there is a computer guests can use
to check email messages or print boarding
passes.

🛏 Mid-City & the Tremé

There's not a whole lot going on sleeping-wise out here, but what's available is nice: historical homes converted into B&Bs and guesthouses that cost a fraction of the rates you'll find in the French Quarter. It's an ideal area to stay in for Jazz Fest – the Fair Grounds are only a short walk away.

TOP CHOICE HOUSE ON BAYOU ROAD B&B **$$**

Map p253 (☎945-0992; www.houseonbayouroad.com; 2275 Bayou Rd; r incl breakfast from $135; P🛜🏊) The true gem of Esplanade Ridge is this 1798 Creole plantation house. It oozes sultry atmosphere, with wide galleries and French doors that open onto thick tropical gardens. Screened porches make it possible to enjoy the chirp of crickets at night without being slaughtered by mosquitoes, and a large swimming pool will keep you cool. Antiques in the three main-house rooms are splashed with natural light from tall windows. Four more rooms in the Kumquat House, also on the grounds, are in no way a compromise, maintaining the same quality atmosphere, style and comfort. For a private and charming experience, a small Creole cottage with its own porch (and your own rocking chair) is also hidden away on the grounds.

DEGAS HOUSE B&B **$$$**

Map p253 (☎821-5009; www.degashouse.com; 2306 Esplanade Ave; r incl breakfast from $200; 🚶🛜) Edgar Degas, the famed French impressionist, lived in this 1852 Italianate house when visiting his mother's family in the early 1870s. During his stay he produced the city's most famous painting, *The Cotton Exchange in New Orleans.* Rooms recall his time here with period furnishings and reproductions of his work. The suites have balconies and fireplaces, while the less expensive garret rooms are the cramped top-floor quarters that once housed the Degas family's servants. Weekend stays include a full hot breakfast; weekdays, fresh baked goods are served continental style. Easels, of course, are available.

INDIA HOUSE HOSTEL HOSTEL **$**

Map p253 (☎821-1904; www.indiahousehostel.com; 124 S Lopez St; dm from $17, d $45; 🛜🏊) Half a block off Canal St in Mid-City, this place has the sort of free-spirited party atmosphere that got you into backpacking in the first place. A large above-ground pool and cabana-like patio add ambience to the three well-used old houses that serve as dorms. Bunk beds include linen and tax. For a unique experience, ask about the private Cajun shacks out back, which come with pet alligators. Guests can use the washer and dryer, and log onto the internet. Children not permitted.

ASHTON'S BED & BREAKFAST B&B **$$**

Map p253 (☎942-7048, 800-725-4131; www.ashtonsbb.com; 2023 Esplanade Ave; r incl breakfast from $170; 🚶🛜) Looking at the detailed plaster ceilings, the ornate stained-glass and the crisp paint and trim, it's very hard to imagine this mansion had a 60ft hole in the front of it after Hurricane Katrina. Nothing to worry about, though; the owners have meticulously restored this 1861 Greek-revival building, furnishing it in a

---

BIDDING FOR A BED

When maximizing quality while minimizing price is your aim, websites such as **Hotwire** (www.hotwire.com) and **Priceline** (www.priceline.com) are an excellent gamble to take. They don't let you see the property name before you commit to paying, but you can choose the neighborhood, star level and amenities before you either bid or buy at up to 50% off the advertised rate. The drawbacks: you can't change your mind (they're nonrefundable) and nonsmoking rooms can't be guaranteed. Still, if you're flexible, the system works. Testing the theory, we 'won' a room at an excellent four-star by Louis Armstrong International Airport for $60 a night.

Even splashing out can be affordable if you find a chichi package auction on **Luxury Link** (www.luxurylink.com). Occasionally there are 'mystery name' properties but quite often the hotels are identified and described (with gorgeous photos to ogle) so you know what you're gambling on. Hmm...maybe we should have tested one of those instead...

luxe style with half-tester canopy beds and claw-foot tubs and today it's better than ever. A hot Creole breakfast and complimentary refreshments throughout the day are included. Ashton's is very well situated if you're in town to experience the delights of Jazz Fest.

HH WHITNEY HOUSE   B&B **$$**
Map p253 ([📱]948-9448; www.hhwhitney.com; 1923 Esplanade Ave; r incl breakfast $150-250;

(➔ 🛈) This 19th-century Italianate beauty is another nice jewel to add to the crown of Esplanade Ridge mansions. There are five rooms over two floors; each has its own style, but all have vintage furniture and antique embellishments. The back garden is a great spot to lounge under the shade of leafy oaks. If you're a *Gone With the Wind* fan, there's an entire suite themed for Scarlett O'Hara, complete with Vivien Leigh portrait.

Understand
New Orleans

New Orleans Today

People still ask New Orleanians, with a concerned look, 'So, how's the city doing?' and they never have to elaborate that they're asking about Hurricane Katrina's impact. And while the answer of the New Orleanian depends on a lot of factors, there is one conclusive statement everyone can agree on: this isn't post-Katrina New Orleans. OK? It's just New Orleans. Whether that new New Orleans is a better place than the old one hasn't been answered yet, but the citizens of the city are trying like hell to make the answer 'Yes.'

Best on Film

A Streetcar Named Desire (1951) Classic Nola drama, with Marlon Brando and Vivien Leigh.

Down by Law (1986) Jim Jarmusch, Tom Waits, Roberto Benigni, a prison break and a swamp.

King Creole (1958) Elvis hits up the old sleazy Quarter.

New Orleans Exposed (2005) Shoestring documentary offers a harrowing look at Big Easy housing projects.

Abbott & Costello Go to Mars (1953) The comic duo thinks they're going to Mars, end up at Mardi Gras and never realize they haven't left Earth.

Best in Print

Bienville's Dilemma (Richard Campanella; 2008) Definitive guide to the city's physical and cultural geography.

A Confederacy of Dunces (John Kennedy Toole; 1980) Quintessential New Orleans picaresque novel.

Nine Lives (Dan Baum; 2009) Nine oral histories form a cross-section of modern New Orleans.

New Orleans Noir (2007) Short stories explore city's dark side.

The Awakening (Kate Chopin; 1899) Love, tragedy and gender roles; one of the first American novels written from a woman's perspective.

Divisions of Income & Elevation

New Orleans was not evenly hit by Hurricane Katrina. Areas such as Lakewood, Gentilly, Mid-City and the Lower Ninth Ward were destroyed. Areas like the Garden District, CBD and the French Quarter were untouched. Guess what we mainly cover in this book? That wealthiest strip, the literal high ground. It's not much higher, but that couple of feet was the difference between a dry living room and flooded attic for thousands. The point: in this city of divisions that play out along ethnic, racial, religious and economic lines, those who had nothing disproportionately bore the brunt of Katrina.

Losing Generations

Based on the most recent census (2010), it is estimated New Orleans lost about 30% of its citizens after Katrina. Most moved to the suburbs and other cities in the American South. In 2000, this was the 31st-biggest city by population in the USA. It is no longer in the top 50. The African American population has dropped from two-thirds to 60% of the population. New Orleans is actually more diverse as a result; whites make up a greater proportion of the population, but so do Asians and Hispanics. But much of the uniqueness of the city's culture is tied up in the rituals, music and folkways of its African Americans. That population not only constricted after the storm; today it is dying too quickly, and too violently. The murder rate of New Orleans is a staggering 50 times the national average, and the vast majority are black-on-black. The main question on the lips of every New Orleanian is: how do we stop young black men from gunning each other down?

Reimagining, Rebuilding, Recreating

So wait: we tell you the city is past Katrina, and then talk about Katrina? There's a reason. The divisions and crime rates we discuss were present before (the murder rate was a little lower, but still atrocious). These were fundamental problems, and the storm bared them to the world. The world didn't sit back. Thousands of volunteer-cum-new-citizens arrived after the storm; thousands of Louisianans saw what was almost lost and decided to make it again, but better. A frontier was open, and young entrepreneurs, artists and service industry members blazed over it. As of this writing, New Orleans has been named one of the top cities for entrepreneurship by *Forbes*. Four out of five James Beard restaurant nominees in the South are here; arts festivals like Prospect and Jazz Fest are the largest they have ever been. Political pundit James Carville commissioned a poll that discovered New Orleanians have more civic pride than citizens of any comparably sized city.

We Dat

The happiest place in the world was New Orleans in late January and February of 2010, when the Saints, carried along by the battle chant 'Who dat!' ('Who dat say they gon' beat dem Saints!') won the Superbowl; mayor Mitch Landrieu, a white politician, was elected with a majority of the black vote; and Mardi Gras happened. All of that happiness, coupled with the innovation and growth that continues to buoy the local economy, contributed to a sense New Orleans was not just back, but way ahead. Then the Deepwater Horizon oil rig blew up and spilled millions of barrels of oil into the Gulf of Mexico, a reminder that down here, neglect of institutions can have catastrophic consequences. But the challenges thrown in this city's face make it more resolute; weeks after the spill, apps were being developed that indicated where to find clean-up spots. New Orleans is the northernmost Caribbean city, the westernmost African one and a unique American experience. The Center for Disease Control and Prevention has named Louisiana the happiest state in the country. New Orleans' citizens want you to discover this truth and share your stories about this special place, where beautiful moments last an eternity. Tell the world: this city was built on low ground, but it always rises.

if New Orleans were 100 people

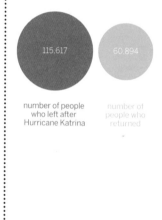

85 would be African American
4 would be White
2 would be Hispanic
9 would be Asian

Hurricane Katrina

115,617

60,894

number of people who left after Hurricane Katrina

number of people who returned

population per sq mile

NEW ORLEANS   USA

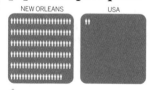

≈ 16 people

History

New Orleans has ever been a place for exiles and seekers: French aristocrats and frontiersmen; rebel slaves, defeated slaveowners and mixed-race children of uncertain status; American explorers, Spanish merchants and Jewish refugees; prostitutes and nuns; musicians, artists, homosexuals and, recently, those seeking to rebuild and revitalize an almost-drowned city.

THE QUALITY OF CREOLE

Throughout all of this history, New Orleans' population has exemplified the quality of Creole: a racial, religious, transnational linguistic mix of settlers who forged a unique identity, a sum of many parts into a greater whole. Many aspects of New Orleans' culture today – street names, food, Mardi Gras – suggest a profound influence left behind by the French and Spanish, who took turns governing this city before the USA absorbed it. It is equally significant that African culture, often with Caribbean influences, has always held a stronger sway here than elsewhere in the US.

Being a major capital of the South has determined many events in New Orleans' history and contributes to its character today, but it is important to note that while this city is geographically Southern, culturally it has always been a place apart. New Orleans has its back to the South and its mouth to the sea, and much of its population has arrived via the latter: international immigrants and refugees and, after 2005, do-gooders and entrepreneurs looking to rebuild.

By North American standards, New Orleans is an old city, and the depth of its history has always been cherished by locals. Even the painful elements of its history – slavery, disease and segregation – have all played a part in shaping one of the most distinct regional identities in the USA.

Alliances between escaped African slaves and Native Americans were not uncommon. Early French settlers also sometimes married Native American women. Today, some 19,000 Louisianans identify themselves as Native American; most are culturally and racially mixed.

TIMELINE	Pre-European Contact	1000	1600s
	Louisiana is populated by thousands of members of the First Nations, who live in villages and large towns in the Gulf Coast region and northern prairies.	The Morgan Effigy, a human death figure carved from a deer antler, is fashioned somewhere near Pecan Island in southwest Louisiana.	European explorers search for the entrance to the Mississippi River. Control of this access point would essentially provide command of the interior of the North American continent.

NATIVE INHABITANTS

Louisiana was well settled and cultivated by the time of European arrival. Contrary to the myth of hunter-gatherers living in a state of harmony with the forest, local Native Americans significantly altered and impacted their environment with roads, trade networks and substantial infrastructure. They were, however, susceptible to European diseases; the germs brought by early explorers wiped out thousands of Native Americans. Ironically, by the time the French arrived with the goal of colonization, the region had probably reverted to something like a state of nature due to the massive deaths caused by introduced diseases.

After 1700, Europeans documented numerous direct contacts with local tribes. A confederation known collectively as the Muskogeans lived north of Lake Pontchartrain and occasionally settled along the banks of the Mississippi River. The Houma nation thrived in isolated coastal bayous from Terrebonne to Lafourche up until the 1940s, when oil exploration began in southern Louisiana and disturbed their way of life.

FRENCH & SPANISH NEW ORLEANS

Europeans knew control of the mouth of the Mississippi equaled control of the interior of the continent, but the Mississippi eluded ships on the Gulf until 1699, when Canadian-born Pierre Le Moyne, Sieur d'Iberville, and his younger brother Jean-Baptiste Le Moyne, Sieur de Bienville, located the muddy outflow. They encamped 40 miles downriver from present-day New Orleans on the eve of Mardi Gras and, knowing their countrymen would be celebrating the pre-Lenten holiday, christened the small spit of land Pointe de Mardi Gras. With a Native American guide, Iberville and Bienville sailed upstream, pausing to note the narrow portage to Lake Pontchartrain along Bayou St John in what would later become New Orleans.

Iberville died in 1706, but Bienville remained in Louisiana to found Nouvelle Orléans – named in honor of the Duc d'Orléans (Duke of Orléans) – in 1718. Bienville chose a patch of relatively high ground beside the Bayou St John, which connected the Mississippi to Lake Pontchartrain, thereby offering more direct access to the Gulf of Mexico. Factoring in the site's strategic position, Bienville's party decided to overlook the hazards of perennial flooding and mosquito-borne diseases. Engineer Adrien de Pauger's severe grid plan, drawn in 1722, still delineates the French Quarter today.

From the start, the objective was to populate Louisiana and make a productive commercial port, but Bienville's original group of 30

Early settlers planned a canal to link the Mississippi River to Bayou St John and, eventually, Lake Pontchartrain. The proposed canal was never built, but after the Louisiana Purchase, its location – Canal Street – became the border between the French Quarter and the American Sector, where Americans settled in what is now Uptown.

1690s	1718	1750s	1762
French fur traders establish small villages and forts in the south Louisiana bayous, paving the way for the eventual settlement of New Orleans.	Jean-Baptiste Le Moyne de Bienville founds Nouvelle Orléans. The city is founded in its current location for its strategic position controlling the mouth of the Mississippi River.	French Cajuns begin to arrive in southern Louisiana following the British conquest of Canada. The area they settle becomes known as (and is still referred to as) Acadiana.	France hands Louisiana Territory, which has proven to be unprofitable, over to Spain in exchange for an alliance in its wars in Europe.

ex-convicts, six carpenters and four Canadians struggled against floods and yellow-fever epidemics. The colony, in the meantime, was promoted as heaven on earth to unsuspecting French, Germans and Swiss, who began arriving in New Orleans by the shipload. To augment these numbers, convicts and prostitutes were freed from French jails if they agreed to relocate to Louisiana.

The colony was not a tremendous economic success, and women were in short supply. To increase the female population, the Ursuline nuns brought young, marriageable girls with them in 1728. They were known as 'casket girls' because they packed their belongings in casket-shaped boxes (see the boxed text, p55). New Orleans was already establishing itself as, and gaining a reputation for being, a loosely civilized outpost. Looking about her, one recently arrived nun commented that 'the devil here has a very large empire.'

In a secret treaty, one year before the Seven Years' War (1756–63) ended, France handed the unprofitable Louisiana Territory to King Charles III of Spain in return for an ally in its war against England. But the 'Frenchness' of New Orleans was little affected for the duration of Spain's control. Spain sent a small garrison and few financial resources. The main enduring impact left by the Spanish was the architecture of the Quarter. After fires decimated the French Quarter in 1788 and 1794, much of it was rebuilt by the Spanish. Consequently, the quaint Old Quarter with plastered facades we know today is not French, as its name would suggest, but predominantly Spanish in style.

The Spanish sensed they might eventually have to fight the expansion-minded Americans to retain control of the lower Mississippi. So they jumped at Napoleon Bonaparte's offer to retake control of Louisiana in 1800.

Andrew Jackson won a one-sided victory at the Battle of New Orleans in 1815, with nearly 900 British versus 13 US losses. Ironically, the battle began after the USA and Britain had agreed to end the war. But the victory put a lid on British designs for the Louisiana Territory.

ANTEBELLUM PROSPERITY

While Napoleon Bonaparte was waging war in Europe, the US was expanding westward into the Ohio River Valley. Napoleon needed cash to finance his wars, and US President Thomas Jefferson coveted control of the Mississippi. The deal seemed natural, but nevertheless the US minister in Paris, Robert Livingston, was astonished by Bonaparte's offer to sell Louisiana Territory – an act that would double the USA's national domain – at a price of $15 million.

Little cheer arose from the Creole community, who figured the Americans' Protestant beliefs, support for English common law and puritan work ethic jarred with the Catholic Creole way of life. In 1808 the territorial legislature sought to preserve Creole culture by adopting

1788	1791	1803	1808
On Good Friday, the Great New Orleans fire destroys 856 buildings, which are replaced with Spanish-style construction that characterizes the French Quarter to this day.	Following the slave revolution in Haiti, the arrival of French-speaking migrants, black and white, doubles New Orleans' population and adds a veneer of Caribbean culture.	Napoleon reclaims Louisiana, then sells the territory, which encompasses almost the entire drainage area of the Mississippi River, to the US for $15 million, doubling the nation's size.	As American settlers move into Creole New Orleans, the territorial legislature officially adopts elements of Spanish and French law to preserve its cultural identity.

elements of Spanish and French law, a legacy that has uniquely persisted in Louisiana till today, to the abiding frustration of many a Tulane law student.

New Orleans grew quickly under US control, becoming the fourth-wealthiest city in the world and second-largest port in the USA by the 1830s. The city's population grew as well, and spilled beyond the borders of the French Quarter. Also in the 1830s, Samuel Jarvis Peters bought plantation land upriver from the French Quarter to build a distinctly American section. That plot, beginning with today's CBD, was separated from the Creole Quarter by broad Canal St. Peters married into a Creole family and epitomized the American entrepreneur operating within the Creole host community.

Developers further transformed the 15 riverbank plantations into the lush American suburbs that are now part of Uptown New Orleans. Creole families that benefited from the city's flourishing economy built their opulent homes along Esplanade Ave, from the Quarter to Bayou St John. While the wealthy chose the highest ground, immigrants and blacks expanded into low-lying wetlands.

The late 1850s saw the revival of Carnival. The old Creole tradition, now propelled by Americans, hit the streets of New Orleans as a much grander affair than ever before. Americans also assumed control of the municipal government in 1852, further illustrating the erosion of Creole influence in New Orleans.

SLAVES & FREE PEOPLE OF COLOR

From the beginning, people of African descent were an important part of the city's population; many households in New Orleans included a few slaves. Equally significant, though, was the city's considerable number of blacks who were free in the antebellum period.

The French brought some 1300 African slaves to New Orleans in the city's first decade. In 1724, French Louisianans adopted the Code Noir (Black Code), a document that restricted the social position of blacks, but also addressed some of the needs of slaves (abused slaves could legally sue their masters) and accorded certain privileges to free persons of color. Although the import of slaves became illegal in the USA in 1807, slavery itself remained legal, and thanks to smugglers like Jean Lafitte, by the mid-19th century New Orleans had become the largest slave-trading center in the country.

Slaves in French and Spanish Louisiana were allowed to retain more of their African culture than slaves in other parts of the USA. Drumming and dancing were permitted during nonworking hours, and since

While the evidence is contested, the accepted wisdom in New Orleans is the African musical traditions kept alive inside Congo Sq served as a base for jazz and later forms of homegrown black music.

1815	1820s	1828
General Andrew Jackson defeats the British in Chalmette, just outside the city, at the battle of New Orleans. The battle occurs after the War of 1812 has technically ended.	New Orleans becomes the second-largest immigrant hub in the USA. Many immigrants come from Germany and Ireland; the latter often settled in the area now known as the 'Irish Channel.'	The first synagogue in the city opens for services. New Orleans Jews are a mixture of Spanish, Alsatian and Germanic groups, giving the community a unique cultural makeup.

War of 1812 memorial

the 1740s free blacks and slaves were allowed to congregate at Congo Sq, initially called Place des Negres. Immense crowds, including tourists from the East Coast and Europe, showed up to witness complicated polyrhythmic drumming and dances, which, by European standards, were considered highly exotic and suggestive.

Long before the Civil War, New Orleans had the South's largest population of free blacks. In Creole New Orleans they were known as *les gens de couleur libre* – free people of color. Throughout the 18th and 19th centuries, it was not uncommon for slaves to be granted their freedom after years of loyal service. Sometimes the mixed offspring of slaves and owners were granted their freedom. Skilled slaves were often allowed to hire themselves out, working jobs on the side until they were able to earn enough money to buy their freedom. The Code Noir permitted free blacks to own property and conduct business.

Free blacks identified with Creole culture, speaking French and attending Mass. Trained musicianship was prized among many families, and orchestras of free black musicians regularly performed at wealthy Creole balls. The free blacks of New Orleans were considered a highly cultured class who probably enjoyed a higher quality of life than blacks anywhere else in the US (and even many whites). They were often well educated, and some owned land and slaves of their own. But they didn't share all the rights and privileges of white Creoles and Americans: they could not vote or serve in juries, and while going about their business were sometimes required to show identification in order to prove that they were not slaves.

Subtle gradations of color led to a complex class structure in which those with the least African blood tended to enjoy the greatest privileges (octoroons, for instance, who were in theory one-eighth black, rated higher than quadroons, who were one-quarter black).

Affairs between races were socially accepted in old New Orleans, but interracial marriages were not. The plaçage was a cultural institution whereby white Creole men 'kept' light-skinned black women, providing them with a handsome wardrobe and a cottage in the Vieux Carré, and supporting any resulting children.

A DEMOGRAPHIC GUMBO

The Creoles could only loosely be defined as being of French descent. The progeny of unions between French Creoles and Native Americans and blacks also considered themselves Creole. Still, while the multicultural stew's constituent parts were not necessarily French, they became French in character after exposure to the city. Early German immigrants, for example, frequently Gallicized their names and spoke French within a generation.

Ironically the group that did not assimilate to the French city was French Acadians. The Acadians (forest-dwellers), former residents of Canada, were deported by the British from Nova Scotia in 1755 after

1830s	1840	1853	1857
Marie Laveau markets herself as the Voodoo Queen of New Orleans, popularizing the religion among the upper class and linking it to the city's public identity.	Antoine's opens for business. The restaurant is still open today, the oldest family restaurant in America, and its kitchen is supposedly responsible for dishes like oysters Rockefeller.	A yellow fever epidemic claims the lives of almost 8000 citizens, or 10% of the city's population. Eventually, the outbreak is traced to mosquito-borne transmission.	The Mistick Krewe of Comus launches modern Mardi Gras with a torch-lit night parade. Eventually, hundreds of other 'krewes' will add their imprint to the celebration.

refusing to pledge allegiance to England. Aboard unseaworthy ships they headed south, but the largely illiterate, Catholic peasants were unwanted in the American colonies. Francophile New Orleans seemed a natural home, but even here the citified Creoles regarded them as country trash. So the Acadians, now dubbing themselves Cajuns, fanned out into the upland prairies of western Louisiana, where they were able to resume their lifestyle of raising livestock.

Other former-French subjects arrived from St Domingue (now Haiti). The slave revolt there in 1791 established St Domingue as the second independent nation in the Americas and first black republic in the world. Following those revolts, thousands of slaveholders fled with their 'property' (slaves) to Louisiana, where slave and master bolstered French-speaking Creole traditions. Thousands of former slaves also relocated from St Domingue to New Orleans as free people of color. This influx doubled the city's population and injected an indelible trace of Caribbean culture that remains in evidence to this day. Their most obvious contribution was the practice of voodoo, which became popular in New Orleans during the 19th century.

As the Civil War approached, nearly half of the city's population was foreign born. Most were from Ireland, Germany or France. The Irish, in particular, took grueling, often hazardous work building levees and digging canals and settled the low-rent sector between the Garden District and the docks, still known as the Irish Channel.

Despite the Napoleonic Code's mandate for Jewish expulsion, trade practices led to tolerance of Jewish merchants. Alsatian Jews augmented the small Jewish community in New Orleans, and by 1828 they had established a synagogue. Judah Touro, whose estate was valued at $4 million upon his death in 1854, funded orphanages and hospitals that would serve Jews and Christians alike.

UNION OCCUPATION

As cosmopolitan as New Orleans was, it was also a slave city in a slave state, and it was over this very issue that the nation hurtled toward civil war. On January 26, 1861, Louisiana became the sixth state to secede from the Union, and on March 21 the state joined the Confederacy – but not for long. The Union captured New Orleans in April 1862 and held it till the end of the war.

Major Benjamin Butler, nicknamed 'Beast,' oversaw a strict occupation, but is also credited with giving the Quarter a much-needed clean-up, building orphanages, improving the school system and putting thousands of unemployed – both white and black – to work. But he

> Voodoo is an authentic part of New Orleans life, but not the touristy version of the religion hawked in the French Quarter. If you want to visit an authentic spell shop, stop by F&F Botanica in Mid-City.

> 'Beast' Butler decreed that any woman who insulted a Union officer would be treated as a 'woman of the town plying her avocation' – a prostitute. Toilet bowls around New Orleans were soon imprinted with Butler's visage.

1860s	1862	1870s	1880s
French instruction in New Orleans schools is abolished in 1862. A statewide ban on French education is implemented in 1868, limiting Francophile/phone cultural influence.	New Orleans is occupied by the Union for the duration of the Civil War. Many citizens resent the Northern presence, setting the stage for a difficult postwar reconstruction period.	The 'White League' is formed in post–Civil War years as an often-violent backlash against the election of black politicians and the presence of Northern government officials.	Mardi Gras 'Indians' appear – black New Orleanians dressed in stylized Native American costume, supposedly as a respectful nod to Indian tribes that resisted white conquest.

didn't stay in New Orleans long enough to implement Abraham Lincoln's plans for 'reconstructing' the city. Those plans, blueprints for the Reconstruction of the South that followed the war, went into effect in December 1863, a year after Butler returned to the North.

Reconstruction

The 'Free State of Louisiana,' which included only occupied parts of the state, was re-admitted to the Union in 1862. Slavery was abolished and the right to vote was extended to a few select blacks. But the move to extend suffrage to all black men, in 1863, sparked a bloody riot that ended with 36 casualties. All but two were black.

At the war's end Louisiana's state constitution was redrawn. Full suffrage was granted to blacks, but the same rights were denied to former Confederate soldiers and rebel sympathizers. Emboldened, blacks challenged discrimination laws, such as those forbidding them from riding 'white' streetcars, and racial skirmishes regularly flared up around town.

In the 1870s the White League was formed with the twin purposes of ousting what it considered to be an 'Africanized' government (elected in part by new black voters) and ridding the state government of Northerners and Reconstructionists. By all appearances, the White League was arming itself for an all-out war. Police and the state militia attempted to block a shipment of guns in 1874, and after an ensuing 'battle,' the Reconstructionist Governor William Pitt Kellogg was ousted from office for five days. Federal troops entered the city to restore order.

Although Reconstruction officially ended in 1877, New Orleans remained at war with itself for many decades afterwards. Many of the civil liberties that blacks supposedly gained after the Civil War were reversed by what became known as Jim Crow law, which reinforced and in some ways increased segregation and inequality between blacks and whites.

Civil Rights

With its educated class of black Creoles, New Orleans was a natural setting for the early Civil Rights movement. In 1896, a New Orleans man named Homer Plessy, whose one-eighth African lineage subjected him to Jim Crow restrictions, challenged Louisiana's segregation laws in the landmark *Plessy v Ferguson* case. Although Plessy's case exposed the arbitrary nature of Jim Crow, the US Supreme Court interpreted the Constitution as providing for political, not social, equality and ruled to uphold 'separate but equal' statutes. Separate buses, water fountains, bathrooms, eating places and courtroom Bibles became fixtures of the

White-supremacist groups appeared throughout the South following Reconstruction. In New Orleans, organizations called the Knights of the White Camellia and the Crescent City Democratic Club initiated a reign of terror that targeted blacks and claimed several hundred lives during a particularly bloody few weeks in 1874.

1884

New Orleans hosts the World's Fair in what is now Audubon Park. Although the state treasurer steals most of the event's funding, this marks the beginning of the city's tourism industry.

Exhibit at the World's Fair

1895–1905

Buddy Bolden, who will eventually go insane and die in relative obscurity, reigns as the first 'King of Jazz.' His music influences generations of performers.

C. UPHAM / CORBIS ©

1896

Homer Plessy, an octoroon (one-eighth black), challenges New Orleans' segregation laws. Subsequently, discrimination remains legal under the 'separate but equal' clause.

landscape. 'Separate but equal' remained the law of the land until the Plessy case was overturned by *Brown v the Board of Education* in 1954. Congress passed the Civil Rights Act in 1964.

INTO THE 20TH CENTURY

As the 20th century dawned, manufacturing, shipping, trade and banking all resumed, but New Orleans did not enjoy the prosperity of its antebellum period. Nonetheless, the turn of the century was a formative period: this was when the city morphed from an industrial port into a cultural beacon.

A new musical style was brewing in the city. Called 'jass' and later jazz, the music married black Creole musicianship to African American rhythms. It also benefited from a proliferation of brass and wind instruments that accompanied the emergence of marching bands during the war years. As jazz spread worldwide, the music became a signature of New Orleans much as impressionist painting had become synonymous with Paris.

In the 1930s, oil companies began dredging canals and laying a massive pipe infrastructure throughout the bayou region to the southwest of New Orleans. The project brought a new source of wealth to New Orleans' CBD, where national oil companies opened their offices, but not without significant environmental impact (see p210 for more information).

New Orleans was inundated with military troops and personnel during WWII. German U-boats sank many allied ships in the Gulf of Mexico, but New Orleans was never directly threatened. With war came manufacturing jobs. Airplane parts and Higgins boats, used for shuttling troops and supplies to the beach during the Normandy invasion, were built in New Orleans. For the duration of the war Mardi Gras was canceled.

Andrew Higgins, a New Orleans-based industrialist, was the inventor of the Higgins Boat. Originally designed to transport goods across marshy Louisiana, the boat was converted into the famed LCPV: the 'Landing Craft, Personnel, Vehicle' that brought Allied soldiers to shore from the Pacific Theater to Sicily and Normandy.

Changing Demographics

The demographics of the city were changing. During the 'white flight' years, chiefly after WWII, black residents moved out of the rural South and into the cities of the North as well as Southern cities such as New Orleans. Most whites responded by relocating to suburbs such as Metairie. Desegregation laws finally brought an end to Jim Crow legislation, but traditions shaped by racism were not so easily reversed. In 1960, as schools were desegregated, federal marshals had to escort black schoolchildren to their classrooms to protect them from white protestors. The tragic irony is that as many whites moved their children

1897	1901	1905	1906
Storyville, New Orleans' infamous red-light district, is established. The music played in the best 'clubs' helps popularize jazz with out-of-town visitors (ie customers).	Louis Armstrong is born on August 4. He will go on to reform school and a storied career, becoming one of New Orleans' most famous musical icons.	A yellow fever outbreak prompts a huge public health response: all standing water is drained, sealed or oiled. The disease is effectively banished from the city.	The muffuletta sandwich is invented at Central Grocery. Along with gumbo, po'boys, jambalaya and red beans and rice, this will become one of the signature dishes of the city.

into private schools, so many formerly all-white public schools became nearly all-black.

New Orleans' cityscape also changed during the postwar years. A new elevated freeway was constructed above Claiborne Ave and run through black neighborhoods, largely so white citizens who fled town after desegregation could commute to work easily. High-rise office buildings and hotels shot up around the CBD, and in the mid-1970s the Louisiana Superdome opened.

In 1978 New Orleans elected its first black mayor, Ernest 'Dutch' Morial. Morial, a Democrat, appointed blacks and women to many city posts during his two terms in office and was both loved and hated for his abrasive fights with the City Council. His tenure ended in 1986, and in 1994 his son, Marc Morial, was elected mayor and then reelected in 1998. In 2001 the younger Morial attempted to pass a referendum permitting him to run for a third term, but the city electorate turned him down. Another African American, businessman Ray Nagin, became mayor in 2002.

PRESERVATION & TOURISM

During the first few decades of the 20th century, the French Quarter was an old and crumbling district, with almost all of its buildings dating from before the Civil War, heavily populated by large families of working-class immigrants and blacks. The issue of preservation arose as prominent citizens began to recognize the architectural value of the French Quarter. The Vieux Carré Commission was founded in 1936 to regulate exterior modifications made to the historic buildings. Gentrification began to take its course as wealthy New Orleanians began to purchase property in the French Quarter, driving up the value of real estate. A similar process took place in neighborhoods such as the Garden District and Faubourg Marigny.

As New Orleans accentuated its antiquity, tourism increased. Bourbon St became oriented toward the tourist trade, with souvenir shops and touristy bars opening up along the street. To accommodate the tourist influx, large-scale hotels were built in the heart of the French Quarter in traditional architectural styles. As the oil boom of the 1970s went bust in the 1980s, tourism became the rock of the local economy. Conventioneers and vacationers regularly outnumbered locals on the weekend, spending cash and spilling beer, primarily in the French Quarter.

1917	1927	1936	1955
The Department of the Navy shuts down Storyville – the Red Light district – despite the protests of Mayor Martin Behrman.	During the Great Mississippi Flood, the levee is dynamited in St Bernard Parish, flooding poorer residents' homes to divert water and protect the wealthy in New Orleans.	Vieux Carré Commission is founded to regulate changes to French Quarter exteriors. The Quarter remains to this day one of the oldest preserved neighborhoods in the USA.	Fats Domino records 'Ain't that a Shame.' Along with Dave Bartholomew, Domino helps generate the 'New Orleans Sound' that defined local music in the mid-20th century.

Tourist dollars meant job opportunities for locals, and also helped prop up some of the city's specialty industries, particularly the food scene.

KATRINA

Occupying a low-lying, drained swamp that sits on a hurricane-prone coast, New Orleans has long lived in fear of the one powerful storm that could wipe out the city. On the morning of Saturday August 28, 2005, Hurricane Katrina prepared to lay claim to that title. The storm had just cut a path of destruction across Florida – killing seven people – when it spilled into the warm Gulf of Mexico. It quickly recharged from its trip across land, and morphed from a dangerous Category Three storm into a Category Five monster, the deadliest designation on the Saffir-Simpson Scale of hurricane strength. Computer models predicted a direct hit on New Orleans.

Mayor Ray Nagin ordered a mandatory evacuation, the first in the city's history. Four out of five residents left the greater New Orleans metropolitan area. Nearly 200,000 stayed behind. The holdouts included those who could not find transportation, people who thought the predictions too dire, and those who wanted to protect their homes and stores from looters.

The storm weakened to a Category Three before making landfall near the Louisiana-Mississippi line just before midnight. As the sun rose Monday morning, it was clear Katrina's winds had caused extensive damage – blowing out windows, tearing large sections of the Superdome's roof, and knocking over trees and telephone poles. Yet a sense that it could have been much worse prevailed.

Paul Prudhomme gained international renown while working at Commander's Palace in the Garden District, and then his own K-Paul's, which opened in 1979 in the French Quarter. Prudhomme's promotion of Louisiana food was a major engine for tourism growth in New Orleans in the 1980s.

Storm Surge

But while house-flattening winds are the most celebrated feature of hurricanes, in this case the most deadly aspect was the storm surge, the rising tide of water driven inland by the gales. Katrina's winds pushed water from the Gulf of Mexico up the Mississippi River, into Lake Pontchartrain, and through the canals that lace the city. The levees built to protect the city did not hold. A torrent of water from the Industrial Canal washed away the Lower Ninth Ward; in neighborhoods like Lakeview and Gentilly, houses were submerged when the 17th St Canal and London Ave canal gave way.

In all, four-fifths of the city was submerged in a toxic soup of salt and fresh water, gasoline, chemicals, human waste and floating bodies. The massive pumps that clear the city after rainy days couldn't process the

1960	1965	1970	1978
Federal marshals escort black children into schools as they are desegregated. In the following years, 'white flight' into the suburbs will leave city schools with few white students.	Hurricane Betsy, the billion-dollar hurricane, batters the Big Easy. Improvements to the levee system made following the disaster fail to protect the city in 2005.	Jazz Fest is held for the first time, beginning its long history as a gathering of a few hundred fans celebrating the city's unique musical heritage.	New Orleans' first black mayor, Ernest 'Dutch' Morial, is elected. Despite lingering racial tensions, a dynasty is established: his son, Marc Morial, is elected mayor in 1994 and '98.

volume of water, which rose as high as 15ft in parts of the city, and remained for weeks. Stranded residents found little time to escape. They moved from the 1st floor to the 2nd floor, then the attic. Some drowned there; those lucky enough to find tools to hack through the roof got out, or used cans of paint to dash out crude appeals for help.

The 'Sliver By the River' – Uptown, the Garden district, the French Quarter and parts of the Marigny and Bywater – survived unscathed. Elsewhere, New Orleans reverted to a Hobbesian state of nature. Looters broke into stores, taking necessities such as food and medication, along with luxuries like DVDs and flat-screen TVs. Around 26,000 people took shelter at the Superdome, in increasingly squalid conditions, while others took ad hoc shelter in the Convention Center. Some attempted to walk out of the city across a bridge into neighboring Jefferson Parish, only to find their way blocked by police. Officials said evacuees were not allowed out of the city because the neighboring areas didn't have sufficient facilities to aid them, but also claimed they feared the lawlessness taking hold in New Orleans would accompany the refugees.

The well-to-do sections of New Orleans on higher ground near the Mississippi River – the 'Sliver by the River' – were largely spared Katrina's floodwaters. New Orleans is a basin whose edge (the high part) is the Mississippi River, which did not break the levees. Water overflowed via Lake Pontchartrain and canals.

FROM REBUILD TO RENAISSANCE

Pundits, geophysicists and even then-House Speaker Dennis Hastert (who claimed that rebuilding a city that lies below sea level 'doesn't make sense to me,' before backtracking) seriously debated writing off New Orleans as a lost cause. The city, they said, was – by dint of its geography – not worth rebuilding.

Native wags – such as journalist Chris Rose, a columnist for the *Times-Picayune* and author of post-Katrina memoir *1 Dead in Attic* – have suggested the USA has always distrusted this strange little city with a habit of marching to its own drummer (often enough, during a Second Line following a jazz funeral).

Yet millions of Americans and thousands of New Orleanians rose to the challenge. They waded into basements in 100°F-plus weather and slopped out trash, rubble and corpses, mowed lawns, planted gardens and fixed each other's roofs, sometimes using discarded pieces of swept-away flooring. They celebrated small victories with what beer they could scrape together, and these impromptu parties became their own building blocks of reconstruction, the cultural component of rebirth in a city where enjoying life is as integral as cement.

Helping the locals were huge numbers of volunteers and professionals, many in their 20s and 30s, who fell in love with New Orleans' distinctive sense of place and found a home even as they rebuilt it. So many

1987	2002	2005	2007
The Saints post their first winning season since joining the NFL in 1967; it proves to be their last for many years, earning the team the nickname 'Aints'.	Long-shot Ray Nagin becomes major of New Orleans. Nagin vows to clean up the city, but his term in office has its share of scandals.	The storm surge following Hurricane Katrina floods 80% of New Orleans. The city is evacuated, although thousands who could not or did not leave linger in the city for days.	Republican Bobby Jindal is elected governor of Louisiana, the first Indian American governor of a US state; many consider him an up-and-coming star of the Republican Party.

newcomers opted to stay that local academics suggested the term 'new New Orleanian' become an official demographic. Others just call these fresh neighbors YURPs: Young, Urban, Rebuilding Professionals. Very few seem to begrudge their presence.

Though the rebirth process has been slow, and some of the changes the Storm wrought on this town will be irreversible, the hope of the rebuilders seems to have trumped the pessimism of the naysayers. New restaurants and bars pop up with happy frequency, and the arts scene in particular seems to be turning this town into something of a Southern Left Bank for the 21st century. Young entrepreneurs, attracted by low rents and the city's undeniable culture, are flooding into town; the city was named by *Inc* magazine the coolest startup city in America, and Louisiana was, as of this writing, ranked 7th in the nation in entrepreneurial activity by the Kauffman Foundation. In a revitalized business climate, there is hope that despite her troubled history, New Orleans is becoming a model of not just recovery, but rebirth.

New Orleans History Reads

HISTORY FROM REBUILD TO RENAISSANCE

Feb–Mar 2010

The Saints win the Superbowl, Mardi Gras happens and Mitch Landrieu is elected mayor, the first white mayor to win a broad portion of the black vote.

Apr–Sept 2010

The Deepwater Horizon oil spill pumps 4.9 million barrels of oil into the Gulf of Mexico, becoming the largest, costliest environmental disaster in American history.

2011

The latest census reveals the population of New Orleans has shrunk by 29% since 2000. A corresponding increase in population is noted in some suburbs.

PCN PHOTOGRAPHY / ALAMY ©

The Saints win the Superbowl

Graffiti art by the elusive artist Banksy

Arts & Literature

This is a city of ephemeral moments. A perfect spring day can vanish in a thunderstorm; a perfect meal disappears in a hungry flash; the song that touches your soul is over in minutes. New Orleanians have always tried to capture temporary beauty – to make the temporal eternal – and the act of seizing the loveliness of the world, plus the ability to appreciate said splendor, is integral to the town's character.

The arts of New Orleans go far beyond the proliferation of dabbers you'll meet around Jackson Sq. The history of New Orleans is recorded in brilliant paintings left behind by the French and Spanish, who helped forge an aesthetic that drips with nostalgia and a sort of gothic melancholy. In turn, modern New Orleans is seized, dissected and interpreted by artists exhibiting their work in swish galleries on Julia St and in sawdust-laden experimental studio spaces on St Claude Ave.

The city's creativity is fed by an intense appreciation of art on the part of the locals, who also love a good story. The city's passionate sensuality, sometimes fraught drama and the eccentric cast of characters who call it home make New Orleans an excellent womb for authors and filmmakers. Great novels and non-fiction emerge from the mouth of the river regularly.

Besides some of the areas we mention in this chapter and our Entertainment Overview, check out local schools for more arts events. Tulane (http://tulane.edu/liberal-arts/art), the University of New Orleans (http://finearts.uno.edu) and the New Orleans Center for Creative Arts (www.nocca.com) all regularly exhibit their faculty and students' artwork.

WHERE TO FIND ART

New Orleans is a city of good museums that are generally strong in local and regional art. Reputable galleries are found in great numbers all over town. The city supports several distinct arts hubs. Royal St is the main stem of the mostly mainstream French Quarter arts scene, where savvy self-marketers have set up shop among the expensive antique shops. More down to earth (and lower in price) are the up-and-coming galleries along lower Decatur St. On the strength of the Bywater Art Market and the New Orleans Center for Creative Arts (Nocca; p95), an educational facility for young artists, the low-rent Bywater is a fertile artistic zone. More highbrow are the quality galleries of Julia Row (see p104) in the Warehouse District. Upbeat Magazine St has several dispersed blocks of excellent galleries.

FOLK ART

The South has long been known for its rich folk-art traditions, now fashionably referred to as 'outsider' art, and New Orleans is a good place to seek out reasonably priced works for your collection back home. The very best paintings demonstrate highly individualistic techniques developed in complete isolation from the art world. Many great outsider works are in the Ogden Museum and New Orleans Museum of Art but true gems can also be found in galleries and shops on Magazine St.

A CITY OF STORIES

New Orleans is a city that loves a good story, and perhaps more so, a good storyteller. As many authors as visual artists are attracted to the town, as evinced by the yearly Tennessee Williams Literary Festival (see Month by Month, p21), named for the author who claimed the city as his 'spiritual home'. The following are some works to complement the list of best reads we supplied in New Orleans Today (p188).

➡ **One Dead in Attic** (2006) A collection of Chris Rose's compelling post-Katrina columns, which initially appeared in the *Times-Picayune*.

➡ **Why New Orleans Matters** (2005) Tom Piazza's evocative, almost elegiac overview of New Orleans culture, set in the context of the natural threats hovering in the city's future.

➡ **New Orleans, Mon Amour: Twenty Years of Writing from the City** (2006) Andrei Codrescu's book reads like a love letter tinged with sadness, but it's also filled with humor, irony and appreciation for the city.

➡ **Yellow Jack** (2000) Josh Russell wrote this masterfully imagined historical novel, set in Antebellum New Orleans, which connects multiple skeins – race, disease, photography, love and eroticism – into an emotionally wrenching plot.

New Orleans boasts some fine arts centers that host good gallery nights, including Zeitgeist (p123); the Ashe Cultural Arts Center, which regularly exhibits work created or inspired by members of the black diaspora; and the 3 Ring Circus (www.3rcp.com), an arts education center that hosts regular music and gallery nights.

PUBLIC ART & PROSPECT

Public art is starting to take off in post-Katrina New Orleans, especially since 2009, when the 'Art in Public Places' project resulted in 19 artists being commissioned to create public art throughout the city. Standouts include **No Place Like Nola** in the Botanical Gardens (p143), a conglomeration of 14 birdhouses that references New Orleans architecture and historical structures, and **Watermarks**, 12 posts situated on Elysian Fields Ave that indicate the height of Katrina floodwaters. For a map and description of all works, see the **Arts Council of New Orleans** (www.artscouncilof neworleans.org) website.

In 2008 New Orleans began hosting **Prospect** (www.prospectneworleans.org), which is currently the largest biennial contemporary arts event in the USA. Artists from around the world (and from New Orleans, of course) exhibited work for two months in venues scattered across the city, as well as public spaces; in all, some 100,000 sq ft of gallery space was utilized for the show, dubbed 'Prospect 1.' 2012 saw Prospect 2, and if you visit in 2014 you'll be in town in time for Prospect 3. Even if you arrive before 2014, you might catch 'midway' Prospect shows (for example, there was a smaller Prospect 1.5 held from November 2010 to February 2011).

➡ **New Orleans City Guide** (1938) This guide was penned in 1938 by the Federal Writer's Project, which employed authors following the Great Depression. As a work of history, prose and sheer quality, it stands alone – and has been re-released by Garrett Press.

FILMING THE BIG EASY

Thanks to plush tax breaks, increasing cachet with the creative class and a distinctive cityscape, New Orleans has become a major filming site in the USA. We supplied some good classic New Orleans movies in New Orleans Today (p188), but following are some modern big screen adaptations of the Big Easy worth checking out. Also, make sure to catch *Treme,* the HBO series by David Simon, creator of *The Wire*. Where that show was about the rot within a city, *Treme* is about the renewal of New Orleans and the city's distinct culture. Plenty of bars in town host viewing parties, including Buffa's (p92) at 7pm on Sundays.

➡ **Beasts of the Southern Wild** (2012) A beautifully compelling magical realist romp that follows a sweet girl named Hushpuppy through the imagined town of Bathtub, Louisiana. Shot by a local film collective dubbed Court 13, this film wowed critics at Sundance.

➡ **Jeff, Who Lives at Home** (2011) Indie comedy flick starring Jason Segal, Ed Helms, Susan Sarandon and Judy Greer, about two brothers coming to terms with their respective life crises, set in Baton Rouge and filmed in Metairie.

➡ **The Princess and the Frog** (2009) Disney actually did a great job capturing the magic, color and at least some of the spirit of New Orleans with this supremely family-friendly fable. Plus, the music is pretty great.

➡ **The Bad Lieutenant: Port of Call – New Orleans** (2009) Ignore the weird, overblown title and focus on the weird, overblown content of this trippy, drug-addled Warner Herzog film, starring Nicolas Cage, about bad cops, bad decisions and muddled moral waters.

➡ **If God is Willing and Da Creek Don't Rise** (2010) Spike Lee documentary that focuses on the complicated and often stalled rebuilding process. It's long (four hours), but undeniably comprehensive and powerful.

The Arts Council of New Orleans (www.artscouncil ofneworleans .org), provides a good intro to the city's art scene, while Humid Beings (humidbeings. com) brings fresh, critical voices to local developments – both are required reading for art-philes.

In 2008, British artist/vandal (take your pick) Banksy left 12 works across the New Orleans cityscape. Some paintings were destroyed by local vigilante Fred Radtke, dubbed the Grey Ghost for his habit of covering tags with grey paint. Google 'Banksy New Orleans map' to see locations of the artist's work.

Architecture

New Orleans has the most distinctive cityscape in the USA. This sense of place is directly attributable to its great quantity of historic homes, and the cohesion of so many of its neighborhoods. The French Quarter and Garden District have long been considered exemplars of New Orleans architecture, but send the Tremé, the Marigny or the Irish Channel to another city, and they would stand out as treasure troves of history and heritage.

As of this writing, 143 sites in Orleans parish are listed on the National Register of Historic Places. While we stress that there's more to the city's architecture than the French Quarter and Garden District, those neighborhoods *do* nicely illustrate the pronounced difference between the two 'sectors' of New Orleans: Creole and American.

The Quarter and Creole 'faubourgs' (Marigny, Bywater and Tremé) downriver from Canal St are densely packed with stuccoed brick structures built in various architectural styles and housing types rarely found in other US cities. Cross Canal St and the wide lots and luxuriant wooden houses of the Garden District more closely resemble upscale homes found throughout the South. Uptown, further upriver, the display intensifies to the point of near-gaudiness.

FRENCH COLONIAL HOUSE

Surviving structures from the French period are rare. New Orleans was a French colony only from 1718 until the Spanish takeover in 1762, and twice during the Spanish period fires destroyed much of the town. Only one French Quarter building, the Ursuline Convent (p53), remains from the French period. The convent was built for the climate of French Canada, but the French recognized Caribbean design was more appropriate in New Orleans.

Madame John's Legacy, at 628 Dumaine St, is a good example of a French Caribbean home. Marked by a steep hipped roof, casement windows and batten shutters, it possesses galleries – covered porches – that help keep the house cool in summer. These galleries shaded rooms from direct light and rainfall. Out on Bayou St John, the Pitot House (p145) is another signature French-colonial compound.

Briquette entre poteaux, where brick fills the spaces between vertical and diagonal posts, was common to French-colonial houses. This style endured during the Spanish period, and is visible where stucco is cleared to expose the exterior walls of Lafitte's Blacksmith Shop (p66).

SPANISH COLONIAL HOUSE

During the Spanish period, adjacent buildings were designed to rub shoulders, with no space between, which created the continuous facade of the French Quarter. The signature home of this period is the two-story town house, with commercial space on the ground floor and residential quarters upstairs. The space between houses was a well-shaded, private courtyard used like a family room. A covered space along the back of the house (loggia) served as a sort of courtyard gallery, and within it a curved stairway led to upstairs. Arches, tiled roofs and balconies with ornate wrought-iron railings became common.

CREOLE TOWN HOUSE

Very few buildings survive from the Spanish-colonial period, and not all the survivors reflect the Spanish style. But the Creoles of New Orleans appreciated Spanish architecture and regularly applied its key elements (especially the courtyard, carriageway and loggia) to French Quarter town houses. Most surviving examples date from the American period. An especially elaborate, three-story example of the Creole town house, with key Spanish elements, is Napoleon House (p67).

The French Quarter is also the Maghreb Quarter. Packed town houses are built Spanish-style, with outdoor space reserved for private courtyards and public balconies. This in turn is a North African tradition, inherited from the Muslim conquest of Spain. In Morocco, houses built in this style are called *riads*.

CREOLE COTTAGE

Freestanding Creole cottages are found throughout the French Quarter and Faubourg Marigny. The front of the house usually has two casement doors, sometimes four. These openings are often shuttered to shield the interior space from sidewalk traffic, passing inches away. The airy floor plan is simple as can be, with four interconnected chambers, each with an opening (a door or window) to the side of the house.

SHOTGUN HOUSE

During the latter half of the 19th century, the inexpensive shotgun became a popular single-family dwelling. The name supposedly suggests a bullet could be fired from front to back through the open doorways of all of the rooms, but in truth only the most basic shotgun has doors lined up so perfectly. The standard 'single-shotgun' house is a row of rooms with doors leading from one to the next. As there is no hall, you pass through each room to traverse the house. Shotguns are freestanding, with narrow spaces along either side. Windows on both sides and high ceilings encourage cross-ventilation and keep the rooms cool.

'Double-shotguns' are duplexes, with mirror-image halves traditionally forming two homes. Many double-shotguns have been converted into large single homes. Some shotguns, called 'camel-backs,' have a 2nd floor above the back of the house.

GREEK REVIVAL

Perhaps no style symbolizes the wealth and showiness of mid-19th-century America than Greek revival architecture. The genre, readily recognizable for its tall columns, was inspired by such classics as the Parthenon. Greek revival houses can be found along St Charles Ave in Uptown and in the Garden District. A nice example is the raised villa at 2127 Prytania St.

Gallier Hall, once the City Hall building for New Orleans, marks the epitome of Greek revival pomp and circumstance. It overlooks Lafayette Sq and is used for civic functions today.

FIVE-BAY CENTER HALL HOUSE

The 1½-story center hall house became common with the arrival of more Anglo-Americans to New Orleans after the Louisiana Purchase in 1803. The raised center hall house, found in the Garden District and Uptown, became the most common type. It stands on a pier foundation 2ft to 8ft above ground, and its columned front gallery spans the entire width of the house.

ITALIANATE

The Italianate style, inspired by Tuscan villas, gained popularity after the Civil War. Segmental arches, frequently used over doors and windows, and the decorative box-like parapets over galleries are commonly identified as Italianate features.

Music & Culture

New Orleans without music is Washington without politics, or Paris without fashion. It is inconceivable. In this city of appetites, music feeds the soul. The city's history can be traced in its music. The French and their Creole descendants gave the city two opera companies before any other US city had one. Meanwhile, slaves and free persons of color preserved African music in Congo Sq. These influences inexorably came together when French-speaking black Creoles livened up European dance tunes by adding African rhythms. From there, jazz was an inevitability.

THE RISE & FALL (& RISE) OF JAZZ

A proliferation of brass instruments after the Civil War led to a brass instrument craze that spread throughout the South and the Midwest. Many of the musicians, white and black, learned to play music without learning to read it. Instead they operated by ear and by memory. Improvisation became the default baseline for playing music.

One of the most problematic figures in jazz history is Charles 'Buddy' Bolden, New Orleans' first 'King of Jazz.' Some said Bolden 'broke his heart' when he performed, while others mused that he would 'blow his brains out' by playing so loudly. Between 1895 and 1906, he so dominated the music scene that audiences deserted halls where rival bands were performing when word spread Bolden was playing somewhere else.

Successors to Bolden included Joe 'King' Oliver, whose Creole Jazz Band found a receptive audience in Chicago, thus spreading the good word about jazz across the country. Oliver was soon overshadowed by his protégé, Louis Armstrong, whom Oliver summoned from New Orleans in 1922. Working together, Oliver and Armstrong made many seminal jazz recordings, including 'Dippermouth Blues.'

Pianist Jelly Roll Morton was a controversial character – he falsely claimed to have 'invented' jazz while performing in a Storyville bordello in 1902 – but he had uncommon talents in composition and arrangement. Kid Ory, who hailed from nearby La Place, LA, moved his band to Los Angeles in 1919 and introduced jazz to the West Coast.

Although jazz went into decline for several decades, the genre has experienced a renaissance since the 1980s. In 1982, then 19-year old Wynton Marsalis stormed onto the scene followed by his older brother Branford. Other musicians, who were studying with Wynton and Branford's father, Ellis Marsalis, at the New Orleans Center for the Creative Arts, formed the nucleus of a New Orleans jazz revival. These included pianist-crooner Harry Connick Jr and trumpeters Terence Blanchard and Roy Hargrove.

Many brass bands still play traditional music inspired by marching band arrangements of the 19th century. Others, like the streetwise Rebirth, fuse styles from 'trad' jazz to funk, R&B and modern jazz. In 2012, Rebirth won a Grammy for Best Regional Roots Music for the album *Rebirth of New Orleans*. Rapping trombone player Trombone Shorty jumps between genres like a frog, sometimes bouncing into hip-hop, R&B, and even indie rock. The Soul Rebels also borrow freely from hip-hop for their arrangements.

Buddy Bolden's unstable personality wasn't for show. He went insane while still at the top and was institutionalized for 25 years, oblivious that the very jazz he played and popularized had spread worldwide. He died a forgotten man, and is buried in an unmarked grave in Holt Cemetery.

ZUMA WIRE SERVICE / ALAMY ©

Allen Toussaint performs at the New Orleans Jazz Fest

R&B & FUNK

New Orleans owes its reputation as a breeding ground for piano players to Henry Roeland Byrd – also known as Professor Longhair. His rhythmic rumba and boogie-woogie style of playing propelled him to success with tunes like 'Tipitina' (for which the legendary nightclub is named) and 'Go to the Mardi Gras.'

In the 1960s R&B and New Orleans fell under the spell of Allen Toussaint, a talented producer who molded songs to suit the talents of New Orleans' artists. The formula worked for Ernie K-Doe, who hit pay dirt with the disgruntled, catchy 'Mother-In-Law,' in 1961.

Aaron Neville, whose soulful falsetto is one of the most instantly recognizable voices in pop music, began working with Toussaint in 1960, when his first hit single, the menacing but pretty 'Over You' was recorded. The association later yielded the gorgeous 'Let's Live.' But 'Tell It Like It Is' (1967), recorded without Toussaint, was the biggest national hit of Neville's career. Art Neville, a piano player from the Professor Longhair school, heads up The Meters, whose sound defines modern New Orleans funk.

The best radio stations in New Orleans are WTUL, 91.5, and WWOZ, 90.7. The former is Tulane University's radio station, which plays an eclectic mix of generally high quality tunes. 'O-Z,' as it's called, plays local New Orleans music and is a backbone of the city's musical community.

ZYDECO

Cajun music is the music of the white Cajuns, while zydeco is the music of French-speaking blacks who share the region. They share plenty in common, but the differences are distinct.

Zydeco ensembles originally comprised a fiddle, diatonic button accordion, guitar and triangle (the metal percussion instrument common to symphony orchestras and kindergarten music classes). Zydeco accordionists prefer the piano accordion, and the rhythm section usually includes a *frottoir,* a metal washboard-like instrument that's worn like armor and played with spoons. The end result is a genre of music that is made for dance accompaniment; the Thursday night zydeco party at Mid-City Rock & Bowl (p152) is not to be missed.

Zydeco, it should be noted, is not a static form of music restricted to country dancehalls. Innovators from Clifton Chenier, the father of zydeco, to Beau Joques, Buckwheat Zydeco, Terrance Simien and Keith Frank have incorporated the blues, R&B, funk and soul into the zydeco sound. Baton Rouge rapper Lil Boosie uses zydeco music to propel his lyrics on the appropriately named track 'Zydeco' on the mixtape 225/504.

The 2003 German movie *Schultze Gets the Blues* is the tale of a retired German salt miner and accordion enthusiast who hears zydeco on the radio and embarks on a quest to Louisiana in search of the roots of the music.

HIP-HOP & BOUNCE

The biggest rap star to come out of the Big Easy is Lil' Wayne, whose growling licks and almost stoned-sounding delivery have become the object of veritable idol worship among teenage New Orleanians. Dee-1 is a young local rapper who has gained prominence for his mix of positivity, humor and intelligence – sadly distinctive within modern hip-hop. His singles, 'Blue' and 'Jay, 50 and Weezy' are well-crafted tracks dripping with keen observation and political awareness; this sort of rap has the potential to be preachy, but Dee-1's local roots and masterful flow have afforded him both critical and commercial success.

With this said, when it comes to the pop music train, in many ways New Orleans passed the hip-hop station and got off at bounce. Bounce is the defining sound of young black New Orleans as of this writing. It's a high-speed genre distinct to the city that involves drum-machine driven beats, call-and-response, sexualized lyrics and extremely raunchy dancing. Shows are led by DJs who play a role similar to a selector at a Jamaican dancehall concert.

Although details are fuzzy, it seems the genre was invented in the early '90s. Bounce quickly became the default dance music in many New Orleans clubs, with DJs calling out over the hyperquick 'Triggerman' rhythm that has been sampled into a thousand and one tracks, as dancers got freaky on the floor and called out their wards and projects (pretty much the way bounce parties go off today, too). Pioneers in the genre include Juvenile, Soulja Slim, Mia X and DJ Jubilee, whose track 'Get Ready, Ready' is a good introduction to the genre. There's a weekly Saturday night bounce party at the St Roch Tavern (p93).

External media has dubbed the music of transgender bounce artists like Katey Red, Sissy Nobby and Big Freedia 'sissy bounce' ('sissy' is local slang for queers); while the label has stuck, Katey Red herself has said she simply considers herself a transgender bounce artist.

If you want to listen to bounce music in New Orleans, turn your dial to 102.9 and 93.3. There's mainly commercial hip-hop on these stations, but they play local talent too, and they're good places to find out where bounce shows are happening.

The Environment

New Orleans is shaped by her environment more than most American cities. Consider: while outsiders bemoan the foolishness of placing a city in a low-lying river basin, it was founded precisely here so it could command the mouth of the Mississippi. Nevertheless, the local dance between man and nature has generally been an uneasy one: do nothing and the land is uninhabitable; impact the land too much and the waters will flood elsewhere.

THE LAY OF THE WATERY LAND

Katrina hit during the particularly brutal 2005 hurricane season, when a record 27 tropical storms spawned 15 hurricanes. Of the five to make landfall, two (Katrina and Rita) slammed southern Louisiana within a three-week period. Katrina was by far the most destructive, but Rita was actually stronger.

The first important factor to consider is that New Orleans is surrounded by water. It stands between the Mississippi River, which curls like a devilish snake around much of the city, and Lake Pontchartrain, a large saltwater body connected to the Gulf of Mexico. Swamps and marshes cover much of the remaining area around the city.

The land the city stands on has been wrested from the Mississippi's natural floodplain. The oldest parts of town adhere to the high ground, which is, in fact, made up of natural levees created by the Mississippi depositing soil there during floods. The moniker 'Crescent City' comes from this old footprint on the natural levees, which got its shape by forming along the curve of the river. The high ground in New Orleans is just a few feet above sea level. Much of the rest of the city is below sea level, forming a bowl that obviously remains vulnerable to flooding, despite human-made levees. The city's elevation averages 2ft below sea level. And it is sinking.

A DAM HEADACHE

In the travelogue *Bayou Farewell* (2003), author and journalist Mike Tidwell documents the culture, folkways and natural environment of the vast, yet shrinking, Louisiana wetlands. It's one of the better nonfiction literary insights into Cajun culture.

The US Army Corps of Engineers built and maintains miles of levees which have kept the Mississippi River on a fixed course for more than a century. You'll see the levee from Jackson Sq, in the French Quarter, as it rises like an evenly graded hill and hides the river from view. That's right: as you walk uphill in New Orleans, you're coming *closer* to the water.

Compounding the difficult geography is the weather. New Orleans sits within the Atlantic hurricane zone, and hurricane season lasts approximately half a year here, from early summer to late fall. Hurricanes cause floods by pushing in water from the Gulf (not, as many assume, the Mississippi). Surging gulf waters run through town via the canal system and can be far more difficult to predict than rising river tides. Storm surges rise like tsunamis, lunging upward as they squeeze through narrow canal passageways. River floods, by contrast, can be observed far upstream, often weeks in advance.

The levee system was extensively updated, repaired and built out after Katrina. Hopefully it will stand up to the next storm, but the final test will be whenever a big storm hits, a scenario no one is keen on rushing.

THE BP OIL SPILL

On April 20, 2010, the Deepwater Horizon, an offshore drilling rig owned by Transocean and leased to BP operating in the Gulf of Mexico, exploded after highly pressured gas expanded into the rig and ignited. Eleven men were killed. Two days later, oil from the underwater Macondo Prospect was spotted seeping into the ocean.

In all, 4.9 million barrels of oil were spilled into the Gulf as a result of the Deepwater disaster, the most expensive in US environmental history. The tourism industry of the Gulf states took a significant hit. Wildlife did worse: oil-slicked animal corpses were found (and continue to be found, as of this writing) on beaches in Grad Isle, south of New Orleans, while reports of lesions, missing eyes and other mutations have been attributed to the chemical dispersants used by BP to clear away oil.

At the time of writing, the Gulf of Mexico's tourism and seafood industry seemed to have recovered from the spill (helped along by the $7.8 billion settlement BP paid to those who lost livelihoods as a result of the spill), but its long-term impacts remain to be seen. Oil has entered the food chain via zooplankton, which could have biological impacts five or 10 years (or more) down the road.

THE VANISHING COAST

Some 30 sq miles of Louisiana coast – an area roughly equivalent to the size of Manhattan – are lost each year due to subsidence of the natural floodplains. Erosion is further enhanced by the extensive canal network dredged for oil production – Louisiana produces one-fifth of the nation's oil and one-fourth of its natural gas – whose pipes and rigs are also subject to leaks and spills (see the boxed text, p211). In addition, the wakes of shipping traffic wear away the delicate edges of the canals.

Miles of bird refuges – home to more than half of North America's bird species, as well as freshwater homes to Louisiana's treasured crawfish – are disappearing. Cajun fishermen who maintained a unique lifestyle for generations are vanishing with the ecosystem that once housed them. For New Orleans, the loss of these wetlands makes the city more vulnerable to hurricanes, as the diminishing land buffer enables hurricanes to maintain full strength nearer to the city. For similar reasons, New Orleans will become more vulnerable to storm surges like the one that followed Katrina.

We want to finish this chapter on an upbeat note, but the loss of Louisiana's coast has not only continued unabated since our last edition – it's gotten worse. This is a conservative state where environmental protection laws are unpopular, especially when the affected industries are lucrative oil and shipping. Maybe we'll have better news in the next edition, but in the meantime, we advise you to see the Louisiana wetlands south of New Orleans now. They may well be underwater in a generation.

If you're still interested in the nitty gritty government management of the enormous levee and canal system that keeps southeast Louisiana from becoming the Northwest Gulf of Mexico, check out the Southeast Louisiana Flood Protection Authority – East (www.slfpae.com).

Survival Guide

Transportation

GETTING TO NEW ORLEANS

The majority of travelers to New Orleans will arrive by air, landing in Louis Armstrong New Orleans International Airport (MSY) in Kenner, about 13 miles west of downtown. The airport was originally named for aviator John Moisant and was known as Moisant Stock Yards, hence the IATA code.

Another option is to fly into Baton Rouge (BTR), 89 miles north of the city; or Gulfport-Biloxi (GPT), Mississippi, 77 miles east. Neither of these options is as convenient as a direct flight to New Orleans, but they may be cheaper during big events such as Mardi Gras or Jazz Fest. The problem is getting from these outer airports to New Orleans.

Many travelers drive or bus to New Orleans, which is located at the crossroads of several major highways. Train travel to New Orleans is easy; the city is served by three Amtrak lines. Finally, while New Orleans is the Queen of the Mississippi, there are no riverboats – just ferries arriving from adjacent suburbs.

Louis Armstrong New Orleans International Airport

New Orleans' **airport** (MSY; ☑464-0831; www.flymsy.com) is in the suburb of Kenner, 13 miles (about a 30-minute drive) west of the city along the I-10 freeway. It's a small airport with only two terminals, so it's pretty easy to get around. It's not a major hub, so you'll likely connect here through Atlanta, Houston, Dallas, Chicago or Charlotte.

Shuttle

Most visitors take the **Airport Shuttle** (☑522-3500; www.airportshuttleneworleans.com; one-way/roundtrip $20/38) to and from the airport. It's a frequent service between the airport and downtown hotels, although it can be time-consuming, especially if your hotel is the last stop. At the airport, buy tickets from agencies in the baggage-claim area. For your return to the airport, call a day ahead to arrange for a pickup, which you should schedule at least two hours prior to your flight's departure.

Taxi

A taxi ride downtown costs a flat rate of $33 for one passenger or $14 per passenger for two or more passengers. No more than four passengers are allowed in a single cab.

Car

At the time of writing, car rental agencies were located about 10 minutes from the airport, connected via a free shuttle. Keep this in mind when returning your vehicle. The quickest drive between the airport and

---

CLIMATE CHANGE & TRAVEL

Every form of transport that relies on carbon-based fuel generates CO_2, the main cause of human-induced climate change. Modern travel is dependent on airplanes, which might use less fuel per kilometer per person than most cars but travel much greater distances. The altitude at which aircraft emit gases (including CO_2) and particles also contributes to their climate change impact. Many websites offer 'carbon calculators' that allow people to estimate the carbon emissions generated by their journey and, for those who wish to do so, to offset the impact of the greenhouse gases emitted with contributions to portfolios of climate-friendly initiatives throughout the world. Lonely Planet offsets the carbon footprint of all staff and author travel.

downtown is the I-10. If you're coming from downtown on I-10, take exit 223 for the airport; going to downtown, take exit 234, as the Louisiana Superdome looms before you. Traffic can get very clogged near the Huey Long Bridge.

Bus

If your baggage is not too unwieldy and you're in no hurry, **Jefferson Transit** (www.jeffersontransit.org) offers the cheapest ride downtown aboard its E2 Airport Downtown Express ($2; ⊘5am-9pm Mon-Fri, 6:30am-9pm Sat, 7:30am-9pm Sun). The ride to New Orleans follows city streets, pausing for stops approximately every two blocks. On weekdays the bus goes all the way to Tulane and Loyola Ave, at the edge of downtown and the French Quarter; on weekends it will only get you as far as the corner of Tulane St and Carrollton Ave. From there it's a cheap cab ride to the French Quarter, or you can transfer to a **Regional Transit Authority** (RTA; ☑248-3900; www.norta.com) bus. Bus 27 will get you to St Charles Ave in the Garden District; bus 39 follows Tulane Ave to Canal St, just outside the French Quarter.

Other Airports

It's worth checking out these airports if you plan to rent a car, but probably not otherwise. **Baton Rouge Metropolitan Airport** (BTR; ☑225-355-0333; www.flybtr.com) is 89 miles (and minutes) north of town. **Tiger Airport Shuttle** (☑225-333-8167; www.flybtr.com) provides direct service to downtown New Orleans for $135. **Gulfport-Biloxi International Airport** (BTR; ☑228-863-5951; www.flygpt.com) is about 77 miles/80 minutes east of New Orleans; besides car rentals, the only

ground transportation is taxis, which will cost around $200 to New Orleans.

Greyhound

Greyhound (☑800-231-2222, 525-6075; www.greyhound.com; ⊘5:15am-8:30pm) buses arrive and depart at the **New Orleans Union Passenger Terminal** (Map p244; 1001 Loyola Ave), which is also known as Union Station. It's seven blocks upriver from Canal St. Greyhound regularly connects to Lafayette, Opelousas and Baton Rouge, plus Clarksdale, MS, and Memphis, TN, en route to essentially every city in the USA.

Amtrak

Three **Amtrak** (☑800-872-7245) trains serve New Orleans at the **New Orleans Union Passenger Terminal** (☑528-1610; 1001 Loyola Ave). The *City of New Orleans* train runs to Memphis, TN, Jackson, MS, and Chicago, IL. Alternatively, the *Crescent Route* serves Birmingham, AL, Atlanta, GA, Washington, DC, and New York City. The *Sunset Limited* route between Los Angeles, CA, and Miami, FL, also passes through New Orleans.

GETTING AROUND NEW ORLEANS

Bicycle

On the positive side of the ledger for riders, New Orleans is flat and relatively compact. On the negative side are heavy traffic, potholes and bad neighborhoods, which make fat tires a near necessity. Oppressive summer heat and humidity also discourage a lot of bicyclists.

All state-operated ferries offer free transportation for bikes. Bicyclists board

ahead of cars by walking down the left lane of the ramp to the swinging gate. You must wait for the cars to exit before leaving. Bicycles aren't allowed on streetcars or buses.

Rental

➡ **Bicycle Michael's** (☑945-9505; www.bicyclemichaels.com; 622 Frenchmen St, Marigny; per day $35)

➡ **The American Bicycle Rental Co** (☑866-293-4037; www.amebrc.com; 317 Burgundy St; per day $35)

➡ **Bike NOLA** (☑858-2273; www.bikenola.net; 1209 Decatur St; per hr $6, per day $30)

Boat

Ferry

The cheapest way to cruise the Mississippi River is aboard one of the state-run ferries. The most popular line, the Canal St Ferry, operates between Canal St and the West Bank community of Algiers from 6am to midnight daily. Another ferry stops at Jackson Ave, near the Irish Channel, and leads to the suburb of Gretna. The ferries are free for pedestrians and cyclists, and just $1 for vehicles.

Riverboat

Visitors to New Orleans during Mark Twain's time arrived by boat via the Mississippi River but for now the days of paddle steamboats plying the Big Muddy are over. Majestic America, which operated paddleboat cruises for years on the historic *Delta Queen,* has ceased operations. Unless someone buys up the business, overnight cruises on the Mississippi are a thing of the past. If you're into a short, tourist-oriented sightseeing cruise, short voyage riverboats still ply the river (p53).

Bus

The **Regional Transit Authority** (RTA; ☑248-3900; www.norta.com) offers bus and streetcar services. Fares are $1.25, plus 25¢ for a transfer. Service is decent, but we wouldn't recommend relying solely on public transport during a New Orleans visit.

No buses run through the heart of the French Quarter, so most visitors only use them when venturing Uptown or out to City Park.

Car & Motorcycle

Driving

A car is not a bad thing to have in New Orleans. Having one makes it much easier to fully experience the entire city, from Faubourg Marigny up to Riverbend, and out along Esplanade Ave. If you are planning to spend most of your time in the French Quarter, though, don't bother with a car. You'll just end up wasting money on parking.

Many city streets, even in posh Uptown, are in an atrocious state, and tires have accordingly short life spans. Tricky left turns through very common four-way intersections, and the intersections themselves, can be a hazard. While stop signs are set out in residential areas, not everyone obeys them. New Orleanian friendliness can be annoying if people stop their cars in the middle of a narrow street to chat with someone – every New Orleans driver has a story about this incident. Finally, New Orleans drivers are generally terrible turn signalers.

Visitors from abroad may find it wise to back up their national driver's license with an International Driving Permit, available from their local automobile club.

Parking

Downtown on-street parking is typically for short-term use only. In some parts of town, look for the solar-powered parking meters. One meter often serves an entire block, so don't assume parking is free just because there's no meter on the curb immediately beside where you park. There are also all kinds of restrictions for street cleaning that limit when you can park on certain streets. Be sure to read all parking signs before leaving your car. Enforcement is particularly efficient in the French Quarter, the CBD and the Warehouse District.

Vehicles parked illegally are frequently towed in the Quarter. If you park your car in a driveway, within 20ft of a corner or crosswalk, within 15ft of a fire hydrant or on a street-sweeping day, you will need to pay about $150 (cash or credit card) to retrieve your car from the **Auto Pound** (☑658-7451; 1415 N Claiborne Ave).

Free street parking is available on many blocks in the Lower Quarter (or try along Esplanade Ave). Otherwise, there are plenty of commercial lots scattered through downtown and the French Quarter; expect to pay around $20 to $30 per day, and keep in mind rates skyrocket at night.

Outside the Quarter and Downtown, parking is a cinch. There's plenty of street parking and not many restrictions. With that said, be careful of street parking during Mardi Gras and Jazz Fest, when cops are liable to ticket you for even very minor infractions.

Rental

Most big car-rental companies are found in New Orleans. There's a glut at the airport, but they're located slightly away from the terminal, so factor in the free 10-minute shuttle ride from the rental office to the airport if flying. Typically you must be at least 25 years of age and have a major credit card, as well as a valid driver's license, to rent a car.

Rates go up and availability lessens during special events or large conventions. A compact car typically costs $30 to $40 a day or $150 to $200 a week. On top of that, there is a 13.75% tax and an optional loss/damage waiver (LDW; insurance), usually charged by the day. US citizens who already have auto insurance are probably covered, but should check with their insurance company first.

Agencies in or near the downtown area include the following:

Avis (☑523-4317, 800-331-1212; 1317 Canal St)

Budget Rent-a-Car (☑565-5600, 800-527-0700; 1317 Canal St)

Hertz (☑568-1645, 800-654-3131; 901 Convention Center Blvd)

Streetcar

Streetcars (aka trolleys or trams) have made a comeback in New Orleans, with three lines serving key routes in the city. They are run by **Regional Transit Authority** (RTA; 248-3900; www.norta.com). Fares are $1.25 – have exact change, or purchase a Jazzy Pass (one-/three-/31-day unlimited ride $3/9/55), which is also good on buses. Jazzy Passes can be purchased from streetcar conductors, bus drivers, in Walgreens drugstores and at various hotels. Streetcars run every 15 to 30 minutes, leaning towards the 30-minute end the later at night it gets.

Canal Streetcar Lines

Two slightly different lines follow Canal St to Mid-City. Both run from the French Market and up the levee before heading up Canal St. The Cemeteries line (from 5am to 3am) goes to City Park Ave. More useful for tourists is the City Park line (from 7am to midnight), which heads up a spur on N Carrollton Ave, ending up at the Esplanade Ave entrance to City Park. The cars run from 6am to 11pm.

Riverfront Streetcar Line

This two-mile route (from 7:30am to 10:15pm) runs between the French Market, in the lower end of the French Quarter near Esplanade Ave, and the upriver Convention Center, crossing Canal St on the way.

St Charles Ave Streetcar Line

When the St Charles Ave route opened as the New Orleans & Carrollton Railroad in 1835, it was the nation's second horse-drawn streetcar line. Now it is one of the few streetcars in the US to have survived the automobile era, running from Carrollton and Claiborne, down Carrollton to St Charles, then via St Charles Ave to Canal & Carondelet (it runs 24 hours).

Taxi

If you're traveling alone or at night, taxis are recommended. **United Cab** (522-9771) is the biggest and most reliable company in New Orleans. You might have to call for a pickup, unless you are in a central part of the French Quarter, where it is relatively easy to flag down a passing cab.

Fares within the city start with a $3.50 flag-fall charge for one passenger (plus $1 for each additional passenger). From there it's $2 per mile. New Orleans is small, so don't expect fares to top $20. Don't forget to tip your driver 10% to 15%.

TOURS

Friends of the Cabildo (523-3939; www.friendsofthecabildo.org) conducts excellent historical and cultural tours of the French Quarter (adult/child $15/10) leaving from Jackson Sq. For a more hokey if harrowing experience, **Haunted History Tours** (861-2727; www.hauntedhistorytours.com) are a little cheesy and a lot of fun, and a good way of learning about the city's supernatural side. There are all sorts of options, from vampire tours to romps through city cemeteries that cost around $20. Our favorite bike tours in New Orleans are operated by Confederacy of Cruisers (p88). For more tours, see p54.

Directory A–Z

Business Hours

New Orleans maintains business hours similar to much of the rest of the USA, except when it comes to bars. Stores tend to stay open from around 10am to 7pm or 8pm, and restaurant hours are generally from 10am or 11am to 11pm (sometimes with a break from 2pm to 5pm). Bars tend to open at around 5pm and stay open till the last customer leaves, although official closing times are something like 2am on weekdays and 3am or 4am on weekends. Restaurants are often closed on Sunday or Monday, sometimes both.

Children

Stuffed with zoos, museums, riverboat cruises and the like, New Orleans is great for kids. Wee ones should rarely feel left out of the fun that defines this town. See p24 for some top kid-friendly suggestions.

Babysitting

Most major hotels can offer on-site babysitting arrangements. Smaller hotels are also familiar with parents' needs and can usually provide the name of recommended childminding services. It's worth inquiring about such arrangements when you make your hotel reservations.

Accent on Children's Arrangements (Map p244; ☑800-539-1227; www.accentoca .com; Ste 303, 615 Baronne St) is a service that takes the kids off your hands and engages them in organized activities. This might include a child-oriented tour of the city or educational entertainment. Services can be customized for varying age groups and to meet you and your children's personal needs.

Climate

New Orleans' climate is fairly simple: it's hot and humid in the summer, and not so hot and humid the rest of the year. The humidity is enough to drive some locals out of town for lengthy summer vacations in more pleasant climes, and to keep tourists away. In December temperatures can fluctuate from 40°F (4°C) to 70°F (21°C). Snowfall is extremely rare. The wettest months are July and August and the driest month is October.

Hurricanes can come off the Gulf of Mexico anytime from June to December, though the peak season is in August and September.

Courses

The **New Orleans School of Cooking** (Map p238; ☑620-9464; 800-237-4841; www.new orleansschoolofcooking.com; 524 St Louis St) is a popular and pretty awesome way to learn the ins and outs of one of this city's great exports – its culinary tradition. There's a good variety of courses on offer, but besides the $29 short-cooking demonstration, you'll need a group of eight or more.

Customs Regulations

US Customs (www.customs .gov) allows each person over the age of 21 years to bring 1L of liquor and 200 cigarettes duty-free into the USA. Non-US citizens are allowed to enter the USA with $100 worth of gifts from abroad. There are restrictions on bringing fresh fruit and flowers into the country and there is a strict quarantine on animals. If you are carrying more than $10,000 in US and foreign cash, traveler's checks, money orders or the like, you need to declare the excess amount. There is no legal restriction on the amount that may be imported, but undeclared sums in excess of $10,000 may be subject to confiscation.

Electricity

The electric current in the USA is 110V to 115V, 60Hz AC. Outlets may be suited for flat two-prong or three-prong grounded plugs. If your appliance is made for another electrical system, you will need a transformer or adapter; if you didn't bring one along, buy one at any consumer electronics store (there are several around town).

120V/60Hz

120V/60Hz

Embassies

There aren't any embassies in New Orleans, but several countries have consulates and honorary consuls in town. Canada's nearest consulate is in Miami, FL.

French Consulate (Map p244; ☑569-2870; www.consul france-nouvelleorleans.org; 1340 Poydras St)

PRACTICALITIES

Internet Access
Many hotels offer wi-fi and cable internet access. Wi-fi is available in almost every coffee shop in town, and all branches of the New Orleans public library.

Newspapers
Gambit (www.bestofneworleans.com) Once a week.

The Times-Picayune (www.nola.com) Three times a week.

New Orleans Magazine (www.myneworleans.com/New-Orleans-Magazine) Once a month.

The Lens (http://thelensnola.org) Investigative journalism, online only.

Radio
88.3 WRBH Reading radio for the blind

90.7 WWOZ Louisiana music and community radio

91.3 WWNO NPR (National Public Radio)

91.5 WTUL Tulane Radio

93.3 WQUE Hip-hop

95.7 WKBU Classic rock

Smoking
You can't smoke in restaurants, but you can light up in bars and the bar areas of restaurants. That said, some bars ban smoking. Many hotels offer smoking rooms, but most smaller guesthouses and B&Bs do not.

Time
New Orleans Standard Time is six hours behind GMT/UTC. In US terms, that puts it one hour behind the East Coast and two hours ahead of the West Coast. In early April the clocks move ahead one hour for Daylight Saving Time; clocks move back one hour in October.

Tipping
Tipping is not really optional. In bars and restaurants the waitstaff are paid minimal wages and rely on tips for their livelihoods. The service has to be absolutely appalling before you consider not tipping. Tip at least 15% of the bill or 20% if the service is good. You needn't tip at fast-food restaurants or self-serve cafeterias.

Taxi drivers expect a 15% tip. If you stay at a top-end hotel, tipping is so common you might get tennis elbow from reaching for your wallet. Hotel porters who carry bags a long way expect $3 to $5, or $1 per bag; smaller services (holding the taxi door open for you) might justify only $1. Valet parking is worth about $2, and is given when your car is returned to you.

UK Honorary Consul (Map p244; ☎524-4180; 10th fl, 321 St Charles Ave)

Emergency

Ambulance ☎911

Fire ☎911

Police (emergency) ☎911

Police (nonemergency) ☎658-4000

Rape Crisis Line ☎482-9922, 888-411-1333

Gay & Lesbian Travelers

The gay community in New Orleans is most visible in the French Quarter, to the lakeside of Bourbon St. While there is a strong gay nightlife scene in the city, there is a lot of integration of the straight and gay worlds. This especially applies to live music shows, which are an integral component of going out in New Orleans. Gays are present but keep a lower profile in Faubourg Marigny, Bywater and elsewhere in town. For gay visitors, finding a place to stay, eat or party in New Orleans will not be a problem. See p39 for listings.

Southern Decadence (p22) is a gay festival that draws a huge crowd to the Quarter in late August or early September. Halloween and Mardi Gras also have a strong gay component in New Orleans.

The **Faubourg Marigny Book Store** (Map p242; ☎943-9875; 600 Frenchmen St) is the South's oldest gay bookstore and is a good place to learn about the local scene. Several websites provide information for the gay community in New Orleans, as well as gay travelers.

Ambush Mag (www.ambush mag.com)

Gay New Orleans (www.gay neworleans.com)

Legal Matters

Although it may seem that anything goes, even New Orleans has its limits. Common tourist-related offenses include underage drinking, drinking outdoors from a bottle rather than a plastic go cup, teen curfew violations and (most commonly) flaunting of private parts.

For people aged 21 years or more, the legal blood-alcohol limit for driving in Louisiana is 0.08%; however, you can be cited for driving while impaired even when your blood-alcohol content is lower.

The legal drinking age is 21. Anyone under the age of 18 on the streets after 11pm is violating the city's curfew. Most bars will offer your drink in a plastic cup, so accept it if you're going to wander off with your drink. Bourbon St flashers rarely get in serious trouble for exposing their private parts, but repeatedly doing so in front of the cops is asking for trouble. If you aren't flashing, don't grope those who are. That's a no-no.

The legal age for gambling is also 21, and businesses with gaming devices (usually video poker machines) out in the open are closed to minors. Even cafes with gaming devices are off-limits to minors, unless the games are contained within private rooms or booths.

Medical Services

Excellent medical care is readily available, but the need for medical insurance when visiting anywhere in the USA cannot be over-emphasized. Doctors often expect payment on the spot for services rendered, after which your insurance company may reimburse you. US citizens should check with their insurer before leaving home to see what conditions are covered in their policy.

If you need immediate medical attention and you are in your hotel, your first call should be to the front desk. Some of the larger hotels have agreements with on-call doctors who can make house calls if necessary. In really urgent situations, you can call an **ambulance** (☎911), which will deliver you to a hospital emergency room.

If you can get to an emergency room, your best bet is the **Tulane University Medical Center** (Map p250; ☎988-5263; 1415 Tulane Ave; ☺24hr), located in the CBD.

Pharmacies

Nonprescription medications and contraceptives can be purchased in the pharmacy section of drugstores such as **Walgreens** (☎525-7263; 619 Decatur St) in the French Quarter. Other branches, and pharmacies such as Rite-Aid and Woolworth, are common around the city.

Money

There are three straightforward ways to handle money in the USA: cash, US-dollar traveler's checks and credit or bank cards, which can be used to withdraw cash from the many automatic teller machines (ATMs) across the country. US dollars are the only accepted currency in New Orleans.

ATMs

With a Visa card, Master-Card or a bank card affiliated with the Plus or Cirrus networks you can easily obtain cash from ATMs all over New Orleans.

Changing Money

Most major currencies and leading brands of traveler's checks are easily exchanged in New Orleans. You will also find various independent exchange bureaus. When you first arrive at the airport terminal you can change money at **TravelEx America Business Center** (465-9647; 6am-5pm), which you'll find in the ticket lobby. TravelEx charges a sliding service fee. It also offers travel insurance, photocopies, fax services, emergency cash and wire money transfers. The Money Gram section of the office closes at 4:30pm.

Nearby, **Whitney National Bank** (8:30am-3pm Mon-Thu, 8:30am-5:30pm Fri) also changes money, charging a flat $5 service fee. Other services offered here include cash advances on credit cards, traveler's checks, money orders and ATMs. Since the exchange counters are only feet apart, get quotes from both.

Better exchange rates are generally available at banks in the CBD. Typical opening hours are 10am to 5pm Monday to Thursday, 10am to 6pm Friday and 10am to 1pm Saturday. The main office of **Whitney National Bank** (228 St Charles Ave) buys and sells foreign currency.

Credit & Debit Cards

Major credit cards are widely accepted by car-rental agencies and most hotels, restaurants, gas stations, shops and larger grocery stores. Many smaller restaurants and bars are cash-only. Many recreational and tourist activities can also be paid for by credit card. The most commonly accepted cards are Visa, MasterCard and American Express. Discover and Diners Club cards are also accepted by a large number of businesses.

Traveler's Checks

ATMs and debit cards have nearly rendered traveler's checks obsolete, but if your bank isn't affiliated with one of the common bank networks such as Cirrus or Plus, the old-fashioned way can be pretty handy. Some younger waitstaff and shop clerks might be unsure how to react to them, though.

They're still virtually as good as cash in the USA, and they can be replaced if lost or stolen. Both AmEx and Thomas Cook, two well-known issuers of traveler's checks, have efficient replacement policies.

You'll save yourself trouble and expense if you buy traveler's checks in US dollars.

Post

New Orleans' **main post office** (Map p244; 589-1135; 701 Loyola Ave) is near City Hall. There are smaller branches throughout the city, including the Airport Mail Center in the passenger terminal; inside the **World Trade Center** (2 Canal St); and in the CBD at **Lafayette Square** (610 S Maestri Place). Post offices are generally open 8:30am to 4:30pm Monday to Friday and 8:30am to noon Saturday.

There are lots of independent postal shops as well, including the **Royal Mail Service** (Map p238; 522-8523; 828 Royal St) and the **French Quarter Postal Emporium** (Map p238; 525-6651; 1000 Bourbon St; 9am-6pm Mon-Fri, 10am-3pm Sat). These shops will send letters and packages at the same rates as the post office.

Postal Rates

Postal rates have a tendency to increase frequently, but at the time of writing the rates were 44¢ for 1st-class mail within the USA and 24¢ for postcards.

It costs 75¢ to send a 1oz letter to Canada, 79¢ to Mexico and 98¢ to other countries.

The **US Postal Service** (800-222-1811; www.usps.gov) also offers a Priority Mail service, which delivers your letter or package anywhere in the USA in two days or less. The cost is $4.95 for 1lb. For heavier items, rates differ according to the distance mailed. Overnight Express Mail starts at $15.

Receiving Mail

If you don't want to receive mail at your hotel, you can have mail sent to you at the main post office, marked c/o General Delivery, New Orleans, LA 70112. General Delivery is US terminology for what is known as poste restante internationally. General Delivery mail is only held for 30 days. It's not advisable to try to have mail sent to other post offices in New Orleans.

Sending Mail

If you have the correct postage, you can drop your mail into any blue mailbox. However, to send a package that weighs 1lb or more, you must take it to a post office or postal shop.

Public Holidays

Note that when national holidays fall on a weekend, they are often celebrated on the nearest Friday or Monday so that everyone enjoys a three-day weekend. For further information on New Orleans' holidays and festivals, see p20. The following are all national holidays.

New Year's Day January 1
Presidents' Day Third Monday in February
Memorial Day Last Monday in May
Independence Day July 4
Labor Day First Monday in September
Columbus Day Second Monday in October
Veterans Day November 11
Thanksgiving Fourth Thursday in November

Safety

New Orleans has an atrocious crime rate, and as of this writing, the worst murder rate in the country. The vast majority of violent crime occurs between parties who already know each other, but tourists are occasionally targeted.

Exercise the caution you would in any US city. The possibility of getting mugged is something to consider even in areas you'd think are safe (eg the Garden District). Solo pedestrians are targeted more often than people walking in groups, and daytime is a better time to be out on foot than nighttime. Avoid entering secluded areas such as cemeteries alone.

Large crowds typically make the French Quarter a secure around-the-clock realm for the visitor. However, if your hotel or vehicle is on the margins of the Quarter, you might want to take a taxi back at night. The CBD and Warehouse District have plenty of activity during weekdays, but they're relatively deserted at night and on weekends. The B&Bs along Esplanade Ridge are close enough to troubled neighborhoods to call for caution at night. In the Quarter, street hustlers frequently approach tourists. Walk away.

Pedestrians crossing the street do not have the right of way and motorists (unless they are from out of state) will not yield. Whether on foot or in a car, be wary before entering an intersection, as New Orleans drivers are notorious for running yellow and even red lights.

To see where crime is occurring before you visit, log on to www.crimemapping .com/map/la/neworleans.

Tax & Refunds

New Orleans' 9% sales tax is tacked onto virtually everything, including meals, groceries and car rentals. For accommodations, room and occupancy taxes add an additional 12% to your bill plus $1 to $3 per person, depending on the size of the hotel.

Some merchants in Louisiana participate in a program called **Louisiana Tax Free Shopping** (☑467-0723; www.louisianataxfree .com). Look for the snazzy red-and-blue 'Tax Free' logo

in the window or on the sign of the store. Usually these stores specialize in the kinds of impulse purchases people are likely to make while on vacation. In these stores, present a passport to verify you are not a US citizen and request a voucher as you make your purchase. Reimbursement centers are located in the **Downtown Refund Center** (Map p244; ☑568-3605; Riverwalk Mall; ⊙9:30am-4:30pm Mon-Sat, from 10am Sun) and the main lobby of **Louis Armstrong Airport** (☑467-0723; ⊙8:30am-4:30pm Mon-Fri, 9am-1pm Sat & Sun).

Telephone

New Orleans telephones are run by BellSouth. The **Yellow Pages** (www.yellowpages.com) has business listings. New Orleans' area code is ☑504, which includes Thibodaux and the surrounding area. Baton Rouge and surrounds use the area code ☑225. Area code ☑318 applies to the northern part of the state.

When dialing another area code, you must dial ☑1 before the area code. For example, to call a Baton Rouge number from New Orleans, begin by dialing ☑1-225. At pay phones, local calls start at 50¢, but long-distance charges apply to 'nonlocal' calls even within the same area code – to Thibodaux, for example – and costs rapidly increase once you dial another area code. Hotel telephones often have heavy surcharges.

Toll-free numbers start with ☑1-800 or ☑1-888 and allow you to call free within the USA. These numbers are commonly offered by car-rental operators, large hotels and the like. (Listings in this book omit the '1,' eg ☑800-000-0000.) Dial ☑411 for local directory assistance, or ☑1 + area code + 555-1212 for long-distance directory information; dial ☑1-800-555-1212 for toll-

free number information. Dial ☑0 for the operator.

If you're calling from abroad, the international country code for the USA (and Canada) is ☑1.

To make an international call from New Orleans, dial ☑011 + country code + area code (dropping the leading 0) + number. For calls to Canada, there's no need to dial the international access code ☑011. For international operator assistance, dial ☑00.

Cell Phones

The USA uses a variety of cell (mobile) phone systems, only one of which is compatible with systems used outside North America: the Global System for Mobile telephones (GSM), which is becoming more commonly available worldwide. Many popular phone services, including T-Mobile, Vodafone and Orange, offer GSM service. Check with your local provider to determine whether your phone will work in New Orleans.

Fax

Besides hotel fax machines, services in the French Quarter include **French Quarter Postal Emporium** (Map p238; ☑525-6651; fax 525-6652; 1000 Bourbon St; ⊙9am-6pm Mon-Fri, 10am-3pm Sat), at St Philip St. In the CBD there is a **Kinko's FedEx Office Center** (Map p244; ☑654-1057; fax 525-6272; 555 Canal St; ⊙7am-7pm Mon-Fri).

Phonecards

Phonecards are readily sold at newsstands and pharmacies. They save you the trouble of feeding coins into pay phones, and are often more economical as well.

Toilets

A recording by Benny Grunch, 'Ain't No Place to Pee on Mardi Gras Day,' summarizes the situation in the French Quarter. While tour guides delight in describing the unsanitary waste-disposal practices of the old Creole days, the stench arising from back alleys is actually more recent in origin.

Public rest rooms can be found in the Jackson Brewery mall (Map p238) and in the French Market (Map p238). Larger hotels often have accessible rest rooms off the lobby, usually near the elevators and pay phones.

Tourist Information

Right next to popular Jackson Sq in the heart of the Quarter, the **New Orleans Welcome Center** (Map p238; 529 St Ann St; ☺9am-5pm), in the lower Pontalba Building, offers maps, listings of upcoming events and a variety of brochures for sights, restaurants and hotels. The helpful staff can help you find accommodations in a pinch, answer questions and offer advice about New Orleans.

Information kiosks scattered through main tourist areas offer most of the same brochures as the Welcome Center, but their staff tend to be less knowledgeable.

Information on Louisiana-wide tourism can be obtained through the mail from **Louisiana Office of Tourism** (☎342-8119, 800-414-8626; www.louisianatravel.com; PO Box 94291, Baton Rouge, LA, 70804).

Travelers with Disabilities

New Orleans is somewhat lax in this department. Sidewalk curbs rarely have ramps, and many historic public buildings and hotels are not equipped to meet the needs of wheelchair-users. Modern hotels adhere to standards established by the federal Americans with Disabilities Act, with ramps, elevators and accessible bathrooms. The St Charles Avenue streetcar is now compliant

with the Americans With Disabilities Act. **Regional Transit Authority** (RTA; ☎248-3900; www.norta.com) buses offer a lift service; for information about paratransit service (alternate transportation for those who can't ride regular buses), call the RTA Paratransit Customer Service on ☎827-7433 or visit the website. The Riverfront streetcar line features braille kiosks, platform ramps and wide doors that allow anyone to board easily. While the old cars continue to be used on the Canal St line, wheelchair accessibility will not be available there either.

Visas

A passport with an official visa is required for most visitors to the USA; contact the US embassy or consulate in your home country for more information on specific requirements. Visitors between the ages of 14 and 79 have to be interviewed before a visa is granted, and all applicants must pay fees that stand at $131 (at the time of writing). You'll also have to prove you're not trying to stay in the USA permanently. The US Department of State has useful and up-to-date visa information online at http://travel.state.gov/visa.

If you're staying for 90 days or less you may qualify for the Visa Waiver Program (VWP); at the time of writing, citizens of roughly three dozen countries were eligible. The US Department of State provides useful and up-to-date online information on visa requirements and the VWP at http://travel.state.gov/visa.

Visa extensions are handled by **US Citizenship & Immigration Services** (☎800-375-5283; www.uscis.gov; Metairie Centre, Suite 300, 2424 Edenborn Avenue, Metairie, LA); it's 8.5 miles northwest of the French Quarter in Metairie.

Women Travelers

Intoxicated bands of men in the Quarter and along parade routes are a particular nuisance. Otherwise respectable students and professionals can be transformed by New Orleans in ways not particularly flattering. Women in almost any attire are liable to receive lewd comments. More provocative outfits will lead to a continuous barrage of requests to 'show your tits.' (This occurs on any Friday or Saturday night, not just during Mardi Gras.) Many men assume that any woman wearing impressive strands of beads has acquired them by displaying herself on the street.

Any serious problems encountered should be reported to the **police** (☎911). Abuse hotlines are available, including a **Rape Crisis Hotline** (☎482-9922) as well as the **Metropolitan Center for Women & Children** (☎837-5400).

The New Orleans branch of **Planned Parenthood** (☎897-9200; www.plannedparenthood.org; 4018 Magazine St) provides health-care services for women, including pregnancy testing and birth-control counseling.

Work

Tourism puts butter on most people's bread in this town, and passers-through might score a low-paying job in a bar, restaurant or youth hostel. Overseas visitors must have the proper work visas in order to work in the USA.

Skills in construction, electricity or plumbing are particularly in demand for the foreseeable future. Show up in town with a truck full of tools and very likely you'll find work as an independent contractor.

You probably don't need a work visa to volunteer in the rebuilding effort. Some organizations, such as **Habitat For Humanity** (www.habitat.org), claim to have more workers than they need, but it can't hurt to check.

Glossary

banh mi – Vietnamese sandwiches of sliced pork, cucumber, cilantro and other lovelies; locally called a Vietnamese po'boy

beignet – a flat square of dough flash-fried to golden, puffy glory, dusted with powdered sugar and served scorching hot

boudin – a tasty Cajun sausage made with pork, pork liver, cooked rice and spices

bousillage – mud- and straw-filled walls supported by cypress timbers

briquette entre poteaux – a style of architecture common to French-colonial houses, where brick fills the spaces between vertical and diagonal posts

Cajun (cuisine) – the rustic cuisine of the countryside

calliope – an organ-like musical instrument fitted with steam whistles; historically played on showboats and in traveling fairs

Creole (cuisine) – the rich, refined cuisine of the city

étouffée – a Cajun or Creole stew of shellfish or chicken served over rice

Fais do do – a Cajun dance party

faubourgs – literally 'suburbs,' although neighborhoods is a more accurate translation in spirit

frottoir – a metal washboard-like instrument that's worn like armor and played with spoons

go cup – a plastic cup given to patrons in bars so they can take their drink with them when they leave

gris-gris – amulets or spell bags

jambalaya – hearty, rice-based dish with any combination of fowl, shellfish or meat (but usually includes ham)

krewes – a deliberate misspelling of 'crews'; organizations or groups of people that create floats and stage festivities during Mardi Gras

migas – scrambled eggs mixed with fried tortilla strips

mudbug – a term for crawfish

muffuletta – a round sesame-crusted loaf spread with a salty olive salad and layered with cheeses and deli meats

plaçage – a cultural institution whereby white men 'kept' light-skinned black women as their mistresses

po'boy – a large sandwich made on French bread and overstuffed with a variety of fillings

Santeria – a Puerto Rican religion related to voodoo

Sazerac – a potent whiskey drink that uses rye as its primary ingredient, with aromatic bitters (including the locally produced Peychaud's), a bit of sugar and a swish of absinthe

snowballs – shaved ice in a paper cup doused liberally with flavored syrup

tasso – a cured, smoked piece of ham

Vieux Carré – alternate term for French Quarter; literally 'Old Square'

zydeco – a style of local music that combines French tunes with Caribbean music and blues

Behind the Scenes

SEND US YOUR FEEDBACK

We love to hear from travelers – your comments keep us on our toes and help make our books better. Our well-traveled team reads every word on what you loved or loathed about this book. Although we cannot reply individually to postal submissions, we always guarantee that your feedback goes straight to the appropriate authors, in time for the next edition. Each person who sends us information is thanked in the next edition – and the most useful submissions are rewarded with a selection of digital PDF chapters.

Visit **lonelyplanet.com/contact** to submit your updates and suggestions or to ask for help. Our award-winning website also features inspirational travel stories, news and discussions.

Note: We may edit, reproduce and incorporate your comments in Lonely Planet products such as guidebooks, websites and digital products, so let us know if you don't want your comments reproduced or your name acknowledged. For a copy of our privacy policy visit lonelyplanet.com/privacy.

OUR READERS

Many thanks to the travelers who used the last edition and wrote to us with helpful hints, useful advice and interesting anecdotes:

Bryan Banek, Cathy Goldner, Ine Indesteege, Heather Monell, Azwa Petra and Ken Steyls.

AUTHOR THANKS

Adam Karlin

Thanks for the help and the lagniappe: the Jazzman Andrew Holbein, for many good trips to the pool; Dan Favre, my host and compadre; Trish Kelly for hugs and unfailing smiles; Mike Robertshaw and Nora Ellersten for unflagging support and good neighborliness; Zach Youngerman, my original guide; Robert Fogarty, for his passionate dedication to storytelling and New Orleans; Gerard Cox, a true patriot of the Crescent City; Ben Reese for his enthusiasm for the cause; Bryan Bailey – YYMR, all that needs to be said; mom and dad, for letting me be here (in so many ways); Rachel Houge, my rock, my fire, my river.

Amy C Balfour

Thank you Cat, Susie and the Lonely Planet team for top-notch editing and mapping. A po'boy and beer to master coordinator and King of All Dive Bars, Adam Karlin. Many, many thanks to those who shared the best of New Orleans and guided my research: Dan & Rozanne Whalen, Vanessa Williams, Melissa Smith, Ashley Graham, Rachel Boudreaux, Terry Vosbein, Jeff Kelsey, Ellen Featherstone, Rocco Calamusa and Nancy Eichler. And cheers to Mardi Gras partners-in-crime Beth, Christin and Melissa.

ACKNOWLEDGMENTS

Cover photograph: Tram, New Orleans. John Coletti/Alamy.

THIS BOOK

This 6th edition of Lonely Planet's *New Orleans* guidebook was researched and written by Adam Karlin and Amy C Balfour. The previous two editions were written by Adam Karlin and Lisa Dunford. This guidebook was commissioned in Lonely Planet's Oakland office, and produced by the following:

Commissioning Editors
Jennye Garibaldi, Catherine Craddock-Carrillo

Coordinating Editors
Susie Ashworth, Ross Taylor

Coordinating Cartographers Mark Griffiths, Jolyon Philcox

Coordinating Layout Designer Adrian Blackburn

Managing Editor Anna Metcalfe

Senior Editor Andi Jones

Managing Cartographers
Alison Lyall, Diana Von Holdt

Managing Layout Designer Jane Hart

Assisting Editor Sam Trafford

Assisting Cartographers
Valeska Canas, Alex Leung, Peter Shields

Assisting Layout Designer Wibowo Rusli

Cover Research Brice Gosnell

Internal Image Research
Nicholas Colicchia

Thanks to Lucy Birchley, Ryan Evans, Trent Paton, Julie Sheridan, Gerard Walker

NOTES

Index

Text on screen

DRINKING & NIGHTLIFE

New Orleans Maps

Map Legend

Sights
- Beach
- Buddhist
- Castle
- Christian
- Hindu
- Islamic
- Jewish
- Monument
- Museum/Gallery
- Ruin
- Winery/Vineyard
- Zoo
- Other Sight

Eating
- Eating

Drinking & Nightlife
- Drinking & Nightlife
- Cafe

Entertainment
- Entertainment

Shopping
- Shopping

Sleeping
- Sleeping
- Camping

Sports & Activities
- Diving/Snorkelling
- Canoeing/Kayaking
- Skiing
- Surfing
- Swimming/Pool
- Walking
- Windsurfing
- Other Sports & Activities

Information
- Post Office
- Tourist Information

Transport
- Airport
- Border Crossing
- Bus
- Cable Car/ Funicular
- Cycling
- Ferry
- Metro
- Monorail
- Parking
- S-Bahn
- Taxi
- Train/Railway
- Tram
- Tube Station
- U-Bahn
- Other Transport

Routes
- Tollway
- Freeway
- Primary
- Secondary
- Tertiary
- Lane
- Unsealed Road
- Plaza/Mall
- Steps
- Tunnel
- Pedestrian Overpass
- Walking Tour
- Walking Tour Detour
- Path

Boundaries
- International
- State/Province
- Disputed
- Regional/Suburb
- Marine Park
- Cliff
- Wall

Geographic
- Hut/Shelter
- Lighthouse
- Lookout
- Mountain/Volcano
- Oasis
- Park
- Pass
- Picnic Area
- Waterfall

Hydrography
- River/Creek
- Intermittent River
- Swamp/Mangrove
- Reef
- Canal
- Water
- Dry/Salt/ Intermittent Lake
- Glacier

Areas
- Beach/Desert
- Cemetery (Christian)
- Cemetery (Other)
- Park/Forest
- Sportsground
- Sight (Building)
- Top Sight (Building)

MAP INDEX

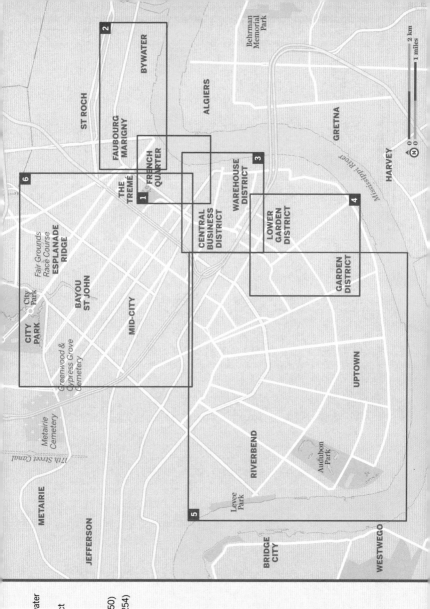

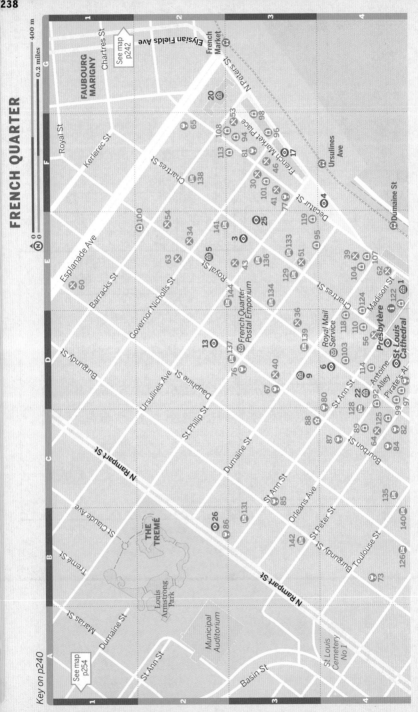

FRENCH QUARTER

Key on p240

See map p254

See map p242

FAUBOURG
MARIGNY

THE
TREMÉ

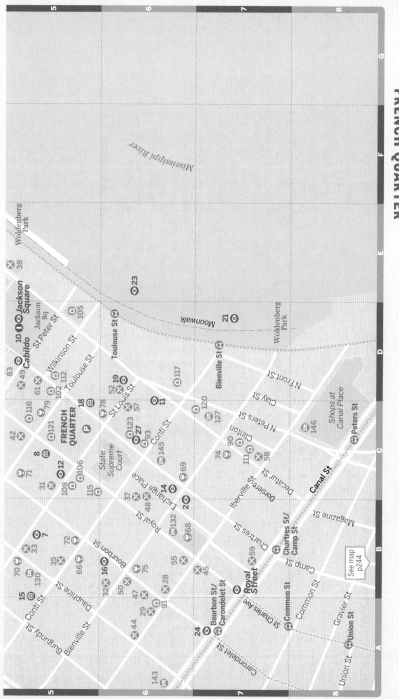

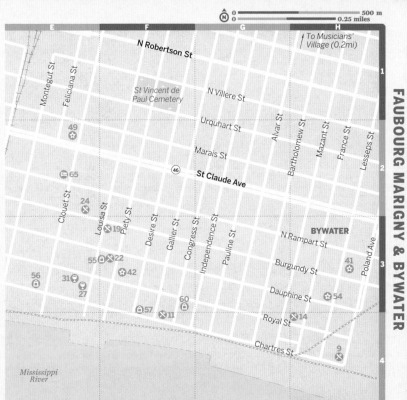

0   500 m
0   0.25 miles

To Musicians'
Village (0.2mi)

N Robertson St

St Vincent de
Paul Cemetery

N Villere St

Urquhart St

Marais St

St Claude Ave

BYWATER

N Rampart St

Burgundy St

Dauphine St

Royal St

Chartres St

Mississippi
River

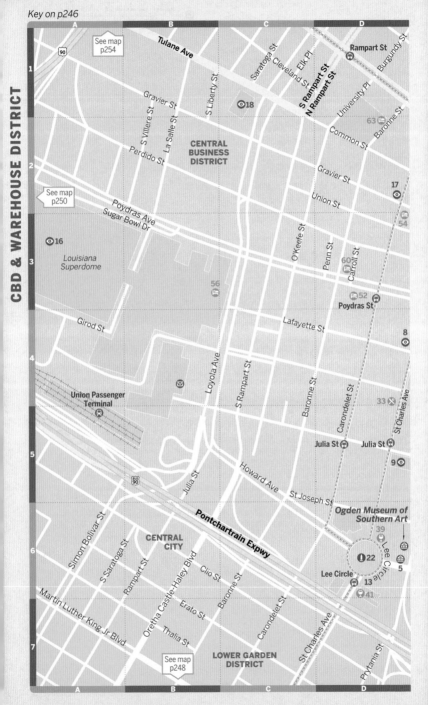

CBD & WAREHOUSE DISTRICT

See map p254

See map p250

See map p248

Tulane Ave

Rampart St

S Rampart St
N Rampart St

Burgundy St

University Pl

Baronne St

Common St

⊙18

CENTRAL
BUSINESS
DISTRICT

Gravier St

S Villere St

S Liberty St

La Salle St

Saratoga St

Cleveland St

Elk Pl

Perdido St

Gravier St

Union St

17 ⊙

54

⊙16

Louisiana
Superdome

O'Keefe St

Penn St

Carroll St

60

52 ⊙
Poydras St

Poydras Ave
Sugar Bowl Dr

56

Girod St

Lafayette St

8 ⊙

Loyola Ave

S Rampart St

Baronne St

Carondelet St

St Charles Ave

33 ⊗

Union Passenger
Terminal

Julia St ⊙ Julia St ⊙

9 ⊙

Julia St

Howard Ave

St Joseph St

Pontchartrain Expwy

Ogden Museum of
Southern Art

CENTRAL
CITY

39

Simon Bolivar St

S Saratoga St

Rampart St

Clio St

Baronne St

Carondelet St

Lee Circle

5

❶22

13
Lee Circle

Martin Luther King Jr Blvd

Oretha Castle Haley Blvd

Erato St

Thalia St

St Charles Ave

Prytania St

41

LOWER GARDEN
DISTRICT

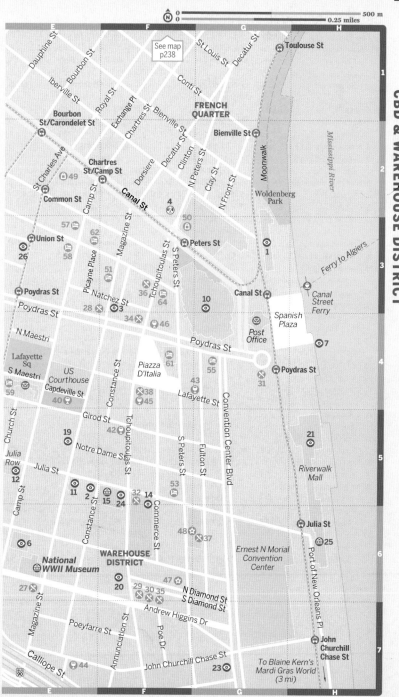

CBD & WAREHOUSE DISTRICT

0 — 500 m
0 — 0.25 miles

See map p238

FRENCH QUARTER

Bourbon St/Carondelet St

Chartres St/Camp St

Common St

Union St
26

Poydras St

Bienville St

Toulouse St

Canal St

Peters St

Mississippi River

Moonwalk

Woldenberg Park

Ferry to Algiers

Canal Street Ferry

Spanish Plaza

Post Office

Poydras St

Poydras St
31

Piazza D'Italia
61

Lafayette St

US Courthouse
Capdeville St
40

Lafayette Sq

Girod St

Notre Dame St
19

Julia St

Julia Row
12

National WWII Museum

WAREHOUSE DISTRICT

Convention Center Blvd

Riverwalk Mall

Julia St
25

Ernest N Morial Convention Center

Port of New Orleans Pl

John Churchill Chase St

To Blaine Kern's Mardi Gras World (3 mi)

N Diamond St
S Diamond St
Andrew Higgins Dr

Poeyfarre St

Calliope St
44

John Churchill Chase St
23

CBD & WAREHOUSE DISTRICT *Map on p244*

GARDEN, LOWER GARDEN & CENTRAL CITY Map on p248

GARDEN, LOWER GARDEN & CENTRAL CITY

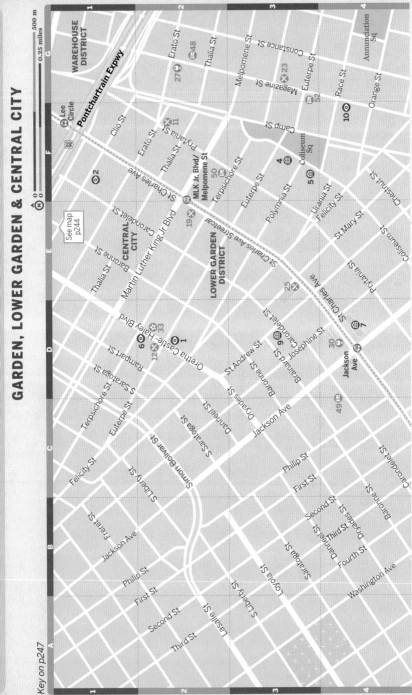

Key on p247

See map p244

Key on p252

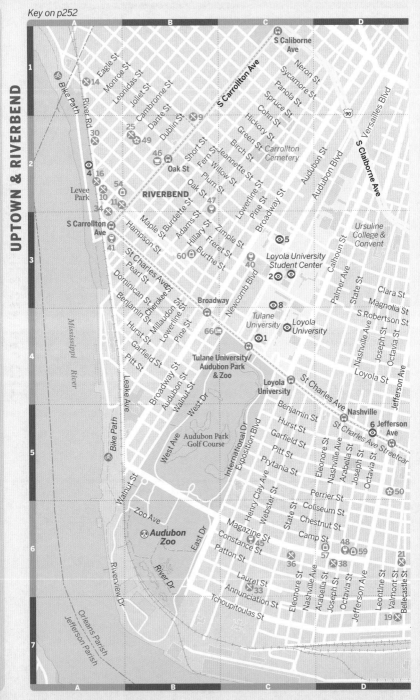

UPTOWN & RIVERBEND

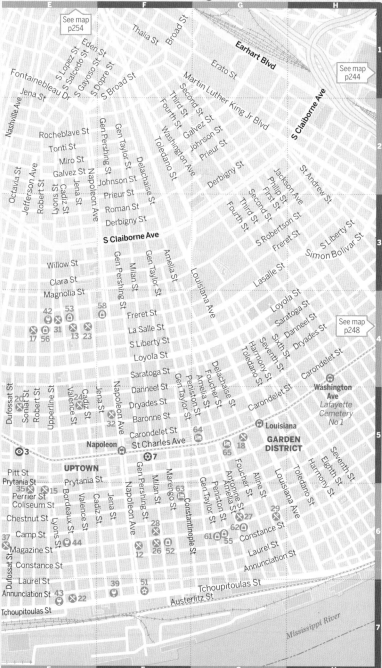

0   1 km
0   0.5 miles

See map p254

See map p244

See map p248

Thalia St
Broad St
Earhart Blvd
Erato St
Martin Luther King Jr Blvd
Fontainebleau Dr
Jena St
Nashville Ave
S Lopez St
Eden St
S Salcedo St
S Gayoso St
S Dopre St
S Broad St
Second St
Third St
Fourth St
Washington Ave
Toledano St
Galvez St
Johnson St
Prieur St
Derbigny St
S Claiborne Ave
Jackson Ave
Philip St
First St
Second St
Third St
Fourth St
St Andrew St
S Robertson St
Freret St
S Liberty St
Simon Bolivar St
Rocheblave St
Tonti St
Miro St
Galvez St
Jena St
Octavia St
Jefferson Ave
Robert St
Lyons St
Cadiz St
Napoleon Ave
Gen Pershing St
Gen Taylor St
Delachaise St
Johnson St
Prieur St
Roman St
Derbigny St
S Claiborne Ave
Willow St
Clara St
Magnolia St
Gen Pershing St
Gen Taylor St
Amelia St
Louisiana Ave
Lasalle St
Loyola St
Saratoga St
Danneel St
Dryades St
Carondelet St
42
53
58
Freret St
La Salle St
S Liberty St
Loyola St
Saratoga St
Harmony St
Seventh St
Sixth St
Toledano St
Carondelet St
17
56
31
13
23
Danneel St
Dryades St
Baronne St
Gen Taylor St
Amelia St
Foucher St
Delachaise St
Carondelet St
Washington Ave
Lafayette Cemetery No 1
Dufossat St
Soniat St
Robert St
Upperline St
Cadiz St
Valence St
Jena St
Napoleon Ave
Carondelet St
St Charles Ave
Peniston St
Amelia St
Louisiana
GARDEN DISTRICT
Seventh St
Eighth St
Harmony St
20
24
32
64
65
18
3
Napoleon
7
Pitt St
Prytania St
Perrier St
Coliseum St
Chestnut St
Camp St
Magazine St
Constance St
Dufossat St
Laurel St
Annunciation St
Tchoupitoulas St
UPTOWN
Prytania St
Bordeaux St
Valence St
Cadiz St
Jena St
Napoleon Ave
Gen Pershing St
Milan St
Marengo St
Constantinople St
Gen Taylor St
Peniston St
Antonine St
Aline St
Foucher St
Amelia St
Louisiana Ave
Toledano St
Harmony St
Lyons St
35
15
63
29
37
44
28
27
62
61
55
12
26
52
39
51
43
22
Laurel St
Annunciation St
Tchoupitoulas St
Austerlitz St
Constance St
Mississippi River